Understanding COM

Ancient Technology in Modern Times

Bruno van Dooren

CopyRight

Understanding COM: Ancient Technology for Modern Times

ISBN: 9789090421346

First Edition

Cover design: Bruno van Dooren

Contents

Foreword

When I first started at Microsoft back in the MS-DOS and Windows 95 days, I found myself dropped right into the COM team. My specific corner of the world was the visual side, dealing with things like the object insertion presentation cache. But you couldn't touch any of that without first passing through the gauntlet of Core COM. I vividly remember staring at IUnknown, trying to wrap my head around v-tables, QueryInterface, class factories, and the dark arts of marshaling. It was, quite frankly, daunting. And the available books on the subject assumed I knew a lot more than I did.

At the time, the computing ecosystem was incredibly diverse, and we were trying to solve the holy grail of software engineering: true binary compatibility across a landscape of rapidly evolving and often incompatible compiler standards. COM was Microsoft's answer to that computing version of the Wild West. And it worked brilliantly. It worked so well, in fact, that it eventually faded into the background. Like a city's potable water infrastructure, you don't think about the details of how the water gets there until you turn on the faucet and nothing comes out.

For COM, that disruption arrived recently. In the summer of 2022, engineers around the world were suddenly faced with the challenge of dealing with DCOM hardening. A technology that had been silently chugging along for decades was suddenly front-page news, requiring immediate attention. As Bruno's friend Carl Daniel aptly put it, at this stage in its lifecycle, COM is less about engineering and more about archaeology.

That is exactly why Bruno van Dooren's Understanding COM is such a vital piece of work. When I was learning COM, we were inventing the rules. Today, you need a guide who can bridge the gap between those ancient foundations and modern, security-first realities. Bruno does an exceptional job of not just hand-waving the magic of the Active Template Library (ATL). Instead, he starts with raw C++ and COM APIs so you can understand exactly what is happening under the hood before introducing templates and macros. He explains why apartment models exist, how proxies and stubs marshal data across boundaries, and how to navigate the complex security models that DCOM hardening now enforces.

This book is the perfect modern companion to the classic, dog-eared copies of Essential COM by Don Box that used to sit on every developer's desk in Redmond. Whether you are a seasoned veteran looking to catch up on two decades of security overhauls, or a newer developer staring down a legacy codebase, you are holding the ultimate survival guide. Welcome to the archaeology dig—you are in excellent hands.

Dave Plummer *Retired Operating Systems Engineer, Microsoft*

Acknowledgments

Writing a book like this is a task that wouldn't have been possible without the help or input of others. Over the years there have been countless people who gave me advice, who taught me something, or helped me along the way. It would be impossible to mention everyone. However, there are a couple of people I want to highlight as instrumental to this book or to my evolution as a software developer.

The first mention should no doubt be my parents, who raised me, put me through college and made sure that I would begin the adventure game of life from a good starting point and with a good set of tools and traits.

Fresh out of college, I started working for ir. Adriaan Brebels who owned and managed a small software engineering startup. The company focused on developing software for test and measurement applications, making software talk to various kinds of data acquisition- and control hardware. Soon after starting, I discovered I had a passion for the lowest levels of software development, and I wanted to do C and C++ projects which was not what the company did. Rather than worry about the business risk, Adriaan helped me secure various challenging projects based on nothing more than the confidence that I would hit the ground running and deliver results. Eventually, this resulted in becoming a Microsoft MVP in the Visual C++ category in 2006.

In modern times, it is considered normal for any technology to be covered by online tutorials, tech blogs, tons of GitHub examples, and so on. However, COM was already past its heyday when all those online resources became a part of life. When it comes to the more in-depth technical resources, they are sparse. Of those, most are out of date. Some don't even compile anymore. Even the official documentation is oftentimes lacking. During the research for this book I discovered there is really only 1 active and authoritative source of COM information and that is Raymond Chen, Senior Software Engineer at Microsoft. Mr. Chen doesn't know me personally and we never had contact. However, his blog is an invaluable resource for anyone who wants to learn about COM in detail. His articles about custom marshaling helped me understand a topic which otherwise would not have made it into the book without skipping the difficult questions.

Finding someone to review this book was similarly challenging. I didn't want to publish this book without having someone at least looking it over to see if it made sense, or if something major was missing. I wanted to find someone who had been actively involved with COM at a low enough level. The problem there is that I was looking for someone who was active as a COM developer 20 years ago, still active enough in development today to read code, willing to spend their free time to read through complex technical topics, willing to respond to the email of a random developer they never met and who asks about a topic they probably haven't thought of for over a decade.

By the time the contents of this book were finished, and it was time to publish, I had almost given up trying to find such a person. I decided to try one last thing, and I emailed retired Microsoft software engineer Dave Plumber whose YouTube channel I follow. Dave has worked on a lot of fundamental Windows OS code and worked extensively with COM. He promptly mailed me back and said "sure, I have a long list of things to get through but I'd be happy to review your book". I can't thank Dave enough for his time. Any and all errors or issues in this book are mine alone of course. I did not ask or expect anyone to review every single thing in this book or chase down every statement to its reference documentation. The purpose of asking for a review was to ensure that I didn't skip anything major and that the overall explanations made sense.

I spent a lot of time over a 4-year period writing this book. I spent an incredible amount of time writing code, writing this book, doing research and experiments. Not all those times were joyful. Many times I was frustrated that I couldn't find a reference for something I thought I knew, or because a proof-of-concept example kept crashing, or because I'd written a chapter only to finally get that proof-of-concept to work properly and realizing my initial understanding was wrong and I had to redact some of what I wrote. Throughout those 4 years, my family was always positive and supportive about this project.

That leaves the most important thank you for last. I will forever be grateful to my wife and daughters who are the light in my life and who carry the burden of always being right.

Introduction

The year is 2026. You might ask yourself why anyone would want to write a book about COM and ATL; Technologies which were already considered arcane when I started learning them in the mid 2000's. Or as my friend Carl Daniel told me several years ago: *"In this part of its lifecycle, COM is less about engineering and more about archaeology"*.

The idea of this book started in the summer of 2022. After more than a decade of not thinking about COM, I was faced with the challenge of dealing with DCOM hardening, like many engineers around the world. Given that I was a bit rusty in my knowledge, I decided to buy the most recent COM bible so that I could familiarize myself with all the changes that had happened in the last 2 decades. And in truth, there are quite a few, including but not limited to:

- Security has been overhauled completely. UAC was added. Some options were added, some options were removed, and there was a massive shift in what is or is not considered best practice.
- 64-bit architecture was introduced in the Windows world. WOW (Windows 32 bit on Windows 64 bit) allows COM to support both architectures. The way this worked was changed several times between Windows XP and Windows 10.
- .NET was added to the landscape, and interoperability between .NET and COM was one of the pillars on which the success of the .NET framework introduction rested.
- The ATL (Active Template Library) gained and lost many features over the years as its relevance waxed and waned.

To my surprise I already had the 2 most recent seminal works in my possession. These are

- "Essential COM" by Don Box (1998)
- "ATL Internals" (2006).

The reality of publishing books about computer technology is that this is mostly done when it makes economic sense. Most books are written about whatever new technology people want to know about because that will lead to the most book sales. Additionally, since new technology often replaces old technology, there is little point in writing about old technology. For example, there is a reason you won't find new books about programming Windows 95 style Virtual Device Drivers. These things no longer exist. Economic relevance and practical relevance usually go hand in hand.

With COM, the situation is different. Most component-based software development is done with technologies such as Java and .NET because that makes the most sense from a software lifecycle perspective. Programming in .NET is not only quicker and cheaper, but there is a massive amount of open source software available with examples, sample code, etc.

However, the type of software that still uses COM today often has very long lifecycles. COM was one of the first technologies that provided a reliable way to reuse code, separate interface from implementation, and hide the details of how or where the actual implementation was running in a client – server setup. Operating systems and industrial process control software for example, have code bases that can be well into the 3d decade of their lifecycle. These systems receive many updates on the front end but if the back end is solid, there is no reason to turn it inside out and replace COM guts with .NET guts, just for the sake of it.

This is especially true for COM, since even today, COM still has a lot of things going for it. For one, COM has stayed stable and backwards compatible for decades. The same COM component that is still silently chugging along after 2 decades would have had to be rebuilt and modified along the way if it was a .NET component .NET has gone through several breaking changes that require components to be recompiled. COM has been so successful in that regard that most people forget it even exists. COM is still very alive and kicking, in the same way that railway or potable water infrastructure is. We don't think about it because when we turn on the faucet, the water is there and we don't wonder about the details of HOW it got there or where it comes from.

That doesn't mean that new software development in COM is still a good idea. There is a reason newer technology came along. Still, there is a massive amount of COM technology still in use and it's not going away any time soon. It still underpins many important applications and subsystems.

In the summer of 2022, after dealing with DCOM hardening I started playing with COM again out of curiosity about the changes. The principles in those old books about COM are still mostly valid, but none of the code compiles cleanly, and several of the programming techniques on display would raise eyebrows today. And of course, the impact of the Windows changes I mentioned earlier is not explained. You can find much online but it's not uncommon to find conflicting or simply erroneous information. This poses a challenge for new software developers who are faced with having to maintain that software.

The plan to write this book was born along the way. With the benefit of hindsight, I can say that this was a much bigger undertaking than I had anticipated. I underestimated the required effort spectacularly. Not only that, but along the way I discovered that I didn't understand COM as well as I thought I did. Doing the research for some of the more advanced chapters of this book was a humbling experience. At the same time, it also gave me a lot of appreciation for just how well designed it is.

With this book, I hope to give people who are new to COM a good entry point to start learning about the technology, both to understand how it works under the hood as well as how to use it successfully, in the same way that Essential COM did almost 30 years ago.

If you have any feedback about this book or a story you want to share, feel free to drop me an email at bruno@iunknown.be

About this book

Writing a book about COM is challenging for many reasons. All other things aside, pretty much every topic is related to all other topics, which makes it hard to write an explanation which doesn't rely on, or refers to things that are further along in the book. After rearranging chapters and content many time, I've managed to build a story that can be read front to back without being forced to look forward or having to accept phrases like '...but this will be explained later'.

This book starts off with setting the historical context in which COM was developed, and how the requirements for code reuse and binary distribution shaped the programming model. After that, there is a section explaining the different concepts without diving into programming just yet. From there, we continue with Interface Definition Language (IDL), the concept of classes and instances, and generally every topic that is important in understanding, building, and using a COM object. That first part of the book uses raw C++ and COM APIs without the use of macros, template libraries or smart pointers. I want the reader to understand exactly what is happening under the hood, even if you wouldn't implement an object in that manner in real life.

For educational purposes, I chose to start the first implementations of the core concepts in a rather naïve manner and then explain the problems and update the implementations along the way. This approach is slightly more verbose and tedious but has the benefit of being able to focus on 1 issue at a time without trying to tackle multiple issues at the same time. Once the basic concepts are established the Active Template Library (ATL) is explored because that is how any C++ COM development is done in real life projects. The power and versatility of ATL are explained by showing how to implement several types of COM object. This chapter also explains how the ATL itself works.

From there, the book turns to more advanced topics such as a deep dive into COM guts, the options for parallelism and asynchronous programming, interoperability with the .NET framework, and a deep dive into COM security. Finally, the book ends with a number of miscellaneous topics. Some of those last topics are not relevant in real world situations anymore, but they are mentioned in earlier books and I didn't want to ignore them completely.

Throughout the book, I use snippets of code to explain a concept. All code in this book comes from Visual Studio projects that are made available for learning, testing, and experimenting. They were built with Visual Studio 2022 in 32-bit and 64-bit configurations. While the code is there for programmers who want to learn COM programming, the book doesn't rely on code for its explanations so if you are reading this book because you want to really understand COM but not necessarily program C++, you can. The companion code for this book is available on GitHub.

https://github.com/brunovandooren/UnderstandingCOM

As was mentioned in the introduction, I still consider 'Essential COM' the foundational work on COM in the time it was written and the decade following its publication. In various parts of the book, the content will deviate from what Don Box explained. These parts will be mentioned explicitly to avoid confusion in case readers compare those sections with Essential COM. That doesn't mean Essential COM was wrong when it was written. It means that in the decades following its original publication, COM has changed significantly in some areas, and some things that were true then are no longer true today.

Code sections in this book use the courier font.

```
//Calculator.h
class Calculator
{
public:
    double Add(double arg1, double arg2);
};
```

Most of the code in this book was written by me or in some cases automatically generated by Visual Studio as part of normal programming activities. These parts are shown without background. Snippets that were copied from a Microsoft header or MSDN under the terms of fair use, have a light grey background and are attributed to either the header file or the webpage where they came from.

```
//combaseapi.h
IUnknown
{
public:
    virtual HRESULT STDMETHODCALLTYPE QueryInterface(
        REFIID riid,
        void **ppvObject) = 0;
};
```

Despite best efforts to make this book free from mistakes, it's certainly possible that there are mistakes, errors or oversights. If / when these are found and reported, they will be listed here.

https://iunknown.be/win32/understanding-com/

Begin at the beginning,

and go on till you come to the end: then stop.

The King of Hearts – Alice In Wonderland.

1

Historical background

A topic like DCOM is challenging to cover for many reasons. Inherently it is a complex topic to begin with. But on top of that, if we look at it from today's perspective, some things seem weird, naïve, limited or even nonsensical.

It pays to keep in mind that the foundations for COM were laid in the early 1990's. The computing landscape was extremely diverse. In terms of hardware, there were companies like Amiga, Atari, Commodore, and many others alongside IBM, all of them making some type of computer. Today, most of these only exist as fond childhood memories among dinosaurs like me, and as names or logos on coveted nerdy t-shirts.

Without losing ourselves in a long list of hardware trivia, let it suffice to say that in that era, a computer with an intel 486DX2 CPU running at 66 MHz was considered a solid performance machine. That CPU could perform 25.6 Mips (Million instructions per second). For reference, my old laptop which I bought in 2016 is an Intel Core i7 6950X, and clocks in at 320440 Mips. The 486 would be paired with 16 Mbyte of memory and be considered powerful. My old laptop has 16 GByte.

Back when people were designing COM, computers were about 10000 times slower and had 1000 times less memory. This was literally a time when developers sometimes counted individual clock cycles to evaluate efficiency or deciding whether an idea was good enough to warrant wasting clock cycles and individual bytes of memory. Things we take for granted today, like memory garbage collection and centralized object management, didn't exist. Implementing them would be prohibitively expensive in terms of resources.

The ecosystem was a lot less homogenous than it is today. In the 90s, Windows ran not only on Intel compatible hardware, but also on Mips, DEC Alpha and PowerPC. Various vendors of programming toolsets competed for adoption by the developer communities. On top of that, there was a landscape of rapidly evolving language standards, most of which were only partially implemented by each vendor. Not only did vendors implement different parts of a language standard, but they often did it in such a way that an average project could only be built with a toolset from that vendor. Even different versions of the same toolset from the same vendor might not be compatible. Most toolsets came with their own runtime libraries for doing things or ways to deal with binary interfaces.

It is against this backdrop of the computing version of the Wild West that all software companies were chasing the dragon of interoperability: the ability to build software that was binary compatible with other software, and the ability to reuse and extend said software. For this book, we're going to start with the concept of a company named MathLibCo making a mathematics library for general purpose computing needs. Software company NumbersInc is making an application to crunch numbers and wants to use that library.

Binary compatibility

MathLibCo develops the source code for an advanced calculator component. Computing languages like C++ only have a source level language definition, not a binary interface definition. For convenience's sake let's assume that compilers are fully standards compliant so they will all compile the same source files.

```
//Calculator.h
class Calculator
{
public:
    double Add(double arg1, double arg2);
};

//Calculator.cpp
double Calculator::Add(double arg1, double arg2)
{
    return arg1 + arg2;
}
```

These source files are part of a C++ project that builds the delivery package for the Calculator class. This package consists of 3 files:

- Calculator.dll. This is the binary package that contains the redistributable implementation of the calculator.

- Calculator.lib. This is a binary static library that the linker can import during the linking process so that the resulting executable contains the appropriate import directives for the code that resides in the dll.
- Calculator.h. This is the original class declaration, which the client compiler needs to understand what a Calculator object looks like, and which methods it exports.

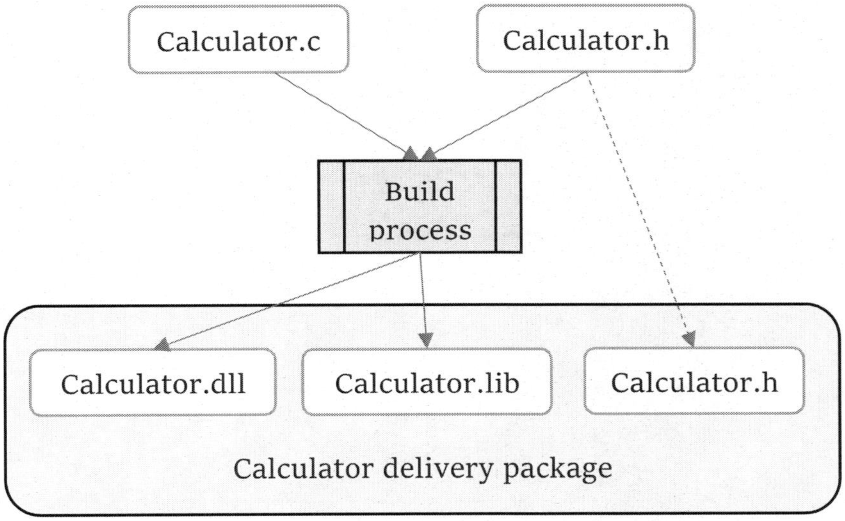

For the sake of correctness: importing and exporting code is a topic which has several aspects and possibilities. There are many things to consider which are not directly relevant here. For the sake of brevity, I'm purposely ignoring things like export and import declarations here, because they're not essential to the point.

Now the testing team at MathLibCo gets the delivery package and decides to build a test application.

```
//Test.cpp
int main()
{
    Calculator calc;
    std::wcout << L"1.0 + 1.0 = "
               << calc.Add(1.0, 1.0)
               << std::endl;
}
```

The compiler takes the Test.cpp file, includes the Calculator.h file and produces an intermediary object file that is passed to the linker. The linker takes that object file, links it with the import directives in the Calculator.lib file and produces the Test.exe executable.

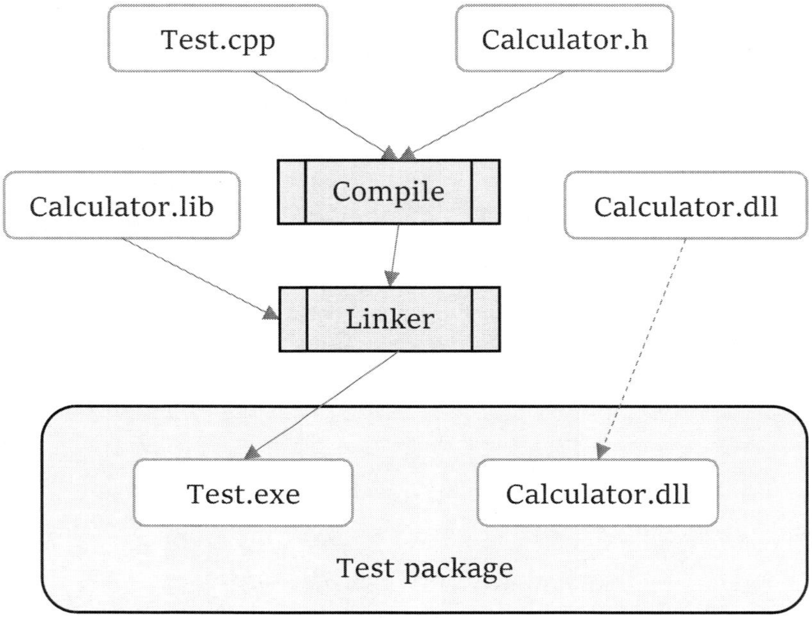

They run the test executable, and it informs the testing team that 1 + 1 is indeed 2. The test is a roaring success. Management is over the moon, the development team gets large bonuses, and no expense is spared to make the launch party rival the decadence of Friday evening trading closing time of a brokerage house in the 80's. The calculator is released to the public.

However, it doesn't take long before problem tickets start rolling in. Some clients report that the Calculator works as expected. Others report that they can build the application but not run it. And some report that they can't even build it. All problems that occur are caused by the fact that the C++ standard is only a language standard. It defines what the source code should look like and what the code means. It says nothing about what that functionality should look like in binary form, nor does it specify how executable code is structured in an executable file or library file. As annoying as it is, there are good reasons for this.

Languages like C++ are machine independent. The same code, compiled on different CPU architectures, should do the same things. This would be impossible if binary compatibility was mandated, because not all architectures do those things the same way. That is why there is a compilation step between the source code and the binary code: to take a platform agnostic statement and turn it into a set of very platform specific binary instructions. No high-level language can have a binary interface definition without tying it exclusively to 1 version of architecture forever.

With today's point of view, you might be thinking: why don't C# and the dotNET framework (to give a random example) have this problem? The answer is very simple. dotNET languages don't compile to machine code. They compile to something called bytecode. You can think of bytecode as a type of platform agnostic assembly language with modern bells and whistles. Bytecode is compiled to actual machine code on-the-fly as it is being executed. That might lead to the following question: ok but why didn't they do that in the early 90's. This question is easily answered by pointing back to the CPU comparison we made earlier. With system speeds being 10000 times slower it becomes understandable that this was simply not feasible.

Symbol names

The problems we are having with the Calculator at this point all stem from the fact that there is no binary compatibility. And this is not limited to compatibility between different platforms. That at least is perfectly logical. You instinctively understand why code on an Intel system compiles to different binary than code on a VMS system. But even on the same architecture, using the same programming language, there was no compatibility. The 90's were a time of rapid expansion in the field of computing. Technologies and languages were invented and discarded as quickly as people could think of them, and there was no uniformity because the entire field was continuously breaking new ground. To quote Sabine Hossenfelder: "*Let a thousand flowers bloom, except most of them are psychedelic mushrooms.*"

Let's look at just function names to get an idea of how things were. Suppose we have the flowing function declaration in our header:

```
void foo(int i);
```

C++ allows function overloading, meaning there can be other functions with the same name. Other versions of the foo function might take an argument type of bool or double. To distinguish between these functions at the binary level, the name of the function is 'mangled'; made unique by encoding the specificity of the arguments into the name, in such a way that they are all unique and the compiler knows which one to use. The term used for this is 'name mangling'. There is no uniform standard for this among compiler vendors.

To give just a couple of examples:

Compiler	Symbol name for void foo(int i)
Microsoft Visual C++ 10	?foo@@YAXH@Z
Borland C++	@foo$qi
GCC 2.9	foo__Fi
Watcom C++	W?foo$n(i)v

The same sort of encoding is used for methods in classes. It quickly becomes obvious why simply distributing a library in binary form is impossible. And this is just looking at symbol names for functions and methods. There are more issues than just the name:

- How methods are arranged in the class relative to the base address
- How member variables are stored relative to the base address,
- ...

None of these things are consistent among compiler vendors. The C++ standard itself was still evolving at the time, vendors didn't implement everything, some things were relatively new, there was no real cooperation between them to come to a consensus on how to do things, etc. Everyone just went with what they thought was best / most efficient / gave them a leg up over others.

There was, however, 1 thing that was common between all major compiler vendors, and that is the way virtual functions were implemented.

Abstract base classes for the win

When a class has a function with a certain name and argument list, functionally that will behave just like a regular method. And if a class derives from that base class, it can use that method just like one of their own.

One of the things a programmer may do is to mark a method as virtual. If a method is marked as virtual, then a class which inherits from that base class can still use that method just like it could in a non-virtual scenario.

However, the derived class also has the option to override that function by providing its own implementation. And then the override will be called. It is important to note that the override will be called whether the function is called through the base class or the derived class.

```
class Base
{
public:
    virtual void Foo(void) {
        std::wcout << L"Base::Foo()" << std::endl;
    }
};

class Derived : public Base
{
public:
    void Foo(void) {
        std::wcout << L"Derived::Foo()" << std::endl;
    }
};


    Derived der;
    der.Foo();
    static_cast<Base&>(der).Foo();
```

Here we have a Base class which implements a virtual function Foo. The Derived class also implements a Foo function with the same signature. As a result, this overrides the virtual one. Whether we call that method via the Derived class instance directly or via the Base class, in both cases the output will be "`Derived::Foo()`".

So how does this work in a practical sense? If a class has a virtual function, the compiler silently slips a pointer into the class's members. This pointer is called a virtual pointer or vptr which is not accessible to the programmer, but only to the compiler. It points to a table or array called a virtual table or vtable.

This vtable contains a function pointer for each virtual function. That pointer points to the most derived method that is to be executed whenever the function is invoked either directly or through a base. A picture will make this clearer.

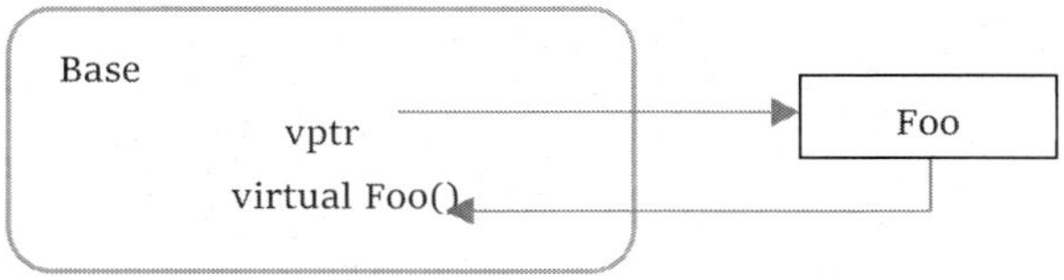

If we use the Base class just by itself, its vptr will point to a vtable where that function is redirected back to Base's own Foo implementation. Even though the implementation details of the function call are different from a non-virtual method, for practical purposes it behaves the same.

Now if we derive from Base, the situation becomes different.

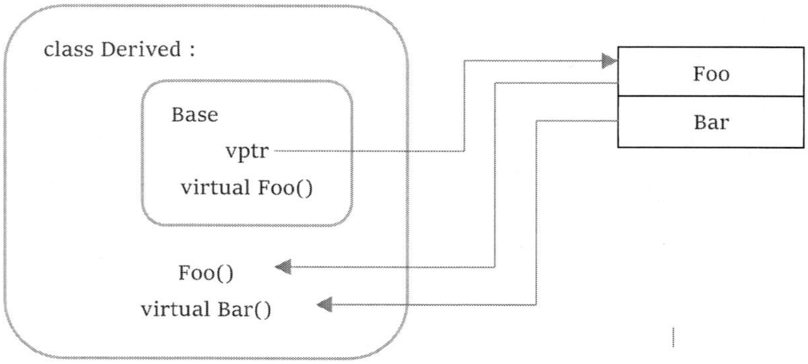

'Derived' has an implementation for Foo, and calls to Base::Foo will be redirected to the version that was implemented by Derived. Derived has a virtual function Bar which is also in the vtable. There is only 1 vptr and 1 vtable because they can be combined. At every level of inheritance any new virtual functions are added to the vtable at the end. From the point of view of every previous class in the inheritance hierarchy, whether the next level exists or not is irrelevant because it doesn't influence how they use the vtable. One further step a base class can take is to declare a function as abstract.

```
class Base
{
public:
    virtual void Foo(void) = 0;
};
```

This simply means that Base has no implementation for Foo from itself. This also means that we cannot make naked instances of Base because something is missing. This is why we call Base an abstract class. It cannot exist by itself. It is literally only a promise that when it is used in an inheritance hierarchy, at some level, the specified functions will exist. Until then, it is impossible to create an instance because there will be nothing for the vtable to redirect to.

A key takeaway here is that it becomes obvious that no amount of name mangling like we saw earlier, is going to matter, because no actual names are going to be used for finding the function. It's all function pointers, and those are compiler agnostic.

Now we can take this concept back to our Calculator class. The convention in DCOM is to call these abstract classes 'interfaces', and their names begin with an 'I'.

```
//IArithmetic.h
class IArithmetic
{
public:
    virtual double Add(double arg1, double arg2) = 0;
};

//calculator.h
class Calculator : public IArithmetic
{
public:
    double Add(double arg1, double arg2);
};

//Calculator.cpp
double Calculator::Add(double arg1, double arg2)
{
    return arg1 + arg2;
}
```

With this implementation, we are on the right track. We can build the Calculator with our toolset of choice, and the client applications can access the Calculator through the IArithmetic interface.

However, the client still cannot create instances of the Calculator class by themselves. After all the client still has no real idea what the actual Calculator looks like. This means that instead of exporting the Calculator class, we must export a function that creates a Calculator instance and returns a pointer to the interface.

```
IArithmetic* GetCalculator(void)
{
    IArithmetic* interfacePtr =
        static_cast<IArithmetic*>(new Calculator());
    if (!interfacePtr) {
        throw std::bad_alloc();
    }
    return interfacePtr;
}
```

We're finally getting to the point where our Calculator company is back in business because all client applications will work with this new approach, regardless of compiler version or vendor.

```
int main()
{
```

```
    IArithmetic* calc = GetCalculator();
    std::wcout << L"1.0 + 1.0 = "
               << calc->Add(1.0, 1.0)
               << std::endl;
}
```

However, we are not out of the woods yet. Everything is indeed working now, but it will all go pear shaped again if something happens that causes GetCalculator to throw an exception.

Note that the example of throwing bad_alloc is a bit contrived because logically, if exceptions are used in this scenario, they would be thrown from within the constructor. However, for the purpose of this example I wanted to make it explicitly visible that exceptions could be generated.

HRESULT instead of exceptions

When it comes to error handling, C++ supports the use of exceptions. And indeed, the Standard Template Library (STL) which comes with the language uses exceptions as the means for error handling. There is however a major problem with exceptions when it comes to building libraries: as with function names, the C++ standard does not specify HOW exceptions are implemented at binary level. And the reason it doesn't do that is the same. C++ is a language specification, not an architectural specification. There are various ways for a compiler to implement exception handling. And unfortunately, this time there was no commonality between different compiler vendors. This means that there is only method for dealing with errors in a way that is compatible with all compilers, which is the good old fashioned return value.

There are many protocols for dealing with error code values. For COM, the HRESULT mechanism was chosen. A HRESULT is a 32-bit value, divided into several fields. One interesting property of HRESULTs is that they can be used not only to communicate errors, but also different types of success codes. The bits in a HRESULT are defined as follows:

Bit	Field	Meaning
31	S - Severity	0 indicates success. 1 indicates a failure.
30	R - Reserved	The 2nd status bit of the NTSTATUS value if an NTSTATUS was mapped to a HRESULT (see bit 28)
29	C - Customer	0 indicates it is a Microsoft code. 1 indicates a 3d party code.

28	N - Reserved	Indicates that an NTSTATUS value has been mapped to a HRESULT.
17	X - Reserved	Reserved for internal use.
26-16	Facility	Identifies the system service responsible for the HRESULT.
15-0	Code	The actual status that was communicated.

To give a couple of examples, let's look at a couple of common values you will likely encounter:

Code	Value	Meaning
S_OK	0x00000000	The operation completed successfully
E_NOTIMPL	0x80004001	The requested operation or feature is not implemented. The severity bit indicates an error. The Facility field is 4 which identifies the COM Interface management service. And the actual error is set to 1.
E_HANDLE	0x80070006	The specified handle is not valid. The severity bit indicates an error. The Facility field is 7 which identifies the win32 subsystem. This makes sense since that is where HANDLE values are managed. And the actual error is set to 6.

At first, HRESULTs can seem a bit weird because they are more complex than a simple code and they can contain a lot of information. However, since so many of them are predefined and commonly used, working with them can quickly become natural.

Because these can contain so much information, they are generally used with 2 C style macros SUCCEEDED(hr) and FAILED(hr) which indicate whether the supplied HRESULT value indicates success or a failure. Armed with this knowledge, we can make our code fully cross compiler compatible.

```
HRESULT GetCalculator(IArithmetic** interfacePtr)
{
    if (interfacePtr == NULL)
        return E_INVALIDARG;
```

```
    try {
        *interfacePtr =
            static_cast<IArithmetic*>(new Calculator());
        return S_OK;
    }
    catch( std::exception ) {
        *interfacePtr = NULL;
        return E_FAIL;
    }
}
```

Instead of being a return value, the interface pointer is now passed via an argument, which also means it must be passed as a pointer to a pointer. If something goes wrong during the creation of the Calculator instance, an exception is thrown from within, and it can be caught so that we can return the appropriate E_FAIL code. If nothing happens, we return S_OK.

We also set the interface pointer to NULL to make it clear that whatever is in the pointer is not valid.

```
int main()
{
    IArithmetic* calc = NULL;
    HRESULT hRes = GetCalculator(&calc);
    if (SUCCEEDED(hRes)) {
        std::wcout << L"1.0 + 1.0 = "
            << calc->Add(1.0, 1.0)
            << std::endl;
    }
}
```

The client side doesn't have to change a whole lot, except the IArithmetic pointer is not passed as an argument, and as a pointer to a pointer. Initializing it to NULL is technically not required because GetCalculator overwrites it, but it is always a good idea to explicitly initialize pointers to NULL.

The argument for using an HRESULT is also valid for any other method call, even the simple Add routine. While adding 2 numbers is unlikely to generate an error, floating point arithmetic has the concept of a 'Not-a-number' value as well as Infinity and adding +Inf to -Inf is undefined. Therefore, it is prudent to simply always return a HRESULT and pass the actual output value(s) via the parameter list, no matter how humble the method. For our contrived example, we'll leave the Add method as is, but keep in mind that it is always best to return a HRESULT. Not only can you then deal with edge cases, but if you ever discover that an existing method has an edge case you didn't anticipate at design time, your interface has the means to deal with it. A hypothetical Add implementation could then look like this.

```
HRESULT Calculator::Add(double arg1, double arg2, double* result)
{
    if (!(std::isfinite(arg1) && std::isfinite(arg2)))
        return E_INVALIDARG;

    if (result == NULL)
        return E_POINTER;

    *result = arg1 + arg2;
    return S_OK;
}
```

Our calculator is starting to look solid. But if you look closely, something is still missing: we need to delete the calculator when we are done using it.

Object deletion

On the surface it seems a trivial problem to solve. It would be trivial to implement the following function and call it a day.

```
void DeleteCalculator(IArithmetic* calculator)
{
    delete static_cast<Calculator*>(calculator);
}

int main()
{
    IArithmetic* calc = NULL;
    HRESULT hRes = GetCalculator(&calc);
    if (SUCCEEDED(hRes)) {
        std::wcout << L"1.0 + 1.0 = "
            << calc->Add(1.0, 1.0)
            << std::endl;
        DeleteCalculator(calc);
    }
}
```

For the problem at hand, it would work very well. But it's not great because it means the application and the library need to always share the assumption that only 1 actor gets a say in when the object is deleted.

That may not seem like a huge deal at first, and for our Calculator, it wouldn't be. But suppose that this is how we do things and deliver the library. This first version is in a simple beta version.

At some point, the math library is updated and comes with a dedicated high performance computing backend. Now, starting the Calculator instance is a big deal because under the hood it connects to that back end, and setting up this connection takes up quite some resources. While the Calculator is running, the back end periodically reports its status back to the Calculator. The client decides they do not need the Calculator anymore and deletes the object right when the back end is accessing the same object. Things go boom because the object the back end it trying to use suddenly ceases to exist.

No one so far considered that the lifecycle of the object could become complex and needs to be arbitrated between different parties. And what's worse, there is no one who could or would have expected this when the client started working with the first IArithmetic implementation. Without other measures, IArithmetic needs to be adapted to make it synchronize its actions with the activities of the back end. This is undesirable because it brings unnecessary complexity with it that has nothing to do with the IArithmetic interface. And worse: even if such a reasonably complex mechanism is implemented, it might all be in vain if the Calculator internally uses another component which exhibits the same problem, and the client application wouldn't even know about it, or be able to coordinate its actions with that internal library.

What we need is a mechanism where every component is 'safe' until no one is using it anymore. This means keeping track of every pointer that exists to our Calculator. And since there is no way of ensuring that those different actors know about each other, really the only place to do so is inside the object (or rather through the object) itself. The only way to make sure an object is only deleted when there are no more extant pointers is to count and keep track of every single place in memory where that pointer exists. With technology and frameworks that were available in the 09's, this means reference counting. The rules are simple:

- Every time an Interface pointer is copied TO a memory location, we add +1 to the object's reference count by calling the 'AddRef' function.
- Every time the owner of a specific pointer is done with said pointer, it needs to 'Release' that pointer to subtract 1 from the object's reference counter.

The reference count is maintained by the instance itself, and if it detects that no one is using it anymore, it can delete itself. Since the client application needs to be able to release the interface pointer, the Release method needs to be available in the interface. The client could also make copies of the pointer, which means the AddRef method needs to be available in the interface as well.

We'll come back to this later but for now let's add those methods in the IArithmetic interface and then implement them in the Calculator.

```
//IArithmetic.h
class IArithmetic
{
public:
    virtual double Add(double arg1, double arg2) = 0;
    virtual int AddRef(void) = 0;
    virtual int Release(void) = 0;
};


//calculator.h
Class Calculator : public IArithmetic
{
    int m_refCount = 0;
public:
    double Add(double arg1, double arg2);
    int AddRef(void);
    int Release(void);
};

//Calculator.cpp
int Calculator::AddRef(void)
{
    return m_refCount++;
}

int Calculator::Release(void)
{
    int tempRefCount = m_refCount--;
    if (m_refCount == 0) {
        delete this;
    }
    return tempRefCount;
}
```

Following the same principles that govern the Add method, the AddRef and Release methods can be called through the abstract base class mechanism. Whenever we call AddRef, the reference count increases. Whenever we call Release, the reference decreases. Once the reference count is 0, the object can delete itself. It can do so safely without having to worry about someone AddRef'ing again when it is in the middle of deleting itself because according to the rules we just formulated, a reference count of 0 indicates that no one is holding on to a valid pointer anymore, so no one can call AddRef anymore.

Note that we use a temporary variable to store the return value in the call to Release because after the instance auto-deletes, m_RefCount should never be touched again

In our scenario, AddRef is called when the first pointer is created and assigned to the client's pointer variable.

```
HRESULT GetCalculator(IArithmetic** interfacePtr)
{
    if (interfacePtr == NULL)
        return E_POINTER;
    *interfacePtr = NULL;


    try {
        *interfacePtr =
            static_cast<IArithmetic*>(new Calculator());
        (*interfacePtr)->AddRef();
        return S_OK;
    }
    catch( std::exception) {
        return E_FAIL;
    }
}
```

The reference count is increased as soon as the copy is made. This is always the responsibility of the actor making the copy. And this needs to be done immediately following the copy. Consider the following snippet:

```
    try {
        *interfacePtr =
            static_cast<IArithmetic*>(new Calculator());
            //do additional work here
            //-> oops, an exception occurs
        (*interfacePtr)->AddRef();
        return S_OK;
    }
    catch( std::exception) {
        *interfacePtr = NULL;
        return E_FAIL;
    }
```

Following the creation of our instance, we do some post-creation configuration work that just happens to throw an exception. We catch the exception, clear the pointer and return a NULL pointer. From the Client's point of view, everything went according to the rules, but now there is a leftover Calculator instance floating around, and it will never delete itself. The reference count is 0, but it has never been increased, and since no one is holding a copy of the pointer value in memory, no one is able to do so anymore. There is a variation of this problem that is more problematic, and easier to miss.

```
try {
    *interfacePtr =
        static_cast<IArithmetic*>(new Calculator());
    (*interfacePtr)->AddRef();
    //do additional work here
    //-> oops, an exception occurrs
    return S_OK;
}
catch( std::exception) {
    *interfacePtr = NULL;
    return E_FAIL;
}
```

Here, we AddRef the instance as we should. The exception is still caught and handled as appropriate, and the pointer is set to NULL as was required, but now, the reference count is 1 yet no one is ever going to be able to call Release because like no one can do so. Not setting the pointer to NULL is also not an option because then, whoever holds it would be made responsible for Releasing it even though we returned E_FAIL. The correct way to deal with this is as follows:

```
try {
    *interfacePtr = NULL;
    //do work here
    //-> oops, maybe an exception occurrs
    *interfacePtr =
        static_cast<IArithmetic*>(new Calculator());
    (*interfacePtr)->AddRef();
    //do additional work here
    //-> oops, maybe an exception occurrs
    return S_OK;
}
catch (std::exception) {
    if (*interfacePtr) {
        (*interfacePtr)->Release();
        *interfacePtr = NULL;
    }
    return E_FAIL;
}
```

We start with putting NULL in the pointer output field. As a result, we can do more work after creating the Calculator instance and AddRef it. Should an exception happen at any point before returning S_OK, there are only 2 scenarios that can happen in the exception handler. Either the pointer is NULL and we know there is no pointer left hanging, or it is non-NULL, and we know we must release it and set it to NULL. On the client's side, things are somewhat simpler.

```
int main()
{
    IArithmetic* calc = NULL;
    HRESULT hRes = GetCalculator(&calc);
    if (SUCCEEDED(hRes)) {
        double result = calc->Add(1.0, 1.0);
        calc->Release();
        std::wcout << L"1.0 + 1.0 = "
            << result
            << std::endl;
    }
}
```

Once we have a valid pointer, we perform the calculation and release the pointer as soon as possible. But here, too, we must take more cases than is obvious at first glance. Admittedly it is farfetched in this case, but stream operators have the potential to throw an exception. Should we do something like this

```
        std::wcout << L"1.0 + 1.0 = "
            << calc->Add(1.0, 1.0)
            << std::endl;
        calc->Release();
```

then at least theoretically, we could end up with a pointer that is abandoned before it has been Released. If you work with raw interfaces like this without using smart pointers, then you need to take special care to avoid situations where exceptions interfere with the responsibilities of pointer management. Additionally, pointer management relies on both trust and goodwill between the object and the client. Clients need to trust that by the time they come into possession of the pointer, its reference count is valid. Libraries need to trust that the Client will call Release exactly once for the pointer it received, and that when any additional copies it makes, AddRef and Release are called for them appropriately.

```
    IArithmetic* calc = NULL;
    HRESULT hRes = GetCalculator(&calc);
    if (SUCCEEDED(hRes)) {
        IArithmetic* calc2 = calc;
        calc2->AddRef();
        calc->Release();
        calc2->Add(1.0, 1.0);
        calc2->Release();
    }
```

In this scenario, it would be 'safe' to skip the calc2->AddRef / calc->Release pair because ultimately it would not affect the lifecycle. However, the more we deviate from the rules, the higher the likelihood that we miss something subtle, and it all goes to pieces. In fact, this is all rather error prone. In realistic environments, you would use specialized smart pointers to take all the pain and possibility for error out of pointer handling, as I will show later in this book. But for the purpose of understanding if is important to know exactly what is going on.

At this point, we have arrived at a solution that is safe to use, is supported by all compilers, and solves every issue we have encountered so far. However, 1 major part is still missing from our puzzle: supporting multiple interfaces.

Supporting multiple interfaces

So far, we've looked at things from the perspective of supporting 1 specific interface. Suppose that our calculator does not only support arithmetic operations, but also goniometric operations via a dedicated ITrigonometry interface. It makes sense to provide specific interfaces for specific functionality. Even if you argue that you could squeeze everything math related into 1 massive, dedicated general purpose ICalculator interface, that will still leave room for a lot of functionality that is not related to math.

Suppose that our library doesn't come with just a calculator, but also a storage interface to provide some type of storage access to temporarily store values in between Client runs. We'd probably have an IPersistentStorage interface or something of that nature. It makes perfect sense that an object implements multiple interfaces.

Schematically, a COM object is represented like this: an opaque object that exposes several interfaces that can be used by a client. And with this drawing it also becomes instantly clear why I sometimes refer to DCOM as 'The ancient art of circles and lollipops'.

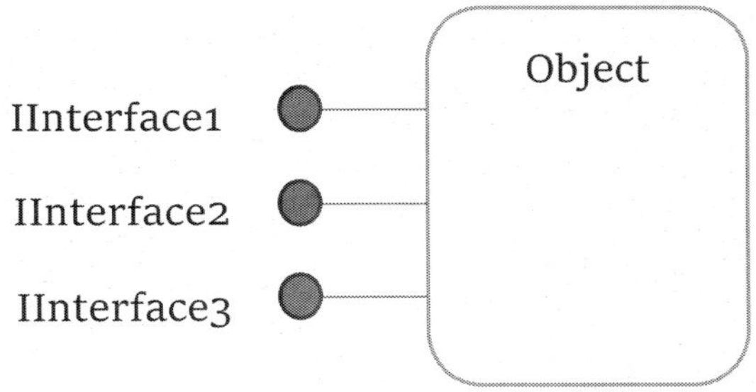

To reiterate: the object is the thing that is created. The interface is the thing that allows us to access that object. An object can have multiple interfaces, and multiple interfaces can be in use at the same time.

> Objects implement specific interfaces to express specific semantics defined by those interfaces.

Similarly, it also makes perfect sense that multiple types of objects implement the same interface. For example, we could have a Translator object that also implements the same IPersistentStorage interface if it has similar storage semantics.

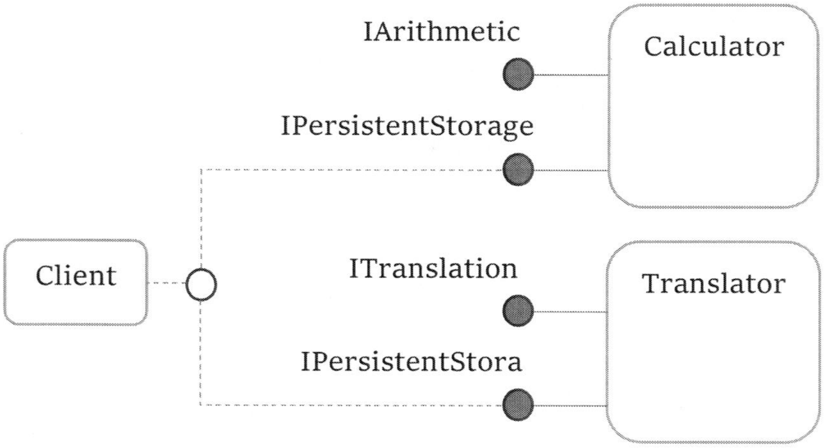

From the point of view of the Client, with only the interface pointer it is essentially unknowable what sort of object is exposing that interface.

> When disparate types of object expose the same interface, they can be handled the same way for the purpose of that interface.

Of course, the client knows what sort of object it has asked to create (by calling GetCalculator in our example) but more generically, from the interface pointer itself it is impossible to know what the object behind it is.

However, we can learn things about the object via the interfaces it supports. If the Client has a way to check if an object exposes IArithmetic, it may not know whether it is 'the' Calculator, but it will know for sure whether the object can be used like one, because interfaces define semantics or capabilities.

This also brings us to the realization that when we create an instance of an object, we only get 1 pointer, for one specific type. In our examples so far, we've always used the IArithmetic interface, and that was fine because there was only 1 interface. If instead, the Calculator would implement 2 interfaces, we need a way to obtain one, using the other. Because remember, we cannot interact with the Calculator itself, only with interfaces. Since we can only switch to a different interface using an existing interface, this is a functionality that ALL interfaces need to support, just like managing the reference count. Without knowing anything specific about an object or the interfaces it exposes, we can say this:

> The absolute minimal level functionality exposed via an interface, by an unknown object, is the ability to manage its existence through the reference count, and the ability to get another interface to the same object.

IUnknown

Finally, we've arrived at the fundamental interface that acts as the lynchpin for everything COM related: IUnknown.

This interface exists for 2 very important reasons. First, it defines the methods for lifecycle management and retrieving interfaces. But second, it unites all COM objects that exist through a single common base class. Various parties including the COM runtime need to hold on to interfaces and manage said interfaces and their underlying objects. Having a single unifying base makes this possible without having to make any other assumptions or forcing objects to implement any non-essential features. If we look in the header file *unknwnbase.h*, we see that it has 3 pure virtual members that we need to implement in any class that inherits from it and interface that inherits from it:

```
//combaseapi.h
IUnknown
{
public:
    virtual HRESULT STDMETHODCALLTYPE QueryInterface(
        REFIID riid,
        void **ppvObject) = 0;

    virtual ULONG STDMETHODCALLTYPE AddRef( void) = 0;

    virtual ULONG STDMETHODCALLTYPE Release( void) = 0;

};
```

We have already discussed the purpose of AddRef and Release so there is no need to cover those details here again, other than to reiterate the rules that govern them:

- When a pointer is copied to a memory location, AddRef needs to be called immediately. This is the responsibility of the actor making the copy.

- When a pointer is no longer needed by its owner, whoever owns it needs to call Release. From that moment on, no one is allowed to use it anymore because the underlying pointer may have been deleted.
- A non-zero return value from either AddRef or Release indicates that at that moment (or at least the moment the return value was generated) the object still exists. A return value of 0 from Release means that that Release call was the one to trigger the delete of the object.

The last rule is formulated a bit weird, but there's a reason for that and we get back to that later.

Our initial implementation is simple and uses the ++ and -- operators.

```
int Calculator::AddRef(void)
{
    return m_refCount++;
}

int Calculator::Release(void)
{
    int tempRefCount = m_refCount--;
    if (m_refCount == 0) {
        delete this;
    }
    return tempRefCount;
}
```

This implementation is problematic because those operators are not threadsafe. If 2 threads would AddRef or Release at the exact same time, the resulting value of m_RefCount would be unpredictable because there is a gap between reading its value and performing the operation on it and writing the result back. In scenarios where concurrent access is not happening, it would be fine. For multithreaded use, this race condition can cause unpredictable behaviour. So, we replace it with the following:

```
ULONG STDMETHODCALLTYPE CalculatorInstance::AddRef(void) {
    return InterlockedIncrement(&m_RefCount);
}

ULONG STDMETHODCALLTYPE CalculatorInstance::Release(void) {
    ULONG retVal = InterlockedDecrement(&m_RefCount);
    if (retVal == 0)
        delete this;
    return retVal;
}
```

Windows has a library of 'Interlocked...' functions that come with the guarantee that whatever they do with the argument is done in an atomic manner. Even 2 concurrent threads trying to perform an operation on the exact same piece of memory will be serialized until 1 thread has completed its operation.

Note that using interlocked functions is not a magic wand that solves all problems. We've mentioned the scenarios where m_RefCount == 1 and one thread tried to AddRef it while another thread calls Release, and Release happens first? That will cause an access violation when the call to AddRef comes through. In the context of COM, those semantics don't make sense. If this scenario plays out, it only means that someone was breaking the rules of COM already. Proper locking and synchronization only help within the framework of rules. They don't help against people intentionally breaking the rules.

That leaves us with the final method we need to explore

```
virtual HRESULT STDMETHODCALLTYPE QueryInterface(
    REFIID riid,
    void **ppvObject) = 0;
```

The argument list is simple enough but can hide a serious amount of complexity. There is the riid parameter of type REFIID, which uniquely identifies the interface we want to use, and the ppvObject parameter, which serves the same function as the interfacePtr parameter in our earlier example. But what is a REFIID?

For programming, as well as designing, we can agree that an object with the name 'Calculator' and an interface with the name 'IArithmetic' make perfect sense.

The problem with good names is that great minds think alike. If I make a Calculator object with an interface called IArithmetic, there is a non-zero chance that someone else with think of those names too. And if the user uses that application on their PC as well as my application, that could cause problems because there is no universal Calculator standard.

That is why DCOM doesn't just use those names. Instead, all names are 128-bit GUIDs which are mathematically guaranteed to be unique. GUID stands for Globally Unique IDentifier. You'll also see the name UUID which stands for Universally Unique IDentifier. Objects have what is called a Class ID (CLSID) and interfaces have an interface ID (IID).

So instead of using those shorthand names like 'Calculator', we use identifiers like CLSID_Calculator with value "D596F767-809D-45C3-947E-012950B5F0C7" and

IID_Arithmetic with value "05DE2CE4-6AAF-4743-A463-51732DF42C5F". Using these identifiers, we can trust that there will never be naming conflicts. They are mathematically guaranteed to be unique whenever or wherever they are generated, so there doesn't have to be a centralized authority in charge of assigning them. You can just use any GUID generation tool like GUIDGen in Visual Studio, and it will give you one whenever you need one, in the form of your choice.

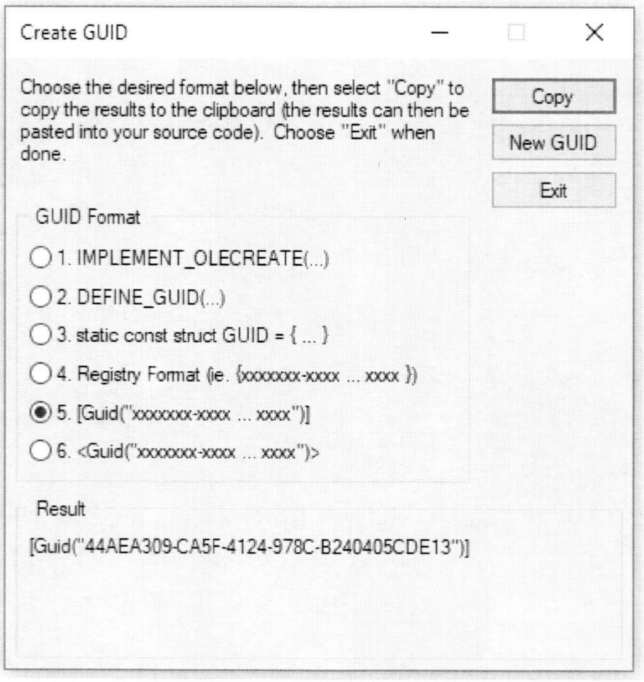

We'll discuss GUID's some more when talking about interface definitions. For now, it suffices that we know what they are. GUIDs have the following type definition:

```
typedef struct _GUID {
    unsigned long  Data1;
    unsigned short Data2;
    unsigned short Data3;
    unsigned char  Data4[ 8 ];
} GUID;
```

The algorithms for generating the data fields are documented in RFC 9562. What is in the data field is not relevant for our purposes. The only purpose of the data is simply to be unique. When you see the datatypes 'REFCLSID' and 'RIID', the REF and R indicate that these parameters are passed as a reference or pointer to this structure.

Armed with this knowledge, we can finally look at how we could implement QueryInterface:

```
HRESULT STDMETHODCALLTYPE CalculatorInstance::QueryInterface(
    REFIID riid,
    void __RPC_FAR* __RPC_FAR* ppvObject)
{
    if (NULL == ppvObject)
        return E_POINTER;

    if (riid == IID_IUnknown) {
        *ppvObject = static_cast<IArithmetic*>(this);
    }
    else if (riid == IID_IArithmetic) {
        *ppvObject = static_cast<IArithmetic*>(this);
    }
    else if (riid == IID_IComServer) {
        *ppvObject = static_cast<IComServer*>(this);
    }
    else    {
        *ppvObject = NULL;
        return E_NOINTERFACE;
    }

    reinterpret_cast<IUnknown*>(*ppvObject)->AddRef();
    return S_OK;
}
```

The first job is to verify that we have a place to write the pointer to. After that, we perform a static cast of our object pointer to the specified interface. If the interface was supported, we AddRef it. If not, we set the output pointer to NULL and return the appropriate error. Setting to NULL is not optional and returning a non-NULL pointer while returning an error code can have unintended side effects. There are 2 peculiarities here: Why do we cast to IArithmetic instead of IUnknown when we request IID_IUnknown, and why does the AddRef happen via reinterpret cast (and why does that even work)? Let's start with the first question.

Suppose our Calculator supports IItf1 and IItfA.

```
class IItf1 : public IUnknown
{
public:
    virtual void Foo( void) = 0;
};

class IItfA : public IUnknown
{
public:
    virtual void Bar( void) = 0;
};
```

```
class Calculator : public IItf1, IItfA
{
public:
    virtual void Foo( void);
    virtual void Bar( void);
};
```

If we draw this schematically, it looks like this:

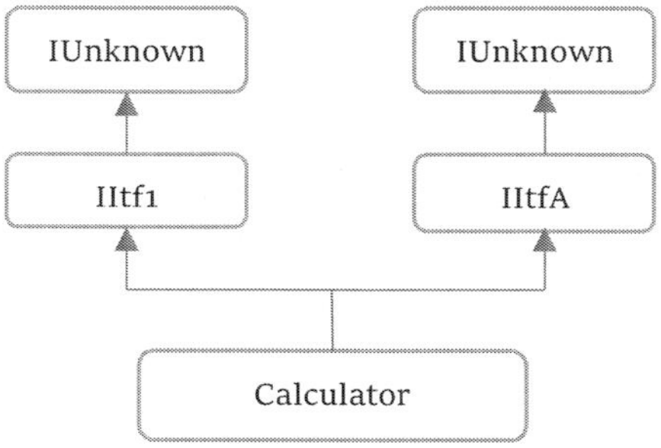

There are 2 Interfaces which derive from IUnknown, so if we try to static_cast Calculator* to IUnknown*, the compiler complains that this is an ambiguous cast. It needs to know 'which' IUnknown we mean. We solve this by casting not to IUnknown, but an interface which inherits from IUnknown. Inheritance is an 'X is a Y' relationship so every IItf1 IS an IUnknown, and every IItf1* IS an IUnknown*. If we look at the vtable explanation from the earlier chapter, this becomes clear.

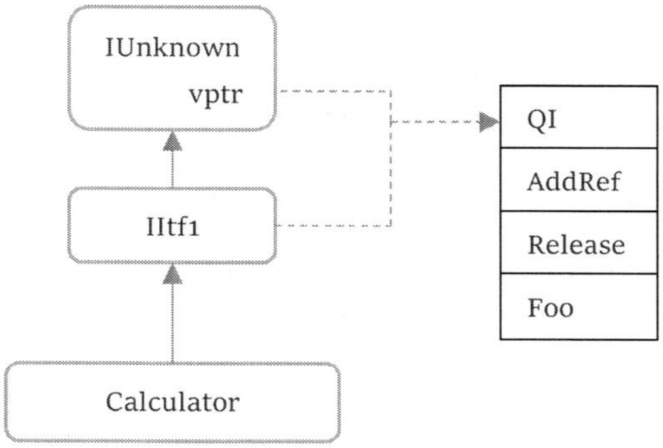

Both IUnknown and IItf1 have the same base address and expect the vptr at the same address. It is therefore perfectly valid to cast Calculator* to an IArithmetic* and pretend it is an IUnknown* because by every measurable property, it really is. Note that for all intents and purposes we could have cast to any other interface supported by our Calculator. To use our contrived example again:

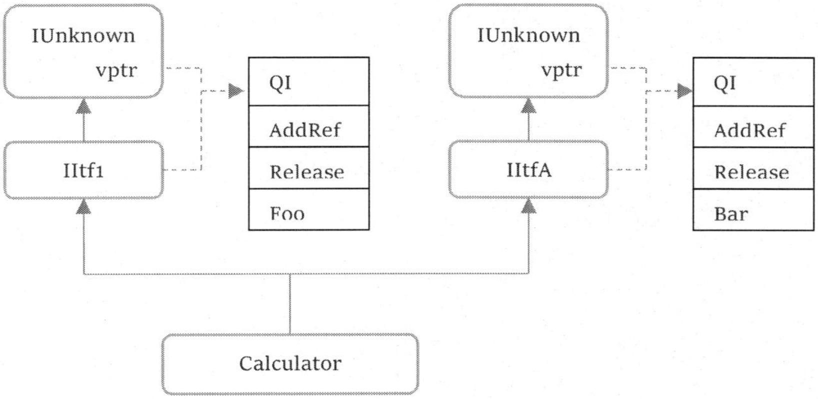

Calculator still has 1 vtable, but in that vtable are the vtables of IItf1 and IItfA. These are independent and in a multiple inheritance situation, there are no guarantees as to which table is located where in the overall table. That is also why multiple inheritance for Interfaces is not allowed. Because that would rely on vendor dependent layout. It is allowed for the final object itself because that is never available to the caller.

If we need to cast to IUnknown* and choose to cast to IItfA* instead of IItf1*, the resulting cast will point to a different vptr, which will point to a different vtable. But that doesn't matter because in both cases, the redirects in that vtable will point to the same implementations of QueryInterface, AddRef and Release. That said, one of the few hard rules is that a query for IUnknown should always return the same pointer. So, it doesn't matter which cast you choose to satisfy that query, but whatever you choose for your object shouldn't change between calls.

The reinterpret cast is easier to explain. Whatever is in *ppvObject is a valid interface pointer. Now we need to AddRef it. Unfortunately, whatever is in there is of type void* and we cannot do anything with a void*. We need to cast it back. A static_cast is impossible for 2 reasons. First, static_cast doesn't allow void* to be cast to a known type, because it has no way to ascertain that said cast is valid. And second, it wouldn't matter if it was because there is no way for the compiler to know 'which' IUnknown* is in *ppvObject and how it relates to the Calculator object.

So we use a reinterpret_cast. This is basically an old C-style typecast where you tell the compiler to just pretend that the specified address has a specific type. And in this case, we get away with that because we cast to IUnknown, and because all interfaces derive from IUnknown, the IUnknown redirects are at the start of the vtable of whatever typecast we used to write *ppvObject. For any other interface we use, using a reinterpret_cast like that would be very dangerous unless we had special knowledge that the cast happens to be true for every possible static_cast we did beforehand. For IUnknown* this is safe. You may be wondering why we don't just call Calculator::AddRef directly. That is certainly a fair question because most of the time it would do exactly what we want. But generally, AddRef and Release should be called through the interface itself.

With every method of IUnknown fully explained, we can now use it in a safe way to switch between interfaces

```
IUnknown* myClassObject = NULL;
HRESULT hRes = GetMyClassObject(&myClassObject);
if (SUCCEEDED(hRes)) {
    IItf1* ift1 = NULL;
    hRes = myClassObject->QueryInterface(
                                IID_IItf1, (void**)&ift1);
    myClassObject->Release();
    if (SUCCEEDED(hRes)) {
        ift1->Foo();
        IItfA* iftA = NULL;
        hRes = myClassObject->QueryInterface(
                                IID_IItfA, (void**)&iftA);
        if (SUCCEEDED(hRes)) {
            iftA->Bar();
            iftA->Release();
        }
        ift1->Release();
    }
}
```

Admittedly, this looks rather messy. The reason is (for now) we are using C style flow control whereby we can only continue with next actions if there was no error in the previous actions. I briefly considered leaving the error flow behind but decided that would set a really bad example. I did leave out the HRESULT checking for the Foo and Bar methods because those errors do not affect the interface lifcycle. Assuming for a moment that all calls return success, this is the lifecycle:

Call	Interface ptr	Refcount
GetMyClassObject	myClassObject	1
myClassObject->QueryInterface	IItf1	2
myClassObject->Release	myClassObject	1
IItf1->QueryInterface	IItfA	2
IItfA->Release	IItfA	1
IItf1->Release	IItf1	0

There are several things we can observe, as expected. With every Interface pointer that was given a valid value, the reference count increases by one. With every Release, it decreases by one. Every interface pointer affects the reference count only, and exactly 2 times. And from this table we can also see that certain actions can be re-ordered without affecting the lifecycle. The following flow is logically identical to the previous one.

Call	Interface ptr	Refcount
GetMyClassObject	myClassObject	1
myClassObject->QueryInterface	IItf1	2
IItf1->QueryInterface	IItfA	3
myClassObject->Release	myClassObject	2
IItfA->Release	IItfA	1
IItf1->Release	IItf1	0

The only 2 things we obviously cannot do is to use a pointer before it has gotten a valid value, and to use it after Release has been called. The former will cause an immediate access violation. The latter, you might get away with in a limited set of scenarios if the reference count hasn't reached 0, but this too falls in the "If you shoot yourself in the foot, you will get hurt" category.

It is also worth mentioning that querying for interfaces can be a dynamic process. Whether an object implements a specific interface or not may not always be a given at design time. Or our code may have the option to use libraries from different providers, not all of which support the same interfaces. It is up to our code to get a pointer to the object (either IUnknown which is guaranteed to exist, or a specific interface we assume exists) and then use QueryInterface to determine which of our expected interfaces exists and then use them accordingly.

When the COM runtime becomes aware of your class object after the server is started, it will perform a list of QueryInterface calls. It will query for IMarshal to see if your class object wants to oversee its own marshaling. It will query for IClassFactory2 to see if your object implements licensing restrictions. It will query for IExternalConnection to determine if it wants to keep track of external connections to perform its own lifecycle management. The list goes on and on. It's a long list. And the COM runtime doesn't care 'why' you want to implement those interfaces or what you do with that information. It will just check whether your object implements it or not. And if it does, it will act accordingly and use that interface as specified in the platform documentation.

Summary

In this chapter we started in the 90's, and explored the road that was taken to go from the need for reusable distributable code, to the foundations of COM. There is of course much more to cover, because COM covers a lot more than just C++ interface design. But with this chapter behind you, you now understand why certain design decisions were made and how COM interfaces work. To recapitulate the key points:

1. All C++ compilers deal with virtual function calls in the same way. So, accessing an object through a virtual base class (also known as an interface) will always work as expected.
2. Objects expose functionality via pure virtual classes known as interfaces through which the object can be accessed.
3. Memory allocation and deallocation need to be done inside the object which exposes the interfaces. To make that possible, objects are created through a 'create...' function call and destroyed when they sense they are no longer in use.
4. Objects manage their own lifecycle through reference counting. Every time a copy of the interface pointer is made, AddRef needs to be called to increase the reference counter. Every time the client is done with the interface pointer, Release needs to be called to decrement the interface pointer. When the reference count reaches 0, the object knows its life is over and should self-destruct.
5. All objects implement IUnknown. The IUnknown pointer serves as the identity of an object.

For more information about IUnknown, check MSDN
https://learn.microsoft.com/en-us/windows/win32/com/using-and-implementing-iunknown

2

Core COM Concepts

Everything we explored so far was to explain where the concept of interfaces comes from and how interfaces are used. But just like 90% of an iceberg is invisible and under water, the same is true for COM infrastructure. To quote Lucy Liu in Kill Bill: "*You didn't think it was going to be this easy, did you*?"

Before we can continue with our Calculator, we need to establish some of the core COM concepts. These are completely transparent when using COM. However, you need to be aware of them if you are building or designing COM objects because the choices you make can have a big impact on performance. An explanation about these topics could have been inserted much later in the book. But then we'd run into terms like proxy and stub without knowing what they are. This may feel like a detour, but it's a crucial detour for understanding what comes later.

Apartments

Back in the 90's, most consumer PCs were single processor machines, with a single core. There were multiple threads alive at any given time, but only 1 was executing. Most programmers were inexperienced with multithreading. Even if you wrote code that could be accessed from multiple threads, you didn't expect it to be executed simultaneously. A single physical CPU could run a single thread. If you really wanted concurrent execution, you had to buy a computer with 2 or more CPU sockets, and 2 or more CPUs. This was not a trivial thing to do because machines like that carried a hefty price tag. And even if you just had a 1 CPU machine, it still wasn't trivial to deal with concurrency issues in a multithreaded environment.

Given the modular and reusable nature of COM, it was entirely possible that the client application would be written by a domain level expert with not a whole lot of experience in thread safety and using COM objects that fully supported multi-threading, or vice versa. It is unrealistic to expect every programmer to become a parallel programming expert or even know what a thread is, or how to program with thread safety in mind. And on the flip side it is unreasonable to expect every COM object to be constrained by existing in a single thread. To solve this problem, the apartment was invented. An apartment can be thought of as an agreement between the programmer of the COM object and the programmer who uses that object. Both parties can declare their concurrency constraints, and the runtime figures out how to deal with that.

There are 3 types of apartment:

1. Single Threaded Apartment (STA)
2. Multi Threaded Apartment (MTA)
3. Neutral Threaded (NTA).

Every thread that uses COM needs to declare whether it belongs to a single threaded apartment or a multithreaded apartment. A thread can exist in only 1 apartment at a given time and must stay there for as long as it is doing anything COM related. We'll ignore Neutral for now.

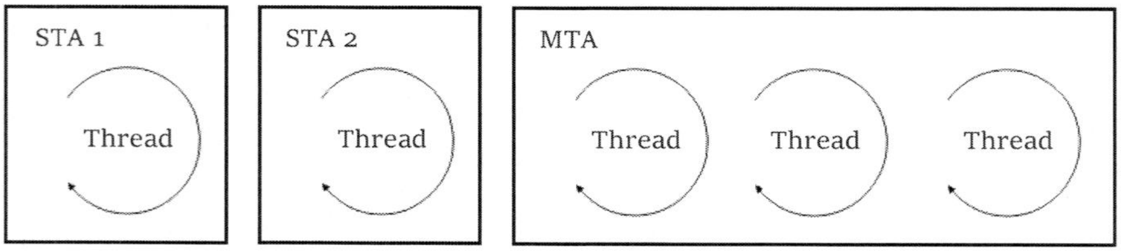

You can think of the apartment as the place where a COM object lives together with the thread(s) on which its interface methods are executed. To phrase that in a different way: there is a guarantee that the COM object is only touched directly by threads that belong to the same apartment. In an STA that means only a single thread. In an MTA, that may be multiple threads, but only those that belong to the MTA.

If someone, somewhere wants to execute a method, the method call must enter the apartment first, after which it can be executed on the thread in that same apartment. For this explanation let's assume that our Calculator object itself supports both single threaded and multithreaded use.

STA threading

To start with the simplest example: Thread 1 creates a Calculator that implements IItf1. The Calculator is now in apartment STA1. If a call to IItf1->Foo() happens from within thread 1 , it gets executed via a direct call through the vtable just like we saw in our earlier examples.

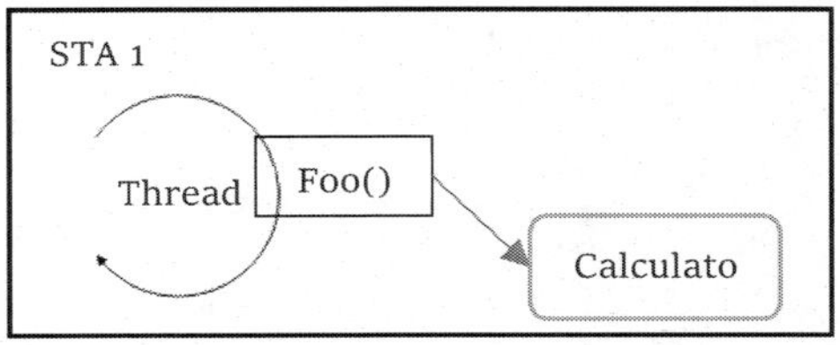

So far, that all makes perfect sense, and looks just like the Calculator examples we saw earlier. It gets trickier when the call originates from thread 2, because the object lives in the STA1 apartment, but the call originates in STA2.

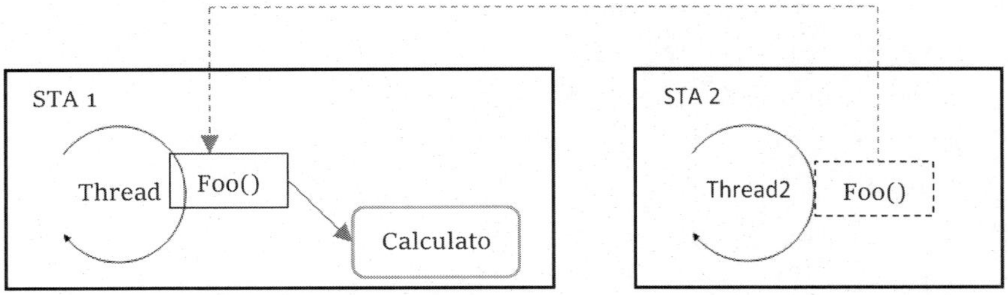

Contrary to the examples we have been playing with so far, the interface pointer we have in thread 2 is not a simple raw pointer. It is a pointer to a proxy object. When thread 1 uses its pointer to call Foo(), this results to an immediate call through the vtable to Calculator::Foo(). When thread 2 tries to do the same, this doesn't happen because it is in STA2, and the call needs to happen in STA1, on thread 1.

To make this happen, the call is transported to STA1 where it is scheduled to be executed on thread 1. After the call is completed, the result is transported back to thread 2 where the call to Foo() is still waiting to complete. It is important to note that while all this is going on, thread 2 is blissfully unaware of what is happening in the background. As far as it is concerned, it calls Foo(), which just happens to take a long time to complete.

2 things stand out here. First, all interactions with the actual object are serialized. There is no possibility of creating a conflict. All interactions are queued and only

processed 1 at a time in thread 1. Thread 1 has a direct pointer but doesn't have to worry about being interrupted or other calls happening at the same time because the out-of-process COM calls are only executed when thread 1 is not doing anything else.

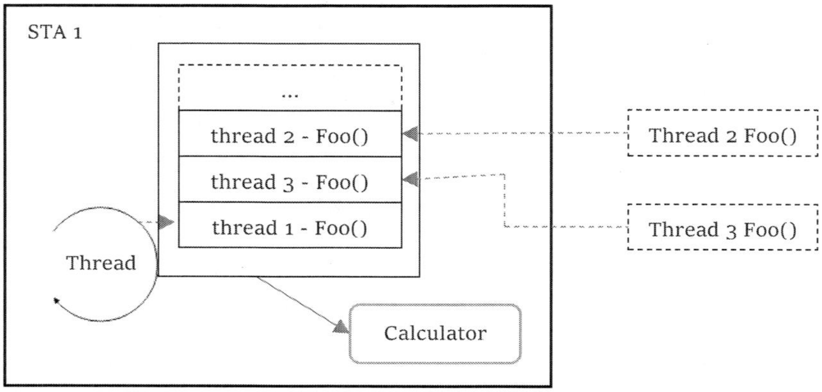

The major benefit is that even if the programmers of either the client or the COM object are not experienced with multi-threaded programming, the use of apartment threading guarantees that calls are executed only 1 by 1 in a serialized fashion. Second, while thread 1 is in the same apartment as the Calculator and thus can perform calls instantly, any other thread is having to halt what it is doing, transport the call to STA1, wait for it to be executed, and then wait for the result to be transported back. It should be obvious that there is a massive amount of overhead in terms of execution times. Btw it's not that those calls don't have an impact on the available CPU time for thread 1. All those out-of-apartment calls are still accounted on the thread. Thread 1 doesn't have to synchronize its calls through the interface because it will never be interrupted while it is doing that. We'll cover the exact details below.

That doesn't necessarily mean that STA threading is slow or inefficient. In many cases, the thread that creates the object is the only one who uses it. In that case, the overhead is no bigger than dereferencing a function pointer through the vptr and the vtable. Another possible scenario is when there are multiple threads interacting with the object, but they only do so occasionally. Again, the overhead would not matter. But in the latter scenario it may not even matter to begin with.

A special case of the STA is the User Interface (UI) thread also known as the main thread. This is the apartment which is used by the Graphical User Interface (GUI) windows which are created by the main application thread, usually upon startup.

Many COM objects exist to support GUI features. Or interact with the GUI. A strict rule of Windows user interfaces is that anything GUI related is only allowed to be accessed by the thread which created the GUI windows. This has been a rule since the inception of Windows and is still an inviolable rule today. One of the reasons is that GUI components use thread local storage, but it also makes logical sense because the win32 API would have to be much more complex to deal with things like one thread updating the text of a textbox while another thread simultaneously deletes the textbox or changes the background color while the first thread is halfway done with painting the background of said textbox. By using the STA paradigm, this is all neatly solved and as an added bonus: should our object need to perform any user interface actions, not only do we not have to invent our own code for transporting those actions to the appropriate thread, but the STA also neatly serializes our actions so that we don't have to worry about clashing with other user interface activity.

MTA threading

A multi-threaded apartment can contain more than 1 thread. Any object created in the MTA can be accessed concurrently by all threads within the apartment. This makes concurrent access efficient and easy from the client's point of view. Of course, this puts a bigger burden on the developer of the object, because the object needs to implement its own locking and synchronization primitives to make sure that its internal state is kept safe.

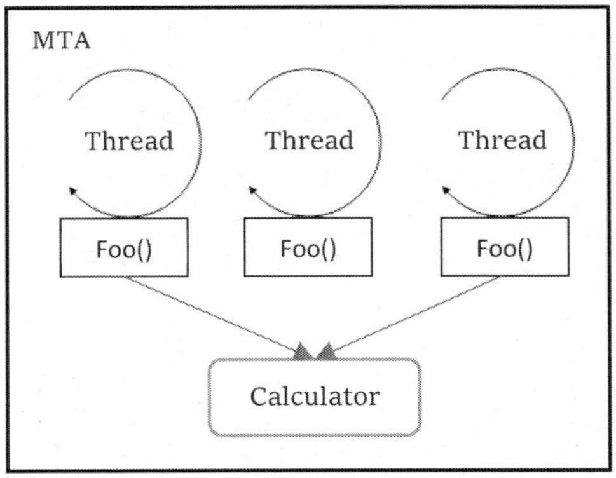

There is no transport of function calls required, nor any synchronization. Foo() can be called by multiple threads at the same time, and it is up to Calculator to make sure this is safe.

Just like with STA objects, MTA objects can be accessed by a thread in a different thread. The situation is very similar to the situation with STA threading. The only difference is that the call is transported into the MTA, where it needs to find a thread to execute on. The COM infrastructure can spin up additional threads or choose to use an existing thread. This is explained in more detail later. No synchronization is performed because the object doesn't require any. This is different from the STA scenario where calls block until they can be executed because there can be only 1 thread in that apartment.

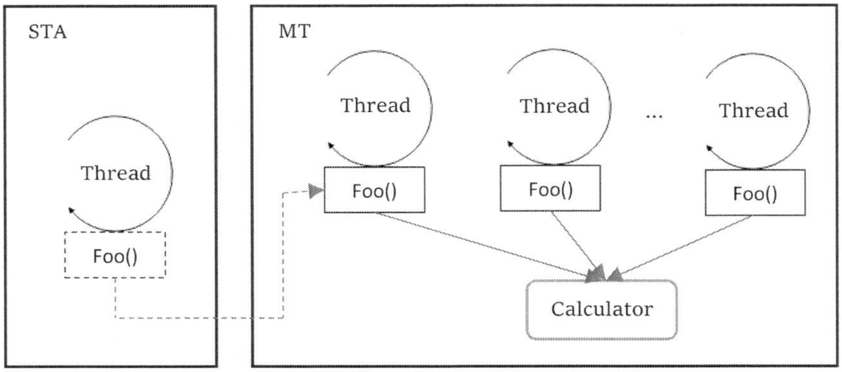

So far we've looked at what happens if an object is created in either type of apartment and then accessed from either inside or outside the apartment. But that was assuming the object supports both types of apartment. However, there is still the scenario where we try to create the object in an apartment it does not support: an MTA object in an STA thread, or an STA object in an MTA thread.

When that happens, the object will not be created in the requested apartment. Instead, a new thread will be spun up and enter an apartment of the correct type. If it's an STA object, the new thread will enter the STA. If it's an MTA object, the new thread will enter the MTA. And instead of making the call directly from the originating thread, the calls will be transported to the apartment of the object, executed, and then the result will be transported back.

NTA threading

NTA is a hybrid between the STA and MTA. The object needs to be programmed as if it is an MTA object, in the sense that it should not rely on being executed in any particular thread so it should not use thread local storage. Calls to neutral objects will not require transport into and out of the apartment. However, access to the object will still be serialized to avoid concurrency problems. In general, this is a performance compromise. The object can be accessed directly without the calls being transported back and forth. But access is still serialized via synchronization locks. The resulting performance is slower than if the client and the object share apartments, yet much faster than if the thread safety had to be implemented via transport.

That said, there is only a limited use for NTA. The invention of NTA came quite a while after people had gotten used to STA and MTA. Method calls are slower than calls from within the same apartment, so NTA is only useful in scenarios where it is certain or at least likely that an object IS going to be used from within different apartment types in the same application. But the use case for using NTA as a sort of faux MTA solution without having to do any synchronization never really caught on because by that time, there were enough known patterns to ensure proper multithreading in a safe fashion.

You might wonder why an object would not specify it supports both STA and MTA if it is safe to use in a completely multithreaded fashion. The answer is that in some cases, an object may start a few additional worker threads to help with various tasks. Those threads may all need to access the object and therefore, things will be a lot simpler and faster if the object is in the MTA. For that reason, an object might specify it only supports MTA, and if an STA thread tries to create it, it will be created in the MTA instead, and the STA thread calls are transported back and forth.

On a final note, it is good to understand that all of the above is invisible to the client. It is merely an implementation detail that will affect performance, but not safety or complexity. So far, we've referred to this mechanism simply as transporting, because that's a neutral expression. The correct term you'll see a lot is marshaling.

Marshaling

The explanation so far has focused on calling methods through a vtable. And that is truth. We've also explained that because of the apartment rules, an object should only be accessed through an interface if the thread doing the access is in the same apartment. That is truth as well. There is only one way to satisfy both requirements, and that is if the interface that is used by the out-of-apartment thread is not directly accessing the object. Instead, it does have a vptr and a vtable, and that vtable has redirects with the correct signatures, in the correct order. Only, those redirects are not direct pointers to the object methods. Instead, they point to a proxy object that is valid for that specific thread. We've mentioned that in COM, interfaces are represented as lollipops. Using that analog, we can think of the proxy as something that looks like that lollipop, behaves like that lollipop, but is not quite 'the lollipop'.

This is important to remember: if your code is executing in a given apartment, and you obtain an interface pointer from the various COM APIs such as CoGetClassObject, CoCreateInstance, or any of the other normal COM related routines, you will not know, nor have to care about whether you get a raw interface pointer or a proxy. This is all handled by COM. Even in scenarios where you want to exchange interface pointers between different apartments you need to use the appropriate APIs, because a particular interface pointer is only guaranteed to be valid in the thread where it was created. You would not know whether you get a raw interface pointer or a pointer to a proxy. All you'll know for sure is that whatever you get is going to be valid for the apartment in which it is used.

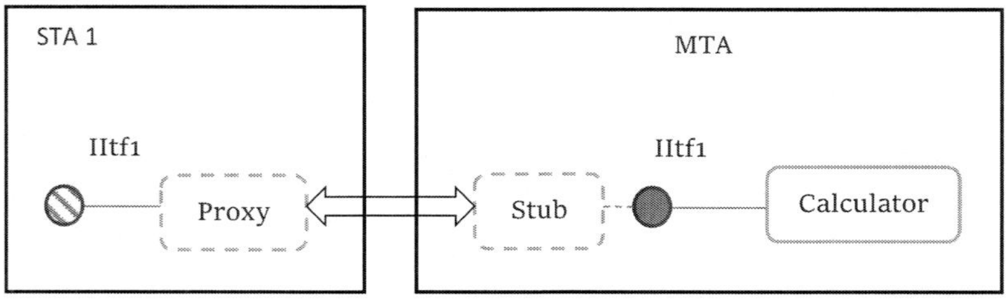

COM is layered on top of the Remote Procedure Call (RPC) protocol. RPC is a technology which is aimed at making distributed applications. It enables server processes to execute code at the request of a client, using proxies and stubs. Stubs are like connection points to the real COM object, providing a connection to a proxy on the client side whereby the client has the appearance of executing the code directly and locally, while RPC uses well-defined connection protocols and libraries in the background to hide the details.

Proxy and stub are 2 sides of the same coin. Sometimes you'll see the term 'proxy' used to indicate both sides. The use of RPC as the communication protocol has the benefit that it can provide this functionality not only between threads in a process or different processes on the same host, but even between threads running on different computers which may even run different operating systems. With this existing infrastructure in place, layering COM on top of RPC is the logical choice.

Since correct behavior depends on COM knowing what apartment a thread belongs to, every thread that interacts with COM needs to initialize with the CoInitialize or CoInitializeEx APIs.

```
//combaseapi.h
WINOLEAPI CoInitialize(LPVOID pvReserved);
WINOLEAPI CoInitializeEx(LPVOID pvReserved,DWORD dwCoInit);
```

CoInitialize is the legacy API which assigns the current thread to an STA. CoInitializeEx does the same thing, except it lets you specify whether the thread apartment is STA, MTA or NTA.

We will revisit this topic much more in depth later, because there is a lot more that can and should be said about marshaling. But for now, it is enough to simply be aware that this mechanism exists and what the high level components are. Otherwise, a lot of other things won't make sense.

Inter-apartment communication

We've mentioned that the interface pointer we get from COM, at any time, is only valid in the apartment in which it was created. The reason is that when the pointer is created, the apartment of the object is known, and the apartment of the caller is known. If a proxy needs to be created, then whatever is 'behind' that interface pointer is set up to be a valid way of executing that call in a manner that complies with the apartment restrictions. Logically, whatever is needed to transport a call from STA 1 to STA 2 is going to be different than what is needed to transport a call from STA 1 to the MTA.

We've briefly mentioned that RPC is used to transport calls between apartments. If the invocation target is an MTA object, the situation is simple. Each process using RPC has 1 or more threads dedicated to calls. These RPC threads are in the MTA by default. This is a good design choice because when a call arrives that is intended for an MTA object, it can be executed immediately on whichever thread it happens to be handled in.

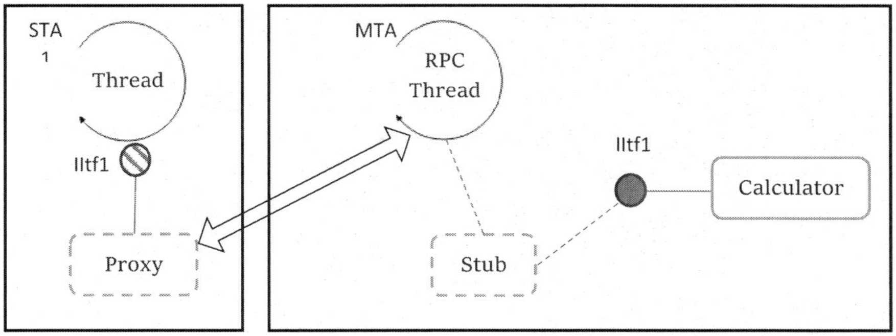

Without getting in too much detail at this point, we can say that the proxy serializes the method call, puts it in an RPC buffer where it is sent to one of the RPC threads. Note that the target MTA can be anywhere: in the same process, in another process, or on another computer. RPC takes care of that technicality. The receiving RPC thread takes that data and executes the call through the stub. It can do this as a direct call because it is in the same apartment as the target object. RPC itself is completely oblivious of the notion of apartments. The RPC threads are in the MTA, but that is really not the same as being aware of apartments themselves. An MTA object can be called directly from other threads in the MTA. By adhering to the convention that those RPC threads are in the MTA, they are allowed to execute calls directly. RPC is a lower-level protocol than COM so it would be meaningless for them to be STA.

If the target is an STA object, the situation is different. The RPC message cannot just be sent to an RPC thread which can then execute the call. The RPC threads are in the MTA, there is no way for them to execute the call. This is where Window messaging comes into play.

In Windows, communication between the operating system, applications, and user interface elements is all implemented via messaging. Due to historical reasons, user interface windows are only allowed to be touched by the thread on which they are created. Without diving into too much detail: user interface elements can only be updated or accessed from inside a single thread. There are several reasons for that. A specific element can only be drawn by a single thread because if 2 threads tried to draw pieces of a user interface at the same time with different info, the result would be a horrible mess of race conditions. Yet protecting every function call in the graphics subsystem with mutexes would be horribly inefficient.

To make that problem go away, all updates are done in the message handling thread. In fact, user interface updates are serialized to solve the same type of problem for which STA was invented. Using the window messaging system to queue COM object method calls on the thread that is pumping the messages for that specific thread is the obvious solution.

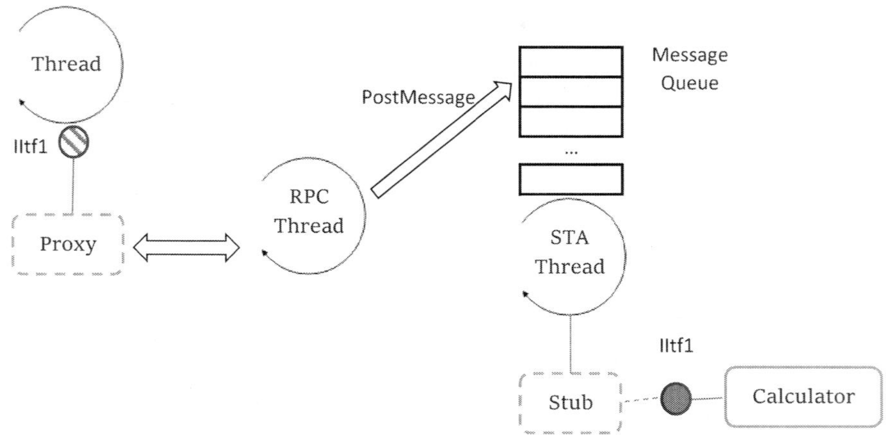

The first part of this diagram is the same as the MTA situation. The Proxy packages the function call into an RPC message, and it goes to one of the RPC threads. However, the RPC thread doesn't execute the call directly. Instead, it posts a message to the message queue of the thread that belongs to the STA of the specified COM object. That message will work itself through the queue, together with all other messages such as GUI updates and operating system messages. Then, when the message is handled, the stub performs the actual function call.

However, for all of this to work, it is critical that ALL threads perform message pumping. If an STA object is only used inside the thread in which it was created, then all calls are direct calls and no messaging is required. So even without messages being pumped, it will work as expected. But as soon as calls originate from another thread, things would grind to a halt.

Even in an MTA thread, messages need to be pumped because an MTA object may be using STA objects directly or indirectly and lack of message pumping would lead to problems. By default, some threads such as manually created worker threads or console application threads are not pumping messages automatically. To deal with that, we use the APIs

```
//combaseapi.h
WINOLEAPI CoInitialize(LPVOID pvReserved);
WINOLEAPI CoInitializeEx(LPVOID pvReserved,DWORD dwCoInit);
```

We already mentioned that these set up the thread to belong to a specific apartment. They also create a hidden window if the thread doesn't have a window associated with it and create a message pump. It is then up to the thread itself to make sure that messages are pumped.

As a minor point of trivia, it must be pointed out that if a thread is performing an alert able wait (a wait operation such as SleepEx or WaitForSingleObjectEx) and the operating system has been given permission to use the thread for other purposes while it is waiting for something, the RPC thread may choose to post an Asynchronous Procedure Call (APC) instead of a window message. An APC is basically a function call that is scheduled in a queue for execution in the specified thread context when the thread itself is in a waiting state.

The effect would be the same because the APC would also be executed on the target thread, at a point in time when it is guaranteed that the thread does not -and cannot -do anything else.

The choice of COM to schedule a call via APC instead of a message is an efficiency improvement in a very specific situation, not something that substitutes the normal way of doing things. On the face of it this is an extremely convenient and efficient way to implement STA guarantees, using already existing functionality, without putting extra requirements on the client programmer. There is, however, a possible problem lurking in the dark.

If the flow of marshaled calls depends on messages being pumped, then it is important that messages ARE being pumped.

For example, a console application does not typically operate in a message driven fashion. It's often built for the purpose of doing a ton of work in a single run without interruption. If the console thread is doing actual work, no marshaling can be done in the background. This can cause problems like time-outs or lost events because any calls from outside the apartment will simply not get a chance to execute on the one and only thread they are allowed to be executed on.

If your console application needs to do large amounts of non-COM related work, it may be a good idea to shunt that work into a worker thread while the main thread in the apartment with the COM objects can process messages. However, given that an application would not create COM objects if it didn't need them to do the work, and we are still talking about STA objects, this does mean that calls from the worker thread then need to be marshaled to the thread handling the messages. Ergo, the requirement to process messages remains. On top of that, marshaling can potentially cause a performance impact. Whether this is going to be a problem or not depends on the use case and performance requirements.

If you want to avoid that overhead and want to keep the main application processing inside the STA thread, you need to define a place in your code where you interrupt your work to deal with incoming window messages. You can combine this with an alertable wait to give your thread an opportunity to wait for user input, for example with a function like this:

```
DWORD WaitProcessIOPumpMessages(DWORD timeoutMilliseconds) {
    DWORD result = MsgWaitForMultipleObjectsEx(
        0,                   // No handles
        NULL,                // No handle array
        timeoutMilliseconds,// Timeout interval
        QS_ALLEVENTS,        // Wait for all types of input
        MWMO_ALERTABLE       // Alertable wait
    );

    if (result == WAIT_TIMEOUT) {
        // Timeout occurred, similar to Sleep(...)
    }
    else if (result == WAIT_IO_COMPLETION) {
```

```
        // An APC was processed
    }
    else if (result == WAIT_OBJECT_0) {
        // A message is available
        MSG msg;
        while (PeekMessage(&msg, NULL, 0, 0, PM_REMOVE)) {
            TranslateMessage(&msg);
            DispatchMessage(&msg);
        }
    }
    return result;
}
```

This function behaves like a SleepEx function would in your console application, except it interrupts its sleep if needed to handle incoming window messages and APCs. In the case of APCs, your code doesn't even have to do anything. Those APCs have been processed while the thread was being co-opted by the system for APC processing. By the time control returns to your code, that has all been done.

Note that this function does NOT act like a true Sleep function because it doesn't resume its sleep if it has been woken up. To turn this into a full-fledged sleep that allows COM processing can be tricky. You'd have to use a high-resolution timer to measure the actual elapsed time between starting the sleep operation and finishing the end of the asynchronous work. And then you'd perform this in a loop until the requested wait period has expired. But even that would not be enough because you'd have to also account for the possible of an 'INFINITE' wait, as well as handling the WM_QUIT, WM_CLOSE, ... messages to make sure the wait operation terminates gracefully. To go into that level of detail would take us beyond the scope of this book. The above function will work for the purpose of defining points in computing intensive code where the thread is given the option to process COM related messages for the purpose of keeping the COM infrastructure happy. You can modify it as needed.

One example of such a modification is the following code if you work a lot with Console style applications. Many console applications show text on screen and then wait for the user to type some input such as a command, a username, ...

You cannot use the standard C++ cin to do so, because it blocks the execution of code until input is received. If you want to wait for input while also processing window messages and APCs, there are several ways you can go about it. One simplistic implementation, based on the code above, would be the following function which captures a character from the input stream.

```
WCHAR WaitForInput(HANDLE hStdin) {
    while (true) {
```

```
        DWORD result = MsgWaitForMultipleObjectsEx(
          1, &hStdin, INFINITE, QS_ALLEVENTS, MWMO_ALERTABLE);

        if (result == WAIT_OBJECT_0) {
            // Console input is available
            INPUT_RECORD inputRecord;
            DWORD eventsRead;
            if (ReadConsoleInput(
                  hStdin, &inputRecord, 1, &eventsRead) &&
                  eventsRead > 0) {
                if (inputRecord.EventType == KEY_EVENT &&
                      inputRecord.Event.KeyEvent.bKeyDown) {
                    return inputRecord.Event.KeyEvent.uChar.UnicodeChar;
                }
            }
        }
        else if (result == WAIT_OBJECT_0 + 1) {
            // A window message is available
            MSG msg;
            while (PeekMessage(&msg, NULL, 0, 0, PM_REMOVE)) {
                TranslateMessage(&msg);
                DispatchMessage(&msg);
            }
        }
        else if (result == WAIT_IO_COMPLETION) {
            // An APC was processed
            continue;
        }
        else {
            return L'\0';
        }
    }
}
```

The above code is a possible implementation of a console input loop which also processes window messages and APCs in the background. You'd use such a loop like this.

```
int main()
{
    HANDLE hStdin = GetStdHandle(STD_INPUT_HANDLE);
    if (hStdin == INVALID_HANDLE_VALUE) {
        std::wcerr << L"Error getting stdin" << std::endl;
        return 1;
    }

    std::wcout <<
       L"Press any key (press 'q' or Escape to exit):" <<
       std::endl;

    while (true) {
```

```
        WCHAR ch = WaitForInput(hStdin);
        std::wcout << L"You pressed: " << ch << std::endl;
        if (ch == L'q' || ch == VK_ESCAPE) {
            break;
        }
    }
}
```

Of course, in a console application, ideally you also need to set up control handlers for termination events such as pressing Ctrl + break or Ctrl + C. Exploring the full set of paradigms for console input is beyond the scope of this book. The main purpose of the preceding examples is to show that marshaling requires you to abide by a couple of rules to make sure the background infrastructure works as expected.

Moving the COM functionality into a worker thread and creating the objects there is certainly an option because it would break the console input away from the COM requirements, though remember that you'd still need to make sure that window messages and APCs are processed in that thread. Note that it is not a hard requirement to process APCs. Only window message processing is mandatory. But if you are going to use synchronization primitives to block execution for extended periods of time, you need to use alertable functions to allow the handling of APCs.

If your program only consists of a single console thread and doesn't use multithreading and doesn't use functionality that requires COM marshaling, you might get away with ignoring everything I just said and pretend the window messaging requirements don't exist. Chances are your program works as expected. However, that would still be a risky thing to do because the COM objects you're using (and which are opaque to you) might do things internally that require messaging or rely on other COM objects you don't know about. This situation is not dissimilar to traffic rules. If everyone stops for a red light and only proceeds when the light turns green, there should be no accident. And running a red light or turning right on red may not have adverse effects in many cases, but that doesn't mean it's always going to end well, even if you establish through testing that it seems to have no apparent consequences.

Memory management

At this point, we've talked about marshaling interfaces and function calls. However, there is still a huge elephant in the room that until now, I've ignored completely. Let's look back at the hypothetical Add routine:

```
HRESULT Calculator::Add(double arg1, double arg2, double* result)
{
    if (!(std::isfinite(arg1) && std::isfinite(arg2)))
```

```
        return E_INVALIDARG;

    if (result == NULL)
        return E_POINTER;

    *result = arg1 + arg2;
}
```

The client-side invocation could look like this:

```
    double result;
    hRes = calc->Add(1.0, 1.0, &result);
```

There are 2 input arguments, which are added together and the result is written in the Result variable. On the surface, everything seems completely trivial. But we just spent the past dozen pages talking about how function calls can be transported to another apartment, and the other apartment can be in a different thread, different process, and even on a different machine with a different architecture. That begs the question: how do the input parameters get from the caller to the callee, and how does the result arrive back on the client side?

If they are both in the same apartment, things are simple. We've already mentioned that when the method call happens in the same apartment, the call is an actual, direct call. This means that the input values are passed via the calling conventions of a normal function call, and the address pointer that the server uses to write the output value is the actual memory location in the client, provided during the function call.

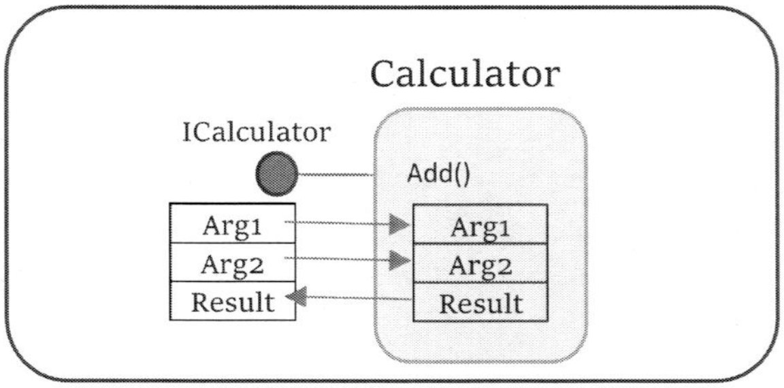

If they are in a different apartment, there is a lot more activity going on behind the scenes, with the marshaler doing a lot of heavy lifting. Consider the following example.

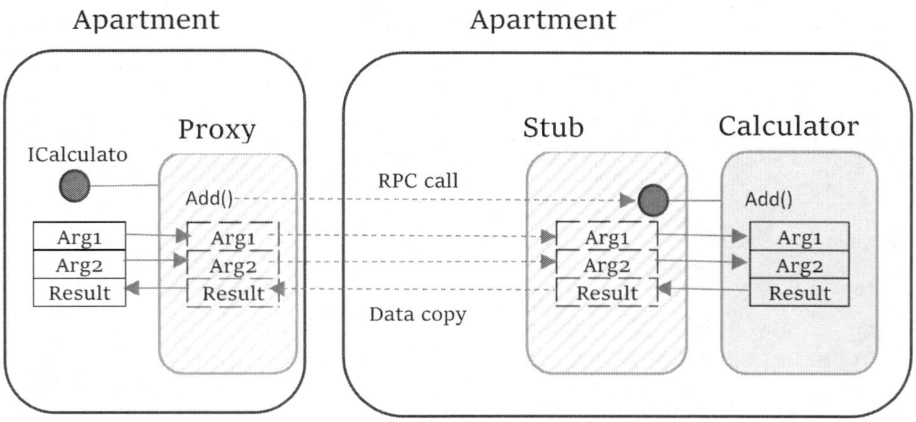

When a caller calls ICalculator::Add, it invokes the method in the proxy. The proxy has memory locations for each of the variables. Arg1 and Arg2 are copied as part of the function call and packaged into the RPC function call which is transmitted to the target apartment where the call is unpackaged. The pointer to the result will be kept locally because there is nothing useful that can be done with it in the stub. Instead, a new memory location is allocated for the result to be written in by the actual Add call.

The stub provides the input arguments to the actual method invocation and then sends the output value back to the RPC caller, where the proxy will copy it into the designated variable whose pointer was supplied as part of the original client-side method call.

The above representation is a simplified example that ignores potential optimization of data copies and temporary variables. The main point is that the proxy provides memory management support alongside the remoting of the method invocation itself to make the entire call transparent. It is worth repeating that in normal circumstances, we don't need to write any code to implement marshaling. Our development tools will generate all that code for us. And that's a good thing because converting a function call to RPC wire format can be tricky and error prone.

The server implementation itself is unable to influence this process. It merely executes a method call with the supplied parameters. It has no knowledge on where the call originates or how / which data is copied before and after the call. It doesn't know or care. For simple plain old data (POD), this is trivial enough. It's just a handful of bytes that need to be copied, and the number of bytes is determined by the data type.

Suppose that we have a use case where we do not simply copy the data back and forth. Instead, we want to receive a pointer to the data. For example, our interface receives a pointer to a spacetime coordinate. This is a scenario that is common in the win32 landscape (receiving a pointer, not necessarily the spacetime coordinate). A naïve implementation could look like this:

```
HRESULT STDMETHODCALLTYPE IOTesterInstance::GetCoordinate(
    /* [out] */ PSPACETIME_COORDINATE* coordinate)
{
    if (*coordinate != NULL)
        return E_POINTER;

    *coordinate = new SPACETIME_COORDINATE();
    memset(*coordinate, 0, sizeof(SPACETIME_COORDINATE));

    (*coordinate)->x = 42;
    (*coordinate)->y = 43;
    (*coordinate)->z = 44;
    (*coordinate)->t = 45;

    return S_OK;
}
```

The reason this cannot work is that the server is not passing a pointer back to the client. Instead, it is passing a pointer to the marshaler. The marshaler will transfer the contents to the client-side proxy as an RPC message and then deallocate the memory. Care needs to be taken so that memory is not leaked. Memory allocated by `new` needs to be deallocated by `delete`, via the same heap manager.

Even if the 2 apartments involved are in the same process and everything is developed in C++, there is no inherent guarantee that caller, callee, and proxy will be using the same runtime libraries and same heap managers. They need to agree to use a set of routines to safely manage memory and transfer memory ownership. By using the following set of COM APIs, all dynamic COM memory inside a process is managed by the same heap manager and the callee and marshaler can swap ownership between themselves in the stub just like a caller and a marshaler in the proxy.

```
//combaseapi.h

LPVOID CoTaskMemAlloc(
    SIZE_T cb);

LPVOID CoTaskMemRealloc(
    LPVOID pv,
    SIZE_T cb);

Void CoTaskMemFree(
    LPVOID pv);
```

`CoTaskMemAlloc` allocates memory, and `CoTaskMemRealloc` can resize previously allocated memory. When the memory ownership is transferred, it can be freed using `CoTaskMemFree` no matter where it was originally allocated. Armed with that knowledge, we can update the example.

```
//Server side
HRESULT STDMETHODCALLTYPE IOTesterInstance::GetCoordinate(
    /* [out] */ PSPACETIME_COORDINATE* coordinate)
{
    if (*coordinate != NULL)
        return E_POINTER;

    const int coordinateSize = sizeof(SPACETIME_COORDINATE);
    *coordinate = (PSPACETIME_COORDINATE)CoTaskMemAlloc(coordinateSize);
    if (!*coordinate)
        return E_OUTOFMEMORY;

    (*coordinate)->x = 42;
    (*coordinate)->y = 43;
    (*coordinate)->z = 44;
    (*coordinate)->t = 45;

    return S_OK;
}

    //Client side
    PSPACETIME_COORDINATE coordinate = NULL;
    hRes = ioDirTest->GetCoordinate(&coordinate);
    if (SUCCEEDED(hRes)) {
        //do something useful with the coordinate
        CoTaskMemFree(coordinate);
    }
```

When implementing the interface contract that has a pointer to something as an output parameter, the COM object allocates the memory and the caller frees it. In a healthy system with proper error handling, every call to `CoTaskMemAlloc` in the COM object is paired with a caller side call to `CoTaskMemFree` and vice versa.

The beauty of this arrangement is that while the caller and callee don't have any knowledge about each other, this approach will always work as expected. If the marshaler is involved, it will do the data copying and allocate / free memory as needed in between. In scenarios where the marshaler isn't involved because they are in the same apartment, the `CoTaskMemAlloc` / `CoTaskMemFree` pattern still works the same way because in that scenario, the COM memory manager is just used as any other shared heap.

Aggregation

COM revolves around the concept of dealing with objects. From that perspective it makes sense that the notion of code reuse was one of the design goals early on.

The C++ style of inheritance that is commonly used in code libraries and which COM uses for interfaces, is not an option when dealing with actual COM objects. In terms of inheritance, the only concepts that were transferable are interfaces, not objects themselves.

But those are merely implementation details. Inheritance is just one possible implementation of the concept 'X is a Y'. That can also be implemented in another manner.

Suppose another company named CalculusInc wants to build a more advanced calculator that is not only an arithmetic calculator but also performs trigonometric operations as defined by an ITrigonometry interface.

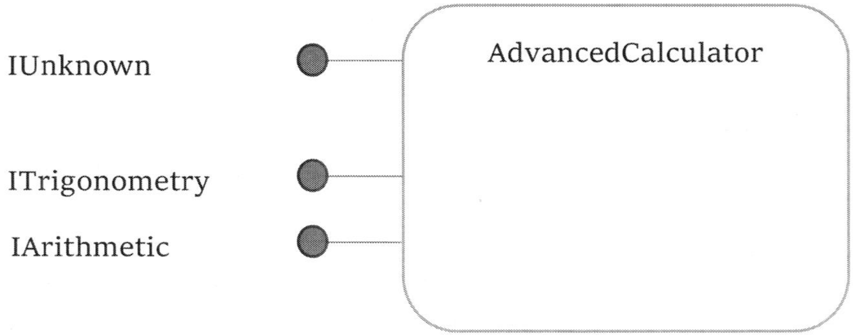

One approach would be for CalculusInc to design an object that implements both the ITrigonometry and IArithmetic interface and then develop both implementations themselves. But obviously, that would involve a lot of work and MathLibCo is renowned for their library implementation, which is already an industry standard. Rather than reinventing the wheel, CalculusInc decides to make a deal with MathLibCo and to use the existing Calculator object as one of the foundations for their more advanced object. From the client's point of view, this will be indistinguishable from a situation where the new object would implement both interfaces itself.

The simplest solution would be to have AdvancedCalculator implement the IArithmetic interface as well that exposes dummy methods, create a Calculator instance internally, and simply do a 1 to 1 mapping for each method that is defined in the interface. This requires the least amount of complexity because the ITrigonometry and IArithmetic interfaces both exist on the same object, and all standard IUnknown behavior will work as expected. This type of implementation is known as Containment. The outer interface is the same as the inner interface, and calls are forwarded as needed.

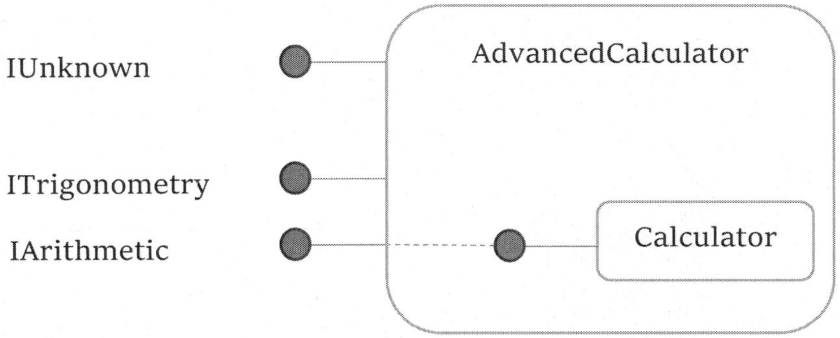

It is impossible for the user of the object to know whether AdvancedCalculator implements both interfaces itself, or whether it encapsulates another object to provide the interfaces it doesn't implement itself. From a client's perspective, this makes it super easy to deal with encapsulated objects.

But there are problems with this. First, it can quickly become a lot of tedious overhead to perform a 1 to 1 mapping, especially if the number of interfaces grows, and there are lots of method calls to map. Even if we'd develop a wizard for this in our development environment, there is a hard limitation. This would only work if we can identify ALL possible interfaces at design time, because there needs to be an explicit mapping.

In situations where we want encapsulated objects to expose their interfaces directly as part of the identity of the outer object, or in cases where objects are encapsulated dynamically based on runtime information, the simple solution of exposing dummy interfaces will stop working. Instead, the higher-level object must make the encapsulated objects part of its identity so that the interfaces of the inner object are exposed directly.

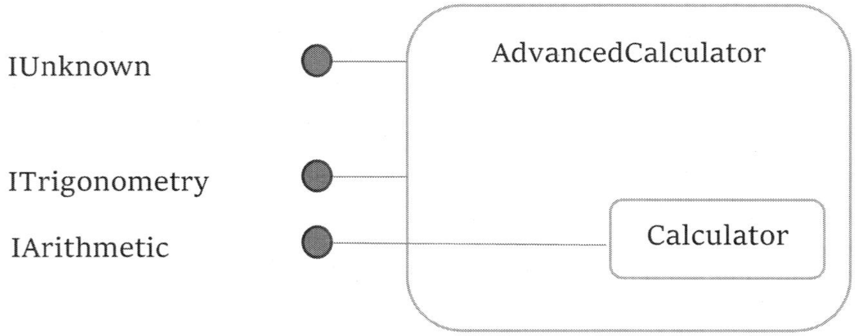

But there is a snag.

From an outsider's perspective, there is only 1 IUnknown pointer. If a client performs a QueryInterface on an IArithmetic interface for IUnknown, then the resulting pointer must be the same pointer as when the same operation is performed on the ITrigonometry interface. And what's more, if the client calls a QueryInterface on an IArithmetic interface for ITrigonometry, even though the Calculator object hasn't the faintest idea what it is.

Similar problems exist with lifecycle management. The Calculator object which supports the IArithmetic interface must somehow entangle its lifecycle management with that of the encapsulating object. Just because there are no more external clients of the Calculator object doesn't mean it can be allowed to terminate.

All these things combined means that COM objects need to explicitly support the requirements for aggregation to make it possible. Based on whether an object is aggregated or not, its behavior must change. An object that supports aggregation must support 2 different scenarios.

Aggregated	Non-aggregated
Inner object exists only as part of an outer object.	Object is standalone
Inner object defers the IUnknown methods to the outer object	IUnknown methods are implemented internally.
The identity of the object is the IUnknown pointer of the outer object	The identity of the object is the IUnknown pointer of the inner object

Implementing this is less straightforward than it sounds, not because it is conceptually difficult, but because there are several sneaky gotchas. We'll go into the implementation details later. For now, it is important to understand the concept.

Aggregation is one of those ideas that sound powerful, but their real-world use is rather niche. Containment is used more often than aggregation because it is so much simpler to design and to implement. However, in the COM infrastructure itself, aggregation is used more often.

A good example of this is the Proxy Manager object which manages the proxies for individual interfaces and aggregates them into a single Proxy Manager object as needed. A proxy manager is the object that manages all interface proxies for a specific remote object instance. The reason for the 1 to 1 relationship is that the implementation details and the specific parameters for RPC communication depend on exactly where the source and the target apartments are located and that can be different for different instances of the same class object.

COM objects are opaque. A Proxy manager can never know in advance which interfaces are implemented on a COM, so it needs to be able to 'grow' its identity with every new interface that is marshaled for the first time.

And because all Interface Proxy objects support aggregation, QueryInterface works as expected. They all defer to the proxy manager which can then resolve the request and aggregate new proxy objects as needed.

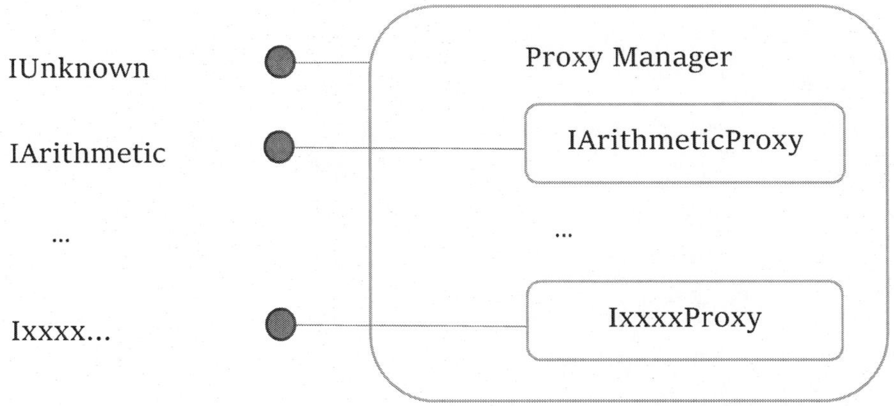

There is another significant benefit to aggregating proxies like this. All Proxy Managers implement other interfaces aside from the ones they're acting as proxy for.

If someone is using an interface pointer, they may really be dealing with a proxy, even if they don't know it. But if it IS a proxy, it will have an RPC connection to a remote object in another apartment, and that connection is subject to security settings that can be managed. To do so, a Proxy Manager implements the IClientSecurity interface.

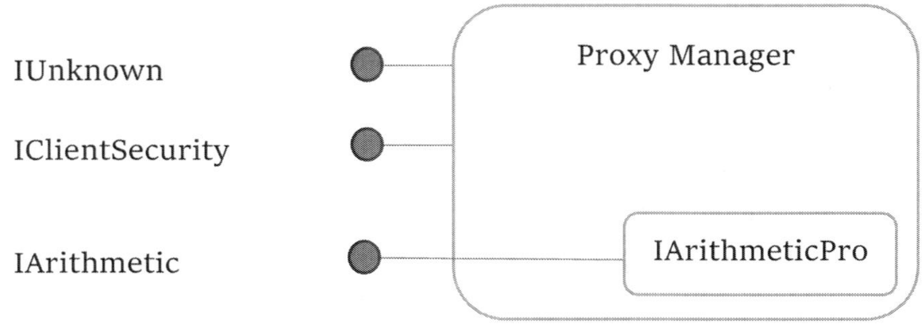

If a program needs to perform security related actions of modify security settings that concern the connection between the interface proxy and the remote object instance, all it needs to do is query the interface for IClientSecurity and even though the remote object doesn't even know about that interface, and IClientSecurity is not listed as an interface that is exposed by the remote object, the aggregation rules cause the proxy to defer the QueryInterface call to the Proxy Manager, who will return an interface pointer to its own implementation of IClientSecurity.

Summary

In this chapter we covered made a small but essential detour from the Calculator application and looked in detail at how threading is done in the world of COM, as well as how memory is managed in calls across apartment boundaries.

We also introduced several new terms. The process of transporting calls and data across apartment boundaries is called 'marshaling'. The source side of this process is often referred to as the Proxy, and the target side as the Stub. In documentation, the term 'Proxy' is sometimes used to cover both sides or to refer to this general arrangement of transport. However, they all refer to the process of marshaling. In general -unless you are implementing custom marshaling- you'll never have to think about how this is done, because the runtime does it all for you.

We also explained the concept of aggregation and how it is used with proxy objects.

With this out of the way, we can start working on our calculator in earnest.

3

Interface Definition Language

In theory, nothing is stopping anyone from manually creating all the declarations, adding the various attributes and typing out all identifying data that would make it possible for every development environment to have a mutual understanding of what the interface exactly looks like at the byte level. But that would be very tedious and error prone. Especially since the resulting definitions would have to be rewritten for every new type of language. One of the design goals was to allow binary distribution and development platform independence. Someone programming an application in Java would need different declarations than someone working with C++. Making and keeping large sets of declarations 100% correct and compatible would be its own level of nightmare. And if it turns out there is an incompatibility, who would be correct? The discussions could be endless.

Instead, we use a language which was designed to be universal, aptly named 'Interface Definition Language' or IDL. IDL is used to describe interfaces and data types in a language independent way for the purpose of letting languages communicate with other languages, possibly on another platform. A declaration in such a language would be the universal truth and can be interpreted by language specific tools to automatically generate the appropriate declarations and type definitions for that specific language.

The Microsoft tool for that language is MIDL. It takes a descriptive IDL type definition, which is then transformed into files that contain type information, which can then be used by development environments for building applications. IDL files have the '.idl' extension and contain type declarations that loosely resemble C++ syntax.

MIDL creates 2 types of files. The first is a collection of C files and header files that can be added to projects that either implement those interfaces, or that interact with programs or components which implement those interfaces. And this is very convenient for C or C++ programmers but doesn't really help developers who work with scripting languages, or Visual Basic, C# or any of a myriad other possible environments.

That is why aside from those headers and source files, MIDL also creates a type library with the .tlb extension. A type library can be thought of as conceptually similar to an IDL file, but in a binary form. Where an IDL file is meant by necessity to be written and read by humans, a TLB file is meant to be convenient for computer programs such as compilers, scripting environments, and development tools including MIDL itself.

Declaring Interfaces

Declaring an interface in IDL looks a lot like declaring a C++ class, with the difference that you don't specify public or private inheritance. IDL definitions are meant for interface specifications, and if something is private, then by default it couldn't be part of a public interface. The `interface` Keyword specifies that IArtithmetic is an interface that must inherit (either directly or indirectly) from IUnknown. Because this is yet a simple interface, it derives directly from IUnknown. Remember that interfaces cannot use multiple inheritance because it would leave the vptr and vtable layout undefined.

```
interface IArithmetic : IUnknown
{
    HRESULT Add(
        [in] double Arg1,
        [in] double Arg2,
        [out] double* Result);

    HRESULT Subtract(
        [in] double Arg1,
        [in] double Arg2,
        [out] double* Result);
}
```

One very noticeable difference compared to C++ is that IDL has the notion of parameter directionality. Parameters can be either input, output, or both. We specify that via attributes between square brackets. IDL interfaces can support the use of properties alongside methods.

```
interface IArithmetic : IUnknown
```

```
{
    HRESULT Add(
        [in] double Arg1,
        [in] double Arg2,
        [out] double* Result);

    HRESULT Subtract(
        [in] double Arg1,
        [in] double Arg2,
        [out] double* Result);

    [propget] HRESULT LastResult([out, retval] double* pVal);
    [propput] HRESULT LastResult([in] double newVal);
}
```

At first it may seem like a violation of the vtable principle that it would be somehow possible to read or write data values. However, this is only syntactic sugar. Behind the scenes, a MIDL creates 'get' and 'set' accessor function definitions that implement the actual data access. The C++ definition of that syntactic sugar is as follows

```
    virtual /* [propget] */ HRESULT STDMETHODCALLTYPE get_LastResult(
        /* [retval][out] */ double *pVal) = 0;

    virtual /* [propput] */ HRESULT STDMETHODCALLTYPE put_LastResult(
        /* [in] */ double newVal) = 0;
```

We know from the historical introduction that interfaces have GUIDs associated with them. Like everything else in IDL, this is declared with the help of attributes.

```
[object, uuid (713E70B0-8E41-482C-80AB-0258CAA5350B)]
interface IArithmetic : IUnknown
{
    HRESULT Add(
        [in] double Arg1,
        [in] double Arg2,
        [out] double* Result);

    HRESULT Subtract(
        [in] double Arg1,
        [in] double Arg2,
        [out] double* Result);

    [propget] HRESULT LastResult([out, retval] double* pVal);
    [propput] HRESULT LastResult([in] double newVal);

}
```

`object` is used to indicate that the interface is a COM interface, with the `uuid (713E70B0-8E41-482C-80AB-0258CAA5350B)` to uniquely identify itself as the IArithmetic interface. As far as interfaces are concerned, this is pretty much everything there is to the principle. And like C++ declarations, the choice to have different IDL files for different declarations or to group multiple declarations together in a single IDL file is mainly one of style.

The final thing to note here is that similar to the need to include headers with base definitions in a C++ .h file, an IDL declaration needs import directives for base types before the actual declarations too.

```
import "oaidl.idl";
import "ocidl.idl";
```

IDL import directives are like C++ style include statements. They contain a massive amount of type definitions for various datatypes and interfaces that are commonly used in COM. A complete listing of everything in those idl files is beyond the scope of this explanation. Suffice it to say for now that these files contain many declarations for commonly used interfaces and data types. An interface as trivial as our IArithmetic would not need them but just like a Windows C++ application that includes windows.h by default, these 2 IDL files are commonly imported by default because many real-world interfaces require something in them.

Declaring objects

Having declared the interface(s) we want to implement, in theory we have all the information we need to use those interfaces. But that is not enough in real life. If someone is developing an application that uses those interfaces to work with some code library or software component, they need more. They need to be able to say 'I want to work with THIS specific implementation of those interfaces' before they can do anything useful. Similarly, the library developer needs to have a way to say 'THIS particular object implements THESE specific interfaces, and has THIS `uuid`'

If 2 different companies implement the same set of interfaces, they will use the same IDL interface definition files. Yet each will have their own separate IDL file to declare the details of their implementation. As developers of a calculator object implementation, we create Calculator.idl. The process is like defining an interface. It starts with the imports. This time we also must include the IDL file containing the declaration of our IArithmetic interface.

```
import "oaidl.idl";
import "ocidl.idl";
import "IArithmetic.idl";
```

Unlike C++ includes, imports are not transitive. IArithmetic.idl also imports oaidl.idl and ocidl.idl, but that doesn't automatically pull them in when compiling Calculator.idl. Declaring an implementation is trivial.

```
[uuid(5AB4FB62-13B0-4370-AD0E-C9E6F989815F)]
coclass Calculator
{
    [default] interface IArithmetic;
}
```

In IDL, a `coclass` is defined as an implementation of a set of interfaces, that allows the use of QueryInterface between a set of interfaces. And just like every interface has a unique identifier, so does every implementation. Because eventually, someone is going to want to say, 'create an instance of THIS particular class'. GUIDs are used here as well for the same reason we use them for interfaces. If we used human readable names, there would be multiple implementations with an obvious name like 'AwesomeCalculator'.

Unlike interfaces, a class can implement (inherit from) multiple interfaces. This does not pose the multiple inheritance problem because no one outside the library has direct access to the actual object, so it doesn't matter that the layout of the object is compiler dependent. An interface can also be marked as default. This will have no effect on C++ applications or other strongly typed languages, but scripting languages can use that attribute to know which interface they can use without having to explicitly query for it.

COM classes can exist on their own or can be part of a set of COM classes that belong together. In either case, there needs to be some sort of container to physically contain their implementation, like a DLL or EXE file. And it should come as no surprise that while this file must have a human readable name, it must also have some sort of name that is guaranteed to be unique.

```
[
    version(1.0),
    uuid(9E9AADC9-2686-4A99-A9FE-A155E0E39E34),
    helpstring("Mathematics library")
]
library MathLib
{
    importlib ("stdole32.tlb");

    [uuid(5AB4FB62-13B0-4370-AD0E-C9E6F989815F)]
    coclass Calculator
    {
```

```
        [default] interface IArithmetic;
    }
}
```

The declaration for the library that contains our calculator class is adorned not just with the GUID that we assign to it, but also a human readable description as well as a version number.

Because our library uses standard COM types and interfaces, it also imports stdole32.tlb which contains those type definitions. Stdole32.tlb contains things like the IUnknown interface, base type definitions and other things that need to be agreed upon by every implementation of a COM class.

Unlike interfaces, a class can implement multiple interfaces. This does not pose the multiple inheritance problem because no one outside the library has direct access to the actual object so it doesn't matter that the layout of the object is compiler dependent. An interface can also be marked as default. This will have no effect on C++ applications or other strongly typed languages, but scripting languages can use that attribute to know which interface they can use without having to explicitly query for it.

Importing IDL vs. Type Libraries

It might seem weird that some things are distributed or imported in IDL source files like oaidl.idl and ocidl.idl on one hand, and some things in a binary format stdole32.tlb file on the other hand.

One major difference is that what is inside stdole32.tlb is the binary type information that is required by interpreted environments to even be able to work with COM itself. I.e. to understand what an IUnknown looks like for example. Supplying that information in a TLB means it is 1 frozen set of information that can be used by MIDL as well as any scripting environment, interpreted language or other type of runtime environment that needs to understand core COM.

There is also the fact that IDL files are most convenient for programmers who implement COM classes and interfaces, and TLB files for programmers who simply use these classes and interfaces. Any project which builds COM components will also create TLB files to be used by client applications. In that regard, it makes sense to distribute base types for implementations in IDL files, and the true, immutable base for COM itself as TLB.

Data types

So far, we've restricted our interfaces to plain old data (POD) types like int and float for the same of simplicity. At this point we've covered enough to implement our Calculator project.

However, things like arrays, string and structures are so common that we need a few words to outline the way these are used because you'll encounter them in any real-world IDL file. If you want to learn more about how various data types are handled in IDL declarations, you can just keep going. If you're anxious to continue with the Calculator project, you can skip the section on datatypes and go straight to next section where we'll compile the IDL to turn it into actual code.

The goal of this section on data types is not to cover every individual data type in depth, but to highlight the more common types you will encounter and what the points of attention are.

Arrays

In many real-world interfaces, parameter lists contain arrays of values. In the world of C and C++, an array is simply a pointer to the memory location of the first value in the array. Indexing into the array is done by calculating the address of each element in the array, based on the offset and starting address. While different environments may implement arrays with different semantics, such as 1 based indexing instead of 0 based indexing, every environment treats it as a block of memory in which indexing is performed.

In COM or IDL documentation you may encounter more formal names to indicate what sort of array is being used. There are 3 terms you may encounter: Fixed, Conformant, and Varying.

A fixed size array is the simplest, because the size is known as part of the type itself. The IDL declaration for a method using an array like that is as follows:

```
HRESULT PassArray(
    [in] double Values[10]);
```

The resulting C++ declaration is equally simple:

```
virtual HRESULT STDMETHODCALLTYPE PassArray(
    /* [in] */ double Values[ 10 ]) = 0;
```

And while different environments may treat arrays in different manners, the type information is unambiguous.

Conformant arrays are a different beast. 'Conformant' means that the size of the array is not known at compile time. This means it is not part of the type definition and needs to be communicated at runtime. Given that the only way to communicate anything about a runtime call is through the parameter list of the call, there needs to be a way to communicate unambiguously which parameter that is going to be.

In the world of C++, the programmer is doing some thinking (hopefully) both during the development of the client application, as well as during the development of the COM component. A documentation reference to designate which parameter contains the size, suffices. A hypothetical method declaration could suffice if both sides were implemented by C++ programmers, because in both cases the programmer would understand what to do.

```
HRESULT PassArray(
    [in] double Values[],
    [in] int NumElements);
```

For many environments such as Microsoft Excel and VB however, arrays are stored in a different manner than in the world of C. It is not enough that the programmer using a scripting language knows this, the runtime itself needs to understand that if one parameter is an array, one of the other possible parameters needs to be that array's size. And it needs to be able to figure this out from the type definition. Note that there are also other reasons why this needs to be in the type definition even for pure C++ environments but we cover those in the next chapter. For now, we simply focus on the fact that the need for unambiguity means that relationship needs to somehow be part of the type. In IDL, we can do that with more attributes.

```
HRESULT PassArray(
    [in, size_is(NumElements)] double Values[],
    [in] int NumElements);
```

This attribute will logically link the array to a parameter that specifies how many elements are in the array. And because this will be baked into the type information in the TLB file, it can be interpreted by any other runtime environment. The resulting C++ declaration still looks as you would expect because in C++, there is no one to do anything with the additional type info.

```
    virtual HRESULT STDMETHODCALLTYPE PassArray(
```

```
        /* [size_is][out][in] */ double Values[  ],
        /* [in] */ int NumElements) = 0;
```

Varying arrays are similar to conformant arrays, with the difference that there is a way to indicate how many elements are actually used / have a value. This may seem redundant when you could also achieve the same thing manually. However, an array could be passed into an object with x number of elements, upon which the object could put in a different number of elements. For example, we could do that if we pass in a C style string, which may be altered by the object. For example, the object could be a string manipulation library which converts all characters to upper class.

```
HRESULT ToUpper(
    [in, out, size_is(MaxChars), length_is(*UsedChars)]
        wchar_t Characters[],
    [in] int MaxChars,
    [in, out] int *UsedChars);
```

This approach differs fundamentally from the previous one because it distinguishes between the size of a buffer, and how much data is in it. This is especially useful if the array can contain different amounts of data in either direction, and it is not possible to deduce from the data itself if an element has valid data or not. For example, a '0' might mean that there is no data there, or it might mean that the data is '0'. This is much less hypothetical than it may seem, because for example some types of string may contain '0' as data instead of terminating character.

Strings

Speaking of strings, it is a good time to expand that topic a bit further. After all, in real world applications, strings are among the most important data types and at the same time one of the most abused and misused ones.

The example we just discussed works just fine if the programmers building the code are C++ programmers for both the object and the application which uses it. A C style string is basically nothing but an array which contains the individual characters of a string, with a final '0' character to mark the end of the string.

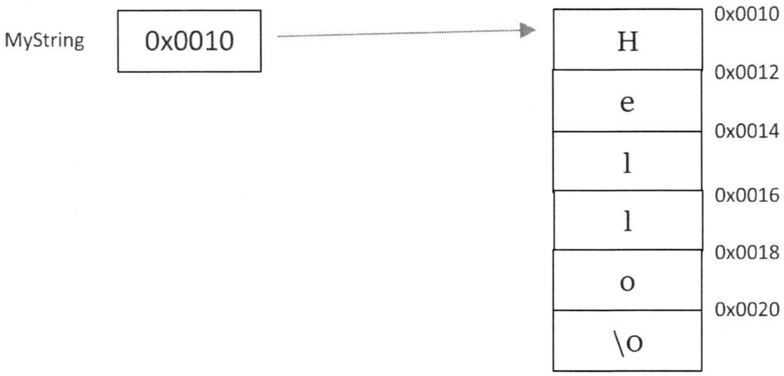

For as long as C strings have been used, programmers and system administrators have cursed the problems associated with them. If string manipulation and the use of arrays like this require the use of a '\0' character to mark the end of the string, then it's easy to understand that mayhem may ensue if it is accidentally or intentionally absent.

Additionally, for C++ programmers the use of strings like this may be intuitive and common sense, but for client applications like Excel, they wouldn't automatically know when something is a string, following string semantics, or simply a raw buffer of characters. To that end, there is an attribute that can be used to put disambiguate the type information to make this clear.

```
HRESULT PassString(
    [in, string] wchar_t* Name);
```

By telling MIDL it is a string, not only will the type information reflect this knowledge, but MIDL will also not need to be told that Name is a pointer to an array and not just a character. Instead, it will work on the assumption that anyone can start at the specified memory location and continue reading until a '\0' is encountered.

However, there is a better way to do things. The COM standard specifies 16-bit Unicode (UTF-16) as the string format for wide-character strings. Without getting too far ahead of ourselves, we can say that UTF-16 is the standard string type to use in interfaces, and it is used by COM internally for all string passing. That's also why the preceding example used a `wchar_t*` datatype. By using UTF-16, all internal string manipulation supports both ANSI (8 bit) character strings as well as all Unicode.

In an ideal world, we'd also be able to specify the total buffer size to add an extra level of safety to the interface definition but MIDL doesn't allow the use of both `string` and `size_is` because that could lead to confusion. To support a safer handling of strings, the world of COM strings revolves around a datatype known as BSTR (B string). If we follow the rabbit hole of type declarations for BSTR through the headers, we see the following:

```
typedef WCHAR OLECHAR;
typedef OLECHAR *BSTR;
```

A BSTR is essentially just like a `wchar_t*` in the way you use it. But the 32-bit memory location right in front of the first character is guaranteed to contain the size of the memory block that was allocated for the string, in number of bytes, NOT including the terminating '\0'

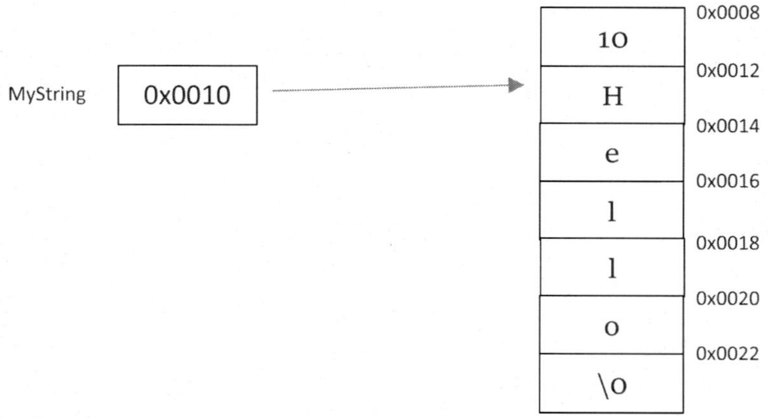

This means you can treat a BSTR like a `wchar_t*` but you can never use a `wchar_t*` like a BSTR and attempting to do so will result in undefined behavior, depending on just what happens to be in the memory location right before the first character.

An observant reader may have noticed that the memory locations in the BSTR example are slightly off from the ones in the `wchar_t*` example. This is because for the purpose of memory efficiency, variables need to be aligned to addresses that are a multiple of their size. The memory location for the number of bytes is 32 bits. This means that it needs to be placed on a 4-byte boundary, whereas an independent `wchar_t*` could start on any 2-byte boundary.

The BSTR data type relies on data being correctly configured to a memory location BEFORE the pointer. This relationship is implied, rather than an explicit type definition. Because of that, there is a small family of helper APIs for allocating and deallocating BSTR data types like the CoTaskMemXxxx routines. These are the 2 main ones:

```
//oleauto.h
BSTR SysAllocString(const OLECHAR * psz);
BSTR SysAllocStringLen(const OLECHAR * strIn, UINT ui);
void SysFreeString(BSTR bstrString);
```

These functions will take all the tedious error prone work of managing the memory in front of the pointer out of our hands and ensure that BSTR behavior is correct and predictable. Additionally, when we use BSTR in our interfaces together with the `[in]` and `[out]` direction specifiers, any marshaling that needs to be performed can be done safely without risking problems from having to manually update pointer values and size parameters.

A hypothetical situation could be as follows:

```
    BSTR bstr = SysAllocString(L"Hello");
    itf->SendMessage(bstr);
    SysFreeString(bstr);

    BSTR bstr2 = NULL;
    itf->GetMessage(&bstr);
    wcout << bstr2 << endl;
    SysFreeString(bstr);
```

Supposing itf is an interface to a COM object in another apartment, we don't have to worry about marshaling all info correctly because the Proxy will know what to do with a BSTR and there is no explicit memory manipulation required. The same goes for data that is received via the hypothetical GetMessage function. Note that the pointer value of bstr2 may be a different one after the function call.

Depending on what you are doing, there is no need to choose BSTR over simple LPWSTR. However, because the length is explicitly tied to the string, they are safer to use and easier to marshal around

Structures

Like any non-trivial C program, you'll often see structures used in IDL to group sets of variables that logically belong together.

```
typedef struct __SPACETIME_COORDINATE
{
    double x;
    double y;
    double z;
    double t;
} SPACETIME_COORDINATE, *PSPACETIME_COORDINATE;
```

This makes it convenient to pass them around in method calls. Technically it is possible to pass these structures themselves by value, but that is very rarely done because it's so inefficient. If we have structures containing many members, everything will have to be copied during every function call. Instead, the common approach is to always pass them by pointer

```
HRESULT SendCoordinate(
            [in] SPACETIME_COORDINATE * coordinate);
```

With the typedefinition of our structure we can also do this in a slightly different way that is very commonly used in the C and C++ world.

```
HRESULT SendCoordinate(
            [in] PSPACETIME_COORDINATE coordinate);
```

Unlike parameters in a method call, structure members do not have in or out attributes. When a structure is used as a parameter, the entire structure is designated for input and / or output.

Variant

A variant is a true 'one size fits all' datatype. It was designed specifically to make it easier to pass data of varying data types through the same interface, as well as make it easier for languages like VBScript and JavaScript to perform late binding of parameters (evaluating the type of a variable the moment it is used, and not during a compilation step).

A Variant is a structure with as first value an enumerated type that specifies what exact datatype is being passed. The data part is a C++ union of every possible supported data.

I am not copying the type definition here because it would literally take up 3 pages, simply because every possible data type is represented. A Simple example should clarify how to use one. Suppose we call some method that expects the data to be passed in a VARIANT, and we want to pass a BSTR

```
VARIANT var;
var.vt = VT_BSTR;
var.bstrVal = SysAllocString(L"Hello world!");
interface->SendSomething(var);
SysFreeString(var.bstrVal);
```

The first thing to do is to specify what type of value we are going to put in the VARIANT. The code which receives the value cannot deduce that for themselves because a VARIANT is a union, meaning all members simply look at the same value but as a different type.

Then we set the value, using the correct way to allocate the BSTR, and call the appropriate method. After we are done using the VARIANT, we also need to manually clean up that BSTR. This is all fine and dandy, but suppose we get data in a VARIANT, and it can have different types:

```
VARIANT var;
interface->GetSomething(&var);
if(var.vt == VT_BSTR) {
    wcout << var.bstrVal << endl;
    SysFreeString(var.bstrVal);
}
if(var.vt == VT_R8) {
    wcout << var.dblVal << endl;
}
```

We must manually account for all possible options. Even if we're not interested in the string values, we must deal with properly deallocating them. Of course, it is contrived to propose a method where we don't know what we are getting. But it's easy to consider a scenario where we have a method for setting instrument settings of some measurement device, and some of the settings are doubles, some are text, some are Boolean, ...

There are various types of value we can store in a VARIANT which require manual actions, even IUnknown pointers! It is painfully obvious that manually dealing with all possibilities is extremely tedious and error prone to cover every scenario. Thankfully, there is no need to do everything by hand. There is a comprehensive set of helper classes available as part of the Active Template Library (ATL). For now, it is enough to simply understand what a Variant is so that you can recognize it when reading IDL files.

Compiling the IDL

To do something useful with the IDL files, they need to be compiled. There are 2 ways we can turn the IDL into something usable. The first is to run midl.exe on the command line for each IDL file.

```
midl /env x64 /h "IArithmetic.h" /W1 /I"..\IDL" /char signed /tlb
"Calculator.tlb" /target "NT60" /nologo
```

This command line is made up with the following arguments.

Argument	Description

`/env amd64`	The resulting code will compile for amd 64-bit environment. This is what you choose for 64-bit Windows platforms. For 32-bit Windows it would be `/env win32`
`/h "IArithmetic.h"`	The generated header file will be generated with this name.
`/W1`	Display warnings that can cause application errors.
`/I"..\IDL"`	Additional include files can be found in ..\IDL
`/char signed`	Specifies that the default C-compiler type for char is signed. This setting helps match C compiler types to MIDL types where char is used.
`/tlb "Calculator.tlb"`	Generate a type library
`/target "NT60"`	Target Windows Vista or higher.
`/nologo`	Disable the copyright banner.

Alternatively, you can also add those IDL files to our project in Visual Studio and let Visual Studio do the heavy lifting. When IDL files are added to the project, the project properties get another tab called 'MIDL'. VS automatically knows what to do but depending on your project requirements. A minor point concerning this is that if you add IDL files to your project, for some reason Visual Studio decides that when MIDL generates the C++ header files, the name of the generated header should have '_h' added to the base name. For example, IArithmetic.idl will compile to IArithmetic_h.h.

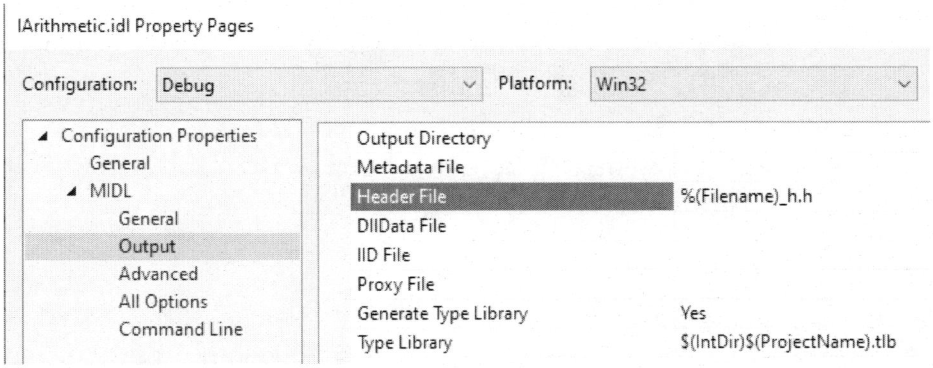

This is not what you want because MIDL then runs for Calculator.idl, the generated header Calculator_h.h still has an include directive for IArithmetic.h without the '_h'. That will lead to compiler errors. This is easily fixed by modifying the project setting.

After MIDL has run (either manually or by VS) we end up with the following files:

- IArithmetic.h and Calculator.h. These are the declarations of the interface and the COM class that we need for implementing our class object and class instances.
- IArithmetic_i.c and Calculator_i.c. These files contain the definition of the class ID CLSID_Calculator and interface ID IIDInterface. These files need to be added to our project build and compiled and linked into our project. Note that if your project settings involve precompiled headers, you need to switch off precompiled headers for those .c files or they will not compile.
- IArithmetic_p.c. This file contains the code for the proxy and stub which are used for marshaling interfaces and data between apartments within the same process, between different processes, and even different hosts. It needs to be added to the VS project for building the proxy. All the tedious and error-prone coding that would have to be done for using the interface across an RPC channel is in this file. There is no Calculator_p.c file because the calculator object itself is never exposed via proxy.
- Dlldata.c. This file needs to be added to the proxy project as well. It exports the required functions that are used for registering, loading and using the proxy. A proxy is a COM object itself. Because the behavior of this COM object is well known, and fully defined by the interfaces, no manual coding has to be done. The only thing we need to do is to build the DLL and register it afterwards. This DLL is often referred to as the proxy DLL, and it can be built completely with only the files that are generated by MIDL.
- LocalServer.tlb. The files we discussed so far are all suitable for use with C or C++ compilers. There are many programming languages and tools that do not know what to do with these files. For example, Visual Basic or C #. For such languages or environments, type libraries are used. A tlb file contains the exact type definition, IDs, and all other information that that is necessary to unambiguously describe the interfaces and classes. With this information, a development environment will be able to convert data from C++ types to its internal representation.

Summary

In this chapter we discussed the basic concepts of the IDL syntax and the anatomy of an IDL file. We now have the necessary pieces to finally build our Calculator COM object.

4

Implementing a COM object

We already know that there is a way for COM objects to be created and that we interact with them through interfaces which are virtual base classes without having to care about details like threading. That leaves us with the question: "where do these objects exist, physically?" Or more practical: "We started on this journey for building a binary reusable object that a client application can leverage. How is the object physically packaged to make this possible?"

We already know that there must be a way for the object to exist in a different binary than the client application. After all, redistribution is one of the core requirements. On the other hand, a COM object itself may use other COM objects from the same library in some way, so it follows that logically a COM object may also exist in the same binary. This is where COM continues the abstraction. In the second chapter we covered that marshaling is implemented using the RPC protocol, which supports calling across process boundaries and physical hardware.

Given that architectural freedom, it makes sense that it is generally unknowable where an object resides, just like it is generally unknowable in which apartment an object resides. Objects can exist in the client's address space, they can live in a separate executable, and even on another computer entirely.

The binary where a COM object is hosted is called a server. This server is typically a DLL or an EXE file. In the COM world you will also encounter files with the OCX extension. An OCX file is binary compatible with a DLL file and exports the same symbol. It is possible to change the OCX file extension to a DLL extension, and everything will still work. However, some tools may be confused. The different file extension indicates that the COM objects inside have a Graphical User Interface (GUI). COM objects with a GUI are sometimes referred to as 'ActiveX'.

As a note of trivia: If you see the word 'Active' in front of a Windows related word, it generally means the word originated in the early 2000's when Microsoft slapped that word on many things, like how the term '.NET' was shoehorned into many names to indicate it was the hot new tech. The distinction between both extensions is not an enforced one. Objects in a COM DLL can have a GUI but that is optional. Objects in an OCX file typically have one, and those are often referred to as ActiveX.

A lot has been written over the decades, and terminology is not always used consistently, but the word 'server' usually refers to the binary file (the DLL or EXE) that implements the COM object. The word 'client' is used for the process that creates and uses the object.

In COM terms the server is often referred to as 'In-process' or 'Out-of-process'. In the scenario of an in-process server, the object lives inside a DLL that is loaded into the address space of the client. There is an obvious performance benefit to this because data that is passed between the client and the server doesn't have to travel between address spaces. The downside is that if something bad happens inside the server, it will take the client down with it. Additionally, there is the matter of trust. If a process consents to injecting a DLL in its own address space, the code in the DLL has full access to that address space, and executes under the client's credentials, even if those are elevated credentials.

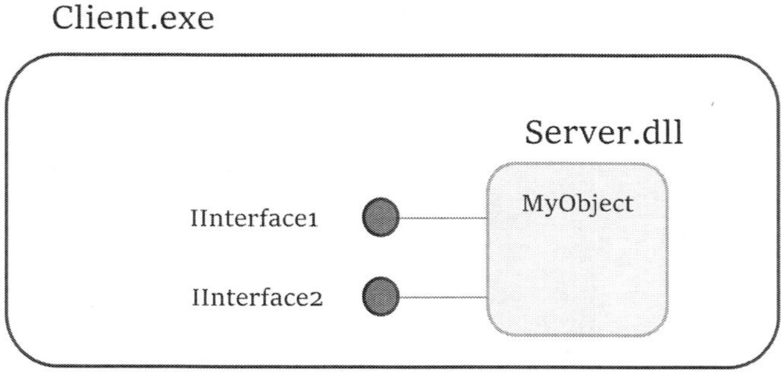

The drawing above reflects the situation if the object and its callers exist in the same apartment. If that is not the case, then for the caller in other apartments, the situation involves a proxy object like explained in detail in the previous chapter. This proxy exists in a separate DLL (the name of said DLL typically involves the word Proxy) and it is made entirely using files that were generated by MIDL.

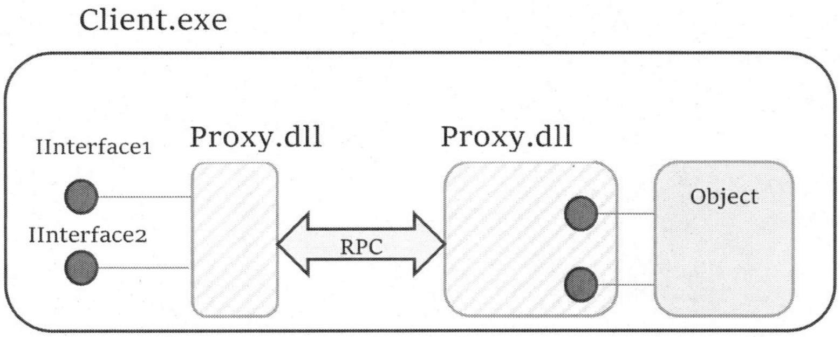

With an out-of-process server, the object lives in its own address space, hosted in a separate executable. It is worth noting that by default both scenarios are handled by the same proxy DLL. Calls are transferred from apartment A to apartment B. Where these are located is a runtime detail that the client typically isn't aware of. It is also possible for the server to be a separate executable.

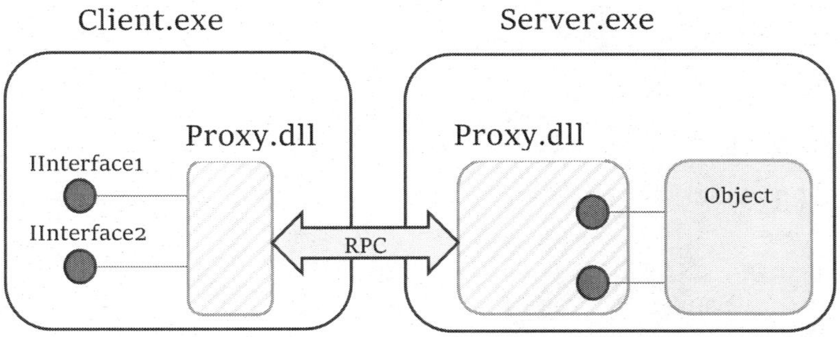

In this scenario, there is a clear separation between the client and the server. This increases reliability and enforces code security boundaries but comes at the cost of having to marshal calls between processes which can cause significant overhead. It also makes lifecycle management of the server object more complex because the lifecycle of the object needs to be tied to- and synchronized with the lifecycle of the server process.

You'll also note that the out-of-process scenario looks a lot like the scenario of an in-process server whose class object resides in a different apartment. That is because when it comes to marshaling, for COM these are logically equivalent. Data goes from one apartment to another apartment through an RPC channel. Where that apartment physically resides is a trivial implementation detail that neither the client nor server cares about. It will obviously have a performance impact and a security impact. But from a COM perspective, there is no difference.

In the Windows world, the out-of-process server can be further split into 2 kinds: regular applications and Windows Service applications. From a COM perspective they are very similar but there are a couple of differences that are interesting from a use-case point of view so I will treat them separately. Aside from the fact that each of them needs to be implemented differently, they have slightly different lifecycle and performance considerations.

The following table highlights the differences between these 3 options and gives some notion as to when each type is generally appropriate.

In-process
The COM object resides in a DLL which is loaded in the address space of the client. Depending on threading requirements, there may be zero overhead in calls to the object. From a security perspective, the client application is vulnerable to the DLL and executes with the client's credentials. Components like this are ideal for building user interfaces and data management because data is kept local to the same memory space. It's also ideal for scenarios where you want to extend application functionality via a plug-in architecture.
Out of process application
The COM object resides in a separate executable. All client calls are marshaled across process borders. The address space is separate and whether the server executable is running with client credentials is configurable. Aside from the security requirements, there are other reasons to implement an out-of-process server. One common reason is that the executable can be used independently. Examples are programs which can perform a command line task or provide a user interface for an external instrument like an electric multimeter or other consumer device. In such scenarios, the COM interface may be a way to make that functionality available for integrating in larger distributed applications as well as standalone use.
Windows Service
From a COM point of view there is not a whole lot of difference between a Windows Service application and a regular command line app or GUI based Windows application.

However, a COM object running in a Windows service would be the only class object with that ID on the system. Any client with permission to use the object would access that object in that service. This makes such a server ideal for 2 scenarios:

- The COM interface can be used as a simple channel to get status information about the service. Hosting the COM object is then not the main purpose of the service, but rather a very convenient means to share information and possibly accept control commands while the service takes care of its primary purpose.
- The service controls 1 resource as a singular actor, because that resource only allows for 1 actor to be in full control. In such cases, the service is that single actor, maintaining 1 internal state, and any client connections can only act under supervision and control of the service which decides what is allowed when, and by whom. An example could be a service that is in control of the management of a complex piece of hardware and synchronizes commands with each other as well as the internal state of the external hardware.

In terms of lifecycle management, there are also differences with regular out-of-process application servers. The COM service manager can start the Windows service upon request, and the service can implement COM lifecycle management to shut down when there are no more external connections. But it is also possible to put the lifecycle in the hands of the Windows administrator in cases where the service has a functional role independent of client connections. In such cases, the service would be started automatically or manually as configured and only start / stop at the request of the operating system or an administrator.

There is no single right or wrong approach here. What you implement and how you design the service lifecycle scenarios depends on user requirements, not on hard COM requirements.

Setting up the development environment

You can build COM projects in many different environments, with the freedom to choose the compiler, tool chain and even operating system of your preference. This versatility is one of the main strengths of COM, and one of the reasons COM exists. In this case we will be working with Visual Studio 2022 and set up our environment accordingly. There are more ways than 1 to organize your build environment and if you're used to different ways of working, that is perfectly fine too. If you're new to this topic or C++ development in general, then the setup below is a good way to start.

We start off with an empty solution for our Calculator.

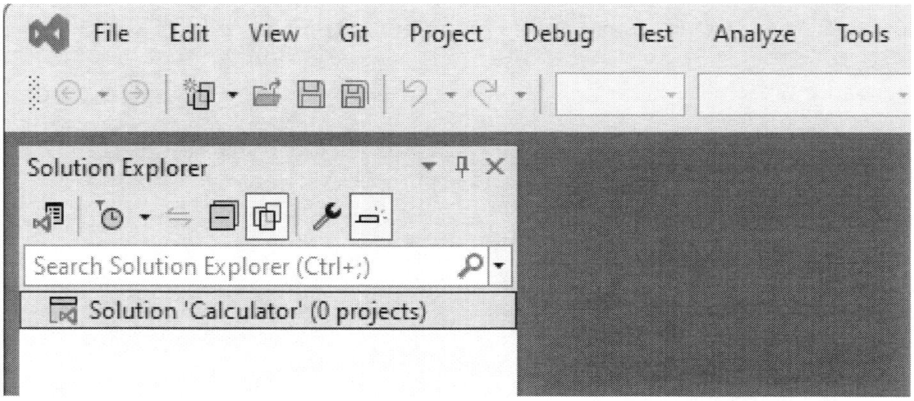

And then add 3 new projects, using the Windows Desktop Wizard for C++ projects, using the following settings:

Name	Type	Options
LocalServer	Console Application	Precompiled headers
LocalService	Console Application	Precompiled headers
InProcServer	Dynamic Link Library	Precompiled headers

Also add 1 empty new project.

Name	Type	Options
Proxy	Dynamic Link Library	<NONE>

On disk in our solution folder we also add an 'IDL' folder where we're going to store the IDL files for the Server(s) that we're going to build, a 'Generated' folder for the files that are generated by the MIDL compiler, and a 'Common' folder for source files that will be used in multiple projects. This way, it is easier to cleanly keep the different project separated. The folder we'll be working in looks like this

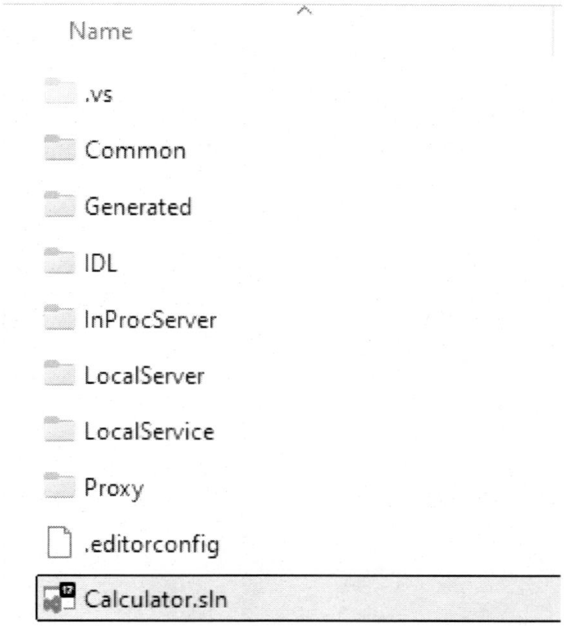

Since we're not using any wizards at this point, we're going to have to set a couple of project options manually. Some project settings only become available after IDL files to the project, so the first thing we do is right click the Proxy project, add a new filter called 'IDL' and add the IDL files as existing objects. We also create a 'Generated' filter in each project.

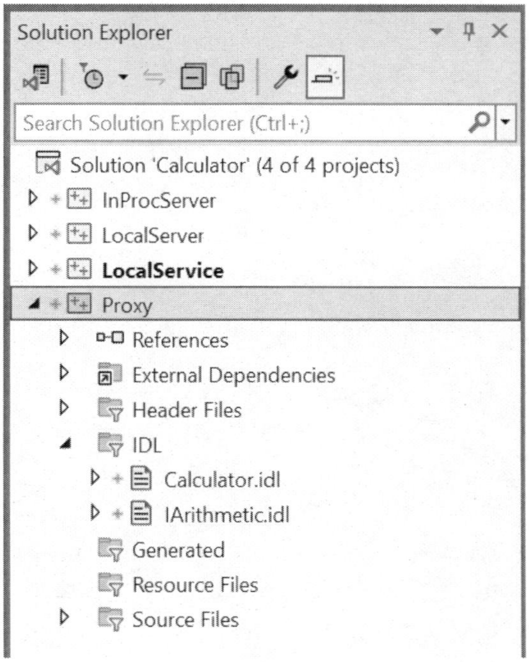

In principle, the IDL files can be added to each project which then uses them to generate the relevant headers and source files. However, the downside is that you have the potential to configure different compilation settings which might lead to hard to diagnose errors. Not every project may have an in-process server or a service or an out-of-process server, but every project will have a proxy project. So, by default, that is a good choice to add the IDL files for compilation.

The options we need to modify, need their new setting both in Debug and Release configuration, as well as 32-bit and 64-bit builds. The most convenient way to set them is to right click each project when you're setting them and making sure that you select 'All configurations' and 'All platforms' when changing those settings.

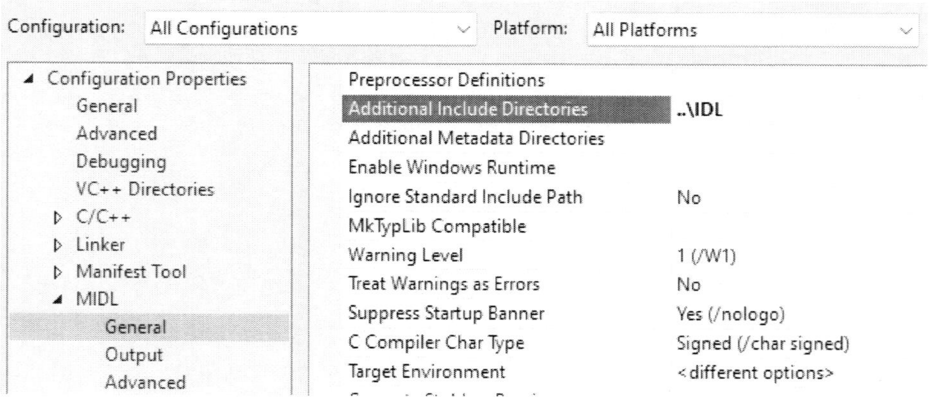

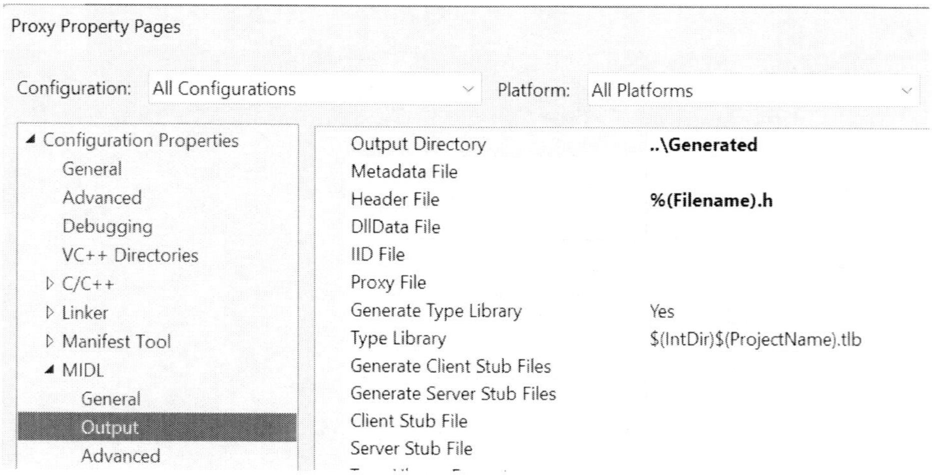

After doing this for all projects, do a build of the solution and verify that everything compiles cleanly. As a result of the MIDL compilation pass, a bunch of header files and C files will be created in the 'Generated' folder. The following files need to be added to each project. While it is not strictly required, adding them underneath the 'Generated' filter makes it convenient to separate user code from generated code.

It's also not mandatory to add the header files but it's convenient for educational purposes because you can quickly open them to inspect the generated code.

Name	File	
LocalServer LocalService InProcServer	Calculator.h IArithmetic.h	Calculator_i.c IArithmetic_i.c
Proxy	Calculator.h IArithmetic.h	Calculator_i.c IArithmetic_i.c IArithmetic_i.c Dlldata.c

It is not really required to add the header files because they're not compiled but it is convenient to be able to open them in Visual Studio for looking at type information. As we mentioned before, there are multiple ways to set up an environment.

In Visual Studio we typically work with C++ projects, not C projects, when building COM projects. With C++, it is common to use precompiled headers to optimize the build process. This setting is enabled by default because it allows a programmer to create a precompiled header with include files that are common for the project. This way, all those commonly used headers go through the compiler only once, instead of once per source file. When the project includes Windows.h or other significantly large or complex headers, this can have a significant impact on build times.

The problem is MIDL doesn't know or care about precompiled headers. But compiling a source file that doesn't use them, in a project that is configured to use them, will cause compilation errors. If the number of files is small, the simplest way is simply to multi-select them in Solution Explorer, right-click and open the properties page, and change the precompiled header specification for those files.

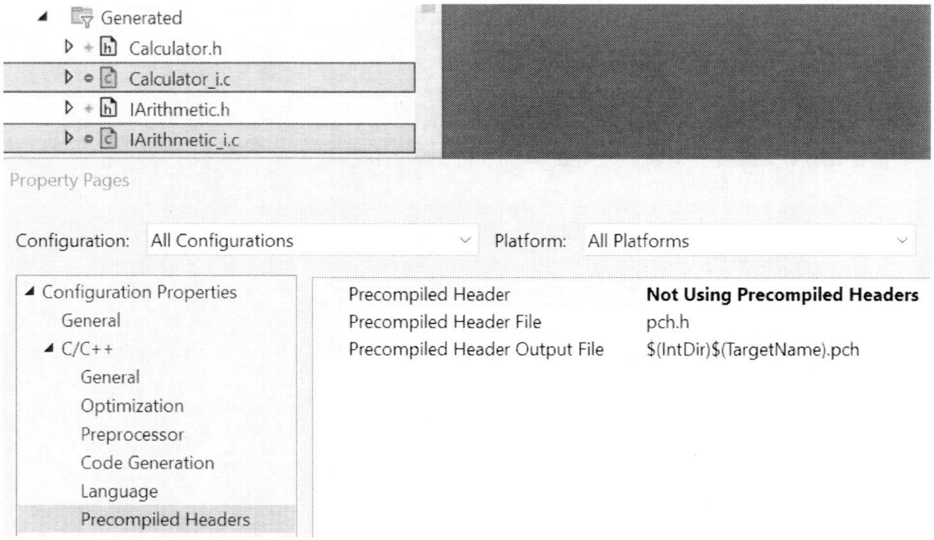

If you're dealing with many files and want to change this for all of them without multiselect, you can do this by closing Visual Studio and editing the project files (*.vcxproj) files in notepad.

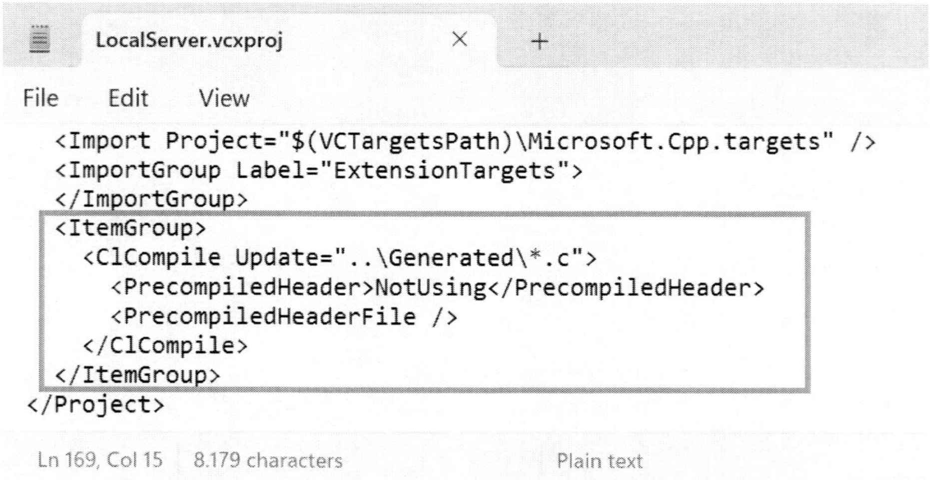

Add the highlighted text right before the end of the project settings. Visual Studio reads the file in a top-down manner and add / remove settings and file references whenever changes are made. By adding this small section, any precompiled header setting is overridden for all *.c files in the 'Generated' folder. One of the reasons this rule is convenient is that the rule will be in effect automatically if you add more files to the project later. There are other ways to implement custom compiler settings as well, working with Visual Studio customization or custom build rules, but that topic goes beyond the scope of this book.

For the Proxy project, changing this is simpler, because the Proxy started as an empty project and it doesn't have to account for cpp files which might demand them. It will only have C++ files so the setting can be changed at the project level.

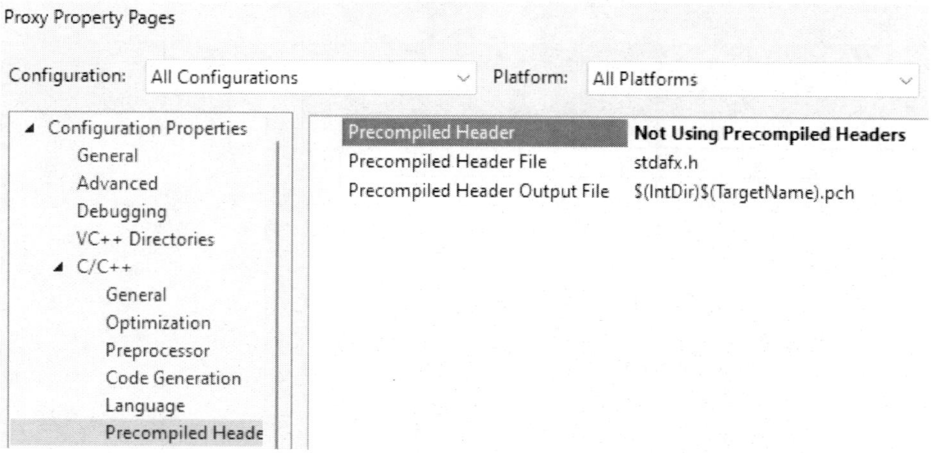

On the Proxy project we also need to link against the RPC library rpcrt4.lib because it contains the code for the proxy and the stub which use RPC. The other projects don't need that because they only use COM APIs and don't know or care about RPC.

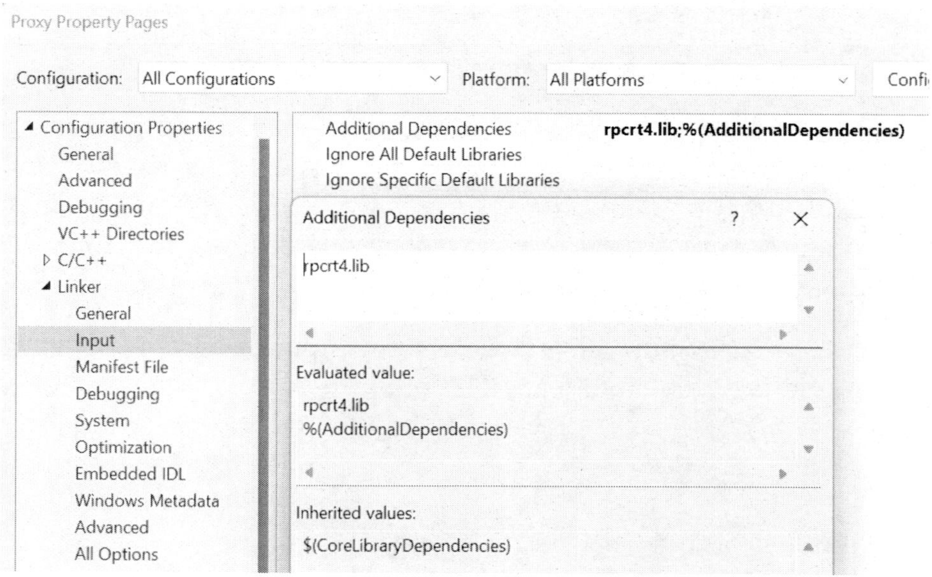

That just leaves the compiler include folders to take care of. Files that are common to all projects are stored in the 'Common' folder. Generated files are in the 'Generated' folder. These folders need to be added to the projects as additional include directories because they are outside the normal list of include directories. This setting needs to be configured for all projects.

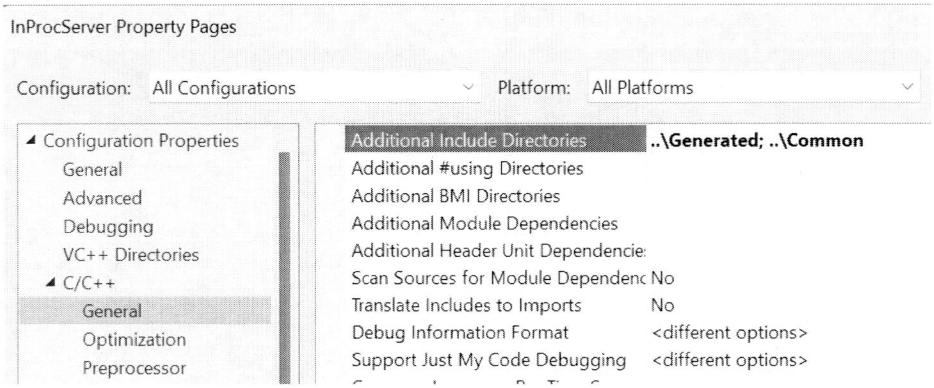

We also want to make sure that the files we build will have a sensible name. By configuring the following setting, the solution name is prefixed to the project name.

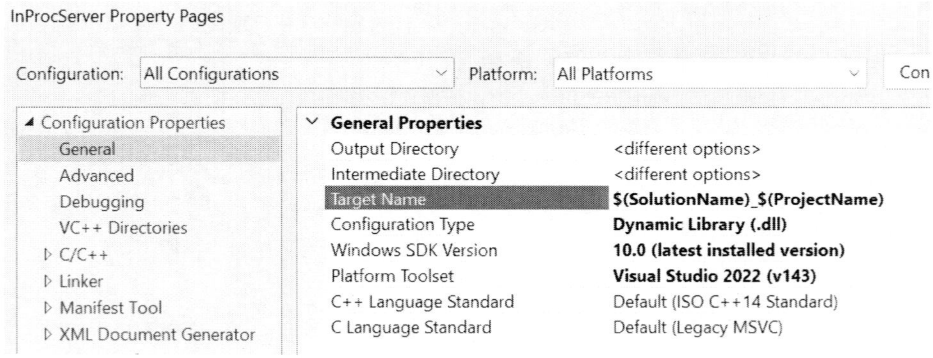

This way, the files we build will have names like 'Calculator_Proxy.dll' which makes it easier to avoid conflicting names if files are placed together in a folder. Of course, depending on other factors you may want to configure a different name or add even more information in the name.

And finally, since the proxy project started as an empty project, we need to specify that the build target is a DLL, not an application.

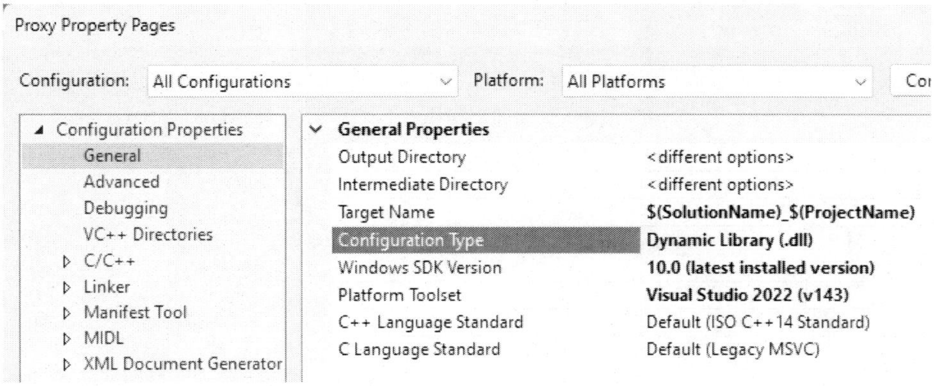

That concludes the project related settings for now. The server projects were all configured with the option of using precompiled headers. Since we will be working with COM, we need to include Ole2.h which contains the declaration of all COM related APIs we're going to need.

```
#ifndef PCH_H
#define PCH_H

// add headers that you want to pre-compile here
#include "framework.h"

#include <Ole2.h>

#include <iostream>
#include <string>
using namespace std;

#endif //PCH_H
```

In the example projects, we will be making use of the standard C++ wstring a lot for the purpose of logging, so it makes sense to add iostream and string to the precompiled header because they're going to be needed all over. However, that is for the purpose of the Calculator servers. Depending on the project you're working on, there will be extra headers as well. The final touch is to rename the dllmain.cpp file that was generated for the InProcServer project. In the EXE projects, the main file has the name of the project. For DLL projects, that file is named dllmain.cpp by default but we rename it to InProcServer.cpp to make the naming more consistent.

That is enough for now to get things started. The IDL files are added to the proxy project, so the proxy project is the logical place to start building. It's the easiest project of them all because there isn't any custom coding to do. And if we're going to test one of our servers, we need the proxy to be there so let's start with that.

Building the Proxy

We've mentioned the proxy several times already. Some interfaces like for example IClassFactory and IUnknown are well known interfaces, and they have standard marshalers because COM is literally built around them (and many other well-known interfaces), and it knows what to do. If our Calculator COM server only supported well-known interfaces, no additional proxies would be needed. However, since IArithmetic is a non-standard interface, the COM infrastructure doesn't know how to proxy by default. Luckily, this is one of the few things in COM that is simple.

The proxy for marshaling an interface is itself a COM server that is implemented as an in-process server in a dedicated DLL which supports all interfaces that are exported by the COM server supported by the proxy. The good thing is that we don't have to worry about any of that. The requirements for a Proxy are well known and is all generated by MIDL. We briefly discussed those files already when covering the different files that were generated. All we need to do is to add those files to an empty DLL project.

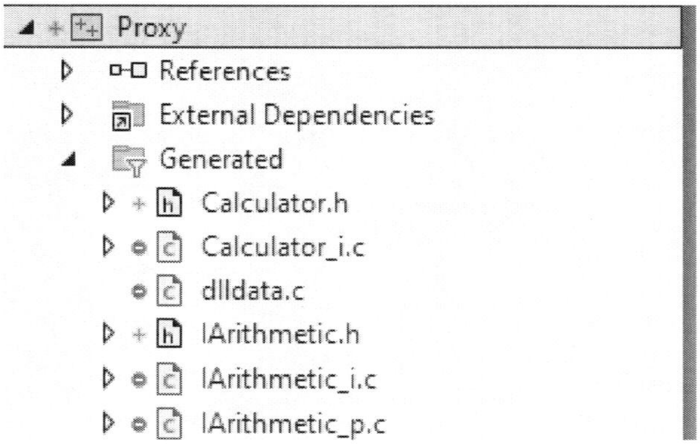

Add the PROXY_EXPORTS and the REGISTER_PROXY_DLL macros to the preprocessor definitions. Note that you cannot do this for all configurations at once. Depending on the active configuration and platform, there will be a variety of preprocessor directives already that are required for that specific configuration, so rather than doing 1 setting for all possibilities at once, you need to set them individually.

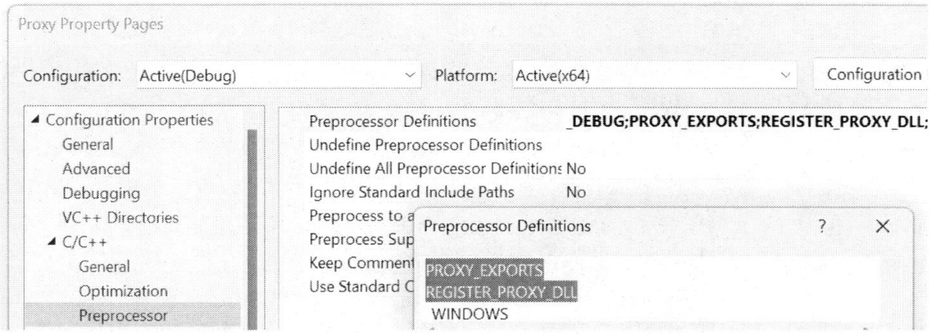

PROXY_EXPORTS will cause the compiler to generate the function bodies and export directives for DLLGetClassObject and DLLCanUnloadNow functions. Originally, these were the only 2 functions for COM DLLs. With Windows 95, 2 additional functions DllRegisterServer and DLLUnregisterServer were introduced to facilitate the registration of COM DLLs.

To generate and export these functions, the REGISTER_PROXY_DLL macro needs to be defined. We will cover these 2 functions and some other peculiarities in full detail in the next chapter about registration. The only reason they are mentioned here already is that we need to explicitly take steps to make sure the proxy works as expected. That is all there is to the proxy DLL. It is a COM DLL no different than the in-process server we're about to build next.

But before we get to do that, we'll have to understand what exactly it is that we'll be implementing.

Classes and instances

It is unfortunate and perhaps caused by COM predating widespread use of C++, that there are some terms in COM that have different meaning than in the rest of the C++ world. In C++, a class is the type definition and an object is an instance of that class. In COM, we talk about class objects, and instances.

While it is not strictly required, the convention is that any DCOM object (the Calculator in our example) consists of 2 parts: a class object and 1 or more class instances. The class object is most closely involved with things such as lifecycle management, registration, connection management and things like that. The instances provide the actual functionality of the supported interfaces. In practical C++ terms, the Class Object is implemented as a C++ class, and the Class Instance is implemented as another C++ class. From a logical point of view, these 2 together represent 1 COM object.

In theory, nothing is stopping you from only implementing a class object, have it support the IArithmetic interface, and use it as a singleton. Or you could implement everything in 1 big class of which the first instance would also work as a class object and the next ones only as instance. COM is pretty relaxed in terms of what it allows you to do. Whatever you create by freewheeling like that may not be able to work together with the rest of the COM ecosystem, but it would work with your own client, if your client is coded to the paradigm you implement on the server side.

For real-world application, it is often an extremely good idea to follow the standard way of doing things. Not only will it mean you have the entire internet and Microsoft documentation / examples to fall back on for reference, but your objects will also be able to integrate seamlessly with the rest of the COM world.

There is also a more practical reason to follow this paradigm. The class object does all the work regarding lifecycle management of the server and deals with things like external connection management. The instance otoh will typically implement the actual functionality we want to expose. Based on what type of COM server we implement, lifecycle management will have to be done differently. The functional part, however, will still be the same. By following the class object / class instance paradigm, it is very easy to support different types of COM server because those differences only require changes to the class object.

With the implementation we are going to do here, the class object will be implemented in a C++ class named CalculatorClass. The class instances will be implemented in a C++ class named CalculatorInstance. Because each of these needs to follow the rules for COM class, they both need to implement IUnknown. That is one of the few hard rules. Additionally, our CalculatorClass class object will implement the IClassFactory interface to support the standard Class object / class instance paradigm. This is a COM requirement for coexisting with the COM landscape. If your implementation works like this, all tools that work with COM objects can use it.

With all that said, let's start with the CalculatorInstance because that is the easiest. It is the thing that implements the actual functionality we want to implement. It implements the IArithmetic interface so that's what the instance needs to derive from.

The C++ definition of this interface was created by MIDL and looks as follows:

```
IArithmetic: public IUnknown
{
public:
    virtual HRESULT STDMETHODCALLTYPE Add(
        /* [in] */ double Arg1,
        /* [in] */ double Arg2,
```

```
        /* [out] */ double *Result) = 0;

    virtual HRESULT STDMETHODCALLTYPE Subtract(
        /* [in] */ double Arg1,
        /* [in] */ double Arg2,
        /* [out] */ double *Result) = 0;

    virtual /* [propget] */ HRESULT STDMETHODCALLTYPE get_LastResult(
        /* [retval][out] */ double *pVal) = 0;
};
```

Note the accessor methods which simulate reading and writing a property value. All interface methods are abstract and need to have an override in the CalculatorInstance.

```
class CalculatorInstance : public IArithmetic
{
private:
    ULONG m_RefCount;
public:
      CalculatorInstance();
protected:
      ~CalculatorInstance();

public:
    //IUnknown methods
    HRESULT STDMETHODCALLTYPE QueryInterface(
        REFIID riid,
        void __RPC_FAR* __RPC_FAR* ppvObject);
    ULONG STDMETHODCALLTYPE AddRef(void);
    ULONG STDMETHODCALLTYPE Release(void);

    //ICalculator methods
    HRESULT STDMETHODCALLTYPE Add(
        double Arg1,
        double Arg2,
        double* Result);
    HRESULT STDMETHODCALLTYPE Subtract(
        double Arg1,
        double Arg2,
        double* Result);
    HRESULT STDMETHODCALLTYPE get_LastResult(
        double *pVal);

};
```

Implementing IUnknown

There are no surprises in the method declarations for our CalculatorInstance. The only peculiarity is that the destructor is protected. This is to ascertain that these objects cannot be deleted by anyone but themselves. The implementation of the various methods poses no surprises anymore at this point. We've covered the IUnknown methods earlier.

```
ULONG STDMETHODCALLTYPE CalculatorInstance::AddRef(void)
{
    return InterlockedIncrement(&m_RefCount);
}

ULONG STDMETHODCALLTYPE CalculatorInstance::Release(void)
{
    ULONG retVal = InterlockedDecrement(&m_RefCount);
    if (retVal == 0) {
        delete this;
    }
    return retVal;
}
```

From a purely technical point of view, the argument can be made that IF an implementation is only going to support STA threading, there is no need to use the interlocked functions to guarantee thread safety. After all, COM will ensure that methods are only executed inside the correct STA apartment, in which case these IUnknown methods will never run the risk of being executed simultaneously. But many implementations of COM objects support both MTA and STA threading, in which case this level of safety is needed.

```
HRESULT STDMETHODCALLTYPE CalculatorInstance::QueryInterface(
    REFIID riid,
    void __RPC_FAR* __RPC_FAR* ppvObject)
{
    if (NULL == ppvObject)
        return E_POINTER;

    if (riid == IID_IUnknown) {
        *ppvObject = static_cast<IArithmetic*>(this);
    }
    else if (riid == IID_IArithmetic) {
        *ppvObject = static_cast<IArithmetic*>(this);
    }
    else    {
        *ppvObject = NULL;
        return E_NOINTERFACE;
    }

    reinterpret_cast<IUnknown*>(*ppvObject)->AddRef();
    return S_OK;
}
```

The QueryInterface yields no surprises. It was already covered in the introductory chapter.

The CalculatorClass has no role related to the custom interfaces that we have implemented. Instead, it does inherit from the IClassFactory interface for implementing the standard class object / class interface paradigm. IClassFactory derives from IUnknown.

```
class CalculatorClass : public IClassFactory
{
private:
    ULONG m_RefCount;

public:
      CalculatorClass();
      ~CalculatorClass();

public:
      //IUnknown methods
      HRESULT STDMETHODCALLTYPE QueryInterface(
            REFIID riid,
            void __RPC_FAR* __RPC_FAR* ppvObject);
      ULONG STDMETHODCALLTYPE AddRef(void);
      ULONG STDMETHODCALLTYPE Release(void);

      //IClassFactory methods
      HRESULT STDMETHODCALLTYPE CreateInstance(
            IUnknown* pUnkOuter,
            REFIID riid,
            void** ppvObject);
      HRESULT STDMETHODCALLTYPE LockServer(
            BOOL fLock);
};
```

The QueryInterface implementation presents nothing unusual.

```
HRESULT STDMETHODCALLTYPE CalculatorClass::QueryInterface(
    REFIID riid,
    void __RPC_FAR* __RPC_FAR* ppvObject)
{
    if (NULL == ppvObject)
        return E_POINTER;

    if (riid == IID_IUnknown)
    {
        *ppvObject = static_cast<IClassFactory*>(this);
    }
    else if (riid == IID_IClassFactory)
    {
        *ppvObject = static_cast<IClassFactory*>(this);
    }
    else
```

```
    {
        *ppvObject = NULL;
        return E_NOINTERFACE;
    }

    reinterpret_cast<IUnknown*>(*ppvObject)->AddRef();
    return S_OK;
}
```

You might just think that the reference counting will be the same as well, but that would be wrong. Instances are created and destroyed dynamically, as requested by a client. For class objects, that approach doesn't really make sense. Class objects typically exist as long as their server is loaded. Their lifecycle is tied intimately to the lifecycle of the server. It doesn't make sense to have them self-destruct dynamically. The class object is typically implemented as a stack based static object which logically cannot be dynamically destroyed. From this, you can go forward in a couple of ways.

One option would be to implement reference counting methods without returning 0. These methods still follow the required semantics. The actual return value doesn't convey any meaning whatsoever. Only their non-zero'ness does.

```
ULONG STDMETHODCALLTYPE CalculatorClass::AddRef(void) {
    return 2;
}

ULONG STDMETHODCALLTYPE CalculatorClass::Release(void) {
    return 1;
}
```

The problem is that this is only true in isolation. Logically, if the reference count of the class object does NOT affect the lifecycle of the class object and thus the server, there needs to be another way to do so. The problem is that some COM APIs may expect the reference count to matter. Because of reasons like this, the more correct implementation is

```
ULONG STDMETHODCALLTYPE CalculatorClass::AddRef(void)
{
    return InterlockedIncrement(&m_CoRefCount);
}

ULONG STDMETHODCALLTYPE CalculatorClass::Release(void)
{
    return InterlockedDecrement(&m_CoRefCount);
}
```

This is like instance reference counting, except the object is not deleted when its reference count reaches 0. Exactly how this ties into the lifecycle is explained in detail when we get to server lifecycle management.

Implementing IClassFactory

Aside from IUnknown, IClassFactory is probably the most implemented interface in the COM landscape. There are many reasons for that. Any COM class object needs to implement some kind of interface for creating instances, so it may as well be IClassFactory. It's worth repeating that COM doesn't force you to implement IClassFactory and make a distinction between a Class Object and a Class Instance. COM is a technology and doesn't really care what you do if you follow the basic rules. But aside from the technical requirements, much of the COM ecosystem expects IClassFactory to be implemented in class objects they are expected to work with and not implementing it means your server cannot be part of that ecosystem.

IClassFactory implementations have 2 main responsibilities: creating instances and providing a locking mechanism for the COM runtime to ensure that the server stays in memory. Locking is the simplest one on the face of it, but there is a nuance that is easily missed. So far, we've only talked about reference counting for the instances and the class objects as reasons for a COM object to stay alive / exist. But the COM server itself also needs a reference count to stay alive. Or rather, there needs to be a mechanism to control the lifetime of the server module, and this needs to exist outside of the reference count of class objects and their instances. Intuitively, you'd think that if there are no more outstanding references to class objects and instances, there is no reason for the COM server to continue its existence.

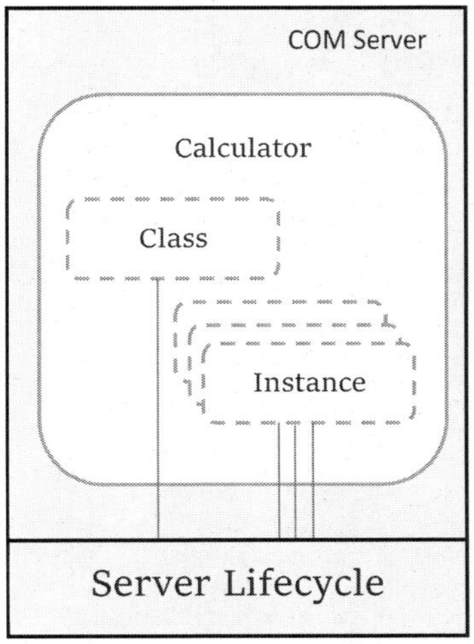

And that is true, in the sense that the server's lifetime needs to extend at least to the lifetime of the objects inside the server. But that is not the entire picture because the documentation for IClassFactory states that a client or the COM infrastructure itself can use IClassFactory::LockServer to lock the server into memory even if the last outstanding reference has been released. In this scenario, all reference counts are 0 and the server could be unloaded, but someone -not the COM object- decided via a call through the class object that the server should stick around for a while longer. At this point it may seem redundant as to why this is even a requirement, because with what we've seen so far, we could achieve the same thing by simply holding on to the class object.

This is a matter of semantics. From a theoretical perspective a client doesn't gain anything by locking the server and then releasing the class object because it needs to remember it did this and get a new class pointer at a later point to unlock it again. This will become apparent when we implement the actual servers.

Historically the LockServer method is intended as a way for a client application to ensure that the server will stay alive even if no one is using it. This can be useful in scenarios where the COM object is used only intermittently. Without the ability to lock the server, a scenario could happen where the reference count drops to 0, the server gets unloaded or shuts down, and almost immediately there is a new activation request which would require the server to be reloaded or restarted. Not only could the performance overhead be significant, but there can be race conditions between loading and unloading DLL files which could lead to application crashes. From a purely functional perspective, the same could be achieved by getting and holding on to an interface pointer, but that is conceptually a different way of working.

In any case, with the introduction of IClassFactory, the client or the COM runtime is yet another party that has a hand in the lifecycle of the server, through manipulation of the class object.

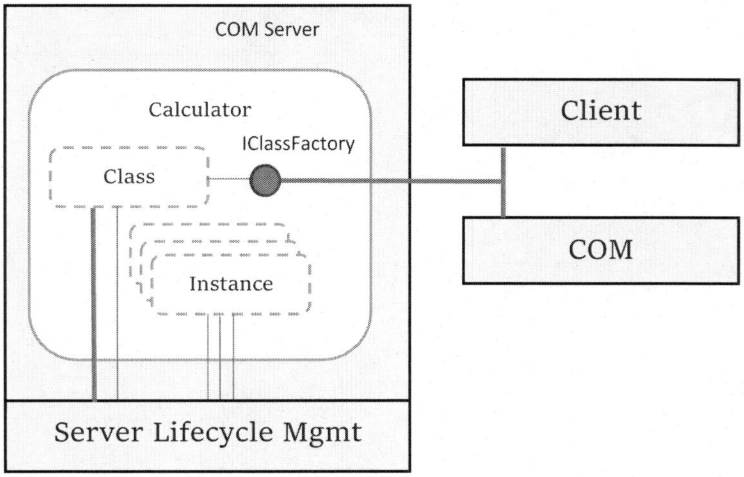

That doesn't fit in with the model we've seen so far, which means the lifecycle should rely on more than just the reference counts of the COM objects. Since the call comes through the class object, you might be tempted to just AddRef the class object to achieve the same result.

The reason it is a bad idea to AddRef the class object in this manner is if you tie the lifecycle of the server to the reference count of the class object and you implement IClassFactory::LockServer in a way that AddRefs the class object reference count, you will (or may) end up with a situation whereby no one has any references anymore, but the reference count is still non-zero. This is a violation of the reference counting rules and simply very confusing. Clearly, a better approach is needed.

When all is said and done, each of the 3 things that we mentioned explicitly controls the server lifecycle conditions. And logically, since a server is either a DLL or an executable (a singular binary module) it is perfectly reasonable to control the lifecycle through a global object. The use of global objects is generally discouraged for good reasons. In this case, however, I find it acceptable because, from the point of view of a COM object, there is only ever 1 server and it always exists. Being able to call on the server at any point is a natural state of being. We can use the server object for other things like logging, but for this purpose, only the locking matters.

```
class Server
{
private:
      ULONG m_LockCount = 0;

public:
      ULONG LockModule(void);
```

```
        ULONG UnlockModule(void);
        ULONG GetLockCount(void);
};


ULONG Server::GetLockCount(void)
{
    return m_LockCount;
}

ULONG Server::LockModule(void)
{
    return InterlockedIncrement(&m_LockCount);
}

ULONG Server::UnlockModule(void)
{
    return InterlockedDecrement(&m_LockCount);
}
```

Locking and unlocking a server to determine whether it needs to continue living or not is conceptually similar to keeping a reference count to determine whether an object needs to stay alive or not so we can use the same mechanism. Note that the `GetLockCount` api is only to be used for informational purposes. The multithreaded safety is only guaranteed between `InterlockedIncrement` and `InterlockedDecrement`.

Now it is just a matter to figure out where to increase or decrease the module lock. There are 3 conditions that -in general- demand that the server module is locked into memory:

1. There are instances in existence.
2. There are references outstanding to the class objects.
3. The server was explicitly locked through IClassFactory::LockServer.

For object instances, the situation is easy. Their existence is always temporary. The server only needs to exist as long as they do, so we can lock and unlock in the constructor and destructor.

```
CalculatorInstance::CalculatorInstance()
{
    g_Server.LockModule();
    m_RefCount = 0;
}

CalculatorInstance::~CalculatorInstance()
{
    g_Server.UnlockModule();
}
```

Class objects are typically implemented static objects. These exist as long as the server itself. This means we cannot use their existence as a condition to control the lifetime of the server via the constructor and destructor, but a non-zero reference count is a reason to make sure the server module doesn't cease to be.

```
ULONG STDMETHODCALLTYPE CalculatorClass::AddRef(void)
{
    g_Server.LockModule();
    return InterlockedIncrement(&m_CoRefCount);
}

ULONG STDMETHODCALLTYPE CalculatorClass::Release(void)
{
    g_Server.UnlockModule();
    return InterlockedDecrement(&m_CoRefCount);
}
```

And that finally brings us to the method that started this whole tangent. With the global server object in place, IClassFactory::LockServer is trivial.

```
HRESULT STDMETHODCALLTYPE CalculatorClass::LockServer(
    BOOL fLock)
{
    if (fLock){
        g_Server.LockModule();
    }
    else{
        g_Server.UnlockModule();
    }

    return S_OK;
}
```

With this, we have locking covered. Server locking is implemented and used seamlessly to control the server lifetime together with instance reference counting and class object reference counting.

The CreateInstance method contains a lot more complexity. Note that this is a barebones implementation for the sake of clarity. There is some extra code in there that only comes into play when dealing with out-of-process servers.

```
HRESULT STDMETHODCALLTYPE CalculatorClass::CreateInstance(
    IUnknown* pUnkOuter,
    REFIID riid,
    void** ppvObject)
{
    HRESULT hres = S_OK;
    *ppvObject = NULL;
```

```
    CalculatorInstance* calculator = NULL;

    if (NULL != pUnkOuter)
        hres = CLASS_E_NOAGGREGATION;

    if (SUCCEEDED(hres)){
        calculator = new CalculatorInstance();
        if (NULL == calculator)
            hres = E_OUTOFMEMORY;
    }
    if (SUCCEEDED(hres)){
        calculator->AddRef();
        hres = calculator->QueryInterface(
            riid, ppvObject);
        calculator->Release();
    }

    return hres;
}
```

There is a lot going on here. After some initialization of variables, we check if we support aggregation or not. Aggregation is a way for an 'outer' object to control an 'inner' object (the object we are trying to create here) to appear as 1 big object. It is the COM equivalent of the outer class deriving from an inner base class so that the derived class appears to be 1 class that exposes the same functionality as the base class, as well as its extra functionality. For now, we have decided that our class doesn't support aggregation and if someone tries to aggregate it, we fail the request.

With that out of the way, we create our calculator instance. If that succeeds, we AddRef the newly created instance. The rules of COM say that we must do that because the newly created object's pointer was written into a memory location. Therefore, there is a reference, and the reference count should reflect that. Bad things can happen if we fail to do so.

A dynamic object (an object which is created and deleted on demand instead of statically allocated) with a reference count of 0 is in limbo. Consider the following: we leave the reference count at 0 and then leave the responsibility of calling AddRef to QueryInterface. That will work. At first. In a couple of months, we decide that some object state data needs to be loaded and we insert a 'Load' function between the object creation and the call to QueryInterface. The Load function does some COM related actions and hands off the interface pointer to some COM related persistence functions. And like a good COM citizen, it AddRefs and Releases the pointer. AddRef takes it to 1, Release brings it to 0, and boom, the object self-deletes. Meanwhile no one has noticed that this happened, the pointer is then passed to QueryInterface, and bad things happen.

Having AddRef'ed the pointer, we can safely perform QueryInterface and since we are done with our copy of the newly created object, we Release it. At that point, 2 things can happen.

```
calculator->AddRef();   // 0 -> 1
hres = calculator->QueryInterface(
    riid, ppvObject);   // 1 -> 1 or 1 -> 2
calculator->Release();  // 1 -> 0 or 2 -> 1
```

Either the call to QueryInterface was successful and we returned the specified interface pointer back to the caller with a reference count of 1. Or it wasn't, in which case our Release drops the reference count to 0 and the object self-destructs cleanly. In both cases, proper COM semantics are observed, and everything was performed in a way that is guaranteed to be safe.

And that is all there is to it for now. There are additional details to be worked out concerning lifecycle management but that will come in the next chapter.

Implementing IArithmetic

After dealing with IClassFactory and IUnknown, that just leaves the IArithmetic implementation on the Class Instance which is equally trivial.

```
HRESULT STDMETHODCALLTYPE CalculatorInstance::Add(
    double Arg1,
    double Arg2,
    double* Result)
{
    if (!(std::isfinite(arg1) && std::isfinite(arg2)))
        return E_INVALIDARG;

    if (NULL == Result)
        return E_POINTER;
    *Result = Arg1 + Arg2;
    return S_OK;
}

HRESULT STDMETHODCALLTYPE CalculatorInstance::Subtract(
    double Arg1,
    double Arg2,
    double* Result)
{
    if (!(std::isfinite(arg1) && std::isfinite(arg2)))
        return E_INVALIDARG;

    if (NULL == Result)
```

```
        return E_POINTER;
    *Result = Arg1 - Arg2;
    return S_OK;
}

HRESULT STDMETHODCALLTYPE CalculatorInstance::get_LastResult(
    double* pVal)
{
    if (NULL == pVal)
        return E_POINTER;
    *pVal = m_LastResult;
    return S_OK;
}

HRESULT STDMETHODCALLTYPE CalculatorInstance::put_LastResult(
    double newVal)
{
    m_LastResult = newVal;
    return S_OK;
}
```

And that's it. If you compare this code to the original example we used as an educational vehicle, it is identical.

Building an in-process server

Now that we have the barebones code for the COM object figured out, we can build it into a server. In this part we don't have to focus on the IArithmetic interface because we have that part done. This next part is all about packaging in a binary somehow, so that it may be used in a client application.

As mentioned earlier, there are different kinds of server. We start with an in-process server because it is the easiest implementation so it's a good place to start. With an in-process server, the class object is implemented in a DLL which is loaded directly into the memory space of the client. This is the most performant way for a client to interact with a COM server. If the threading requirements of the client and the server match, then the client will access the server directly through a raw pointer without anything in between, and a method call will only take nanoseconds, no different than if you'd call any other function that is in the same memory space.

The flip side is that if either the client or the server does something wrong, the resulting crash will take them out both, and neither can expect a graceful shutdown. Additionally, if there are multiple clients, then each of them will host their own copy of the server and instantiate their own copy of the class object. Whether this is a problem or a feature depends on the circumstances.

For example, if you are making an interface to a piece of instrumentation hardware that is stateful, then having multiple instances connected to it without knowledge about each other is probably not a good idea. On the other hand, if you are implementing a middle tier that is a black box abstraction layer for interacting with remote databases and implementing business logic, then that is the ideal use case for objects that don't have to know about other clients. And in fact, separating them may be a good idea for the purpose of user isolation, resilience, and load balancing.

Implementing the server is trivial. Any DLL that hosts a class object needs to export 2 functions:

```
STDAPI DllGetClassObject(
        _In_ REFCLSID rclsid,
        _In_ REFIID riid,
        _Outptr_ LPVOID FAR* ppv);

STDAPI DllCanUnloadNow(void);
```

The purpose of the first one is obvious. The client has loaded the DLL for a given class object and is now requesting a pointer to said class object.

```
STDAPI DllGetClassObject(
    _In_ REFCLSID rclsid,
    _In_ REFIID riid,
    _Outptr_ LPVOID FAR* ppv)
{
    if (NULL == ppv)
        return E_POINTER;

    static CalculatorClass computerClass;
    if (rclsid == CLSID_Calculator)
        return computerClass.QueryInterface(riid, ppv);

    *ppv = NULL;
    return CLASS_E_CLASSNOTAVAILABLE;
}
```

There is not a whole lot to say here except that the class object is implemented as a static stack object, meaning there is only 1, and it will exist as long as the DLL is loaded in memory. And that brings us to the second function.

DLLCanUnloadNow is a function that is called to determine if it is safe to unload the DLL if it is no longer in use. As we saw in the previous chapter, this is where the server lock count comes into play. We only allow the server to be unloaded if the 3 conditions (class object refences are 0, there are no instances, no server lock is applied) are true.

```
STDAPI DllCanUnloadNow(void)
```

```
{
    return g_Server.GetLockCount() == 0 ? S_OK : S_FALSE;
}
```

The lifecycle of an in-process server is simple. When the client asks for the class object, the COM runtime loads the applicable DLL and calls DLLGetClassObject. Unloading the DLL is done at the client's request or when COM performs a deallocation of unused DLLs that can be unloaded during a housekeeping cycle, via the APIs

```
//combaseapi.h
WINOLEAPI_(void)
CoFreeUnusedLibraries(
    void
    );

WINOLEAPI_(void)
CoFreeUnusedLibrariesEx(
    _In_ DWORD dwUnloadDelay,
    _In_ DWORD dwReserved
    );
```

When someone calls these functions, the COM runtime calls DLLCanUnloadNow to determine which DLLs are no longer needed. Those that report they are no longer in use will then be removed from the client's address space. DLLCanUnloadNow can also be called during the last call to CoUnInitialize. So, keep in mind that in the latter case, if the process is no longer hosting COM, your DLL might be unloaded regardless of what you return. This is another of those situations where breaking the rules of COM can have unforeseen consequences.

Unfortunately, as simple as this is, in multithreaded scenarios, the following is a possible (and not the only) scenario in which race conditions present themselves. Consider the situation where we have received a pointer to the class object, and when we are done with it, we Release.

```
ULONG STDMETHODCALLTYPE CalculatorClass::Release(void)
{
    g_Server.UnlockModule();
        //DllCanUnloadNow is called in another thread
        //right between these 2 statements
    return InterlockedDecrement(&m_CoRefCount);
}
```

If that happens, theoretically the DLL could be yanked out of the process, which would cause a crash because code was still executing inside the DLL. You could look at that code and argue that if you reverse the order of the module unlock and the interlocked decrement, we avoid this scenario. But that's not true. Suppose we use a temporary variable to swap the order of those statements.

```
ULONG STDMETHODCALLTYPE CalculatorClass::Release(void)
{
    ULONG temp = InterlockedDecrement(&m_CoRefCount);
    g_Server.UnlockModule();
        //DllCanUnloadNow is called in another thread
        //right between these 2 statements
    return temp;
}
```

If DLLCanUnloadNow is called in another thread when the return call is still happening, code is still executing in the DLL and if the DLL is unloaded, there will be an application crash. But this is not the only such scenario. We could be calling DllGetClassObject via one of the COM APIs to get the class object, just while in another thread, someone else is calling DLLCanUnloadNow via another COM API like CoFreeUnusedLibraries at the same time.

Since DllGetClassObject and DLLCanUnloadNow can be called simultaneously in different threads, you might wonder if it is necessary to synchronize them using a mutex for example. The answer is that this still wouldn't make them safe. Yes, you can protect the function bodies with synchronization primitives, but both functions need to eventually return a value, and it is impossible to synchronize the return calls. The chances are small, but in theory it is perfectly possible for DllGetClassObject to return a pointer to the class object just as DLLCanUnloadNow returns S_OK to indicate the DLL can be unloaded.

In this case, the decision was made to not put synchronization in place because there really is nothing much to synchronize with. GetLockCount only returns the value of an integer which is updated through interlocked functions. That is as safe as it gets. Nothing else is going on and putting synchronization boundaries around reading a value from memory is redundant.

A COM server itself cannot solve this situation because the fundamental problem exists in the level of software that is using the server. We could implement synchronization here but that would not solve the problem. It would only make the problematic window smaller. And as it happens: the solution to that problem (DllGetClassObject racing against DLLCanUnloadNow) is readily available!

The client itself knows the way it will be using the COM object. Or rather, the programmer building the client application knows how the client application will be using the COM object. If a client is using the class object intermittently, potentially from multiple different threads, then the client itself can call IClassFactory::LockServer on the class object to lock the server into memory when it starts using the class object and then use it again later to unlock it when it knows it is completely done. This way, there will be no race conditions.

There is a little bit more that can be said about this topic. Back when COM was a hot topic, the COM infrastructure was made more robust over time to deal with possible problem scenarios. For example, in 'Essential COM', Don Box notes that starting with Windows NT 4.0 SP2, COM added a heuristic: if it detects that a DLL has been accessed from multiple threads, it defers unloading instead of immediately unloading an unused DLL when CoFreeUnusedLibraries is called. Instead, it delays the unloading until a subsequent call is made to CoFreeUnusedLibraries, creating a safety window to reduce the risk of race conditions. While it is undoubtedly true that various such heuristic safety implementations exist, this is all undocumented in official documentation.

In principle, the COM infrastructure is in a position where it can completely avoid this problem. Only COM is supposed to call the DllGetClassObject and DLLCanUnloadNow functions, in response to various COM related APIs being called by the client. If COM itself would serialize the way it accesses those functions, that problem could be avoided. However, there are a couple of things to be mindful of. First, COM was built in the 90's to be lightweight technology that could run on the computers at that time. And in a running Windows system where COM is also used for a lot of things going on internally, serializing unrelated things may have a significant performance impact. And secondly, in a more complex COM object hierarchy, loading a COM server in memory and getting the class object may cause other supporting COM servers to be loaded and potentially unloaded as a result. This can rapidly give rise to an explosion in synchronization scenarios that would need to be accounted for. Not only would this too have an impact on performance, but it might also break backwards compatibility for existing implementations.

The race conditions I described I this chapter seem theoretical to the point where they strain credulity. And it is not unreasonable to assume that COM is at least sensible in how and when it does cleanup cycles. This is all undocumented but there are several measures we could think of that COM can take to avoid serious issues and as long as you let COM take care of the housekeeping, there tend to be no problems.

A COM DLL is typically small compared to other things. We're talking about an order of magnitude that can still be measured in Kilobytes. On a computer that has gigabytes of RAM, worrying about Kilobytes is not only pointless, but if you try to be too creative, you risk creating more problems than you solve. If you really want to, it is possible to create multithreaded races between DllGetClassObject and DLLCanUnloadNow for the purpose of crashing the application. If it is possible to intentionally create such a disaster, this means it's also possible to accidentally create one. And given the potential to save a few Kilobytes on one hand, and the time needed to implement manual cleanup cycles in such a way that you're not risking problems, it is safe to say that we no longer live in an era where it is sensible or even justified to spend developer time to keep memory consumption to a minimum at the Kilobyte granularity.

Note that there are safeguards in place to ensure that servers will eventually get released if the application which locked them terminates unexpectedly. The COM runtime keeps track not only of locks but also reference counts associated with a client process. If an application terminates unexpectedly, there is a garbage collection process that detects this and takes appropriate action to make sure that resources are not kept alive indefinitely.

With DllGetClassObject and DLLCanUnloadNow fully implemented and understood it seems that everything is in order. The final thing we need to do is add a module definition file to the DLL project in which we are building our in-process server, to tell the linker that it needs to export those functions.

```
LIBRARY
EXPORTS
        DllGetClassObject    PRIVATE
        DllCanUnloadNow      PRIVATE
        DllRegisterServer   PRIVATE
        DllUnregisterServer PRIVATE
        DllInstall          PRIVATE
```

Building an out-of-process server

As the word says, an out of process server runs in a different process from the client that is using its COM object. This means that every single method call needs to be marshaled and sent via RPC to the remote process. The act of invoking a remote method call is several thousand times slower than dereferencing a raw pointer of an in-process COM object. But as we saw earlier, there are some valid use cases.

Whatever the case may be, you want to implement your COM objects in a separate process. The first thing you need to do is to Initialize the main application thread for COM. This is something we don't need to do in the in-process server because the in-process server DLL will be loaded into the client process, in a thread that is initialized by the client (or the COM infrastructure acting in that thread).

For our scenario, we only have our own object to consider. In such cases, MTA can be beneficial because it allows your objects to use worker threads without losing performance to unneeded marshaling. The downside is that this comes with the requirement to make sure that your object is safe for multi-thread use and has the necessary logic to deal with concurrent calls of any kind.

```
HRESULT hRes = CoInitializeEx(0, COINIT_MULTITHREADED);
if (FAILED(hRes)) {
    return hRes;
}

CalculatorClass calculatorClassObject;
```

It should be noted that from the client's point of view, it doesn't matter what the server process chooses for apartment type. Every call is going to be marshaled between apartments either way. Choosing COINIT_MULTITHREADED here is only going to make dealing with worker threads a lot easier and avoids having to marshal inside the server when doing that.

The class object itself is treated as a stack object, just like we did in the in-process server. The reason is that just like in that scenario, our class object sticks around for as long as the application is running. Note that the same application can host multiple class objects. If so, their lifecycles are inherently tied together because if the application shuts down, all class objects go down with it. Likewise, if 1 class object locks the server into existence through its IClassFactory interface, all other class objects stay in memory too.

The next step is to inform the COM runtime that we are in fact hosting the class object with class id `CLSID_Calculator`. This is done through the CoRegisterClassObject API. Obviously, if the server is started in response to a client request for a COM object with a specific CLSID, COM will expect that there will be a COM object with that class ID. But until we hand over the pointer, COM will not be able to interact with it. The COM infrastructure handling that client request will start the executable and then wait for a while until it's being given an interface pointer. Initializing the internal state of your server may take time. If this takes too long, eventually the client call fails with an error like RPC_S_CALL_FAILED or REGDB_E_CLASSNOTREG. There is no documented timeout value, so it is impossible to say exactly how much time you have. However, keep in mind that at this point in the server lifecycle, you're only setting up the class object, and possibly starting some worker threads, but not do a whole lot of real work yet so as long as you don't do anything wildly unexpected, this should not be an issue.

```
hRes = CoRegisterClassObject(
    CLSID_Calculator,
    static_cast<IClassFactory*>(&calculatorClassObject),
    CLSCTX_LOCAL_SERVER,
    REGCLS_SUSPENDED | REGCLS_MULTIPLEUSE,
    &dwReg);
```

The first 2 parameters are the class ID and a pointer to the class object. This gives COM an easy way to associate the server process with the CLSID of that specific COM object and its interface pointer.

The CLSCTX enumeration parameter can have many different values to support a wide variation of scenarios. For our server, we just use `CLSCTX_LOCAL_SERVER` to indicate that the class object is running in a local server.

The REGCLS enumeration has to do with the behavior of the server if the class object is not only used by outside callers but also in-process. For our purposes, we specify `REGCLS_SUSPENDED | REGCLS_MULTIPLEUSE` to indicate that the class object can be used multiple times, and it remains suspended until we resume it. The reason for starting it suspended is twofold. First, if we register multiple class objects, this is more efficient because the class IDs are all registered at the same time instead of requiring multiple round trips. Second, there is an inherent race condition that could otherwise happen. Suppose that we register several live class objects. There is an inherent race condition. Consider the following scenario:

1. Class object A is registered.
2. Class object A is used briefly by a client.
3. Class object A determines whether it has been used, and is no longer in use, and is therefore initiating module shutdown.
4. Class object B is registered but the module continues to shut down.

To avoid such scenarios, the class objects are registered 1 by 1 in a suspended state, and then we start them all at once. As a sidenote, COM holds requests for STA class objects on pause until the thread's message pump starts handling messages, which normally is after all class objects. Calls to MTA objects could theoretically arrive after the first call to CoRegisterClassObject finishes, which is why they are registered in a suspended state until they can all start at the same time.

```
if (SUCCEEDED(hRes)) {
    hRes = CoResumeClassObjects();
    if (SUCCEEDED(hRes)){
```

```
        g_Server.WaitForShutdown();
    }
    CoRevokeClassObject(dwReg);
}
```

If the resume operation succeeds, the thread is halted to wait for the server to shut itself down when all the criteria are met for it to terminate its lifecycle. As discussed earlier, that wait operation is done in a manner that window messages and APCs will be processed. When the shutdown signal happens, `CoRevokeClassObject` is used to inform the COM runtime that this server is no longer hosting the class object for `CLSID_Calculator`. It is the responsibility of the server to make sure that every successful call to `CoRegisterClassObject` matches a corresponding call to `CoRevokeClassObject`. The body of the server is no more complex than this collection of calls:

```
HRESULT hRes = CoInitializeEx(0, COINIT_MULTITHREADED);
if (FAILED(hRes)) {
    return hRes;
}

CalculatorClass calculatorClassObject;

DWORD dwReg = 0;
hRes = CoRegisterClassObject(
    CLSID_Calculator,
    static_cast<IClassFactory*>(&calculatorClassObject),
    CLSCTX_LOCAL_SERVER,
    REGCLS_SUSPENDED | REGCLS_MULTIPLEUSE,
    &dwReg);

if (SUCCEEDED(hRes)) {
    hRes = CoResumeClassObjects();
    if (SUCCEEDED(hRes)){
        g_Server.WaitForShutdown();
    }
    CoRevokeClassObject(dwReg);
}
```

Lifecycle management needs to be implemented differently from in-process servers though. This is where things get sticky. Unlike a DLL server which is loaded into the client process space where it can reside at leisure without having to do anything, the out-of-process server is responsible for its own lifecycle management. It needs to implement 'some' kind of behavior to determine if it needs to continue running or not, unlike the in-process server which only must inform anyone who wants to know whether the server is locked or not. How this is done is left up to the implementer to decide.

In general, it is reasonable to assume that if the server is started for the purpose of using its class object(s), then it should stop if the following conditions are true:

1) The module was not locked explicitly.
2) There are no class instances still in existence.
3) No one is using the class object(s).

Now that sounds similar enough to the requirements for an in-process server. But there is a twist. We supplied a pointer to the class object to `CoRegisterClassObject`. And like a good COM citizen, when that routine makes a copy of the pointer for its own purposes to hold on to, it calls AddRef. Similarly, `CoRevokeClassObject` calls Release. So, maintaining the effect of the class object the lock count via AddRef / Release is not an option because the module will be locked in `CoRegisterClassObject` and not unlocked until shutdown is in progress. But shutdown will not happen until it is unlocked. Clearly, AddRef and Release of the class object cannot be allowed to affect the module lock, so we let the code reflect that.

```
ULONG STDMETHODCALLTYPE CalculatorClass::AddRef(void)
{
#ifdef _USRDLL
        g_Server.LockModule();
#endif
    return InterlockedIncrement(&m_CoRefCount);
}

ULONG STDMETHODCALLTYPE CalculatorClass::Release(void)
{
#ifdef _USRDLL
        g_Server.UnlockModule();
#endif
    return InterlockedDecrement(&m_CoRefCount);
}
```

The calls to LockModule and UnlockModule in the constructor and destructor of the class instances remain valid so we don't have to make any changes there. Contrary to the DLL situation, the process needs to take control of its own lifecycle. The main thread is performing the wait operation, so it needs to be triggered when the module is unlocked. This means we need to make the following change.

```
ULONG Server::LockModule(void)
{
    ULONG lockCount = CoAddRefServerProcess();
    return lockCount;
}

ULONG Server::UnlockModule(void)
{
```

```
    ULONG lockCount = CoReleaseServerProcess();
    if (0 == lockCount)
        ShutdownServer();

    return lockCount;
}

ULONG Server::ShutdownServer()
{
    return SetEvent(this->m_ShutdownEvent);
}
```

If the count reaches 0, we need to fire the shutdown event that the main thread is waiting for. However, like the situation with the in-process server, there is a race condition that needs to be managed. When the module lock count reaches 0, we initiate the irreversible shutdown of our server. That could happen from a different thread, if our server is complex there may be a lot of cleanup involved, etc. There is going to be a delay between the initiation of the shutdown sequence, and the call to `CoRevokeClassObject`.

Suppose that a new client sends a request for our class object right between the initiation of the shutdown and the call to `CoRevokeClassObject`. The COM runtime will happily oblige, and bad things will happen. No matter how we implement the shutdown sequence, this window is unavoidable because our server needs to synchronize its own activities with outside requests from the COM infrastructure. Thankfully, there are APIs to help us out.

```
//combaseapi.h
WINOLEAPI_(ULONG)
CoAddRefServerProcess(
    void
    );

WINOLEAPI_(ULONG)
CoReleaseServerProcess(
    void
    );
```

The functions `CoAddRefServerProcess / CoReleaseServerProcess` do the same thing as our InterlockedIncrement / Decrement pair, which is to maintain an atomic module lock count. On top of that, whenever it notices that the reference count has dropped to 0, it automatically suspends the class objects hosted in our server process and informs the COM runtime that this process is no longer hosting the registered class objects, which will make the COM runtime launch another out-of-process server, leaving this one alone to finish its shutdown sequence. To implement this, we need to make a small modification to our lock / unlock calls.

```
ULONG Server::LockModule(void)
{
#ifdef _USRDLL
    return InterlockedIncrement(&m_LockCount);
#else
    ULONG lockCount = CoAddRefServerProcess();
    return lockCount;
#endif
}

ULONG Server::UnlockModule(void)
{
#ifdef _USRDLL
    return InterlockedDecrement(&m_LockCount);
#else
    ULONG lockCount = CoReleaseServerProcess();
    if (0 == lockCount)
        ShutdownServer();
    return lockCount;
#endif
}
```

That leaves us the following situation, where the class object reference count does not affect the server lifecycle.

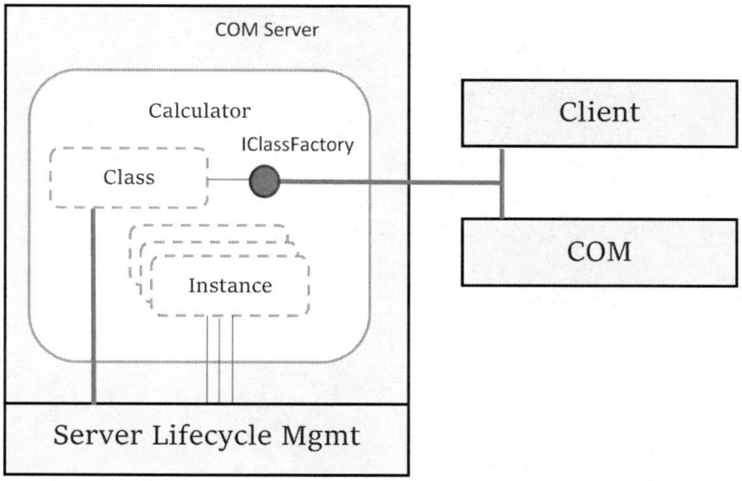

This is where IClassFactory::LockServer comes into play again. And this is where it becomes obvious why it exists on a class object interface. Consider what could happen without that method:

1. Client A requests a pointer to the class object.
2. COM launches the exe and passes a marshaled pointer to A.
3. Client B requests and gets a marshaled pointer to the class object.

4. Client A creates an instance. This brings the module lock to 1.
5. Client A uses and releases the instance. The module lock drops to 0, and shutdown is initiated.
6. Client B tries to create an instance -> bad things happen.

It would essentially be impossible for client B to guarantee it could ever be sure it would be able to create an instance, based on timing. That is one of the reasons why the LockServer method exists. Clients don't have to call it themselves. If they did, Client B would still be in a race to call LockServer before Client A releases its instance and unlocks its hold over the server. The timelines would be tighter, but there is still the potential for things like that to happen. COM does the locking for us. Whenever an IClassFactory interface is marshaled, COM calls LockServer on it with fLock set to TRUE. When the proxy is released, COM calls LockServer on it with fLock set to false. The proxy itself always returns S_OK. Clients don't have to call it themselves because it would be completely redundant and only increase the potential for errors.

However, there is even more we can do to control the lifetime of our COM server with more granularity. COM has an interface specifically designed to keep track of external connections: IExternalConnection. This interface has only 2 methods.

```
//objidlbase.h
IExternalConnection : public IUnknown
{
public:
    virtual DWORD STDMETHODCALLTYPE AddConnection(
        _In_  DWORD extconn,
        _In_  DWORD reserved) = 0;

    virtual DWORD STDMETHODCALLTYPE ReleaseConnection(
        _In_  DWORD extconn,
        _In_  DWORD reserved,
        _In_  BOOL fLastReleaseCloses) = 0;

};
```

Theoretically, this interface supports 3 types of external connection: Weak, Strong, and Callable. According to the documentation, only 'Strong' is ever used so there is not much point in talking about connection types. When an external caller makes a connection, AddConnection is called by the stub manager. When an external connection disappears, ReleaseConnection is called. When the last external connection is removed, the stub needs to be destroyed by the class object by calling `CoDisconnectObject` if `fLastReleaseCloses` is TRUE. If an object does not expose IExternalConnection, the stub manager manages the stub lifetime internally. If it supports that interface however, that responsibility falls on the class object.

Armed with that knowledge, we can make the following changes to our class object:

```
class CalculatorClass :
    public IClassFactory, IExternalConnection
{
}

DWORD CalculatorClass::AddConnection(
    DWORD exconn,
    DWORD dwreserved)
{
    DWORD retVal = 0;
    if (exconn & EXTCONN_STRONG) {
        g_Server.LockModule();
        retVal = InterlockedIncrement(&m_ExtRef);
    }

    return retVal;
}

DWORD CalculatorClass::ReleaseConnection(
    DWORD extconn,
    DWORD dwreserved,
    BOOL fLastReleaseCloses)
{
    DWORD retVal = 0;
    if (extconn & EXTCONN_STRONG)
    {
        g_Server.UnlockModule();
        retVal = InterlockedDecrement(&m_ExtRef);
        if (0 == retVal && FALSE != fLastReleaseCloses)
        {
            CoDisconnectObject(
                 static_cast<IExternalConnection*>(this), 0);
        }
    }
    return retVal;
}
```

You'll notice that there are 2 things going on at the same time, and they are largely unrelated. The first thing is that each call to AddConnection will increase the module lock count, and each call to ReleaseConnection will decrease the module lock count. In that sense, these 2 methods replace the functionality that was provided by the class object AddRef / Release calls in the in-process server. In essence, while there is someone externally holding on to the class object, the class object will keep the module locked into existence.

The second thing is that a separate reference count is maintained for the class object: the external reference count. According to the documentation, after the last external connection disappears and the stub is destroyed, the object should shut down. That is not quite true for class objects in an out-of-process server. Because there may also be outstanding class instances, and we certainly don't want to shut down when there are still clients using class instances.

And just because we destroyed the stub doesn't automatically mean the object has to die. If the stub is destroyed and the client still has an active instance, the server stays alive. If another (or the same) client then requests a reference to the class object, a new stub will be created by the stub manager, and the number of external connections will increase again. In terms of lifecycle, it is important to distinguish between the lifecycle of the stub which is managed through IExternalConnection only and the lifecycle of the server, which is managed through the module lock, which is affected by more than just IExternalConnection.

Note also that IExternalConnection can also be implemented on class instances for the same purpose. On a class object of an out-of-process, IExternalConnection helps with lifecycle management of the server and works with the server reference count. On a class instance it could be used for the purpose of responding to the last client losing its connection without necessarily relying on the instance reference count. For example, the object could have a non-zero reference count because the reference is held internally in the server somewhere without necessarily requiring an external connection.

There is just one more thing that requires explanation: the module lock counting and the shutdown signal. As was mentioned earlier, if we detect the 0, we have the obligation to initiate shutdown because our server simply cannot do anything useful anymore. Given that the shutdown is something we need to wait for, it is natural to build our functionality on top of existing Windows synchronization primitives like events.

```
ULONG Server::ShutdownServer(){
    return SetEvent(this->m_ShutdownEvent);
}
```

The code for waiting otoh is quite a bit more complicated, as was explained in the section about marshaling.

```
ULONG Server::WaitForShutdown(void)
{
    while (!IsShutdownInitiated()) {
        DWORD result;

        result = MsgWaitForMultipleObjectsEx(
            1,                  // 1 handle
```

```
            &m_ShutdownEvent,    // Shutdown event
            INFINITE,            // Timeout interval
            QS_ALLEVENTS,        // Wait for all types of input
            MWMO_ALERTABLE       // Alertable wait
        );
        if (result == WAIT_IO_COMPLETION) {
            // An APC was processed
        }
        else if (result == WAIT_OBJECT_0) {
            // A message is available
            MSG msg;
            while (PeekMessage(&msg, NULL, 0, 0, PM_REMOVE)) {
                TranslateMessage(&msg);
                DispatchMessage(&msg);
            }
        }
    }
}
```

With this code in place, we have a fully functional out-of-process server. In existing COM servers, you could find code similar to this:

```
bool Server::IsShutdownInitiated(void)
{
    return WAIT_OBJECT_0 ==
        WaitForSingleObject(m_ShutdownEvent, 0);
}

HRESULT STDMETHODCALLTYPE CalculatorClass::CreateInstance(
    IUnknown* pUnkOuter,
    REFIID riid,
    void** ppvObject)
{
    HRESULT hres = S_OK;
    *ppvObject = NULL;

    g_Server.LockModule();
    if (g_Server.IsShutdownInitiated())
    {
        hres = CO_E_SERVER_STOPPING;
    }
    else
    {
        CalculatorInstance* calculator = NULL;

        if (NULL != pUnkOuter)
            hres = CLASS_E_NOAGGREGATION;

        if (SUCCEEDED(hres))
        {
            calculator = new CalculatorInstance();
            if (NULL == calculator)
```

```
                hres = E_OUTOFMEMORY;
        }
        if (SUCCEEDED(hres))
        {
            calculator->AddRef();
            HRESULT hres = calculator->QueryInterface(
                                    riid, ppvObject);
            calculator->Release();
        }
    }

    g_Server.UnlockModule();
    return hres;
}
```

This is a technique described in 'Essential COM' to account for the possibility of an activation request being handled just as the server shutdown has been initiated. The module is locked immediately, and then the actual CreateInstance code is executed if the server is not yet shutting down. The LockModule call will see to it that the instance creation will finish safely before UnlockModule is being called. It is important to remember that at the time, the COM infrastructure was a lot more fragile and a lot less out developed than it is today.

With today's infrastructure, the documentation for IClassFactory states that the LockServer functionality is handled by the stub manager before the IClassFactory interface is being marshaled to the client. The very fact that someone is holding an IClassFactory pointer to create an instance is de facto proof that the module is locked as long as that pointer is not released. The above code should never be necessary in this era. This is doubly true because there is also our IExternalConnection implementation which keeps the module locked while anyone is holding a marshaled connection to our class object. We also have `CoAddRefServerProcess` / `CoReleaseServerProcess` which are fully synchronized with COM to remove those types of race conditions from the server lifecycle management.

Special tricks and contortions like above should no longer be needed if you make use of the 'modern' tools that the COM API makes available for you (modern is a relative concept when talking about COM). But many COM projects have roadmaps spanning decades. They have been migrated from one version of Visual Studio to the next since the dawn of time and may still have internal plumbing that originated in the era when the COM infrastructure was more fragile. If you see such things, understand that this made sense at the time, but it is no longer needed today if those newer APIs and interface are used.

The only possible scenario where such a thing might conceivably happen is if a worker thread inside the MTA hosting our server happens to be holding a non-marshaled IClassFactory pointer. Such a pointer would not have the protection of LockServer being called automatically, and it would also not affect the external connection counting. It is conceivable, though not likely, that it could attempt to create an instance just as the last external connection is being released and the server initiates its shutdown. Granted, in a complex server that does a lot of cleanup work, the actual shutdown could take a lot of time, and a call to IClassFactory::CreateInstance could happen through that unmarshaled interface. In that case, there are 2 things that need to be considered. The first is that to guarantee that this method is completely free from race conditions, the LockModule and UnlockModule methods need to use critical sections around the bodies of those methods like this:

```
ULONG Server::LockModule(void)
{
#ifdef _USRDLL
    return InterlockedIncrement(&m_LockCount);
#else
    EnterCriticalSection(&m_CritSectionLockModule);
    ULONG lockCount = CoAddRefServerProcess();
    LeaveCriticalSection(&m_CritSectionLockModule);

    return lockCount;
#endif
}

ULONG Server::UnlockModule(void)
{
#ifdef _USRDLL
    return InterlockedDecrement(&m_LockCount);
#else
    EnterCriticalSection(&m_CritSectionLockModule);
    ULONG lockCount = CoReleaseServerProcess();
    if (0 == lockCount)
        ShutdownServer();
    LeaveCriticalSection(&m_CritSectionLockModule);

    return lockCount;
#endif
}
```

CoAddRefServerProcess and CoReleaseServerProcess APIs are safe for multithreaded use. But the fact that the result of CoReleaseServerProcess triggers a Windows event in a separate call, makes the entire concept susceptible to the following race:

Thread A	Thread B
Releases its last external connection and triggers UnlockModule	Executes CreateInstance
UnlockModule calls CoReleaseServerProcess	
	LockModule calls CoAddRefServerProcess
	IsShutdownInProgress returns false
ShutdownServer is called	
	Normal CreateInstance functionality is executed.
	…
	Bad things happen.

Is this farfetched and unlikely? Absolutely. But when it comes to multithreading, something is either threadsafe or not. Almost threadsafe is not threadsafe. Then again, the 2nd consideration is this: on modern versions of Windows, the only way something like this race can even happen is from worker threads inside the MTA. If for some reason you feel that this is something you need to implement like that, there is no single 'off the shelf' solution that magically makes everything safe. The above code will work as intended with that critical section added. But the only reason it would be necessary is your worker threads are actively doing things with the IClassFactory interface while your server has already decided to shut down. In that case, you will also need to implement a notification mechanism to notify those threads, have them shut down in an orderly fashion, and synchronize their shutdown with the general server shutdown. There are no 'off the shelf' recipes for this so even if you start with this implementation, you will still need to expand this code and implement threadsafe shutdown protocols.

With this implementation, we have a fully functional out-of-process server that properly manages its own lifecycle.

Building a Windows service

From a COM point of view, there isn't a big difference between a regular out-of-process server and a Windows service. Sure, a Windows service comes with more management tools for your convenience, and it requires a bit more coding. But from a COM point of view, it's pretty same-ish except that a Windows service is always running with a dedicated user account, and there's only 1 of them. If you think of a COM Windows service as an out-of-process server, it is similar except every client on the system connects to the same class object.

The biggest difference is conceptual. If you program a Windows service, that means the service is an actor with certain responsibilities, regardless of whether a user is currently using its functionality.

Suppose that our computer connects to a process control network with a lot of industrial controllers. In such networks, there are often pieces of software monitoring and managing the activities of those controllers, loading data, logging activity to various databases, etc. That would be a natural situation for a Windows service because even if there are no users interacting with the controllers for control or monitoring purposes, there is a lot of housekeeping work that needs to be done.

Or think back to our example of a computer with 256 CPU cores for number crunching workloads. Instead of having an out-of-process server starting up and shutting down every time someone needs to crunch numbers (which may involve a lot of initialization work) there could be a Windows service that performs all that initialization at startup, and then host a class object that is sitting there, ready for when someone needs it. It would even be trivial to have it start the first time it is used (the COM runtime does that for us) and then run for a certain amount of time and shut down if it has been idle for a specified interval.

There is a second interesting aspect of hosting a class object in a Windows Service. Imagine that we have a service of which the workload is entirely unrelated to user input or users doing things. But you want to get information on what it is doing, monitor its activities, maybe display some things in a systray status application. In that case the Windows service could host a COM object solely for clients to connect to it and get information, something which is otherwise impossible or would require another information storage technology such as a database or the registry, or rather complex inter process communication mechanisms.

Windows services have gotten a lot of new features since the early days, and the service handler can respond to a wide range of events such as network changes, device changes, and many more. It is beyond the scope of this book to cover the finer details of Windows service development.

For our Calculator service, we are going to build a service that will respond to start and stop control events, as well as pause and resume requests. Pausing and resuming is optional for a service, but it ties in neatly with COM functionality so our service does that too.

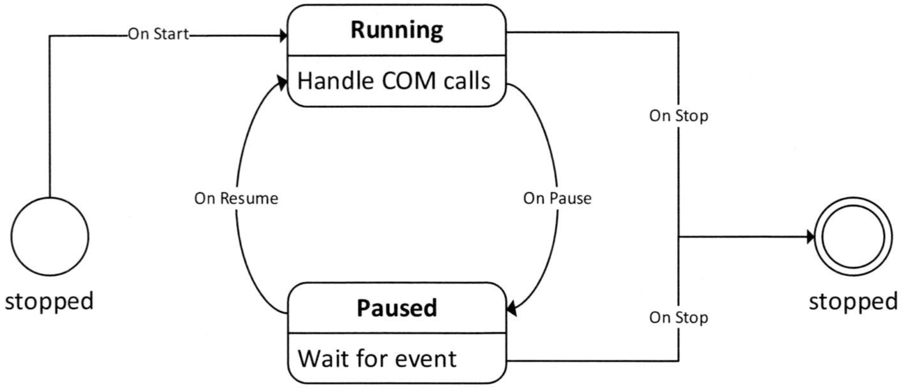

Obviously, a real service would have a lot of other activity happening in parallel and there would be a lot more complexity in the state diagram. Our service will still just act as a Calculator and handle COM calls so not a whole lot of complexity is needed.

For regular applications, everything starts with a 'main' function which contains (indirectly) all code of that program. For services, there is a 'ServiceMain' function that has the same role. It is possible for multiple services to exist in a single executable, each of them with their own servicemain function. You can think of them as independent services which just happen to share an address space, but which are otherwise unrelated.

The prototype for the servicemain function is even the same as that of the main function we're used to.

```
//winsvc.h
typedef VOID (WINAPI *LPSERVICE_MAIN_FUNCTIONW)(
    DWORD   dwNumServicesArgs,
    LWPSTR   *lpServiceArgVectors
    );
```

There is still a normal main function of course, because in the end a service still starts the same way as any other executable. But that main function typically doesn't do a whole lot. Its sole job is to register and start the 'real' ServiceMain functions. For most services, there is just a single ServiceMain function in the process, but the Windows service architecture is built around the idea of a collection of services, whether there is 1 or more service. Each ServiceMain function is responsible for its own handling of service commands. When our service starts, that main function is registered and started, and control dispatching starts dispatching to those functions

```
const LPWSTR g_ServiceName = L"Calculator Service";
```

```
int wmain(int argc, WCHAR* argv[])
{
    SERVICE_TABLE_ENTRY services[] =
    {
        {(LPWSTR)g_ServiceName,
           (LPSERVICE_MAIN_FUNCTION)ServiceMainFunction},
        {NULL, NULL}
    };

    if (StartServiceCtrlDispatcher(services) == FALSE)
    {
        return GetLastError();
    }

    return 0;
}
```

That is literally all there is to the main function. The ServiceMain Function otoh has quite a bit more going on and is in fact almost identical to what we had for our previous out-of-process server.

```
VOID WINAPI ServiceMainFunction(DWORD argc, LPWSTR* argv)
{
    DWORD Status = E_FAIL;
    CalculatorClass calculatorClassObject;

    // Register our service control handler with the SCM
    g_StatusHandle = RegisterServiceCtrlHandlerEx(
                                         g_ServiceName, ServiceCtrlHandler,
NULL);
    if (g_StatusHandle == NULL)
        return;

    if (SetStatus(SERVICE_START_PENDING, 1, true))
        return;

    if (g_Server.Initialize(L"Calculator_V1_LocalService.txt", NULL)) {
        SetStatus(SERVICE_STOPPED, 1, false);
        return;
    }

    HRESULT hRes = CoInitializeEx(0, COINIT_MULTITHREADED);
    if (FAILED(hRes)) {
        SetStatus(SERVICE_STOPPED, 2, false);
        return;
    }

    DWORD dwReg = 0;
    hRes = CoRegisterClassObject(
        CLSID_Calculator,
        static_cast<IClassFactory*>(&calculatorClassObject),
        CLSCTX_LOCAL_SERVER,
```

```
        REGCLS_SUSPENDED | REGCLS_MULTIPLEUSE,
        &dwReg);

    if (FAILED(hRes)) {
        SetStatus(SERVICE_STOPPED, 3, false);
        return;
    }

    hRes = CoResumeClassObjects();
    if (FAILED(hRes)) {
        CoRevokeClassObject(dwReg);
        SetStatus(SERVICE_STOPPED, 4, false);
        return;
    }

    SetStatus(SERVICE_RUNNING, 1, true);
    g_Server.WaitForShutdown();
    CoRevokeClassObject(dwReg);
    SetStatus(SERVICE_STOPPED, 5, false);
}
```

The flow of COM APIs is exactly like in the regular out-of-process server. The 2 main differences have to do with service management. During service startup, and at various points in the life of our service, we need to inform the Windows service control manager (SCM) what is going on. During service startup, we must inform it about how things are progressing and whether we are starting, running, or stopped. Informing the service manager is easy. For example, this is the code for informing it about startup:

```
bool SetStatus(DWORD state, DWORD checkPoint, bool allowControls)
{
    SERVICE_STATUS serviceStatus;
    serviceStatus.dwServiceType = SERVICE_WIN32_OWN_PROCESS;
    serviceStatus.dwCurrentState = state;
    if (allowControls)
        serviceStatus.dwControlsAccepted =
        SERVICE_ACCEPT_STOP |
        SERVICE_ACCEPT_SHUTDOWN |
        SERVICE_ACCEPT_PAUSE_CONTINUE;
    else
        serviceStatus.dwControlsAccepted = 0;

    serviceStatus.dwWin32ExitCode = NO_ERROR;
    serviceStatus.dwServiceSpecificExitCode = NO_ERROR;
    serviceStatus.dwCheckPoint = checkPoint;
    serviceStatus.dwWaitHint = 0;

    if (!SetServiceStatus(g_StatusHandle, &serviceStatus)) {
        DWORD retVal = GetLastError();
```

```
        if (retVal == ERROR_INVALID_HANDLE)
            return true;
        else if (retVal == ERROR_INVALID_DATA)
            return true;
        else
            return true;
    }

    return false;
}
```

The reason for putting that code in a helper function is that we need to cover a couple of scenarios, and having all that code interspersed with the main code can be error prone and make the code difficult to read. The main features are that we can communicate to the Windows Services SCM what state the service is currently in (for example SERVICE_START_PENDING) and which controls -if any- we accept from the service manager (SERVICE_ACCEPT_STOP, SERVICE_ACCEPT_SHUTDOWN, SERVICE_ACCEPT_PAUSE_CONTINUE). More options are possible. Our Calculator service only accepts the ones shown in the diagram earlier. Other than that, the code is almost an exact copy of the regular out-of-process server, except for the registration of the control handler. The Windows service manager needs to have a way to pass control commands to our service. That's why we register our service control handle callback function with the RegisterServiceCtrlHandlerEx API.

```
ULONG WINAPI ServiceCtrlHandler(
    DWORD dwControl,
    DWORD dwEventType,
    LPVOID lpEventData,
    LPVOID lpContext)
{
    switch (dwControl)
    {
    case SERVICE_CONTROL_STOP:
    case SERVICE_CONTROL_SHUTDOWN:
        SetStatus(SERVICE_STOP_PENDING, 1, false);
        g_Server.ShutdownServer();
        return NO_ERROR;

    case SERVICE_CONTROL_PAUSE:
        SetStatus(SERVICE_PAUSE_PENDING, 1, false);
        CoSuspendClassObjects();
        SetStatus(SERVICE_PAUSED, 2, true);
        return NO_ERROR;

    case SERVICE_CONTROL_CONTINUE:
        SetStatus(SERVICE_CONTINUE_PENDING, 1, false);
        CoResumeClassObjects();
```

```
        SetStatus(SERVICE_RUNNING, 2, true);
        return NO_ERROR;

    default:
        return ERROR_CALL_NOT_IMPLEMENTED;
    }
}
```

That is the bare-bones implementation of our Calculator service. Giving intermediate status updates to the SCM is not mandatory. If processing is done sufficiently fast, there is no point in using the PENDING states and using checkpoint values. If much processing is needed, for example to bring all worker threads to a stable state in response to a SERVICE_CONTROL_PAUSE command, then it is necessary to give the SCM intermediate updates, so it knows the service doesn't hang. And that is all there is to a minimal Windows COM service. The STOPPED status is not reported in the handler. That is done in the ServiceMainFunction where the STOPPED status is reported after revoking the class objects.

In terms of lifecycle management and behavior, this chapter covering Windows services is less fleshed out than the previous chapters. Right now, our service isn't much more than a glorified out-of-process server with a fancy way of starting and stopping. The reason for not being authoritatively fleshed out is that there are multiple valid approaches you might select, simply based on what the service is designed for, and what the normal use cases are. Let's look at the implementation we have so far. Regardless of whether the service is started in response to a COM Launch request, or as part of normal Windows startup, or manually by the administrator, in this case the following will happen.

1. The service starts and registers a class object.
2. The service enters a wait cycle and normal COM functionality can start
3. The service will stop if
    a. It receives a shutdown control from the operating system or a stop command from the administrator. OR
    b. It sends its internal shutdown event because there are no more outstanding external connections, module locks or instances, and the final unlock automatically triggers the shutdown.

Is this a good thing? Regrettably, there is no authoritative answer. The only one who can answer that question is whoever is designing the service because they are in control of the use cases. The above scenario is perfectly valid for a Windows service which normally starts only in response to a COM launch request. If such a service has no reason to exist outside its use by clients, then this is exactly what you would expect.

When no one is using it anymore, it shuts down just like any other out-of-process application. On the other hand, if the service performs vital tasks independent of the clients and the COM interfaces are only for interacting with the service, then this is a terrible implementation. For such cases, we need to ensure that the service lives out its normal lifecycle and only stops in response to operating system or administrator requests. That would be easy to implement because we already have a module locking mechanism in place to do that. It is as trivial as modifying the ServiceMainFunction as follows:

```
VOID WINAPI ServiceMainFunction(DWORD argc, LPWSTR* argv)
{
    //removed code
    //...

    g_Server.LockModule();      //<-- lock before wait
    g_Server.WaitForShutdown();
    //removed code
}
```

While this lock operation should technically be matched with a corresponding call to `g_Server.UnLockModule()` , in practice this won't make a difference because we revoke the class object and explicitly signal the shutdown event. This is a rather terminal way to end things. Objectively, if we get a shutdown or stop command, and we're going to wait until all client connections are gone, we could be waiting for a long time. And if we're going to want to implement a more graceful shutdown protocol, it will take a massive amount of coding complexity. In that case we're going to have to keep track of clients, implement ways to notify them and have them acknowledge those notifications, track shutdown progress… which is generally not a good use of developer resources. There is no inherent requirement for gracefully disconnecting clients. That said, it should be noted that if the service is working with important data that needs to be persisted or with external IO that needs to end gracefully, proper thought should go into designing the shutdown protocol for the sake of avoiding data corruption. As was mentioned several times, all these design considerations depend greatly on what you are trying to achieve and what the hard requirements are.

When we lock the module before entering the wait cycle, then no matter what happens in terms of external connections or class factory locking, there will always be at least 1 lock outstanding: the one we set right before entering the wait. This modification also raises the question: does locking the module really guarantee it will stay in memory?

It's true that the COM server is locked. But if an administrator decides it is time to shut down the service, the service WILL shut down, regardless of outstanding locks. Technically, a service -can- refuse to listen to shutdown or stop commands, but while that is technically feasible, we're going to operate on the premise that any programmer implementing a COM service is not going to purposely subvert SCM commands. So, if the administrator sends a `SERVICE_CONTROL_STOP` command, the service will initiate a service shutdown.

This may seem problematic from an application point of view, but the reality is that the administrator should always have an overriding say in lifecycle management. Even if the service would ignore the control messages from the SCM, the administrator could still kill the process. And even if we prevent that using various dubious programming techniques, in the end the service will still shut down if the operating system itself is shutting down. And again, we're working on the premise that we're not actively trying to mess things up.

In normal circumstances the service control handler we've shown above will remove normal COM activities from playing any deciding role in lifecycle management of the service. The extra lock operation during startup ensures that and startup and shutdown of the service are controlled solely by the administrator or the operating system, just like other services.

But what if we want to do the opposite? Instead of taking lifecycle control away from normal COM routine, we want to make sure that the service is only running if it needs to perform COM activities. If someone should start it outside the times when it is needed for COM, it needs to shut down. Going back to the first version of our service doesn't work, because in that version it will start up and wait for a client to unlock after locking, for the last external connection to disappear, or the last instance to be released. If no one ever establishes a connection, that means the wait will last indefinitely (or until the administrator or operating system intervenes). This can be solved with a temporary lock that causes the following behavior:

1. LockModule
2. Wait x seconds
3. UnlockModule

At that point, there are two possibilities. If no one has connected to the COM server, the unlock in step 3 is recognized as the last unlock, the shutdown event is fired, and the service shuts down because it has no work to do. On the other hand, if someone did connect to it and is using the class object or an instance, the UnlockModule does nothing except decrementing the global module lock. The service will still go on and as soon as the last external connection disappears and the last lock is gone, it will shut down. One way to implement this is by using a Windows timer.

```
DWORD Server::SetTemporaryLock(ULONG seconds)
{
    m_Unlocktimer = SetTimer(NULL, 0, seconds * 1000, NULL);
    if (m_Unlocktimer == NULL)
        return GetLastError();
    LockModule();
    return NO_ERROR;
}
```

Timers can be created with a callback function that executes when the timer does. But we already have a message loop in place in our implementation of `WaitForShutdown` so we can use that to handle the timer event. We just create a timer that fires a window message, which we can then catch.

```
ULONG Server::WaitForShutdown(void)
{
    //removed some code

        else if (result == WAIT_OBJECT_0) {
            // A message is available
            MSG msg;
            while (PeekMessage(&msg, NULL, 0, 0, PM_REMOVE)) {
                if (msg.message == WM_TIMER &&
                        msg.wParam == m_Unlocktimer) {
                    KillTimer(NULL, m_Unlocktimer);
                    UnlockModule();
                    break;
                }
                TranslateMessage(&msg);
                DispatchMessage(&msg);
            }
}
```

We catch the timer message, and if the timer that fired the event is our unlock timer, we perform the unlock and kill the timer to prevent it from firing again and causing multiple unlocks. That leaves 1 final change to be made.

```
VOID WINAPI ServiceMainFunction(DWORD argc, LPWSTR* argv)
{
    //removed code
    //...

    g_Server.SetTemporaryLock(5);     //5 seconds
    g_Server.WaitForShutdown();
    //removed code
}
```

At this point we have covered 3 distinct lifecycle use cases. There are more variations possible. Services run outside the control of non-elevated users. And as stated, a COM service can be used by multiple users, for various purposes. How a service is expected to behave is ultimately a matter for the designers to decide, which is why a COM service requires more care during the designp hase than a regular out-of-process server, even though the actual COM objects may be very similar.

Surrogate servers

There may be times when a client application requires the use of a specific COM server but doesn't want to have that server running in its own address space. Obvious reasons include security (the client address space may contain sensitive data) or stability (a specific in-process server may not be very stable). Whatever the reason may be, most servers are distributed only as in-process servers, in the form of a DLL that needs to be loaded in an address space.

However, thanks to the concept of apartments and marshaling, where any server runs in the physical sense is an implementation detail that the client doesn't really know or care about. An in-process server needs 'a' process to host it. It doesn't have to be the client process. This is where the concept of surrogates comes into play.

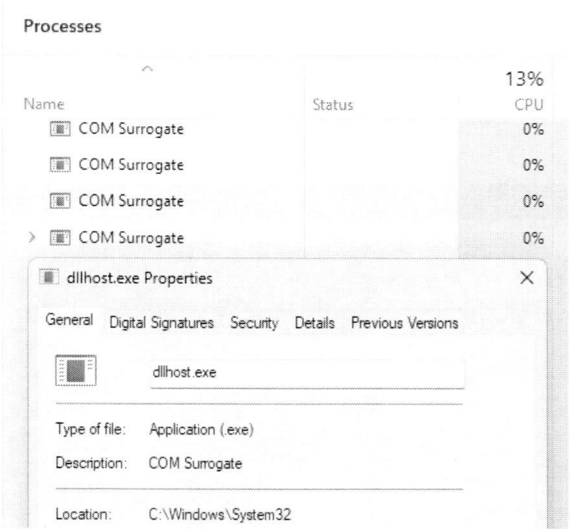

When a client requests an activation or an out-of-process server, COM checks the registration information for the requested class ID. It will first attempt to locate an out-of-process server to start. If it doesn't find one, it will launch an executable whose sole purpose is to load and host the in-process server for the duration of its lifecycle. Lifecycle management of any in-process server is performed through the DLLGetClassObject and DLLCanUnloadNow functions and is therefore identical for every server. Windows comes with a default surrogate server that can be used without having to do anything. At any point in time, there are probably a couple of surrogates active on a given Windows system.

As a developer you don't have to do or configure anything special to make use of the default surrogate process. It is possible to specify a different surrogate executable than the standard one. Logically it would have to be developed and distributed with the in-process server, if it was built with specific functionality or features to facilitate that specific server. But in that case, it would make more sense to supply an actual out-of-process server. Surrogates are not the preferred method for running a server out of process. With a regular out-of-process server, the executable can be used as a stand-alone program that can interact with other applications. With a surrogate this is not possible. Additionally, the lifecycle management implemented by a surrogate is rather generic. There is no fine-grained control over the lifecycle, which may have an impact on overall system resources, as well as resources which are kept needlessly in use by the server as while ng as it is alive.

If out-of-process use is a scenario you foresee and want to support, supplying a purpose-built server is always better than shoehorning the in-process server into a surrogate process.

Activation and Launch

Now that we've seen the 2 scenarios for DCOM server configuration (in-process and out-of-process), we need to look at the next question: how does it all work in a practical sense?

When client.exe starts and requires an in-process server, somehow it needs to load and properly initialize server.dll. If client.exe needs an out-of-process server.exe, server.exe needs to be started and initialize its object(s). Or if server.exe is already running, client.exe needs to be able to set up communication to it.

This is where the COM Service Control Manager (COM SCM) comes into play. It is an unfortunate name because there is also a Service Control Manager for Windows service applications, and they are unrelated to each other. Commonly, the SCM for Windows Services is just called 'Service Control Manager' while the SCM for COM is commonly referred to as the COM SCM.

When a client makes a request for a specific out-of-process server, the COM SCM checks if the server is already running in the requested context for that user. If it is not, then the COM SCM will start the server by launching the exe or starting the service if the caller has the correct permissions. That part of the process is called

‘Launch’ and the permission to do so is called ‘Launch Permission’. It only applies to out-of-process servers.

The term ‘Activation’ refers to the process of using the class object (to create instances). Access to the class object is governed by ‘Activation Permission’. Note that some documentation uses very ambiguous language to talk about activation. Some sources describe Activation as “Creating an instance of the (class) object” and in the context of COM and C++, this is very dubious language. It’s tricky to find an authoritative definition of that word but it boils down to the ability to use the class object.

For in-process servers, it is certainly correct to talk about Activation in the meaning of ‘starting to use the class object’ but for in-process servers, the security settings governing Activation and Launch are ignored. The reason behind this is most likely that security is used to govern what a process is or is not allowed to do in another process. An in-process server exists in a program’s own process space, and as such it is not isolated from anything inside the process. There is no separate permission for allowing the client to load an in-process server. This will be discussed in more depth in the chapter about security.

Summary

In this chapter we set up the development environment for starting our Calculator server project, using the IDL files we created in the previous chapter.

We covered building the proxy, as well as the 3 different types of server: in-process, out-of-process application, and out-of-process Windows Service. We briefly covered surrogates which can act as an out-of-server body for an in-process server.

And finally, we described Launch and Activation; 2 topics which take us seamlessly to the next chapter, which covers how to register our servers in such a way that COM can know where to find them and what to do with them.

5

Server registration

In the previous chapter we covered the different ways we can build a COM server. We've seen 3 types of server that all host the same implementation, but in different packages, for different purposes, with different lifecycle requirements:

- In-process: the server is loaded in the client application.
- Out-of-process: the server is hosted in a different application.
- Out-of-process windows service: the server is hosted in a Windows service application.

Even though each of these can exist in coexistence with the others, that is not commonly done for the simple reason that COM servers are designed for a purpose. That purpose often dictates the appropriate deployment package. It is possible to deploy all 3 options side by side. Our own Calculator has all 3 types for educational purposes but it's hard to imagine why that would make sense in a real-life application.

We know that a COM object has a GUID, a human readable name, a physical location on disk, permission lists for Launch and Activation, and several other pieces of information that belong together so that the COM Runtime and COM SCM know what to do.

That leaves us with the question of where all this information is stored, and how it is structured in a manner that allows the COM infrastructure to put all these puzzle pieces together. The answer, as with most things on a Windows system, is this is all stored in the registry. When COM needs to perform any COM related lookup, it consults the well-known registry key HKEY_CLASSES_ROOT (HKCR).

All objects have a GUID as their formal name. But that is hardly a convenient way to deal with objects as a developer. As a C or C++ programmer, you have the luxury of being able to link against the MIDL generated *.c files and use symbol names like CLSID_Calculator in your code. But even that only works if your client always connects to the same server. Many industrial environments have distributed applications that interact with components from different vendors that all implement the same interfaces such as Ole for Process Control (OPC). The first link in the chain of configuration data is the Program ID of the COM server, aka the ProgID. That is available directly under HKCR. For our calculator, there is a registry key which acts as the entry point for looking up information about the Calculator COM server

HKCR\Mathlib.Calculator.1

In that registry key there is a default value with the short name of the calculator, which is only used for informational purposes.

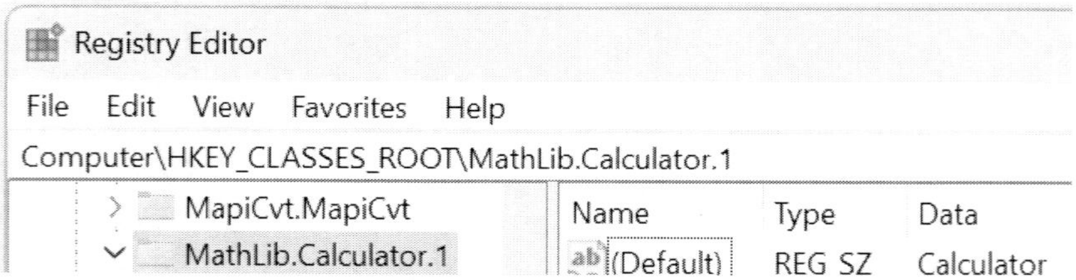

The important information is in the subkey

HKCR\Mathlib.Calculator.1\clsid

which has a default value that is the GUID of the class object.

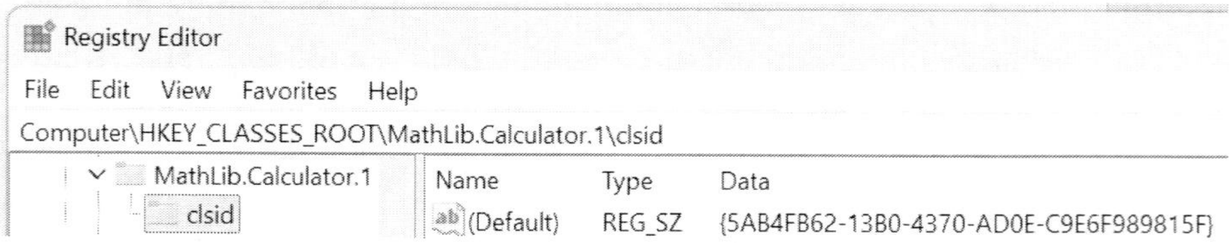

When a client application or COM itself wants to obtain the class id for a named class, it can use the API

```
//combaseapi.h
WINOLEAPI
CLSIDFromProgID(
    _In_ LPCOLESTR lpszProgID,
    _Out_ LPCLSID lpclsid
    );
```

to translate the human friendly name to the actual COM name. Because it is not uncommon for distributed applications to be created from components that change over time, being able to use these friendly names is important to administrators and users, even if it doesn't really matter a lot to the developers. Note that some classes do not have a program ID in place. One reason can be that the class objects are part of a larger collective of objects that exist solely to support a higher-level object that is exposed to the world, but which are not intended to be used or configured independently.

The ProgID is also a built-in way for COM to do versioning. When you perform the lookup for a ProgID, COM will test that name to see if it is an alias. It will attempt to open a CurVer key to find the 'current' version of the requested program ID. This enables a primitive version of side-by-side installation. This gives people administering a system a limited means of configuring which server is used if multiple versions of object are installed, if the client application uses the program ID and not the class ID directly. Theoretically, a versioning scheme like this allows objects to be installed side by side but this only works if their installers are well designed and don't overwrite each other's files.

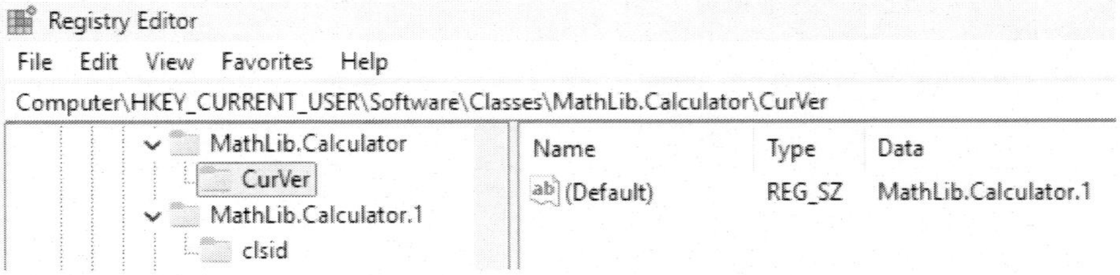

With a way to establish the class id established, the next link in the chain is to find the details of the class. This can be found with the shortname of the Calculator class object as shortname, under

HKCR\CLSID\{clsid}

The CLSID key is listed under HKCR as a special container under which all possible class IDs are stored.

The HKCR\CLSID\{clsid}\progid registry key points back to the program id of the class. This way, it is trivial to perform the lookup in the reverse direction with another API, at least if there exists a program id for that class id.

```
//combaseapi.h
WINOLEAPI
ProgIDFromCLSID(
    _In_ REFCLSID clsid,
    _Outptr_ LPOLESTR  FAR * lplpszProgID
    );
```

Underneath HKCR\CLSID\{clsid} there exists at least 1 key that links the class object to the binary package containing the COM server. In this case, that is the InprocServer32 key whose value is the path the DLL containing the in-proc server.

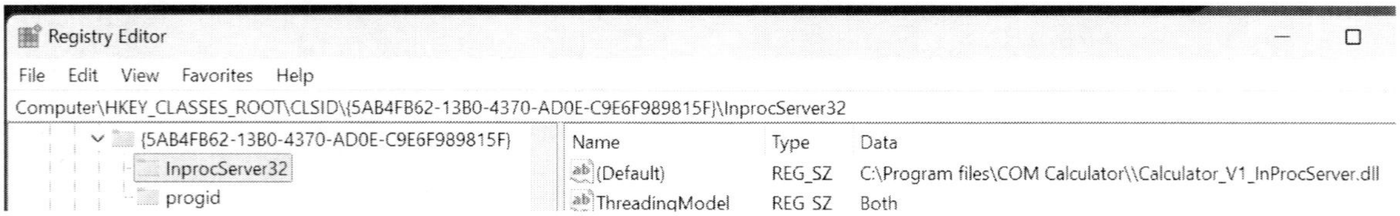

Any class object needs a key to define the binary file in which it resides. The following keys are possible:

Key	Value
InprocServer32	Path to the DLL for the in-process server
LocalServer32	Path to the executable for the out-of-process server. This path may contain command line arguments.

There are also obsolete keys such as InprocServer and LocalServer, which were originally used with 16-bit COM servers. These can no longer be used natively on Windows. A modern 64-bit Windows system can run 32-bit executables via something called Windows on Windows (WOW or WOW64). Running 16-bit executables or loading 16-bit DLLs is not possible like this. Using them on a 64-bit operating system requires a virtual DOS environment which is not available without custom setup and then remoting the calls to the server running on that system. Setting this up is outside the scope of this book. To quote an old college professor of mine: This is left as an exercise for the reader.

The InprocServer32 type can optionally have a ThreadingModel value to configure the apartment requirements. The following options are allowed:

Key	Value
Apartment	The server supports the STA apartment model.
Free	The server supports the MTA apartment model.
Both	The server supports both STA and MTA apartment models.
Neutral	The server supports the NTA apartment model.
<none>	If no ThreadingModel is specified, the server is loaded in the first apartment that was initialized in the process. This is sometimes called the main STA or the host STA.

For out-of-process servers, specifying this option would be meaningless. When the server executable of an out-of-process server is launched, it is the server which will initialize the apartment of its threads and decide on which thread the object is created. The COM runtime has no say in this. It also makes no practical difference for the client because any interface pointer must be marshaled to that external executable.

Note that the out-of-process server in this case is a regular server, not a Windows Service. The registration of a COM server that resides in a Windows Service is made in a different section of the registry we'll cover shortly.

With this information, COM has everything it needs to respond to queries for a class object. If your COM server only uses well known interfaces such as IClassFactory, this is enough to function. But things will grind to a halt as soon as the first custom interface needs to be marshaled. That will result in an error because we haven't told COM yet where the proxy DLL for the custom interfaces is.

Interface Proxy DLLs

COM looks up interfaces by GUID. For every interface that requires marshaling, there is (or should be) an entry

HKCR\Interface\{interface guid}

For the IArithmetic interface that is exposed by the Calculator class, the following key exists:

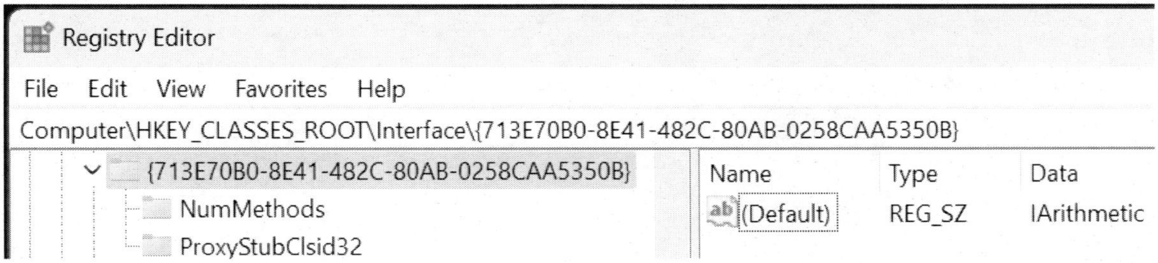

For each interface for which a proxy is installed, there is such an entry. As was shown earlier, the proxy DLL for an interface is itself a COM server with a class object that contains the code to translate method calls to RPC data packets and back. Like any other class object, it needs to have a class ID. This is stored under the ProxyStubClsid32 key.

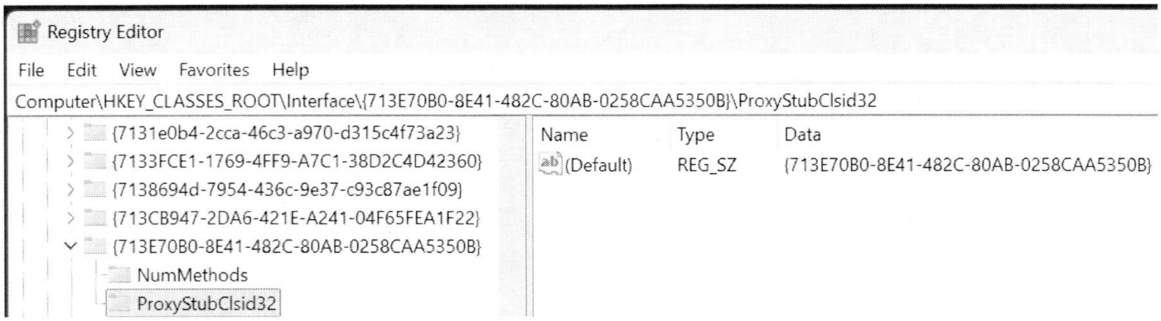

It may seem odd that the class id for the proxy class object is the same as the interface ID. This might seem a violation of the concept that a GUID should uniquely identify something. However, the GUID was specifically created for that interface. Since every GUID is unique, it is impossible for that GUID to conflict with any other class object and it is safe to use as class ID as well. If you implemented your own proxy DLL, you could generate a new GUID. If you use the proxy code that was generated by MIDL, by default the GUID of the first interface is re-purposed as class id. Additional interfaces that are covered by the same proxy will refer to the same class ID. If we look up that class ID, we see this it is an in-proc server which supports both STA and MTA threading models.

At this point you may start to wonder how this is going to work if 2 different vendors have a COM server that supports the same interface, and both install a Proxy DLL to handle marshaling for that interface. The answer is that whoever is the last to write to the specified registry key, is the one who wins. However, that is not the problem it appears to be.

COM interfaces are mandated to be immutable. This means that once an interface definition is released to the world, that specific GUID is always going to identify 1 unique interface definition that is byte by byte compatible with every implementation of that interface in the world.

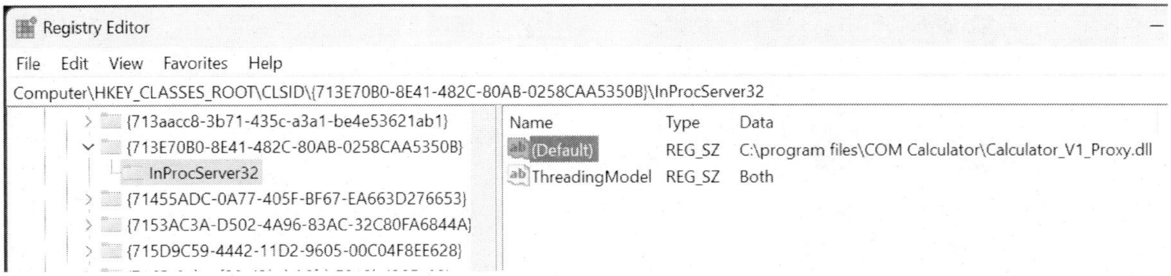

There is an important observation to make here: There is only 1 proxy for each interface. It doesn't matter who made the COM server for which the proxy is used. And it doesn't matter who built the proxy. The COM specification is precise to bit level. Whatever interface was specified in IDL, no matter who compiles it, it will be bit by bit compatible with that interface no matter for which class object in which COM server the interface is being marshaled.

This highlights another reason for interfaces to be immutable. Once an interface has been released to public, it is never allowed to change. That GUID must always identify 1 unique interface definition that is bit by bit compatible with every implementation of that interface in the world.

Imagine for a moment that we don't abide by that requirement and there is a class object A that implements IItf1 which has a Foo method with 1 parameter. It also installs the proxy DLL for IItf1. We then install a COM server from a different vendor with class object B that uses the modified IItf1, and it too installs a proxy. The new proxy would just overwrite the entry that is already there, and suddenly class object A stops working because it can no longer work with the proxy. Alternatively, if the installer sees that the proxy is already installed and foregoes the installation of the proxy DLL, then class object B won't be able to work with the proxy. Interfaces need to be immutable not only because the vtable layout can never be allowed to change, but also because every single bit of information concerning the interface has an effect on the marshaling process and it is critical that ANY Proxy DLL that is installed for a specific interface is valid for everyone who implements or uses that interface.

This also means that if you install a COM server as part of an overall installation or setup, there may be issues if during the uninstall process the installer removes the proxy DLL and the HKCR\Interface\{interface guid} registry key. You could argue that if the setup encounters such a situation during installation, it should create a backup of the information that there and restore it when its own components are uninstalled. That, too, is not without issues. What should the uninstaller do if the software that installed the original proxy DLL is uninstalled at some point? Once you start to 'what if' every conceivable scenario, you quickly realize that COM was never designed with those things in mind.

This is why applications in a COM environment, especially the more complex ones, often have a 'repair' option, and one of the things it does is to re-register the various components to make sure that things like uninstalls of other software do not leave permanent configuration damage to the system.

Type libraries

Earlier in the process when we used MIDL to generate the various header files and c files, a type library file was created as well. A type library (*.tlb file) contains all relevant information for applications that are developed in environments other than C or C++.

These type libraries can be distributed manually for use by developers, like how IDL files can distributed for development purposes. But it's also possible to register them in the registry. This is especially useful for scripting languages and environments that figure out the marshaling and type conversion at runtime instead of compile time. Additionally, development environments like Visual Studio use Type Library information from the registry to understand the various interfaces, methods and properties associated with a COM object. Type libraries have their own subkey at

    HKEY_CLASSES_ROOT\TypeLib\{Library ID}

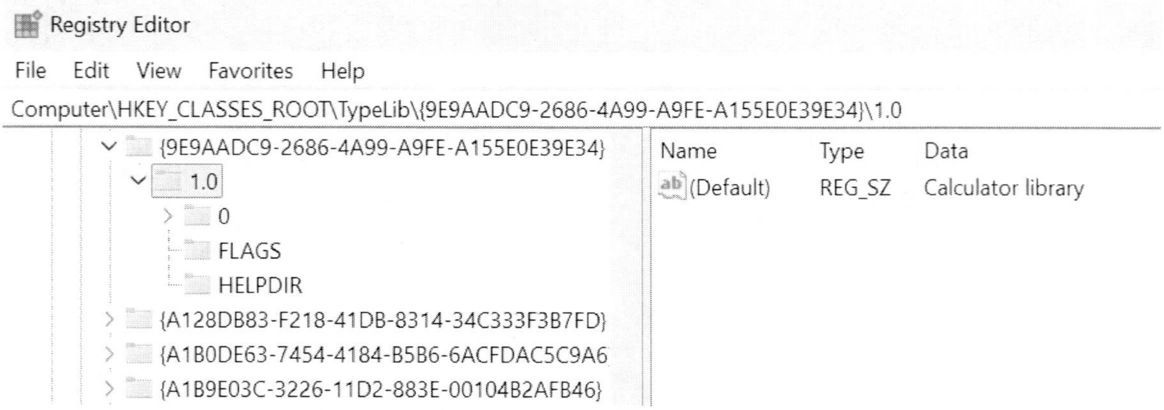

That key contains various information about the type library, including its location.

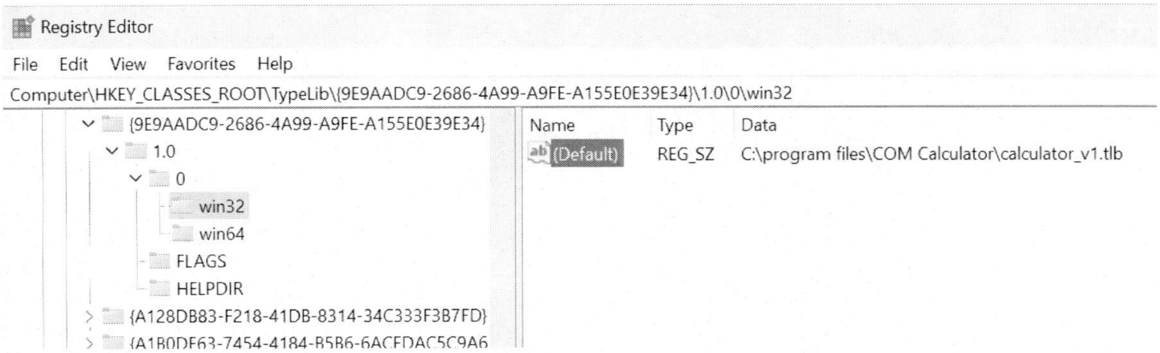

The Type Library registration itself has subkeys for pointing to 64- and 32-bit versions of the type library. When we compile an IDL file with MIDL, we can specify an architecture, and this may affect the generated code files. But COM itself is platform agnostic. IDL files contain type information and meta data that is converted to code files and a type library. A type library can be converted back to IDL. Therefore, it seems odd or redundant to distinguish between 32- and 64-bit versions. If the version you register is the 64-bit version, make sure to also register the 32-bit version. They can even be the exact same file! The reason for making sure that both are registered is that there are many legacy tools involved in the COM ecosystem. Some of them explicitly reference the win32 versions and refuse to use the type library if only the 64-bit version is registered, even though the type information inside is platform agnostic. Visual Studio itself is guilty of this.

To create a logical link between an interface ID or class ID, additional registry keys can be created under the class registration and interface registration.

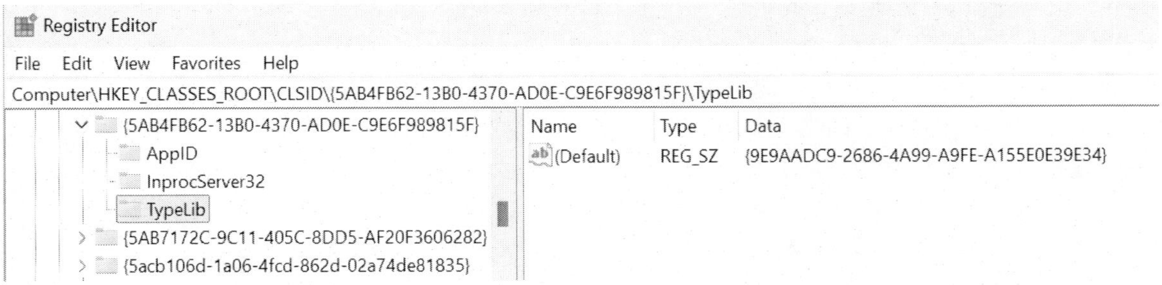

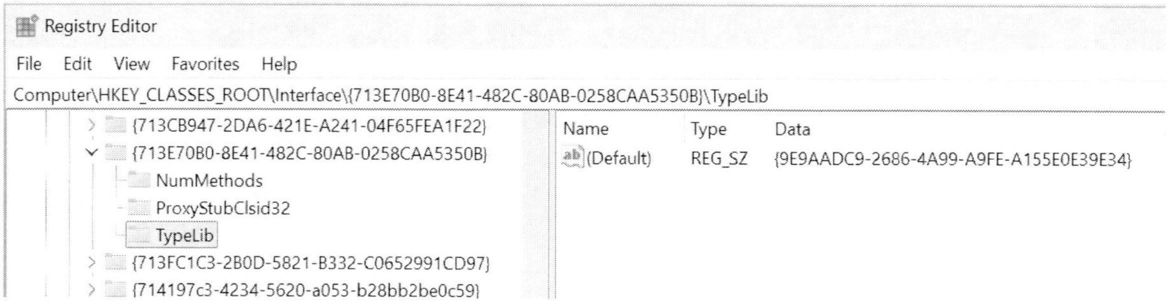

With this information in place, there is a strong link between the class, the interfaces, and the type library they are contained in. Here, too, is the same potential for overwriting information that exists for the proxy. But as with the proxy configuration, there is some resilience because if the interface contract was honored, then in principle it shouldn't matter where the type information for the interface comes from.

Interfaces can be implemented by multiple class objects, leading to multiple type libraries. Suppose a competing implementation of the IArithmetic interface is installed on the system and registers its proxy as well as its type library. The original type library is still registered on the system with its unique library ID, and if a class object has a TypeLib subkey pointing to that library, that will be unaffected by the new type library.

Application ID

The information that was explained up to this point is all related to the COM server, and how the class object, interfaces, proxy and type information are tied together. In other words, everything related to types and where type information is located. What we haven't yet discussed is configuration of the executable side of things, such as permissions, protocol configuration, the identity used by the COM server to execute, and so on. In other words, all the information you need when you stop thinking in the abstract about circles and lollipops and start thinking about actually configuring components to run in a specific way.

For this purpose, there is the concept of an Application ID (AppID). The AppID is the configuration name for the server hosting the class object. Or more specifically, it is the name under which the configuration data for the COM server is stored in the registry.

```
HKCR\AppID\{App ID}
```

This name can be either a GUID or a human readable name. The benefit of a GUID is that it is unique. The benefit of a human readable name is that when you're using visual tools, it's a lot easier to navigate the data or quickly find it in the registry during development phase. Let's go with a GUID for now. The class ID has a value to identify the AppID that contains the COM server runtime settings

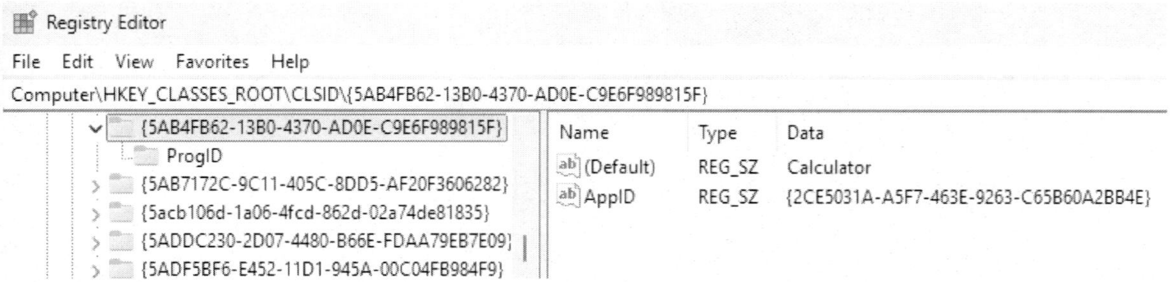

These settings are available under the AppID registry key where all application specific settings are stored.

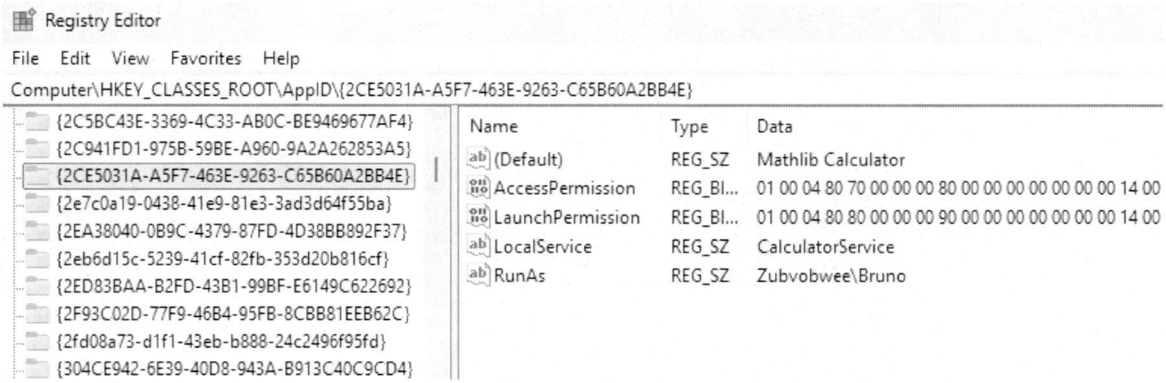

The default value is the human friendly name of the application. Other values may be added as needed. An example of this is the identity of the user account under which the COM server is launched.

This is also a good time to point out the configuration for a COM object that is hosted in a Windows service. Unlike in-process servers or regular out-of-process servers which have a key directly under the CLSID key, the link between the COM object and the server is made via the AppID entry. When an out-of-process server is requested, COM looks at the class ID and checks if an AppID key can be found. If the AppID is found and it contains a LocalService record, that is the out-of-process server that will be launched, even if a LocalService entry exists under the class ID. Unlike InProcServer32 and LocalServer32, LocalService is a value, not a key.

The LocalService value is the name of the Windows service that will be started if permissions are configured correctly. To be precise, this name is the one that must match a service configuration under the

Computer\HKEY_LOCAL_MACHINE\SYSTEM\CurrentControlSet\Services\

registry key in the HKEY_LOCAL_MACHINE hive where all other Window service configuration is stored.

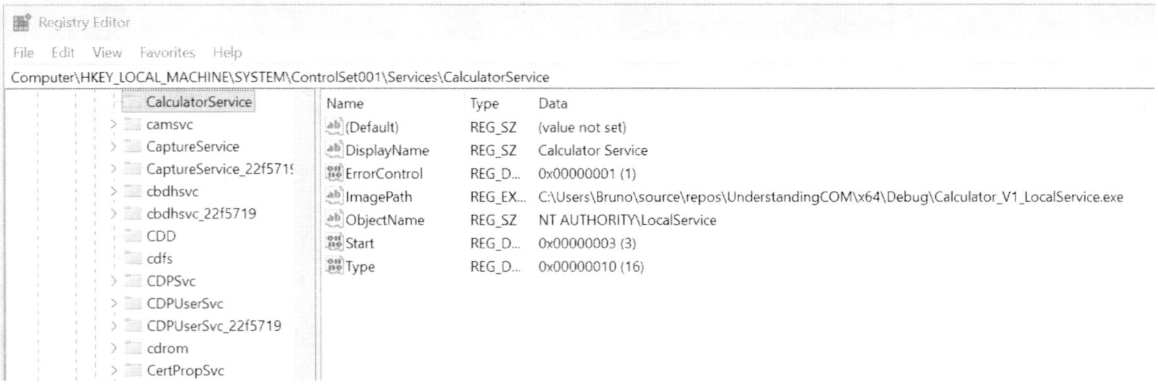

Some of these settings can be configured directly in the registry. However, for most settings it is more common to use the DCOMCnfg tool that is part of Windows. It is an old tool which hasn't been developed as fully as you might expect but it is the only built-in tool that is available. As such it is still used a lot. Using DCOMCnfg, we can configure the application settings for the COM server in a GUI.

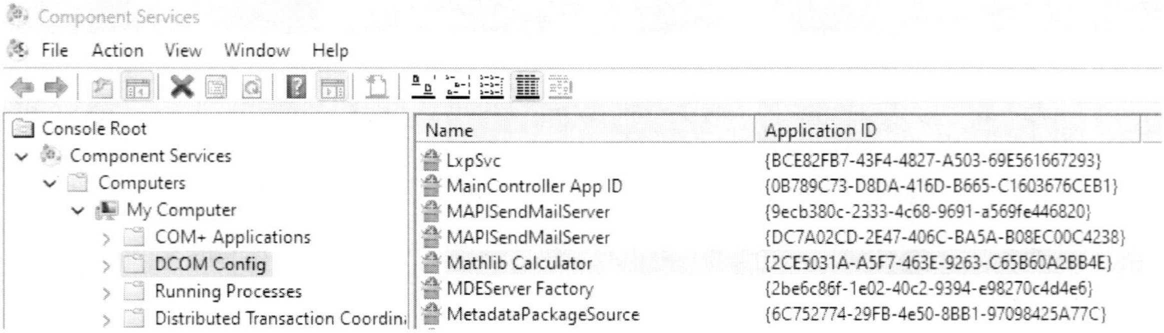

Even though the registry uses the GUID to link the ClsID entry to the AppID, the default value of the AppID is used as display name so it is still easy enough to find the Calculator application.

How the AppID and DCOMCnfg are used to configure specific scenarios is explained in the next chapter. For now, the key takeaway is that the HKCR\AppID\{App ID} key needs to be created and configured as the AppID value under the HKCR\ClsID\{Class ID}.

HKEY_CLASSES_ROOT revisited

If we summarize the previous sections in a high-level drawing, it would look something like this:

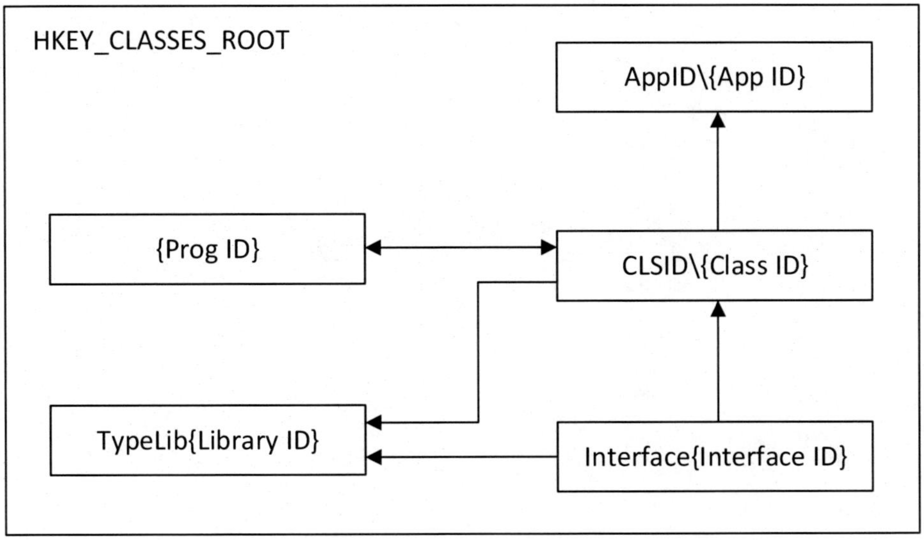

1. Class objects are identified by a Class ID and a program ID that can be translated from one into another. The class ID entry identifies the server(s) in which it resides and the threading requirements.
2. Classes may or may not have an Application ID which acts as a coat hanger for information that pertains to runtime requirements for the server hosting the class object(s).
3. An interface proxy is a class object itself, and a link exists to find that class object based on the Interface ID.
4. To help dynamically typed environments figure out type information, class objects and interfaces can be linked to a Type Library with a library ID.
5. The links are directional. If you want to follow a link in a direction that is not supported by the data entries, the only option is to iterate over all entries.

So far so good, and this picture is easy to understand. However, HKEY_CLASSES_ROOT is not a distinct registry hive. It is a view that is created with information from 2 other hives:

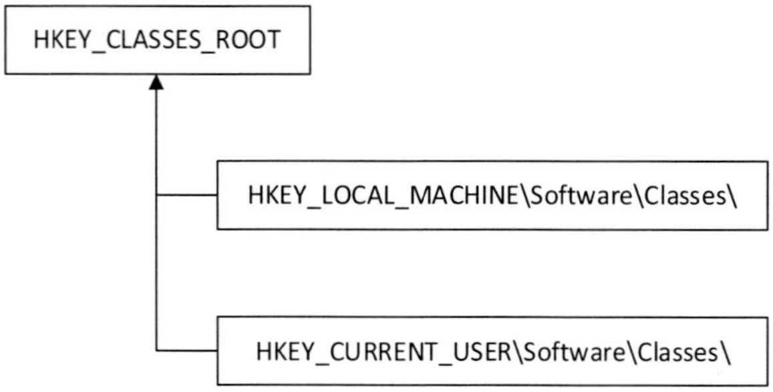

When the HKEY_CLASSES_ROOT view is generated, the information in the HKEY_CURRENT_USER hive takes precedence. This applies to all types of registered information but if we look at the class registration as an example, this is the situation.

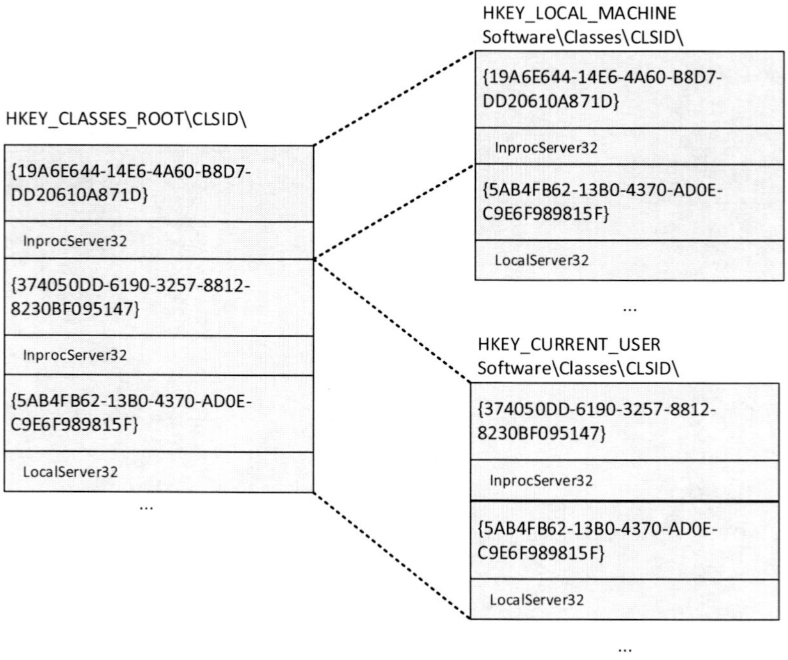

The same class could be configured differently in the different hives. If the HKLM registration has a LocalServer32 entry and the HKCU entry has an InprocServer32 entry, the class registration projected in HKCR will have both entries. If the hives have conflicting entries, then the entries under HKCU will win.

But this is still only half of the picture. On any 64-bit system, Windows supports both 64 bit and 32-bit applications, running side by side. This is especially convenient for COM applications. COM supports marshaling data and calls to any platform that follows the COM requirements. A 64-bit application can use a 32-bit server and vice versa. Both versions can exist side by side on the same system. To this end, HKCR has the following entry

HKCR\WOW6432Node

Which acts as a root for all 32-bit COM configuration information. However, this is where things get a little messy because some things in some subkeys of the WOW6432Node key of the HKLM and HKCU registry hives, some of the information is redirected, and some is shared between architectures. It is important to understand the difference. Note that this applies only to 32-bit binaries on a 64-bit system.

Redirection
With redirection, the system detects when a 32-bit application wants to access a specific configuration key and silently redirects the operation to the equivalent key under the WOW6432Node. For example, when a 32-bit application opens registry key HKLM\Software\MySettings, the registry redirector will silently route the request to key HKLM\Software\WOW6432Node\MySettings. This way, the 32-bit version and 64-bit version will each have their own copy, which can have different values even though both address their copy with the same name.

Sharing
With a shared key, both architectures use the same key.

Redirection and Reflection
This is not used anymore, but before the Windows 7 / Windows 2008 Server R2 Windows system, a process known as Redirection and Reflection was used. In older documentation you might still encounter the symptoms of this so I will briefly describe the background.

In this scenario, the redirection still happened behind the scenes, but there is also an additional synchronization step that copied the values between both keys. This way, both versions could be written to independently, using the same names. Yet they will always have the same value.

This is fundamentally different from a shared key because the synchronization agent could have a list of rules as to which information was to be reflected, and which wasn't. For example, in Windows Vista, registry keys underneath CLSID were reflected only if they had a LocalServer32 subkey. If you registered an out-of-process server \Software\Classes \CLSID\{CLSID} under either HKLM or HKCU, those changes were reflected between architectures. COM is architecture independent, and therefore a request for an out-of-process server is architecture independent. The only requirement from the client is that it runs in a separate address space. To that end, either a 32 bit or 64-bit version will work. So, it makes sense at least from a practical point of view. However, as logical as this sounds, it could lead to issues because while the Interface subkey was reflected too, the actual proxy DLL might not be found because a proxy DLL is architecture dependent. I am unaware of the decision making that led to reflection being phased out. My personal guess is that the collection of rules governing reflection gave rise to too many edge cases and scenarios that exhibited unintended side effects. With Windows 7 and newer versions, keys are either shared completely or redirected entirely, leading to much clearer behavior.

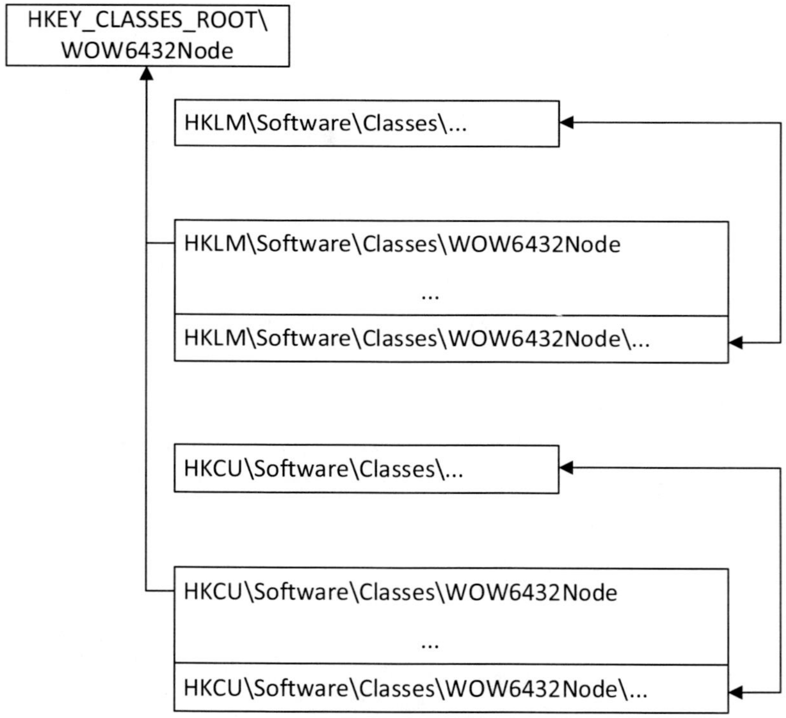

The HKLM\Software\Classes\WOW6432Node and HKCU\Software\Classes\WOW6432Node are mapped into HKCR\WOW6432Node, like the 64-bit situation. However, because of the redirection or sharing rules, some of that information the same as the regular 64-bit information.

The following registry keys are shared:

- \Software\Classes\AppID. AppID settings determine how the server should run, which network protocols are used for remote calls, where the server should run (locally or on a remote computer) etc. None of these settings are affected by the architecture of the server. To give an example: if a non-standard port range is specified for network communication, those settings depend on the firewall(s) having been configured for the non-standard port ranges or protocol choices. And DCOM is architecture agnostic. It would make no sense to support different settings for 32-bit and 64-bit version.
- \Software\Classes\TypeLib. Type libraries contain detailed information about the types contained within. This information will be correct regardless of architecture because that is the point of having them. It's what makes marshaling between architectures and platforms possible.

The following registry keys are redirected:

- \Software\Classes\Interface
- \Software\Classes\ClsID

Depending on the age of COM documentation, the registry location that is specified for 32-bit registration information may be HKLM\Software\WOW6432Node\Classes instead of HKLM\Software\ Classes\WOW6432Node. If you check this with a registry tool such as regedit, you will see that both appear to exist. However, the former is a symbolic link to the latter. These symbolic links exist for backwards compatibility with legacy applications that use hardcoded paths. Your code should never refer to WOW6432Node locations directly anyway and instead let the win32 API handle those redirections internally as will be explained in the next section.

Before we move on, we need to briefly revisit Type Library registration. We know that Type Libraries are shared between 64 and 32 registry locations.

It is also worth noting that while the HKCU\Software\Classes\AppID registry key is merged into HKCR\AppID and can even override data coming out of HKLM\Software\Classes\AppID in the HKCR view, it is not actually honored by DCOM. Instead, when it comes to the AppID data, DCOM refers directly to the data in HKLM and just ignores HKCU or the HKCR mappings. There are multiple possible reasons for this.

Whatever settings are in the HKLM AppID section have been configured by an administrator, and deal with settings that may have an impact on security. We will cover security in more detail later, but as an example let's consider a COM server that may have been configured with a restriction on who is allowed to launch it. If the HKCU AppID settings could override the HKLM settings, any user with a bit of knowledge could override those restrictions by creating the relevant registry entry, and there would be nothing an administrator could do to prevent that.

Another security related scenario involves a user with Admin credentials on a system where UAC is enabled. With UAC, that user would be using the computer as an ordinary user, and any applications that start under reduced credentials can write to the user part of the registry where normally they wouldn't be able to do harm. But if that user starts an application which uses COM and the HKCU settings were to come into play, then a bad actor could sneakily escalate their influence from the level of a regular user to the level of an administrator, and this would clearly be a violation of the entire reason UAC exists.

There are more restrictions still. For example, a class object in HKCU may have an AppID entry, but that doesn't mean that DCOM just blindly uses all those settings. Consider the scenario where an AppID setting exists to configure that ServerA is launched with certain credentials. This may be a perfectly safe thing to do. The server may exist solely to host a class that starts or stops a system service. This is typically an action that requires administrator permission. Having a class object that only starts and stops that service, and then configuring it to run with administrator permissions, could be one way to support such scenarios. The 'RunAs' registry key is stored under the AppID setting AppIDServerA. Nothing is preventing users from registering SneakyServerB in the HKCU hive and setting its AppID key to AppIDServerA. If the system would then blindly honor those settings, it would launch SneakyServerB with administrator credentials. This would clearly be a gross security violation. Unfortunately, many things that pertain to AppIDs and their relationship to HKCU are -not- explicitly documented so if your application makes use of such things as AppIDs under HKCU or for classes under HKCU, be sure to test extensively with a proof-of-concept setup to verify that what you have in mind is supported.

Supporting HKCU registration (or HKLM registration for that matter) is a design choice. If you develop a component that is used for administrative purposes, and it requires administrator rights, supporting per-user registration may be pointless or even confusing. Likewise, you might choose not to provide HKLM registration if for example your application does not need special permissions, and it is designed as part of a 'portable' executable that is intended to be run without needing installation by a privileged account. I'm not saying that's a good reason to specifically refuse to support HKLM installation. But it would work within the restrictions that go with HKCU registration.

Self registration

Based on the previous sections, we need to create the following registry entries in either HKLM or HKCU:

\Software\Classes\{ProgID}		
<default value>	REG_SZ	Shortname of the calculator
\Software\Classes\{ProgID}\ClsID		
<default value>	REG_SZ	Calculator Class ID
\Software\Classes\CLSID\{ClsID}		
<default value>	REG_SZ	Shortname of the calculator
AppID	REG_SZ	Calculator APP ID
\Software\Classes\CLSID\{ClsID}\{ProgID}		
<default value>	REG_SZ	Calculator Prog ID
\Software\Classes\CLSID\{ClsID}\[InprocServer32|LocalServer32]		
<default value>	REG_SZ	Depending on the key, this is either the path of the DLL or the path of the executable with optional command line args/
ThreadingModel	REG_SZ	The apartment model(s) supported by the class object.
\Software\Classes\AppID\{AppID}		
<default value>	REG_SZ	Application configuration name (for DCOMCnfg)
LocalService	REG_SZ	Name of the service, if the COM server is a Windows Service. If a service is registered for the COM object, it will take precedence for out-of-service registration over a LocalServer32 entry under the CLSID.

Depending on circumstances, these keys are added to either HKLM for servers that are globally accessible on the computer, or HKCU for servers that are accessible only to the user. It is not needed to refer to the WOW32Node registry locations directly. The registry API will do that redirection transparently, based on the architecture of the code from which it is used.

Sometimes the argument is made that doing all of this with a dedicated installer would be preferable because at a higher level it's a lot clearer what happens. Even today with advanced installers, the fact remains that COM is susceptible to information being overwritten. We already mentioned that this is the case for the interface proxies or type library references. So, the ability to repair the settings for a single server remains a benefit for systems administrators.

Arguably we could create a script or program to configure / repair / remove all settings but one of the principles of COM is self-registration. Any COM server needs to support the ability to add or remove its configuration information to the system.

There is not 1 universal way to add this information to the registry. A program can do it any way it wants. The only requirement is that a server can register and unregister itself, for both registry hives. The code for doing this is very generic. Sadly, there is no API to take that task out of our hands. There are several helper routines you might find on the internet or pieces of code to start from. For this book I wrote a helper class. At the core of things, registration is just a registry update based on a bunch of parameters.

Registry transactions

Before moving on to the registration process, a brief interlude is needed. In the process of writing this book, I tried to keep things as much on topic as possible but here it is justifiable to take a short detour because it addresses a pet peeve of mine: processes that make configuration changes but do not deal gracefully with failure halfway through the process.

Since Windows Vista, there is support for performing registry operations under a kernel transaction. Using transactions, various registry changes and (optionally) file system changes can be grouped together and be either committed or rolled back as a singular change. At the time of writing, Microsoft has deprecated file IO transactions because the developer uptake was limited and the functionality had a lot of nuances. However, registry transactions are still fully supported. As it turns out, all COM related registration information is registry based so there is no real reason to avoid them.

Using registry transactions involves a bit more programming but has the great benefit that after all registry updates are either committed or rolled back as 1 atomic block of changes. It either succeeds or doesn't, but under no circumstance are partial changes left behind.

Registry corruption can be a difficult situation to recover from, and difficult to diagnose from a variety of symptoms. The certainty of using registry transactions is well worth the little bit of extra work it takes. The boilerplate for such operations looks like this:

```
HANDLE transaction = CreateTransaction(
```

```
                                  NULL, NULL, 0, 0, 0, 0, NULL);
if (transaction == INVALID_HANDLE_VALUE)
{
    return GetLastError();
}

//Do work here

if (retVal == 0) {
    CommitTransaction(transaction);
}
else {
    RollbackTransaction(transaction);
}

CloseHandle(transaction);
```

There are various options that can be specified when creating a transaction.

```
//ktmw32.h
HANDLE
APIENTRY
CreateTransaction (
    IN LPSECURITY_ATTRIBUTES lpTransactionAttributes OPTIONAL,
    IN LPGUID UOW OPTIONAL,
    IN DWORD CreateOptions OPTIONAL,
    IN DWORD IsolationLevel OPTIONAL,
    IN DWORD IsolationFlags OPTIONAL,
    IN DWORD Timeout OPTIONAL,
    _In_opt_ LPWSTR Description
    );
```

Most of them are reserved and should be 0 or NULL. Only the following are applicable:

- lpTransactionAttributes: determines whether the handle can be inherited by child processes. For simple COM registration inside a single process, this can be NULL.
- CreateOptions determines whether the transaction can be distributed or not. A distributed transaction can be used for integration with other transaction managers such as the SQL server transaction manager and others. Since only the local registry is involved, this can be 0.
- Timeout: it is possible to specify a time in which all actions should be finished. We specify 0 (which is equivalent to INFINITE) because updating a registry will resolve itself one way or another in a fraction of seconds.

- Description: The description can be useful when debugging complex software and having to work with the handle table. For this purpose, however, NULL is good.

When working with transactions, it is important to note that the IO operations themselves are agnostic of transactions. The transaction is linked to a handle when it is created or opened. Any operations that are performed on the handle, are then covered by the transaction. Because modifying the parameters lists for the existing APIs was impossible while maintaining backwards compatibility, Microsoft created various new APIs that are nearly identical to existing ones, but with an additional transaction parameter.

```
//winreg.h
WINADVAPI
LSTATUS
APIENTRY
RegCreateKeyTransactedW (
    _In_ HKEY hKey,
    _In_ LPCWSTR lpSubKey,
    _Reserved_ DWORD Reserved,
    _In_opt_ LPWSTR lpClass,
    _In_ DWORD dwOptions,
    _In_ REGSAM samDesired,
    _In_opt_ CONST LPSECURITY_ATTRIBUTES lpSecurityAttributes,
    _Out_ PHKEY phkResult,
    _Out_opt_ LPDWORD lpdwDisposition,
    _In_        HANDLE hTransaction,
    _Reserved_ PVOID  pExtendedParemeter
    );
```

As opposed to

```
//winreg.h
WINADVAPI
LSTATUS
APIENTRY
RegCreateKeyExW(
    _In_ HKEY hKey,
    _In_ LPCWSTR lpSubKey,
    _Reserved_ DWORD Reserved,
    _In_opt_ LPWSTR lpClass,
    _In_ DWORD dwOptions,
    _In_ REGSAM samDesired,
    _In_opt_ CONST LPSECURITY_ATTRIBUTES lpSecurityAttributes,
    _Out_ PHKEY phkResult,
    _Out_opt_ LPDWORD lpdwDisposition
    );
```

The only difference is the transaction parameter and a reserved extended parameter that must be NULL. Going into the full set of options for the various registry APIs is beyond the scope of this book. Suffice it to say that all transacted APIs function like the 'Ex' versions of the APIs.

For registration purposes it helps that we only have to write string values.

```
int WriteRegKey(HKEY Key,
    wstring SubKey,
    wstring ValueName,
    wstring Value,
    HANDLE Transaction)
{
    HKEY hKey = NULL;
    long result = RegCreateKeyTransactedW(
        Key, SubKey.c_str(),
        0, NULL, REG_OPTION_NON_VOLATILE,
        KEY_WRITE | KEY_READ,
        NULL,
        &hKey,
        NULL, Transaction, NULL);

    if (result != ERROR_SUCCESS)
        return GetLastError();

    result = RegSetValueEx(
        hKey,
        ValueName.c_str(),
        0,
        REG_SZ,
        (const BYTE*)Value.c_str(),
        (lstrlen(Value.c_str()) + 1) * sizeof(WCHAR));
    RegCloseKey(hKey);

    if (ERROR_SUCCESS != result) {
        result = GetLastError();
    }

    return result;
}
```

For every write operation, we open the registry key in a transacted manner and perform a write operation. We know from the earlier chapter that most values are stored in a dedicated key, so the overhead from opening and closing a key for every write operation is not too bad in practical terms. And since we're only talking about a handful of keys on a one-off basis, the convenience of a high-level helper outweighs the marginal inefficiency.

There is one more operation we will need, and that is establishing whether a key exists or not. That will become important during the un-registration process. The code is even simpler than the write operation.

```
DWORD RegKeyExists(
    HKEY root,
    const wstring regKey,
    HANDLE Transaction,
    bool& exists)
{
    HKEY hregKey = NULL;
    int retVal = RegOpenKeyTransactedW(
        root,
        regKey.c_str(),
        0, NULL,
        &hregKey,
        Transaction,
        NULL);

    if (ERROR_SUCCESS == retVal) {
        RegCloseKey(hregKey);
        exists = true;
    }

    else if (ERROR_FILE_NOT_FOUND == retVal) {
        exists = false;
        retVal = ERROR_SUCCESS;
    }
    return retVal;
}
```

For the sake of keeping the error handling trivial at the level where this function will be called, the key existence is communicated using a boolean, and the return value will be an error only in case of actual error. One peculiarity deserves to be mentioned: if you check for the existence of a key and you are working with transactions, you need to use the transacted API and supply the ongoing transaction. That is the only way to get a yes or no answer about the existence of a key, with the changes in the ongoing transaction considered. If you delete a registry key under a transaction and then check whether it exists or not with a non-transacted API, it will report true because the transaction isn't committed.

As for deleting a registry key, one regrettable fact is that while Microsoft implemented a transacted delete function, they did not provide a transacted function that deletes a registry key with subkeys. However, there is a way around that limitation.

```
DWORD RegDeleteTreeTransacted(
        HKEY regKey, wstring subkey, HANDLE transaction)
{
```

```
    HKEY hKey = NULL;
    long result = RegCreateKeyTransactedW(
        regKey, subkey.c_str(),
        0, NULL, REG_OPTION_NON_VOLATILE,
        KEY_WRITE | KEY_READ,
        NULL,
        &hKey,
        NULL, transaction, NULL);

    if (result != 0)
        return GetLastError();

    result = RegDeleteTreeW(hKey, NULL);
    RegCloseKey(hKey);

    if (result == 0) {
        result = RegDeleteKeyTransacted(
            regKey,
            subkey.c_str(),
            KEY_WRITE | KEY_READ,
            0,
            transaction,
            NULL);
    }

    if(result != 0)
        result = GetLastError();

}
```

As mentioned earlier, operations themselves don't know about transactions so if we open a transacted registry handle first, then we can use that to call the regular RegDeleteTreeW function. A side effect of that function is that it doesn't delete the root of the tree that was deleted so that must be deleted separately.

Server registration

Armed with these 3 helpers and an understanding of what they do, we can now implement the ServerRegistration class. Note that I present this class just as a convenient way to configure the registry for the manually built servers. No doubt not all corner cases are covered, but for real-life scenarios, this is covered by ATL classes so covering every possible scenario here is not a requirement.

```
ServerRegistration::ServerRegistration(
    wstring ClsID,
    wstring ProgID,
    wstring ShortProgName,
    wstring AppID,
    wstring ApplicationName,
    wstring ModulePath,
```

```
    wstring ModuleCOMType,
    wstring ThreadingModel)
{
    m_ClsID = ClsID;
    m_ShortProgName = ShortProgName;
    m_ProgID = ProgID;
    m_ModulePath = ModulePath;
    m_ModuleCOMType = ModuleCOMType;
    m_AppID = AppID;
    m_AppName = ApplicationName;

    //Software\Classes\CLSID\{ClsID}
    m_clsidKey = L"Software\\Classes\\CLSID\\" + ClsID;

    //Software\Classes\CLSID\{ClsID}\progid
    m_clsidProgid = m_clsidKey + L"\\ProgID";

    //"Software\Classes\Library.ClassObject.Version
    m_progidkey = L"Software\\Classes\\" + ProgID;

    //"Software\Classes\Library.ClassObject.Version\{clsid}
    m_progidclsid = m_progidkey + L"\\clsid";

    //"Software\Classes\AppID\{AppID}
    m_appidkey = L"Software\\Classes\\AppID\\" + m_AppID;

    //If we register a service, the link to the service is not made under
    //the CLSID but under the AppID
    //Software\Classes\CLSID\{ClsID}\[LocalServer32|InProcServer32]
    //or
    // Software\Classes\APPID\{AppID}\
    if (ModuleCOMType != L"LocalService")
    {
        m_serverKey = m_clsidKey + L"\\" + ModuleCOMType;
    }
    else
    {
        m_serverKey = m_appidkey;
    }

    m_ThreadingModel = ThreadingModel;
}
```

The constructor receives the individual IDs and names. Using those names, it formats the various key names where data is added. This ensures that the internal consistency of the registration data is accurate.

```
DWORD ServerRegistration::RegisterServer(bool perUser)
```

```
{
    HKEY regroot = perUser ?
                   HKEY_CURRENT_USER : HKEY_LOCAL_MACHINE;

    HANDLE transaction = CreateTransaction(NULL, NULL, 0, 0, 0, 0, NULL);
    if (transaction == INVALID_HANDLE_VALUE) {
        return GetLastError();
    }

    int retVal = 0;
     if (retVal == 0) {
        retVal=
WriteRegKey(regroot,m_clsidKey,L"",m_ShortProgName,transaction);
    }
    if (retVal == 0) {
        retVal= WriteRegKey(regroot,m_clsidKey,L"AppID", m_AppID,
transaction);
    }
    if (retVal == 0) {
        wstring valueName = L"";
        if (m_ModuleCOMType == L"LocalService") {
            valueName = L"LocalService";
        }
        retVal= WriteRegKey(
                      regroot,m_serverKey,valueName,m_ModulePath,
transaction);
    }
    if (retVal == 0 && m_serverKey.find(L"InProc") != wstring::npos) {
        retVal = WriteRegKey(regroot, m_serverKey,
                             L"ThreadingModel", m_ThreadingModel,
transaction);
    }
    if (retVal == 0) {
        retVal = WriteRegKey(regroot,m_clsidProgid,L"",m_ProgID, transaction);
    }
    if (retVal == 0) {

retVal=WriteRegKey(regroot,m_progidkey,L"",m_ShortProgName,transaction);
    }
    if (retVal == 0) {
        retVal = WriteRegKey(regroot, m_progidclsid, L"", m_ClsID,
transaction);
    }
    if (retVal == 0) {
        retVal = WriteRegKey(regroot, m_appidkey, L"", m_AppName,
transaction);
    }
    if (retVal == 0) {
        retVal = AddExtraConfig(transaction);
    }

    if (retVal == 0) {
```

```
        CommitTransaction(transaction);
    }
    else {
        RollbackTransaction(transaction);
    }

    CloseHandle(transaction);
    return retVal;
}
```

There is nothing complex going on here. Based on whether the registration is per user or not, the appropriate root key is selected. And then all aforementioned keys are created within the boilerplate of a kernel transaction. The one odd thing is the call to AddExtraConfig that doesn't seem to do anything.

```
    virtual inline DWORD AddExtraConfig(HANDLE transaction) {
        return NO_ERROR;
    };
```

And indeed, it doesn't do anything, because it is a placeholder for a method that might do something useful if the ServerRegistration class is used as a base class. That way, if a specific registration implementation requires additional configuration to be added to the registry for its own purposes, it can be added in an override method which will automatically be added to the base registration process.

The un-registration process is similar in nature.

```
DWORD ServerRegistration::UnregisterServer(bool perUser)
{
    int retVal = 0;

    HKEY regroot = perUser ? HKEY_CURRENT_USER : HKEY_LOCAL_MACHINE;

    HANDLE transaction = CreateTransaction(NULL, NULL, 0, 0, 0, 0, NULL);
    if (transaction == INVALID_HANDLE_VALUE)
        return GetLastError();

    //Remove the serverkey for this server
    //We canot remove anything else because there might be other servers
    //registered for the same CLSID
    if (m_ModuleCOMType == L"LocalService") {
        HKEY hKey = NULL;
        LSTATUS result = RegCreateKeyTransactedW(
        regroot, m_serverKey.c_str(),
        0, NULL, REG_OPTION_NON_VOLATILE,
        KEY_WRITE | KEY_READ,
        NULL,
        &hKey, NULL, transaction, NULL);

        retVal = GetLastError();
```

```
        if (0 == retVal)
            RegDeleteValueW(hKey, L"LocalService");

    }
    else if (m_ModuleCOMType == L"LocalServer32" ||
        m_ModuleCOMType == L"InProcServer32") {
        retVal = RegDeleteKeyTransacted(
                            regroot, m_serverKey.c_str(), 0, 0, transaction,
NULL);
    }

    if (retVal == 0)
        CommitTransaction(transaction);
    else
        RollbackTransaction(transaction);

    CloseHandle(transaction);
    return retVal;
}
```

If you look at this code carefully, you'll notice that it isn't balanced with the registration side. There is no call to a placeholder to remove extra configuration information. The reason is that unlike adding servers for a given CLSID, if we remove a server, there is no clean, convenient way to know for sure that there aren't other servers still relying on the existence of those registry keys.

For example, if we remove the registration of an out-of-process server, it's trivial to check that there is no in-process server. But there may still be a LocalService linked to the AppID. Or we might be cleaning up a 32-bit version of a server and be tempted to clean up the AppID because there is no 32-bit server left. But since some parts of the registry are shared between versions, cleaning up the 32-bit information might destroy the registration for the 64-bit version that is still registered.

It's things like this where it becomes obvious that some parts of the COM experience were bolted on over time to make things work, without solving the underlying complexities and dependencies in a manner that makes the impact of changes obvious. That is why the code for removing registration only removes the specific part we know we can remove, without touching anything else.

To make using the ServerRegistration class convenient, we inherit from it and supply the necessary constants.

```
class CalculatorRegistration :
    public ServerRegistration
{
public:
    CalculatorRegistration(
```

```
        wstring ModuleCOMType, wstring modulepath);
};

CalculatorRegistration::CalculatorRegistration(
    wstring ModuleCOMType, wstring modulepath) :
    ServerRegistration(
        L"{5AB4FB62-13B0-4370-AD0E-C9E6F989815F}",
        L"MathLib.Calculator.1",
        L"Calculator",
        L"{2CE5031A-A5F7-463E-9263-C65B60A2BB4E}",
        L"Mathlib Calculator",
        modulepath,
        ModuleCOMType,
        L"Both")
{

}
```

This way, all values exist together in 1 location. This reduces the risk of things like copy paste errors, especially when we have more than 1 server type in our solution. With the registration code all taken care of, we can finally implement the registration code in our servers.

In-process server registration

A server should be able to register and unregister itself. However, a DLL by itself is not executable. To facilitate DLL registration, Microsoft made a helper program called regsvr32.exe that exists on all Windows computers. The most basic way to use this is when registering a DLL for global use, in the HKLM hive.

Regsvr32 <dll_path>

Or to uninstall the DLL:

Regsvr32 /u <dll_path>

When invoked with the path of a valid DLL file, regsvr32 loads the DLL into its memory space, and invokes either the DLLRegisterServer function or the DLLUnregisterServer function. These must be exported by the DLL that hosts the server. With the use of the helper class, these functions are trivial to add to the DLL server project.

```
STDAPI DllRegisterServer(void)
{
    CalculatorRegistration registration(
                              L"InprocServer32",
                              g_Server.GetServerModuleName());

    if (NO_ERROR == registration.RegisterServer(false))
        return S_OK;
```

```
    return E_APPLICATION_NOT_REGISTERED;
}
```

Likewise, the un-registration function is trivial to implement.

```
HRESULT DllUnregisterServer(void)
{
    CalculatorRegistration registration(
                                L"InprocServer32",
                                g_Server.GetServerModuleName());

    return registration.UnregisterServer(false);
}
```

We've mentioned the g_Server global variable before as simply a way to interact with the global server state. Global variables themselves are a bad idea in general. The 1 permissible case in which they make sense is if the thing they interact with (in this case the server instance) is always itself globally accessible. Since 'The COM Server' is always a global object from the point of view of the COM objects inside the server, this is one of those permissible cases where a global variable is a sensible idea.

In this case we use it to retrieve the name (full path) of the module in which its code resides. The beauty of using the derived class we made earlier is that we never have to copy that information in different places and thus prevent copy paste errors.

You'll notice that these functions have no support for per-user registration. They were introduced before the Windows 2000 timeframe and were not intended for per-user registration like that. It would have been better if some flexibility had been foreseen in the function prototype, but alas. To help with that, an additional DLLInstall function was introduced.

```
STDAPI
DllInstall(
    BOOL bInstall,
    _In_opt_ PCWSTR pszCmdLine
);
```

This function is intended to be used with regsvr32. The bInstall parameter indicates whether the DLL is being installed (TRUE) or uninstalled (FALSE). The pszCommandLine parameter is optional and can be used when invoking regsvr32 to pass additional instructions to the DLL. To make regsvr32 use this function for registration purposes, it can be invoked like this:

Regsvr32 /i[:cmdline] <dll_path>

Or to uninstall the DLL:

Regsvr32 /u /i[:cmdline] <dll_path>

When the /i switch is specified, regsvr32 doesn't call the DLLRegisterServer or DLLUnregisterServer functions, but only calls the DllInstall function as appropriate. We implement it like this:

```
HRESULT DllInstall(
    BOOL   bInstall,
    PCWSTR pszCmdLine)
{
    CalculatorRegistration registration(
                               L"InprocServer32",
                               g_Server.GetServerModuleName());

    if (!pszCmdLine)
        return E_INVALIDARG;

    wstring cmd(pszCmdLine);
    transform(cmd.begin(), cmd.end(), cmd.begin(), ::tolower);

    if (cmd.find(L"peruser") == 0 || cmd.find(L"user") == 0)
    {
        if (bInstall) {
            return registration.RegisterServer(true);
        }
        else {
            return registration.UnregisterServer(true);
        }
    }

    return E_INVALIDARG;
}
```

There is no standard as to what the arguments should look like. In this design, the decision was made to use DLLInstall purely for the per-user registration, contingent on 'peruser' or 'user' being supplied as the command line string. With this implementation and the DLLRegisterServer and DLLUnregisterServer, our DLL has everything it needs to cover the various scenarios. It would be equally valid to also cover the global registration via DLLInstall. After all the command line string allows for this flexibility. But since both options would need to be executed via regsvr32 commands anyway, there isn't really a point in doing that. As a final note, we do need to add these functions to the .def file for our DLL project to make sure they are exported properly.

```
LIBRARY
EXPORTS
```

```
DllGetClassObject    PRIVATE
DllCanUnloadNow          PRIVATE
DllRegisterServer    PRIVATE
DllUnregisterServer  PRIVATE
DllInstall                 PRIVATE
```

Regsvr32 works by loading the DLL into its memory space and calling the aforementioned functions. A 32-bit module cannot be loaded by a 64-bit executable or vice versa. To account for that, there are 2 versions of regsvr32. For 64-bit versions there is

C:\Windows\System32\regsvr32.exe

And for 32 bit versions, there is

C:\Windows\SysWOW64\regsvr32.exe

It sometimes feels odd to see so many '32' references, and in this case the 64-bit version has 2 '32's in its path, and the 32-bit version has a '64' in its path. The plain names were used for 16-bit versions first, and the '32' versions were introduced for the 32-bit versions to exist alongside the 16-bit versions. But for 64-bit Windows, the approach was made to silently redirect the registry based on the architecture of the application. My guess is that to keep things identical except for the redirection, keeping the existing names (for the registry keys as well as the system folder) was the least bad option.

Out-of-process server registration

For out-of-process servers, no additional tools are necessary. The idea is that a well-behaved COM application supports command line arguments. In theory you can do whatever you want in terms of naming convention. In practice, there are standard commands that are used universally and supporting them makes it easier to play nice with others. For example, if you use the standard ones, tools like Visual Studio will be able to perform a post-build step to register your application, either globally or per-user.

For registration

- RegServer
- RegisterServer
- RegServerPerUser
- RegisterServerPerUser

For unregistration

- UnRegServer
- UnRegisterServer
- UnRegServerPerUser
- UnRegisterServerPerUser

It is good practice to check these flags in a case-insensitive manner because capitalization can often be a personal choice. The command line parsing is performed in a dedicated helper function and is itself rather boring and uneventful

```
StartupReason GetStartupReason(int argc, WCHAR* argv[])
{
    for (int i = 1; i < argc; i++)
    {
        wstring arg(argv[i]);
        transform(arg.begin(),
                  arg.end(),
                  arg.begin(),
                  ::tolower);
        if (arg.find(L"unregserverperuser") >= 0 ||
            arg.find(L"unregisterserverperuser") >= 0){
            return StartupReason::e_UnregisterServerPerUser;
        }
        else if (
            arg.find(L"unregserver") >= 0 ||
            arg.find(L"unregisterserver" >= 0 )){
        return StartupReason::e_UnregisterServer;
        }
        else if (
            arg.find(L"regserverperuser" >= 0 ) ||
            arg.find(L"registerserverperuser" >= 0)){
            return StartupReason::e_RegisterServerPerUser;
        }
        else if (arg.find(L"regserver" >= 0) ||
            arg.find(L"registerserver" >= 0)){
            return StartupReason::e_RegisterServer;
        }
        else if (
            arg.find(L"embedding")){
            return StartupReason::e_Embedding;
        }
    }

    return StartupReason::e_Other;
}
```

We skip the first argument because that is always the full module path and if for some reason someone builds a server with 'RegServer' in the name that could cause some funky problems. Additionally, we scan the arguments in the order where RegServer won't be recognized if the argument under review is RegServerPerUser or

UnRegServer. This way of scanning also removes the problem of having to deal with -RegServer vs /RegServer. When an out-of-process server is started by COM, the argument 'Embedding' is always added to the command line to make it possible for server to always recognize whether they are started for class object activation or another reason.

With that, we can implement the registration in the out-of-process server.

```
int wmain(int argc, WCHAR* argv[])
{
    ULONG error = NO_ERROR;
    StartupReason reason = GetStartupReason(argc, argv);
    if (reason != e_Embedding) {
        CalculatorRegistration registration(
                                          L"LocalServer32",
                                          g_Server.GetServerModuleName());

        switch (reason)
        {
        case e_RegisterServer:
            return registration.RegisterServer(false);
        case e_UnregisterServer:
            return registration.UnregisterServer( false);
        case e_RegisterServerPerUser:
            return registration.RegisterServer( true);
        case e_UnregisterServerPerUser:
            return registration.UnregisterServer( true);
        case e_Other:
            return ERROR;
            break;
        }
    }

    //Do normal out-of-process startup
}
```

There is not much more to say here because we already covered the registration routines earlier. Based on the command line, the appropriate option is executed and the program ends, unless the startup reason is 'embedding', in which case the out-of-process server starts as described before.

Service registration

From a runtime point of view, a Windows service is just a regular executable whose lifetime is controlled in a different manner from other executables. But it is an exe file and can be run from the command line like a regular application. The difference is that unless it is started by the Service Control Manager, the service hooks won't work, and the executable is expected to behave just like a regular application. This makes it easy to add the registration routines.

```
int wmain(int argc, WCHAR* argv[])
{
    ULONG error = NO_ERROR;
    StartupReason reason = GetStartupReason(argc, argv);

        CalculatorRegistration registration(L"LocalService",
                                            L"CalculatorService");

        switch (reason)
        {
        case e_RegisterServer:
            return registration.RegisterServer(false);
        case e_UnregisterServer:
            return registration.UnregisterServer( false);
        case e_RegisterServerPerUser:
        case e_UnregisterServerPerUser:
        case e_Other:
            return ERROR;
            break;
        }
    }

    //Do normal out-of-process startup
}
```

The difference here is that per-user registration is not supported. COM only starts Windows services on request if they are registered in HKLM. There are several reasons for this:

- COM was originally designed to operate in a system-wide context, and Windows Services are still designed to run like this.
- Services operate with a unique name. Allowing services to be registered and managed based on user configuration can create reliability issues or cause various sorts of unexpected behavior.
- Since Windows Vista, services run isolated from user sessions. Bringing things back to a situation where users can affect services would decrease overall security. Services are also often configured to run with different accounts and overall there would be many possible avenues where user control over services could create pathways for security breaches.

Since Windows 10, there is support for per-user services, meaning that a specific service can be configured to run in the background like a regular service, but under the credentials of the logged-on user. But the users themselves have no control over this. Configuration of per-user services is still done at the HKLM level, meaning an administrator must set them up, and the user has no explicit control over this. These per-user services are also not launched by COM.

One thing you could do if there is a compelling use case, is to create a service, configure it as a per-user service, and have it register a class object, exactly like a regular COM service. From a COM perspective, this is no different from hosting a class object in an out-of-process server. Whether this makes sense or not depends on what you are trying to do. If you want nothing else than what you would get from a regular out-of-process server, then there isn't a reason to work with per-user services. Otoh, if you have a background task you want to run and be available in the user context, then you could have a custom class object to interact with that service.

Looking back to the configuration task for out-of-process COM service, registration is only half of the job. Our service isn't registered with a path but a service name. In order for COM to launch the service, the service exe needs to be registered as a Windows service. There are a couple of ways to do this. The easiest is to use sc.exe, which is the supporting application made specifically for managing service registrations. Service registration is relatively simple but there are a couple of things you need to pay attention.

The following command can be used for our service.

```
sc create CalculatorService ^
    binPath= "C:\Path\To\YourExecutable.exe -embedding" ^
    DisplayName= "Calculator Service" ^
    obj= "NT AUTHORITY\LocalService"
```

All services have an internal name to identify them in the registry. Ours is "CalculatorService". This is the reason for not using the module name during registration. Instead of registering the full module path, we register the name which is used by the Windows Service Control Manager to look up the service details in the registry.

binPath is the full path to the service executable. DisplayName is the user friendly name that is visible in services.msc.

And finally, the rather non-intuitive 'obj' parameter is the security principal that is used as the service identity. Services run under their own identity. There are various options. You can configure the service to run with a named user account or one of the built-in accounts. If no account is specified, LocalSystem is used. As a default value, it is no longer appropriate because running a service with full System credentials should never be done unless there is a very good reason. Instead, we use LocalService which has much less privileges.

One important remark is that whatever credentials you use to run the service should have access to the path where the service executable is stored. When everything is registered correctly, the service information is stored in the registry.

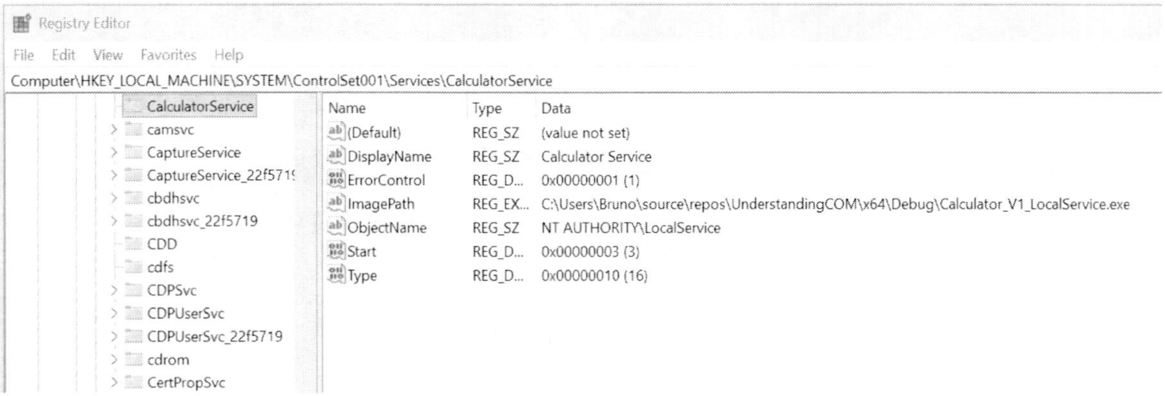

The information is the registry is used by the service control manager and the services.msc mmc.

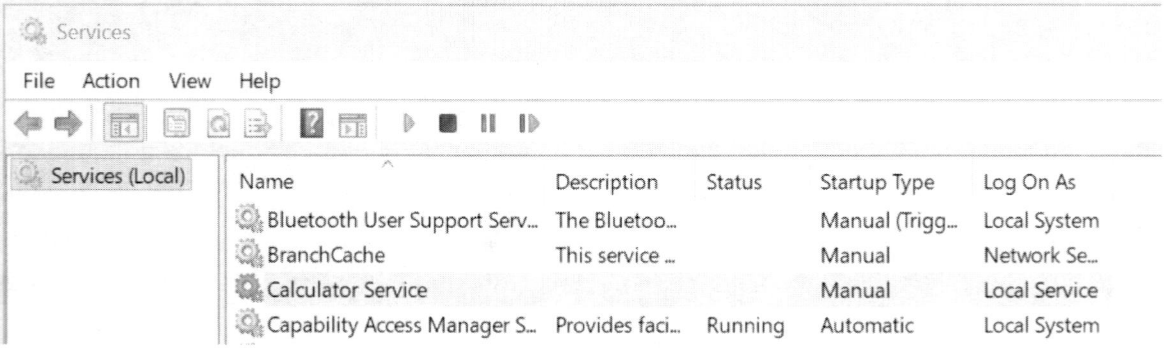

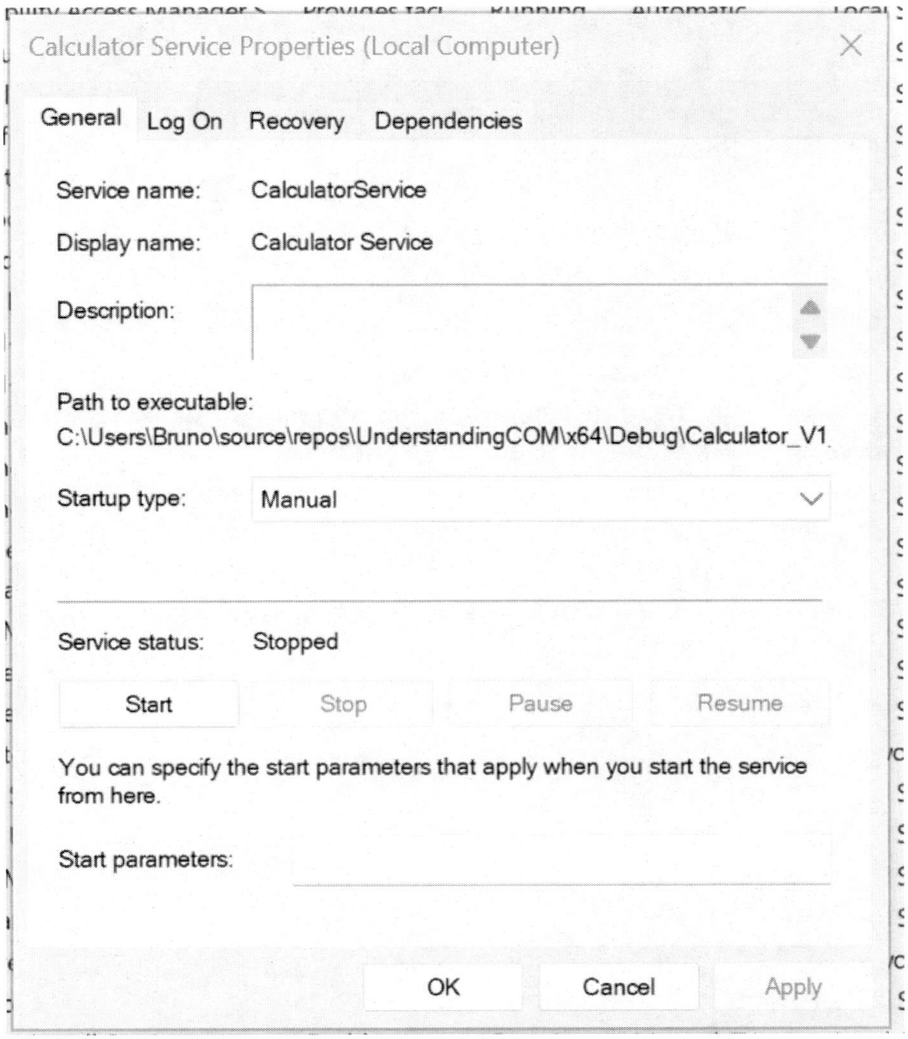

Proxy registration

Proxy registration is just like registering any other in-process server. You register them with regsvr32. But there is a snag. We built the proxy by simply taking the files created by MIDL and building them into a DLL project as-is without adding or changing anything. The problem is that the auto-generated boiler plate code doesn't deal with HKCU.

There are a couple of reasons why this might be the case. To begin with, MIDL was created before per-user registration was a thing. There is a tendency to not change tools as changes happen. For example, DCOMCnfg too doesn't do anything with the per-user registry hive and frankly could be a whole lot more useful overall. The purpose of proxies is also to shuttle calls back and forth between apartments, regardless of where those apartments are. But a per-user registered proxy cannot be used with any apartments not in the current user scope. Not only would a process running with different credentials be able to access the proxy file (or the hive in which it is registered) but it would also be a gross security violation to give user Bob control over a proxy whose code is executed by user Alice. Alice might have their own version of the proxy installed, but there is no guarantee. It's safe to say that per-user proxy registration is not without issue.

That said, there are also use cases where it may do exactly what is expected. When you have a portable application that does not rely on installation by an administrator, any COM components that come with the application may have interfaces that need marshaling only in the context of that user and per-user proxy registration is exactly what is needed. To that end, we can take the existing proxy project with the base boiler-plate code and add the DLLInstall code that is missing. Any attempt to do so will immediately hit a brick wall. To get a decent understanding of what it is we need to implement, we look at the boiler plate code.

```
#include <rpcproxy.h>

#ifdef __cplusplus
extern "C"   {
#endif

EXTERN_PROXY_FILE( IArithmetic )
EXTERN_PROXY_FILE( IComServer )


PROXYFILE_LIST_START
/* Start of list */
  REFERENCE_PROXY_FILE( IArithmetic ),
  REFERENCE_PROXY_FILE( IComServer ),
/* End of list */
PROXYFILE_LIST_END


DLLDATA_ROUTINES( aProxyFileList, GET_DLL_CLSID )

#ifdef __cplusplus
}  /*extern "C" */
#endif
```

The capitalized parts are all C style macros. If we follow the trail of macro declaration turtles all the way down, starting with 'DLLDATA_ROUTINES', we find this bit of macro code:

```
//rpcproxy.h
HRESULT STDAPICALLTYPE DLLREGISTERSERVER_ENTRY() \
    { \
        return NdrDllRegisterProxy(hProxyDll, (const ProxyFileInfo
**)pProxyFileList, pClsID); \
    }  \
```

The DLLRegisterServer function calls the NdrDllRegisterPRoxy win32 API, which has no concept of a per-user registration. The information supplied is the DLL module handle, a list of proxy information structures, and the class id of the proxy class object. The ProxyFileInfo structure contains quite a lot of info.

```
//rpcproxy.h
typedef struct tagProxyFileInfo
{
    const PCInterfaceProxyVtblList *pProxyVtblList;
    const PCInterfaceStubVtblList  *pStubVtblList;
    const PCInterfaceName *         pNamesArray;
    const IID **                    pDelegatedIIDs;
    const PIIDLookup                pIIDLookupRtn;
    unsigned short                  TableSize;
    unsigned short                  TableVersion;
    const IID **                    pAsyncIIDLookup;
    LONG_PTR                        Filler2;
    LONG_PTR                        Filler3;
    LONG_PTR                        Filler4;
}ProxyFileInfo;
```

Here too, is no per-user option, so hijacking the existing code by modifying the registration call is not an option. Replacing the internal implementation of NdrDllRegisterPRoxy is also not a viable option because depending on the internal complexity, this might be non-trivial. NdrDllRegisterPRoxy isn't documented in terms of what it does, so it would also be tricky to guarantee its behavior was fully transferred into HKCU. Luckily, the registry API has a way to help us with that by providing an API that allows an application to redirect a well-known registry key.

```
//winreg.h
WINADVAPI
LSTATUS
APIENTRY
RegOverridePredefKey (
    _In_ HKEY hKey,
    _In_opt_ HKEY hNewHKey
    );
```

This function lets you specify an alternate location for changes that are made in a well known hive, but only for the process in which it is used. The limitation is that the key that must be redirected has to be one of the well-known ones.

For example, it is possible to redirect HKLM to HKCU\TempChanges. With this in place, a creation request for HKLM\Software\Test would result in the registry key HKCU\TempChanges\Software\Test being created. There are a couple of use cases for such behavior. A setup program might use this to redirect the registry IO of various components and then transfer them all in bulk to the 'real' destination when all installers which it fires off internally have finished successfully. Or it could be used to examine changes in a safe and isolated manner.

What it cannot do, sadly, is redirect 1 well known key to another. It is not possible to redirect HKLM to HKCU directly. That would be a nice feature and would make any COM-related changes end up in the correct location immediately. However, this is where the structure of the registry comes to our aid unexpectedly. Because we can redirect HKEY_CLASSES_ROOT to HKCU\Software\Classes. The former is a well-known key, and the latter is not. So it satisfies the requirement of RegOverridePredefKey. And inside the proxy DLL, NdrDllRegisterPRoxy writes to HKCR which translates to the registry key HKLM\Software\Classes. Which means that effectively, all COM related registry updates would go to HKLM\Software\Classes will be transferred into HKCU\Software\Classes.

The really good news is that this allows us to use the high-level calls to DLLRegisterServer and DLLUnregisterServer in the proxy DLL, thereby guaranteeing that whatever changes are necessary, are performed exactly as before, but in a different hive. The full implementation looks like this:

```
HRESULT DllInstall(
    BOOL   bInstall,
    PCWSTR pszCmdLine)
{
    HKEY hkcuClasses;
    LSTATUS status = RegCreateKeyEx(
        HKEY_CURRENT_USER,
        L"SOFTWARE\\Classes",
        0,
        0,
        REG_OPTION_NON_VOLATILE,
        KEY_ALL_ACCESS,
        0,
        &hkcuClasses,
        NULL);

    if (status != ERROR_SUCCESS)
        return HRESULT_FROM_WIN32( GetLastError());

    HRESULT hRes = S_OK;
    status = RegOverridePredefKey(HKEY_CLASSES_ROOT, hkcuClasses);
```

```
    if (status == ERROR_SUCCESS) {
        if (bInstall) {
            hRes = DllRegisterServer();
        }
        else {
            hRes = DllUnregisterServer();
        }
    }
    else
        hRes = HRESULT_FROM_WIN32(GetLastError());

    RegCloseKey(hkcuClasses);
    return hRes;
}
```

The code opens a registry key at HKCU\Software\Classes and redirects HKCR to it. At that point the native DLLRegisterServer or DLLUnregisterServer is called, resulting the proxy being registered per-user. It's important to note that this will not work as a blanket solution if the marshaling needs to be done between different security contexts, so you need to evaluate if adding this functionality makes sense or is even a good idea. If you are developing a software package that is supposed to be portable and installable without admin rights, then per-user registration of the proxy may be useful

Registering a type library

Like servers or proxy DLLs, type libraries can be registered too. This is not strictly necessary for COM to function. It's more for the benefit of scripting environments, development environments, and programs that process type information at runtime. Sadly, unlike regsvr32 for proxies and in-process servers, there is no equivalent for registering type libraries. There is a tool called 'regtlibv12.exe' which can register type libraries. It's not part of a regular Windows install but is available with the Windows SDK or some versions of the .NET framework if you manually install it or extract it from the installer. And on some systems, it is present in one of the .NET folders, but that's not generally useful. Additionally, even if you have it on your system, when you distribute your program (the COM server and the type library) you are not allowed to redistribute regtlibv12.exe for the purpose of registering your type library.

There are a couple of APIs available for registering and unregistering a type library.

```
//oleauto.h
WINOLEAUTAPI
RegisterTypeLib(
    ITypeLib * ptlib,
    _In_ LPCOLESTR szFullPath,
    _In_opt_ LPCOLESTR szHelpDir);
```

```
WINOLEAUTAPI
UnRegisterTypeLib(
    REFGUID libID,
    WORD wVerMajor,
    WORD wVerMinor,
    LCID lcid,
    SYSKIND syskind);

WINOLEAUTAPI
RegisterTypeLibForUser(
    ITypeLib *ptlib,
    _In_ OLECHAR  *szFullPath,
    _In_opt_ OLECHAR  *szHelpDir);

WINOLEAUTAPI
UnRegisterTypeLibForUser(
    REFGUID         libID,
    WORD   wMajorVerNum,
    WORD   wMinorVerNum,
    LCID            lcid,
    SYSKIND         syskind);
```

The registration functions take an ITypeLib pointer which can be retrieved by calling LoadTypeLibEx.

```
//oleauto.h
WINOLEAUTAPI
LoadTypeLibEx(
    LPCOLESTR szFile,
    REGKIND regkind,
    ITypeLib ** pptlib);
```

ITypeLib is an interface pointer to a COM class that holds all relevant configuration information that needs to be registered, and which can be passed to the registration APIs. The un-registration APIs do not take this pointer. Instead, they take the identifying information for finding the appropriate root record in the registry. This information could also be gleaned from the type library itself of course. However, that would mean the type library information can only be removed if the library is still present. And this may not be the case if it was simply deleted, or removed as part of an un-install operation that failed to delete the type library records first.

That is also not the only problematic issue. The registration APIs only create the actual TypeLib entries. They do not create references under the various entries under HKCR\Interface

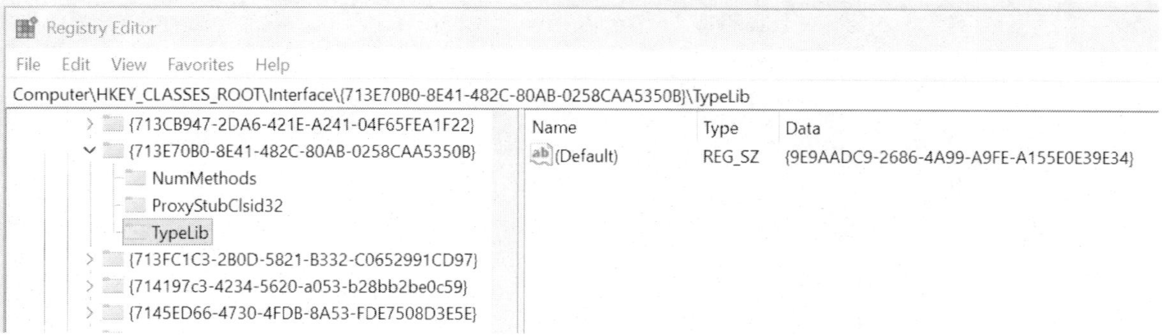

These have to be created manually. Or rather explicitly by an application. But there is no protocol for what to do in case of conflict. You could argue that if the entries don't exist, you create them, and if they do exist, you overwrite them. Given that an interface is immutable, this is not an unreasonable assumption to make. It may not be ideal, but at least the type information should be consistent. The bigger question is: what to do during an uninstall?

If a TypeLib key in HKCR\Interface\ is overwritten, the original contents are gone. There is no sensible way to figure out which other type library has a definition for that interface. During the un-registration process, when we clean up the registry entries, we could check if another version of the type library is still on the system. During un-registration we know the GUID so that is doable. But if there is no other version and then previous reference was to an entirely different type library, there is no other option than to enumerate ALL registered type libraries, load them, and examine the contents.

As mentioned, there is no standard available tool to do any of this. The APIs are there to enable your application to manage the type libraries. This goes beyond self-registration. During the research phase for this book, I found that more people encountered problems related to type libraries and developed an open-source application named 'RegTlb' which is hosted on GitHub. It provides functionality that is similar to what RegSvr32 does for in-process servers. This tool provides the following features:

- Registration of type libraries in either HKLM or HKCU.
- Un-registration of type libraries, either starting from the library file itself or the GUID.
- A way to query the registry for registration information
- A way to query the contents of a TLB file for GUIDs.

It's a pretty basic tool but it works. Admittedly, building COM servers by hand like we've done so far is not something you'd typically do. However, there may still be scenarios where you want to register a type library. For example, you might need to register it on a development machine where you want to build a .NET client without having the actual server installed. To that end, having a simple tool to do so may be convenient. Unlike the SDK tools, The RegTlb hosted on GitHub is licensed under the GPL and may be freely distributed.

Registering Visual Studio output

The self-registration methods we covered earlier is the default method, and it works fine during application installation because it is simple and not too cumbersome. However, during development and debugging, having to manually register the output of your build process can quickly become an onerous task if you are debugging or make regular changes to your servers in small increments.

To help with that, Visual Studio project settings have an option to do this for you after the build step.

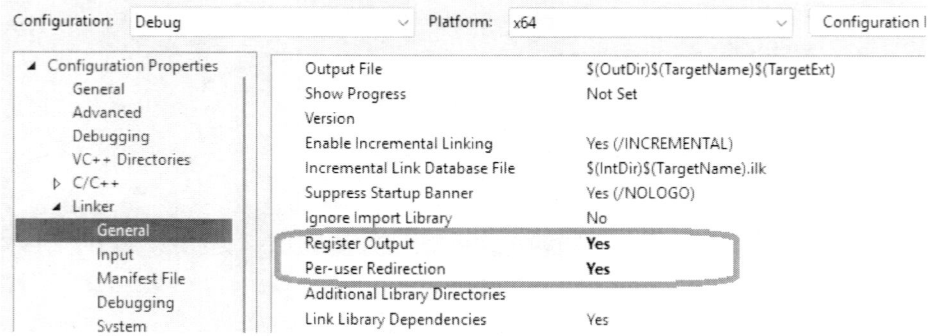

Visual Studio uses these 2 options to determine if it should register the output of your build process, and if so, whether the registration needs to happen in HKLM or HKCU. Note that this is another reason why your server should use the standard command line arguments for registration and un registration. Visual Studio blindly assumes that those are the ones it must use if you work with those project properties.

This is also one of the major reasons for having per-user registration. It is considered bad practice to work with administrator credentials if there is no pressing reason. The per-user option enables you to develop the server and deploy it per-user for testing and debugging purposes, even if that is not the intended use case for the final product.

Note that if you select per-user registration for the Proxy project, this will fail unless you added custom code to the project for supporting per-user registration. Visual Studio doesn't inherently know whether you are building a Proxy or a general purpose in-process server so it will call regsvr32 with the standard options for per-user registration on the assumption that the developer setting this option knew what he was doing.

DCOMCnfg

A final note about registration is that there is a tool for examining the registration information on a system. This tool is DCOMcnfg.

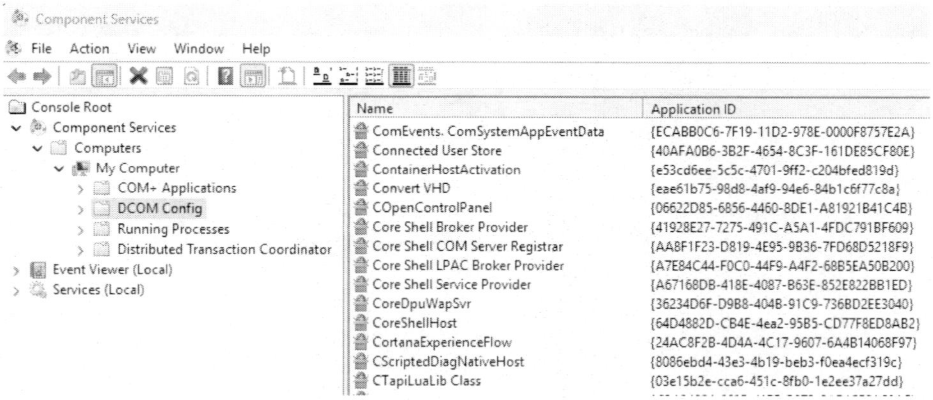

Its main purpose is to configure the AppID settings for a COM Server. For practical purposes, it is mainly used to configure permissions and -if applicable- the user identity of the server. Sadly, it is rather limited in what it does and shows. COM has gone through many changes in terms of architecture and supported settings, but DCOMCnfg has not evolved with those changes.

For example, it does not show CLSID related configuration, nor does it support proper search and sort, which means that finding a specific COM Server can be much more tedious than it should be. It also does not show which settings CAN be configured, what their default values would be and what their purpose is.

Additionally, this tool shows the merged view of HKCR without indication of where the underlying information comes from (HKLM or HKCU) and without indication of whether certain information is applicable. For example, DCOMCnfg will show AppID settings that originate in HKCU even if for security purposes, that is ignored even though it is mapped into HKCR.

As a result of these issues, DCOMCnfg is fairly useless for managing or troubleshooting registration related issues, with the exception of security. The topic of security will be covered in detail, further in the book.

Summary

In this chapter we covered the information that is required for COM to correctly work with servers, interfaces, and settings. We also covered the relationships between different registry locations for storing information, depending on whether it is intended for global use or user specific use.

We also implemented the code for enabling COM Servers to register and unregister themselves from the registry, and the ways in which this is used. With this covered, we can finally build clients and perform some experiments.

For more detailed information about registration information and the registry a lot can be found on the Microsoft website.

https://learn.microsoft.com/en-us/windows/win32/winprog64/shared-registry-keys

https://learn.microsoft.com/en-us/windows/win32/com/registry-entries

Special care should be used in scenarios where 32-bit and 64-bit are mixed, or per-user and per-machine registration. While all of this is possible, it can lead to weird side effects that make you want to pull your hair out and scream WHY!?!?!?!?!? At your computer.

Here are a handful of 'gotchas' I ran into when playing around with the example code for this book:

- HKCR is a virtual hive, which is a merged view of HKCU and HKLM. The merge operation is fully functional but some of it is completely ignored by the system. For example, when launching a LocalService, the system simply ignores HKCR and looks directly at APPID configuration in HKLM.
- The APPID section in general but also individual LocalServer32 entries are reflected. This means that a request for a 32-bit server can still result in the launch of a 64-bit server.
- Removing information from the 32-bit section of the registry can result in the 64-bit section becoming unusable.
- If you are playing with per-user registration of proxy DLLs, weird things can happen if a server runs in a different security context because it will not load

the same proxy. Similar problems may occur if a type library is registered like that.

- The registry will merge what it can. There is no overall sanity checking involved. If, during the development phase of the project, you build and test some piece of code with a per-user registration and you clean up everything except 1 entry in the Interfaces section, that 1 entry will still be merged into HKCR and cause problems.
- The type library registration is shared between the 32-bit and 64-bit registry sections. And the type information inside them is platform agnostic. But the library itself is linked to the architecture for which it is compiled. Legacy tooling may refuse to use a library that was compiled for 64-bit architecture, even when it is properly registered and visible in the 32-bit section of the registry.

All of this is caused by the fact that COM had to react to changes in the Windows system over the almost 4 decades of its lifecycle. Over time, the Windows system changed by adding support for user sessions, network security, process and Windows station separation, support for 32-bit executables on a 64-bit system, and so on. COM had to follow those changes in how it deals with registration information, while still retaining backwards compatibility where possible.

When considering the use cases of your software, try to consider what type of registration it needs and stick with that. Alternatively, if you have a legitimate need to mix different type of registration, Alternatively, if you have a legitimate need to mix different type of registration, be sure to test everything and build in some kind of diagnostic that shows the registration information for your components in the different sections of the registry so that if you need to debug problems or have a user where things don't work as planned, at least you can follow the breadcrumbs.

6

Implementing a client application

Now that we have created a server and registered on the system, we can start building a client application. Like with the server, we're going to start with raw APIs here for the sake of explaining the process in full detail.

Step by step activation

During the implementation phase of the server, we explored the distinction between a class object and a class instance. While it is not typical to do so, we can use them individually for their intended purpose in a step-by-step sequence for the purpose of getting an IArithmetic interface.

Before anything COM related can happen, the client must initialize the COM runtime and tell it which apartment it wants that thread to belong to. In this case we choose the MTA because we know our server supports it.

```
HRESULT hRes = CoInitializeEx(0, COINIT_MULTITHREADED);
if (FAILED(hRes))
{
    cout << "CoInitializeEx failed." << endl;
    return hRes;
}
```

The first step in dealing with any COM server is getting a reference to the class object.

```
//combaseapi.h
HRESULT CoGetClassObject(
  REFCLSID rclsid,
```

```
  DWORD     dwClsContext,
  LPVOID    pvReserved,
  REFIID    riid,
  LPVOID    *ppv
);
```

The first argument is the class ID of the class object we want to get. The second specifies WHAT sort of class object we expect. I.e. the class context. This is a bitmask where we can specify whether we want an in-process server, and out-of-process server, and several activation options. In this case we explicitly request an out-of-process server.

You can create a custom context value with different possible bitmasks. For example you could make a bitmask of `CLSCTX_LOCAL_SERVER | CLSCTX_INPROC_SERVER` and the COM runtime would make a choice for you depending on the availability of the requested server, with a preference for the in-process server. In most circumstances the client would know the environment they are working in and could be more specific but if the specified COM object could be from varying vendors implementing the same interfaces, likewise you could prefer added flexibility.

pvReserved should be NULL. riid is the ID of the interface. Usually this would be IClassFactory, but it can also be IUnknown or IClassFactory2 or any other interface that is implemented by the class object. And finally, the 5th parameter is a reference (pointer to) the interface pointer we request.

As I mentioned earlier it would be valid COM to implement functionality directly on top of the class object and use it as a singleton for example, but that is not common. Our object implements the IClassFactory to allow each client to work with its own instance.

Using the QueryInterface method, we can get a pointer to the class object's IClassFactory interface. Using that interface, we can create an instance and retrieve the IArithmetic interface pointer and perform an arithmetic operation.

Putting it all together, this is what we end up with:

```
IUnknown* iUnknown = NULL;
hRes = CoGetClassObject(
    CLSID_Calculator,
    CLSCTX_LOCAL_SERVER,
    0,
    IID_IUnknown,
    (void**)&iUnknown);

if (SUCCEEDED(hRes)) {
```

```
    IClassFactory* classFactory = NULL;
    hRes = iUnknown->QueryInterface<IClassFactory>(
              &classFactory);
    iUnknown->Release();

    if (SUCCEEDED(hRes)) {
        IArithmetic* iArithmetic = NULL;

        hRes = classFactory->CreateInstance(
                  NULL,
                  IID_IArithmetic,
                  (void**)&iArithmetic);
        classFactory->Release();

        if (SUCCEEDED(hRes)) {
            double result;
            hRes = iArithmetic->Add(1.0, 1.0, &result);
            iArithmetic->Release();
            cout << "1 + 1 = " << result << endl;
        }
    }
}
```

The first order of business is to get the class object. Using that, we can query it for the IClassFactory interface. It is of course possible to immediately request the IClassFactory interface instead of first requesting IUnknown and then querying it for IClassFactory. Here I opted not to, because I wanted to show explicitly that we need to manage each interface pointer directly.

We use the IUnknown pointer to retrieve the IClassFactory pointer. After that we release the IUnknown pointer because that is the last time we need it. Consequently, as soon as we do that, we should never use that pointer again. Once 'Release' has been called on any specific pointer, it should be considered invalid. Here, underlying object is still alive, because there is an IClassFactory pointer that still has a reference count. However, from the point of view of the IUnknown pointer, that is irrelevant because pointers don't know about each other.

Another thing to note is that we only Release the pointer if the return value indicated success. If an error occurred, that pointer should be a NULL pointer and doing anything with that pointer would trigger a NULL reference exception.

Now that we have a pointer to the IClassFactory we can finally create an instance and get a pointer to the desired interface. At this point we can release the last pointer we have to the class object, and we no longer have a connection to the class object itself. However, because there is 1 active interface to an instance, and the lifecycle tracking of the class object relates to outstanding instances, the server will remain alive. At this time, we can use the interface pointer to our instance and perform a calculation. After we're done, we Release the pointer.

This marks the Release of the last pointer to our instance, and the last remaining dependency on the server. The server will now recognize that there is no longer any reason to stay alive and initiate the shutdown sequence we saw earlier.

Sidenote about QueryInterface

You may have noticed that the QueryInterface method call is a template method which takes only 1 argument instead of the 2 we discussed earlier (riid and OutPtr). This is because the C++ implementation of IUnknown takes a bit of error prone tedium out of our hands. The standard says that the riid must be supplied and a pointer returned. The problem there is that the pointer is forced through the interface as a void pointer.

Theoretically if I was copy-pasting code and using the QueryInterface implementation with 2 arguments I could end up with this:

```
IClassFactory* classFactory = NULL;
hRes = iUnknown->QueryInterface(
                    IID_ExtenalConnection,
                    &classFactory);
```

This piece of code would compile cleanly, despite the fact that the pointer type and the CLSID are completely unrelated. In this case the standard is sadly opening the door to countless runtime errors. However, the compiler can help us out here. Thanks to the include files that were generated by IDL, the compiler already knows at this point what the riid is for every interface we are using, so Microsoft implemented a nonstandard __uuidof keyword to retrieve that value for a given type.

```
//UnknwnBase.h
template<class Q>
HRESULT STDMETHODCALLTYPE QueryInterface(_COM_Outptr_ Q** pp){
    return QueryInterface(__uuidof(Q), (void **)pp);
}
```

In case you are unfamiliar with C++ templates, basically this syntax lets us define a method that takes a pointer to a generic type and then calls the 'real' QueryInterface method with the riid for that particular type as first argument.

The cool thing about templates is that these are parsed and generate strongly typed code at compile time, so all type checking is static and therefore 100% correct. This does mean that a new method is created and compiled for each type we use. If you think a bit further you might wonder why this doesn't interfere with the IUnknown interface, because it changes the class layout. The answer is that these additional methods are not virtual, and therefore not in the vtable where they might interfere.

Now you can legitimately ask: fine, but why isn't that the case for CreateInstance where the same scenario happens? The answer is that it would be largely irrelevant. You could make your own template function for that but in real life, as we'll see in next example, we wouldn't take that step-by-step approach of going through the class object first and then creating an instance after. In normal circumstances, calling IClassFactory->CreateInstance is done by the COM runtime, not by the client application.

Querying for an interface otoh is a fundamental thing that happens many times in a C++ based COM application, so it makes sense to build in a template method that is both convenient to use, and safeguards against copy - paste errors.

Activating through CoCreateInstance

I mentioned earlier that following the IClassFactory made it easier for our server to coexist in the standard COM landscape, and one easy example of this is that the previous step process can be fully automated by using the CoCreateInstance api which does all that heavy lifting for us.

```
//combaseapi.h
HRESULT CoCreateInstance(
  [in]  REFCLSID  rclsid,
  [in]  LPUNKNOWN pUnkOuter,
  [in]  DWORD     dwClsContext,
  [in]  REFIID    riid,
  [out] LPVOID    *ppv
);
```

The rclsid and dwClsContext parameters mean the exact same thing as before. pUnkOuter is an interface pointer to use for aggregation which we will conveniently ignore for now because we're not doing that yet. On the surface, riid and ppv look the same as before, but in this case, they are the interface we want on the instance, and a pointer to that interface on the instance.

With that in mind, the code looks like this:

```
IArithmetic* iArithmetic = NULL;
hRes = CoCreateInstance(
    CLSID_Calculator,
    NULL,
    CLSCTX_LOCAL_SERVER,
    IID_IArithmetic,
```

```
    (void**)&iArithmetic);

if (SUCCEEDED(hRes)) {
    double result;
    hRes = iArithmetic->Add(1.0, 1.0, &result);
    iArithmetic->Release();
    cout << "1 + 1 = " << result << endl;
}
```

As you can see, there is almost no boilerplate overhead anymore and after a single invocation of CoCreateInstance we have access to the functional part of our COM server. All in all it is very efficient.

Note that in the background, there is a whole lot of activity going on. If we check the log of our COM server this time, you see that things look similar, but there is a lot more going on in the background which the COM runtime is doing for us.

I've mentioned several times already that implementing standard interfaces makes our server work together automatically with the rest of the ecosystem, and that is what is going on here.

Using functions like CoCreateInstance will let the runtime do most of the heavy lifting and by querying for various interfaces, it determines what it can or should do.

Importing Type Libraries

So far, we've dealt with the interfaces and their identifiers via the .h and .c files that we added to our project. For the server projects, this was not too onerous because we had to use MIDL anyway. A proxy DLL cannot be built without them. And if you're compiling IDL files and building a proxy, re-using those files isn't a big deal.

For a client application, the situation is a bit different. First, the client generally doesn't need to know or care about proxies. Second, the client may have to deal with several objects and their interfaces. It would be very tedious for a client developer to hunt down the right IDL files, put them all in the project, and then add all generated .h and .c files to the project as well. And that is ignoring the fact that servers are typically distributed with their TLB files. IDL file may or may not be provided. And if they're not, then you would need to use MIDL to create the IDL files from the TLB, compile the IDL files to get generated code, etc.

Thankfully, none of that is necessary because the C++ compiler can deal TLB files directly via the #import statement. Typically, the import statement is put in the precompiled header so that it has to be processed only once.

```
#ifndef PCH_H
```

```
#define PCH_H

#include <Ole2.h>
#import "Calculator_V1.tlb"

#endif //PCH_H
```

This is the file that was created as part of the proxy DLL build. Standard include file rules apply: the file must be in the local directory or in one of the include folders.

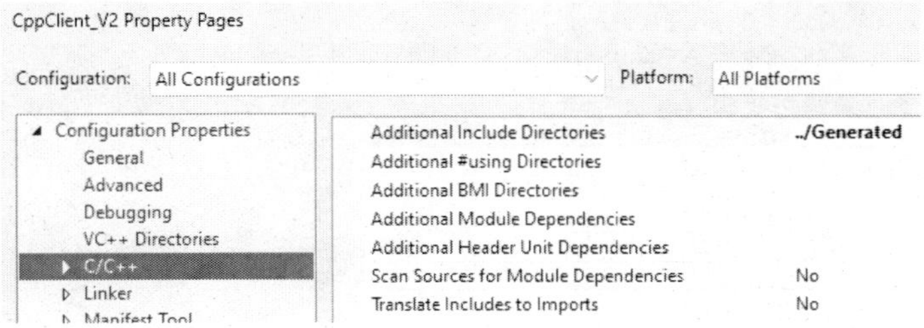

When the specified file is processed, the compiler creates 2 files: Calculator_V1.tlh (TypeLib generated Header) and Calculator_V1.tli (TypeLib generated Inline file). The header file contains a declaration for the imported types that is similar but not identical to the declarations that were originally generated by MIDL. This header is then silently included in place, in the same place the import has performed. If we look at just the code that pertains to the IArithmetic interface, this becomes apparent.

```
_COM_SMARTPTR_TYPEDEF(IArithmetic, __uuidof(IArithmetic));
struct __declspec(uuid("713e70b0-8e41-482c-80ab-0258caa5350b"))
IArithmetic : IUnknown
{
    //
    // Property data
    //

    __declspec(property(get=GetLastResult,put=PutLastResult))
    double LastResult;

    //
    // Wrapper methods for error-handling
    //

    HRESULT Add (
        double Arg1,
        double Arg2,
        double * Result );
    HRESULT Subtract (
        double Arg1,
        double Arg2,
        double * Result );
    double GetLastResult ( );
```

```
    void PutLastResult (
        double pVal );

    //
    // Raw methods provided by interface
    //

      virtual HRESULT __stdcall raw_Add (
        /*[in]*/ double Arg1,
        /*[in]*/ double Arg2,
        /*[out]*/ double * Result ) = 0;
      virtual HRESULT __stdcall raw_Subtract (
        /*[in]*/ double Arg1,
        /*[in]*/ double Arg2,
        /*[out]*/ double * Result ) = 0;
      virtual HRESULT __stdcall get_LastResult (
        /*[out,retval]*/ double * pVal ) = 0;
      virtual HRESULT __stdcall put_LastResult (
        /*[in]*/ double pVal ) = 0;
};
```

There are 2 parts to the declaration. The first is the raw interface. In other words, this is the part that has a 1 to 1 vtable mapping to the original interface. The method names are a bit different, but that doesn't matter. All that matters is the order of the virtual methods, and their signatures. The 2nd part of the declaration is a more user-friendly version that more closely resembles the declaration of the IDL file. For example, the 'LastResult' property has a raw put and get interface that is identical to the original one.

```
      virtual HRESULT __stdcall get_LastResult (
        /*[out,retval]*/ double * pVal ) = 0;
      virtual HRESULT __stdcall put_LastResult (
        /*[in]*/ double pVal ) = 0;
```

The other one doesn't have HRESULT return values and is much more similar to how we would expect a property to behave. These higher-level methods are not virtual, so having them in the interface doesn't interfere with the vtable in any way.

```
    double GetLastResult ( );
    void PutLastResult (
       double pVal);
```

The implementation of those higher-level calls is contained in the TLI file. If we take the 'GetLastResult' method as an example, we can see how that higher level method makes use of the raw methods.

```
inline double IArithmetic::GetLastResult ( ) {
```

```
    double _result = 0;
    HRESULT _hr = get_LastResult(&_result);
    if (FAILED(_hr)) _com_issue_errorex(_hr, this, __uuidof(this));
    return _result;
}
```

The raw method is called directly on the interface pointer. If the method returns an HRESULT to indicates failure, an internal helper function is used to throw a C++ exception that can be caught higher up in the hierarchy. While this is very convenient and using those higher-level methods and properties make your code more readable, there is a tradeoff. If we use code like this, handling C++ exception becomes mandatory. And even more important: if we start doing this, using COM smart pointers to handle all the reference counting becomes mandatory too. If we would use manual AddRef and Release calls in combination with these wrapper methods, then we are back to the same problems that were highlighted in the introduction. The Add and Subtract methods still have the HRESULT return value.

```
inline HRESULT IArithmetic::Add ( double Arg1, double Arg2, double * Result )
{
    HRESULT _hr = raw_Add(Arg1, Arg2, Result);
    if (FAILED(_hr)) _com_issue_errorex(_hr, this, __uuidof(this));
    return _hr;
}
```

However, as you can see from the wrapper, checking the return value becomes pointless because those are not really used anymore. If the method fails, an exception will be thrown before the call returns.

While this is great if we have a codebase that fully supports this paradigm, that is not a given. Especially if we are dealing with an older codebase where we now have to deal with an additional interface. Additionally, suppose that we want to import that type library for the sake of implementing a server? In that case we really don't want to have those higher-level methods available. They clash with the actual methods we want to implement. Sometimes you only want the interface the same way it would be generated from the IDL file by MIDL. Thankfully, we can modify the behavior of the import statement. A typical way to import a type library with those restrictions is the following:

```
#import "Calculator_V1.tlb" raw_interfaces_only, raw_native_types, no_namespace,
named_guids, auto_search
```

- Raw_interfaces_only: create the interfaces without any of the error-handling wrappers.

- Raw_native_types: when working with more complex COM native data types such as a BSTR or Variant, do not substitute them with smart variations.
- No_namespace: do not put the generated code in a separate namespace.
- Named_guids: create GUID variables with default names such as IID_IArithmetic.
- Auto_search: if the type library references other type libraries on which it depends, automatically import those as well.

With those modifications in place, we can compile the precompiled header again and get the following contents in the TLH file.

```
struct __declspec(uuid("713e70b0-8e41-482c-80ab-0258caa5350b"))
IArithmetic : IUnknown
{
    //
    // Raw methods provided by interface
    //

      virtual HRESULT __stdcall Add (
        /*[in]*/ double Arg1,
        /*[in]*/ double Arg2,
        /*[out]*/ double * Result ) = 0;
      virtual HRESULT __stdcall Subtract (
        /*[in]*/ double Arg1,
        /*[in]*/ double Arg2,
        /*[out]*/ double * Result ) = 0;
      virtual HRESULT __stdcall get_LastResult (
        /*[out,retval]*/ double * pVal ) = 0;
      virtual HRESULT __stdcall put_LastResult (
        /*[in]*/ double pVal ) = 0;
};

extern "C" const GUID __declspec(selectany) IID_IArithmetic =
    {0x713e70b0,0x8e41,0x482c,{0x80,0xab,0x02,0x58,0xca,0xa5,0x35,0x0b}};
```

With this set of modifications, the TLI file is no longer generated. It would contain the wrapper methods that put error handling around the raw vtable calls. Since we specified that we don't want that, there is nothing to put in that file anymore. After all this, we can build a new client application in the next section.

Remote Activation

We've seen that CoCreateInstance can be used to conveniently start a COM server. We've also discussed earlier how in principle, it is essentially transparent as to where a COM server is running in the physical sense. A major benefit of COM is precisely that you can build applications with various components distributed across different computers. This is where CoCreateInstanceEx comes in. It does essentially what CoCreateInstance is doing, but with optional parameters

```
//combaseapi.h
HRESULT CoCreateInstanceEx
(
  [in]       REFCLSID     Clsid,
  [in]       IUnknown     *punkOuter,
  [in]       DWORD        dwClsCtx,
  [in]       COSERVERINFO *pServerInfo,
  [in]       DWORD        dwCount,
  [in, out] MULTI_QI     *pResults
);
```

The first 3 arguments are the same as before. CoCreateInstanceEx has the ability to return multiple interfaces in 1 go, instead of having to query for each of them individually. That is why instead of specifying 1 riid and have 1 output pointer, there is a C style array of MULTI_QI structures with a specified number of elements.

```
//objidl.h
typedef struct tagMULTI_QI {
  const IID *pIID;
  IUnknown  *pItf;
  HRESULT   hr;
} MULTI_QI;
```

Since each interface request can fail individually (because it may not be implemented), there is an individual HRESULT for each request. That leaves the pServerInfo variable.

```
//objidl.h
typedef struct _COSERVERINFO {
  DWORD       dwReserved1;
  LPWSTR      pwszName;
  COAUTHINFO *pAuthInfo;
  DWORD       dwReserved2;
} COSERVERINFO;
```

This structure has 2 reserved parameters that should be NULL and 0 respectively. The pwszName argument is used for the name or IP address of the server where we want to run the COM server. pAuthInfo is another structure, which can be used for configuring how the client and server authenticate each other.

```
//wtypesbase.h
typedef struct _COAUTHINFO {
  DWORD           dwAuthnSvc;
```

```
    DWORD           dwAuthzSvc;
    LPWSTR          pwszServerPrincName;
    DWORD           dwAuthnLevel;
    DWORD           dwImpersonationLevel;
    COAUTHIDENTITY *pAuthIdentityData;
    DWORD           dwCapabilities;
} COAUTHINFO;
```

If you do supply a structure, you can explicitly configure which protocols or authentication service are used, which identity is used, and so on. Security will be covered in full later in this book. Instead, we supply NULL for pAuthInfo, and authentication is left to be negotiated between the COM runtimes of client and server, based on system configuration and security policies. With all that said, let's look at the implementation.

```
IArithmetic* iArithmetic = NULL;

COSERVERINFO info;
memset(&info, 0, sizeof(info));
info.pwszName = L"Zubvobwee";

MULTI_QI mqi[1];
mqi[0].pIID = &__uuidof(IArithmetic);
mqi[0].pItf = NULL;
mqi[0].hr = 0;

if (SUCCEEDED(hRes)) {
    hRes = mqi[0].hr;
    if (SUCCEEDED(hRes)) {
        double result;
        hRes = iArithmetic->Add(1.0, 1.0, &result);
        iArithmetic->Release();
        cout << "1 + 1 = " << result << endl;
    }
}
```

This all looks very familiar. We specify that the remote server where the COM server needs to start is called "Zubvobwee" and we request 1 interface pointer, to the IArithmetic interface. Note that we need to check 2 HRESULTs here, because contrary to CoCreateInstance, the final HRESULT for querying for the specified interface, is returned separately. Other than that, for the application itself there is no difference whether the server is running locally in-process, locally out-of-process, or remotely. This is where it becomes obvious why COM is wonderful for building distributed applications.

CLSCTX revisited

During the previous activation scenarios, we used the CLSCTX parameter several times. Without going in too much detail or covering every one of them, there are a couple of things worth mentioning.

The main basic context values are CLSCTX_INPROC_SERVER, CLSCTX_LOCAL_SERVER, and CLSCTX_REMOTE_SERVER. These specify an in-process server, out-of-process server, and a remote server on a different computer. It is perfectly legal to bitwise xor these to say 'all of the above' in which case the COM runtime will choose, based on what's available. In fact, there is a standard value for that: CLSCTX_SERVER. CLSCTX_INPROC_SERVER16 and CLSCTX_INPROC_HANDLER16 are the variants for 16-bit Windows versions. These are obsolete and can be ignored.

CLSCTX_NO_CODE_DOWNLOAD and CLSCTX_ENABLE_CODE_DOWNLOAD disable or enable the ability of the COM runtime to download and install COM servers from Active Directory or the internet as needed. Way back when Windows 2000 was still called NT5, there was the idea that the internet would be a COM infrastructure landscape. In a corporate environment, developers would publish objects in Active Directory, and the runtimes would download code from wherever it was needed and run it upon request. In home computing environments, websites would publish COM servers which would be downloaded or updated on demand, to do all sorts of interesting things. We'd have flowers in our hair and hear 'Spirit in the sky' play in the background. There would be world peace. Of course, the world turned out to be a mean place and remote execution and a living ecosystem of executable code being downloaded on the go lead to exactly the sort of situations you can imagine with hindsight, to the point where many telecom operators even refused to allow RPC traffic even when Windows 2000 was still hot and new. This behavior can be turned on or off. In practice this is not used.

CLSCTX_NO_CUSTOM_MARSHAL tells the runtime to fail activation if custom marshaling would be used. There may be different reasons why an application would want this, but security is the major one. A marshaler would have intimate access to the data being exchanged between client and server. This data may include sensitive information that needs to remain secret. And what would be the point of encrypting sensitive data being exchanged, when an attacker could easily get full access by implementing a custom marshaler? For many applications this wouldn't be useful but if you work with sensitive data, it's a consideration you need to make.

CLSCTX_NO_FAILURE_LOG can disable the logging of activation failures. The documentation advises strongly against this, and I agree because it can make troubleshooting problematic. The only reason I can think of offhand is if you'd otherwise completely spam the logs, but if that is a scenario you need to anticipate, you should probably find a better solution than to attempt incessant activation and silencing the error logging.

CLSCTX_DISABLE_AAA and CLSCTX_ENABLE_AAA are very interesting from a security perspective. These settings disable or enable 'Activation As Activator'. This prosaic description refers to the scenario where an out-of-process server is launched under the credentials of the client. In this situation, you have to establish a level of trust. Does the client have to trust the server to run under its credentials? Suppose the server carries a piece of malicious code that only executes if it detects the caller is running as an administrator? Even without considering malicious intent, it could be a bad decision to let a random piece of code execute with full credentials in case it makes an oopsie and corrupts the system or -worst case- your organization's Active Directory. With these 2 flags, you can explicitly control the scenario. If AAA is disabled, the out-of-process server can only launch if it is configured to run with a specified user account in DCOMCnfg.

CLSCTX_ACTIVATE_X86_SERVER, CLSCTX_ACTIVATE_32_BIT_SERVER (the same value as CLSCTX_ACTIVATE_X86_SERVER), and CLSCTX_ACTIVATE_64_BIT_SERVER relate to the 'bitness' of the server and are only available on 64-bit systems. On a 32-bit platform, obviously everything is 32-bit but a 64-bit system can run 32- or 64-bit code. The server can express its own preference through its registration, but the client can override this if it wants to make a specific choice. In principle, any combination should work because marshaling can take care of most issues. For example, a 32-bit DLL cannot directly be hosted in a 64-bit application. But it can be hosted in a surrogate process and then called by the 64-bit application. However, the choice you make can have a big performance impact and of course, requesting something that doesn't exist will end in failure.

Summary

In this chapter, we built a couple of very simple clients to finally demonstrate how a client can use a COM object. The full example code is available and also contains logging to track exactly what is going on with the reference count, class object, interface queries, etc. It's a good starting point for doing some experimenting to see what the COM runtime is doing under the hood.

7

Aggregation

In the chapter about Core COM Concepts, we discussed aggregation as a way to reuse existing COM objects and expose their interfaces as part of the identity of another object. The object that is being reused is called the inner object. The object that takes on interfaces of the inner object as part of its own identity is called the outer object.

The inner object can choose whether it supports this or not. The outer object determines which interfaces it wants to expose. Even if the inner object exposes many different interfaces, the outer object controls the QueryInterface method so it can decide what to do with the query on an interface-by-interface basis. The outer object is in the driving seat in all regards. The rules of aggregation say that the inner object must defer to all IUnknown methods to the outer object.

To start with, let's go back to the moment of instance creation. For the sake of clarity, the error handling, input validation and other code has been stripped out. The essence of the creation boils down to the following which does what we specified and obeys the rules of COM as we've thus far understood them, while at the same time being completely wrong on many levels:

```
//The class object creates the instance and passes the
//outer pointer to the instance
HRESULT STDMETHODCALLTYPE CalculatorClass::CreateInstance(
    IUnknown * pUnkOuter,
    REFIID riid,
    void** ppvObject)
{
    HRESULT hres = S_OK;

    CalculatorInstance* calculator = new CalculatorInstance(pUnkOuter);
```

```
    if (pUnkOuter) {    //aggregation
        calculator->AddRef();
        hres = calculator->QueryInterface(riid, ppvObject);  //wrong
        calculator->Release();
    }
    else {  //no aggregation
        //....
    }

    return hres;
}


//The instance saves a copy of the pointer to the outer object
CalculatorInstance::CalculatorInstance(IUnknown* pUnkOuter)
{
    m_UnkOuter = pUnkOuter;
    m_UnkOuter->AddRef(); //Wrong
    m_RefCount = 0;
}


//IUnknown methods delegate to the outer object
ULONG CalculatorInstance::AddRef(void){
    return m_UnkOuter->AddRef();
}

ULONG CalculatorInstance::Release(void){
    return m_UnkOuter->Release();
}

HRESULT CalculatorInstance::QueryInterface(
    REFIID riid,
    void** ppvObject)
{
        return m_UnkOuter->QueryInterface(riid, ppvObject);
}
```

The reasons why this naïve implementation is wrong are handled point by point in the next chapters.

Pointer management

When the object is created, it gets a pointer to the outer object, which we store for later use. After all, to be able to delegate e.g. an AddRef call to the outer object, it's vital that we have that pointer. And because we make a copy of that pointer, the normal rules of COM say that we need to AddRef it. This is the first major problem. Consider the lifecycle of the outer object. It will stay alive as long as its reference count is non-zero. The outer object holds a pointer to the inner object and hangs on to it as long as it must exist because it's part of the outer object's identity.

The inner object has a pointer to the outer which it has AddRef'ed. And it must hang on to it for as long as it's alive. Neither the inner or the outer object will even auto-delete because both are hanging on to an AddRef'ed pointer of each other.

This leads us to the first special rule of aggregation: The inner and outer object are not allowed to AddRef each other. The inner object can store the outer unknown pointer safely because the inner object is controlled by the outer. As long as the inner is alive, it follows that the outer pointer is safe to use. Meanwhile the outer object has received a pointer that was AddRef'ed once by the inner object itself during the CreateInstance call. It can safely make a copy of that pointer and Release it when the outer object is self-destructing.

When to defer

The second major problem is the QueryInterface call. The implementation we have properly delegates to the outer object.

```
return m_UnkOuter->QueryInterface(riid, ppvObject);
```

But the outer object will use QueryInterface on the inner object to get the actual interface it wants to be part of its own identity.

```
    if (riid == IID_IArithmetic) {
        m_UnkInner->QueryInterface(riid, ppvObject);
    }
```

Clearly, this will recurse infinitely because the inner and outer object continuously pass the QueryInterface call between them until the call stack explodes. And then there is of course this piece of code

```
    calculator->AddRef();
    hres = calculator->QueryInterface(riid, ppvObject);
    calculator->Release();
```

Which would cause an access violation because the QueryInterface call would be delegated to the outer object, which would try to pass it back to the inner object, except the m_UnkInner pointer isn't yet initialized with a value. This brings us to the next rule of aggregation: The inner object must delegate everything to the outer object, but the outer object must have an IUnknown pointer for the inner object that doesn't delegate back. Instead, it performs the non-delegating operation on the instance. This is also where things get a little dicey, because as is, there is no way for the

QueryInterface method to know in what context it is being called. Something like this cannot work.

```
HRESULT CalculatorInstance::QueryInterface(
    REFIID riid,
    void** ppvObject)
{
    if (m_UnkOuter) {    //aggregation
        return m_UnkOuter->QueryInterface(riid, ppvObject);
    }
    else {  //no aggregation
        //....
    }

}
```

If aggregation is going on, then `m_UnkOuter` is always going to be non-NULL, even when QueryInterface is being called by the outer object and should be non-delegating. There is only one way out of this impasse. There must be 2 implementations of IUnknown: the regular one which delegates everything, and another one that doesn't. Logically, the implementations of those methods need different names.

```
    //IUnknown methods
    HRESULT STDMETHODCALLTYPE QueryInterface(
        REFIID riid,
        void __RPC_FAR* __RPC_FAR* ppvObject);
    ULONG STDMETHODCALLTYPE AddRef(void);
    ULONG STDMETHODCALLTYPE Release(void);

    //non-delegating IUnknown methods
    HRESULT STDMETHODCALLTYPE NDQueryInterface(
        REFIID riid,
        void __RPC_FAR* __RPC_FAR* ppvObject);
    ULONG STDMETHODCALLTYPE NDAddRef(void);
    ULONG STDMETHODCALLTYPE NDRelease(void);
```

The internal variations of these members are not part of the interface signature. They are not virtual. Their implementation is simple enough. It's the one we already had, with a different name. We'll take AddRef as an example.

```
ULONG CalculatorInstance::NDAddRef(void) {
    return InterlockedIncrement(&m_RefCount);     }
}
```

These new non delegating methods are invisible to anyone dealing with the interface of the Calculator object because all exposed interfaces derive from the base IUnknown. A first, naive implementation to support both scenarios (aggregation and no aggregation) would be like this:

```
ULONG CalculatorInstance::AddRef(void) {
    if (m_UnkOuter) {
        return m_UnkOuter->AddRef();
    }
    else {
        return NDAddRef();
    }
}
```

But this still doesn't solve the problem that the IUnknown pointer which is held by the outer object must behave differently from the delegating IUnknown behavior through interface pointers like IArithmetic. What we really need here, is a way to map the internal routines onto an IUnknown vtable and then pass that faux IUnknown pointer to the outer object. There are several ways this could be done, but a common one is to have a tiny class that acts as a faux IUnknown.

```
template<class T> class CNonDelegatingIUnknown : public IUnknown
{
public:
    T* m_Owner;
    CNonDelegatingIUnknown(T* owner) :
        m_Owner(owner) {};

    HRESULT STDMETHODCALLTYPE QueryInterface(REFIID riid, void** ppvObject) {
        return m_Owner->NDQueryInterface(riid, ppvObject);
    }

    ULONG STDMETHODCALLTYPE AddRef() {
        return m_Owner->NDAddRef();
    }

    ULONG STDMETHODCALLTYPE Release() {
        return m_Owner->NDRelease();
    }
};
```

`CNonDelegatingIUnknown` inherits from IUnknown. Because of this, a `CNonDelegatingIUnknown*` can be used as an IUnknown*. Each of its IUnknown method implementations forwards the call to the non-delegating methods of the owning object. The reason for this class being a template class is that the location of those internal functions relative to the base pointer of the class with which it is used (`CalculatorInstance` in this specific case) is implementation dependent, and different for each class that implements those routines. By specializing `CNonDelegatingIUnknown` for the specific class we are using it for, we give the compiler the chance to figure out during compilation by creating a dedicated implementation of `CNonDelegatingIUnknown` for every class with which it is used. We can then modify the class as follows.

```
class CalculatorInstance : public IArithmetic, IComServer
{
private:
    ULONG m_RefCount;
    IUnknown* m_UnkPtr;
public:

    //IUnknown methods
    HRESULT STDMETHODCALLTYPE QueryInterface(
        REFIID riid,
        void __RPC_FAR* __RPC_FAR* ppvObject);
    ULONG STDMETHODCALLTYPE AddRef(void);
    ULONG STDMETHODCALLTYPE Release(void);

    //non-delegating IUnknown methods
    HRESULT STDMETHODCALLTYPE NDQueryInterface(
        REFIID riid,
        void __RPC_FAR* __RPC_FAR* ppvObject);
    ULONG STDMETHODCALLTYPE NDAddRef(void);
    ULONG STDMETHODCALLTYPE NDRelease(void);

    //...

    CNonDelegatingIUnknown<CalculatorInstance> m_NDUnknown;
};
```

The `CalculatorInstance` class gets a member that can act as a non-delegating IUnknown*. This member is initialized with the constructor of the `CalculatorInstance`.

```
CalculatorInstance::CalculatorInstance(IUnknown* pOuter) :
    m_InnerUnknown(this)
{
    m_RefCount = 0;
    if (pOuter) {
        m_UnkPtr = pOuter;
    }
    else
        m_UnkPtr = &m_NDUnknown;
}
```

Based on whether the instance is being aggregated or not, the internal IUnknown* points to the outer object or to the non-delegating implementations of the inner object.

```
ULONG CalculatorInstance::AddRef(void) {
    return m_UnkPtr->AddRef();
}

ULONG CalculatorInstance::Release(void) {
```

```
    return m_UnkPtr->Release();
}

HRESULT CalculatorInstance::QueryInterface(
    REFIID riid,
    void** ppvObject){
    return m_UnkPtr->QueryInterface(riid, ppvObject);
}
```

This is an elegant way to have `CalculatorInstance` implement IUnknown in a way that is simple and redirect appropriately depending on whether the instance is being aggregated. And more importantly, we now have the ability to pass a non-delegating IUnknown* even if aggregation is going on.

Passing the non delegating interface

The only question left is how to pass that non delegating pointer to the outer object? That question has a 2-part answer. It would of course be trivial to give `CalculatorInstance` a method like this

```
IUnknown* CalculatorInstance::GetNDIUnknown() {
    //...
}
```

But we don't need to do this. Very early in this book, we saw that the IUnknown interface pointer of an object must always be the same, regardless of who is using it and where it is being used. Therefore, it follows that the inner IUnknown pointer that is being held by the outer object MUST be used as the identity of the object. With this knowledge, we can modify our code as follows:

```
HRESULT STDMETHODCALLTYPE CalculatorInstance::NDQueryInterface(
    REFIID riid,
    void __RPC_FAR* __RPC_FAR* ppvObject)
{
    //snip
    if (riid == IID_IUnknown) {
        *ppvObject = static_cast<IUnknown*>(&m_NDUnknown);
    }
    //snip
}

HRESULT STDMETHODCALLTYPE CalculatorClass::CreateInstance(
    IUnknown* pUnkOuter,
    REFIID riid,
    void** ppvObject)
{
    //snip
    if (pUnkOuter && (riid != IID_IUnknown))
        return CLASS_E_NOAGGREGATION;
```

```
    CalculatorInstance* calculator = new CalculatorInstance(pUnkOuter);
    if (NULL == calculator)
        hres = E_OUTOFMEMORY;
    if (SUCCEEDED(hres))
    {
        calculator->AddRef();
        hres = calculator->NDQueryInterface(riid, ppvObject);
            calculator->Release();
    }
    //snip
}
```

We've modified the `NDQueryInterface` so that it always returns the same, nondelegating IUnknown pointer. When CreateInstance now returns the pointer to the outer object, it has a proper non delegating pointer to use for querying interfaces and eventually releasing the inner object.

Identity management

The final detail that needs explaining is the check for the requested interface. If aggregation is requested, then the only allowed interface is `IID_IUnknown`. There are 2 good reasons for this. The first reason is that the non-delegating IUnknown is just that: the implementation of a raw IUnknown* without any other members. That vtable has no other members that would e.g. redirect the IArithmetic members.

The second reason is that IUnknown is the only non-delegating interface that should exist, even if we wanted to bother making a non-delegating IArithmetic. Aside from the non-delegating IUnknown, all other interfaces fall back on the regular IUnknown base of Calculator like they should, because the rules of aggregation say that any QueryInterface call through the aggregated object should be delegated to the outer object. That is the entire point of doing all of this.

Now you might wonder what happens if someone queries for `IID_IUnknown`. As it happens, that is never a problem. If a client holds an interface pointer that belongs to the inner object and queries for `IID_IUnknown`, the inner object delegates that query to the outer object, which will satisfy the request for `IID_IUnknown` by returning its own IUnknown* as mandated by COM. This is as it should be because through the process of aggregation, the outer object has taken the interfaces of the inner object and made them part of its own identity.

Alternative implementations

The implementation we just covered uses a template class to ensure the correct mapping of non-delegating methods. In the modern era that is a perfectly acceptable solution. In fact, the ATL is built around the concept of using templates in this manner. But in the early 90's, template programming was still largely compiler dependent, in the sense that most compilers only implemented a limited subset of the language features and often used non-standard syntax. For this reason, many projects used pointer arithmetic to implement similar functionality. The following implementation in Essential COM is one example of this.

```
//Essential COM : page 191 - 192
    class Car : public ICar {
        LONG m_cRef;
        IUnknown* m_pUnkOuter;
    public:
        Car(IUnknown* pUnkOuter);
        // non-delegating IUnknown methods
        STDMETHODIMP InternalQueryInterface(REFIID,
            void**);
        STDMETHODIMP_(ULONG) InternalAddRef(void);
        STDMETHODIMP_(ULONG) InternalRelease(void);

        // snip ...

            class XNDUnknown : public IUnknown {
            Car* This() {
                return (Car*)((BYTE*)this -
                    offsetof(Car, m_innerUnknown));
            }
            STDMETHODIMP QueryInterface(REFIID r, void** p)
            {
                return This()->InternalQueryInterface(r, p);
            }
            STDMETHODIMP_(ULONG) AddRef(void)
            {
                return This()->InternalAddRef();
            }
            STDMETHODIMP_(ULONG) Release(void)
            {
                return This()->InternalRelease();
            }
        };
        XNDUnknown m_innerUnknown; // composite instance
    };
```

This code does something like what our template class does, except it does so through a bit of trickery. XNDUnknown is the non-delegating implementation of IUnknown. In this case it has special knowledge of the layout of Car, because it is a subtype of the Car class. This way it avoids having Car to be a template, at the cost having to be a subtype. Every class which uses this method for implementing a non-delegating IUnknown must have this copy-pasted.

Having established that XNDUnknown understands the layout of the Car class, the only missing piece is that it must know the location of the Car class in memory. This is done via pointer arithmetic. XNDUnknown calculates the difference, in number of bytes, between the Car base and its m_innerUnknown member. Armed with that knowledge, any instance of XNDUnknown can infer the exact location of the Car object of which it is a data member by subtracting the internal offset from its own 'this' pointer.

This technique works but requires some non-intuitive pointer arithmetic. Looking at this code with a modern era perspective, it may seem weird to resort to tricks like this instead of passing the ICar pointer via the constructor. But that requires storing the ICar*, which would increase the amount of memory needed by `XNDUnknown`.In today's world, coding to save individual bytes is no longer as relevant as it once was. Especially when considering that the resulting code is non-intuitive and harder to debug. When weighing the benefit of those memory savings against the hidden cost of making code harder to read and understand, we need to look at things with the right perspective. When Don Box wrote 'Essential COM', 8 to 16 MB of memory in a computer was typical for a solid computer. That's megabytes, not gigabytes, and it was also used for running the operating system and everything else.

If you had an application in the late 90's that made extensive use of COM objects, then the difference of 4 bytes per instance could make a significant difference in memory consumption. Especially if you also had other smart optimizations in other places. Our own `CNonDelegatingIUnknown` class could certainly use the same mechanism to avoid storing the instance pointer. However, with the design perspective of today, there is something to be said for keeping the code straightforward at the cost of storing an extra pointer. To be perfectly honest, in any real-world application where you implement a non-trivial COM object, you'd probably be using something like the ATL to implement your objects. There would have to be a very good reason to start rolling your own COM boilerplate for use in production code.

Summary

In this chapter we explored the process of aggregation, and the requirements that come with identity management in aggregation scenarios, which is different from standalone objects.

Having modified the Calculator project to make it support aggregation, we are perfectly placed to move to the next project and kill 2 birds with 1 stone: to use the ATL to build a more advanced calculator which aggregates the current one.

8

Automation and IDispatch

Everything we covered so far revolves around IUnknown and assumes that the client can work with QueryInterface and knows how to call methods to different interfaces. Generally, this means that the client needs to be built using some sort of development environment because a lot needs to happen to call the 'Add' method. Consider the implementation in C++:

```
hRes = iArithmetic->Add(1.0, 1.0, &result);
```

Using the base IArithmetic pointer, the method call is executed through the vtable, the data values are passed on the stack as 8-byte doubles and returned via the 8-bytevariable pointed to by the result pointer.

The iArithmetic pointer can be obtained through known platform APIs like CoCreateInstance, so that is not going to be a huge deal to implement in a scripting environment. But once it has that pointer, what is the scripting environment going to do with it? Calling the Add method relies on being able to navigate a vtable and knowing where the virtual function pointer for the add method is located. But in a scripting environment 'Add' is just a piece of text. In COM, method names don't really exist. Remember that name mangling is platform dependent which is why method names are not exported for that purpose. Additionally, from the script's point of view, "1.0" could be a float or a double, and there is no real way to know.

Scripting environments support late binding, meaning statements are evaluated when they are executed, instead of early binding which would require some sort of compilation stage.

In theory, a scripting environment could use the registered (hopefully) type library to read type information about the interface, figure out what the exact parameter type is, look up the method name, figure out where in the vtable the relevant method pointer is, put together a stack call frame, and then execute it while manually taking care of any marshaling. It could work but it should be obvious that this is going to be complex and error prone. It also requires a significant amount of developer effort on the part of anyone wanting to add COM support to their environment. And that is of course under the assumption that the scripting environment would know exactly what the GUID is for the interface pointer. If a COM object returns a pointer to an object that was created internally such as a helper object or a sub-object, then the scripting environment would hold a pointer of unknown type and no way to call methods or change to a different interface.

Solutions can be developed to deal with all these issues, but clearly, it's going to be a gargantuan effort. In a time when there was a push to get developers to adopt COM, these problems were going to impact the uptake. To encourage adoption by the popular languages of the time such as VBA, VBScript, and Javascript, Microsoft developed the IDispatch interface as a built-in way to do the things we just listed as problems. Any interface that needs to support late binding can derive from IDispatch. Dispatching is just a fancy name for a mechanism that allows a client to forward an execution request to a server to have it executed on its behalf.

So far, we've mentioned VBScript, VBA and Javascript as client environments that support late binding and which need an IDispatch interface to work. However, PowerShell must be added to that list. PowerShell is the default scripting environment for Systems Administration and general-purpose scripting in Windows environments, so having a way to make your COM object useful in such an environment can be a big deal.

Staying with the theme of the book so far, let's say that we want to implement a calculator, in such a way that it can also be used in a scripting environment such as PowerShell where we want to be able to do something like this

```
$comObject = New-Object -ComObject DispCalc.Calculator.1

[double] $arg1 = 1.0
[double] $arg2 = 1.0
[double] $result = 0
```

```
$comObject.Add($arg1, $arg2, [ref] $result)

"$arg1 + $arg2 = $result"
```

Dispatching in a nutshell

At the core, the dispatching mechanism is simple. The minimum requirement necessary to be able to dispatch methods is that we need a way to translate 'Add' to a method call, and to pass arguments back and forth.

It starts with the creation of the object. The mechanism for this is the same as for all objects and uses CoCreateInstance in the background.

```
$comObject = New-Object -ComObject DispCalc.Calculator.1
```

Everything here was covered previously. In the background, the program ID is translated to a class ID, and CoCreateInstance is called to retrieve a pointer to the dispatching interface. The real work is done when the script encounters the following line.

```
$comObject.Add($arg1, $arg2, [ref] $result)
```

4 different things are happening here:

1) Check whether the object even supports dispatching.
2) Get the type information that describes the interface and its various parameters.
3) Get the list of method names and their dispatch ID (DISPID).
4) Invoke the call.

We've mentioned that in PowerShell, 'Add' is just a piece of text. Through the dispatch interface, powershell will retrieve a list of names, and the DISPID for each method. It will check if the requested method is in that list and generate an error if it isn't. It will then use the interface type description to format an argument list. If the parameter types don't match exactly (or if the value was supplied as a constant expression such as '1.0') it will try to apply the necessary conversions. When all that is done, the script has enough information to use the dispatch interface for executing the method with that specific DISPID value, using the specified list of parameters".

Note that steps 1 and 2 are optional. An object is not obligated to provide type information. Only the mapping of names to DISPIDs and the ability to invoke are necessary. The arguments for an Invoke operation are encoded as variants so if the DISPID is known, the client can encode the information and attempt an Invoke. If the types match or are close enough that conversion is possible (for example sending a float when a double is expected), the call can be attempted. Clients CAN use the type information if it is provided, and they know what to do with it. But equally, developers can use this while developing. When working with objects in PowerShell, it can be convenient to do something like this:

```
$comObject = New-Object -ComObject DispCalc.Calculator.1
$comObject | Get-Member
```

```
$comObject | Get-Member


   TypeName: System.__ComObject#{4ff14d8f-4d38-40d5-af67-e09b7a35bce5}

Name     MemberType Definition
----     ---------- ----------
Add      Method     void Add (double, double, double)
Subtract Method     void Subtract (double, double, double)
```

This is a quick way to discover available methods and their signatures. Depending on how the interface is defined in IDL or how it is compiled, parameter names may or may not be visible for display like this.

These 4 steps that provide the required functionality are defined in the IDispatch interface as follows (annotations removed for clarity):

```
//oaidl.h
interface IDispatch : IUnknown
{
      HRESULT GetTypeInfoCount(
            [out] UINT* pctinfo);
      HRESULT GetTypeInfo(
            [in] UINT iTInfo,
            [in] LCID lcid,
            [out] ITypeInfo** ppTInfo);
      HRESULT GetIDsOfNames(
            [in] REFIID riid,
            [in, size_is(cNames)] LPOLESTR* rgszNames,
            [in] UINT cNames,
            [in] LCID lcid,
            [out, size_is(cNames)] DISPID* rgDispId);
      HRESULT Invoke(
            [in] DISPID dispIdMember,
            [in] REFIID riid,
            [in] LCID lcid,
            [in] WORD wFlags,
            [in, out] DISPPARAMS* pDispParams,
            [out] VARIANT* pVarResult,
            [out] EXCEPINFO* pExcepInfo,
```

```
             [out] UINT* puArgErr);
};
```

With this interface, any late binding environment has everything it needs to retrieve type information, to do something useful with that information. One thing to keep in mind is that this interface was designed with long term compatibility in mind so the interface has several parameters that are not actually used, but which provided the option for use that was not foreseen at the time without breaking compatibility. For example, the interface supports the notion of supporting multiple sets of type information, but this has never come to fruition.

Defining the interface

Like IUnknown, IDispatch is meant to be used as a base class by any interface that wants to support the dispatching mechanism. It starts with IDispatch as a base class.

```
[
        object,
        uuid(4ff14d8f-4d38-40d5-af67-e09b7a35bce5),
        dual,
        nonextensible,
        oleautomation
]
interface IDispCalculator : IDispatch
{
};
```

The declaration of our IDispCalculator interface in IDL looks similar to what we had before, with a couple of notable differences. After the object and uuid attributes, there are a couple of new attributes.

'dual' refers to binding type. So far, all our interfaces have derived directly from IUnknown or another interface that derives from IUnknown. They support early binding, meaning the layout of the vtable and method invocation are figured out at compile time. To support this, MIDL generates header files and a type library containing the necessary information to make this possible. Our new `IDispCalculator` derives from `IDispatch`, which is recognized by MIDL as meaning that the object will be supporting late binding. Unless we specify that `IDispCalculator` supports both, the information for late binding is the only thing that would be generated. The 'dual' attribute serves that purpose.

`'nonextensible'` is an optional attribute that indicates that the interface is fixed, and no new members will be added. On the face of it, this seems redundant. Any early binding interface relies on a fixed vtable and should never change, once it is released. The idea that a keyword is needed to indicate it doesn't, seems silly. However, supporting early binding isn't mandatory, and a late binding interface can change. That is one thing where a late binding has an edge of early binding: because a dispatching mechanism is in place that figures out things at runtime instead of compile time, there is a disconnect between the identification of the method to execute, and its actual execution. This is a dynamic process, and as such there is no technical reason why it could not support interfaces whose functionality changes between script runs. Based on whether the interface is marked as nonextensibe or not, a client environment can decide whether it can keep certain dispatching information in a cache for optimization or not. In today's world of computing performance, caching such information doesn't really make much sense anymore but in the late 90's it could make a measurable difference.

'`oleautomation`' is another optional attribute. You can use it to specify that the arguments of the methods in the interface are all of a type that is automation compatible. Automation compliance is important because it's what allows scripting environments to convert to and from known types. In general, dispatching interfaces should always work with data types that are specified as automation safe, but it's not strictly enforced. The `oleautomation` attribute instructs the MIDL compiler to validate this. Using non-automation compliant types such as handles, complex structs, non-safe interface pointers or arrays will trigger errors or warnings, as appropriate for the seriousness of the problem. Defining the methods of the interface is similar to the original calculator, with a small difference.

```
[
	object,
	uuid(4ff14d8f-4d38-40d5-af67-e09b7a35bce5),
	dual,
	nonextensible,
	oleautomation
]
interface IDispCalculator : IDispatch
{
	[id(1)] HRESULT Add(
				[in] DOUBLE Arg1,
				[in] DOUBLE Arg2,
				[out] DOUBLE* Result);
	[id(2)] HRESULT Subtract(
				[in] DOUBLE Arg1,
				[in] DOUBLE Arg2,
				[out] DOUBLE* Result);
};
```

Every method must be assigned a DISPID because these are the identifiers that the `GetIDsOfNames` method will return for the methods in the interface. If we look at the generated TLB file with OleViewer, we see this relationship. Without these identifiers, PowerShell would simply report that the 'Add' method is not implemented on the COM object because it would find no DISPID for a method with that name.

Defining the COM object that implements this interface is done as follows.

```
[
	uuid(2b97fbfc-c11d-46ed-89ca-1f2942b7854d),
	version(1.0),
]
library DispCalcServerLib
{
	importlib("stdole2.tlb");
	[
		uuid(6bd32af8-dd7d-4b68-8691-011a6704d9ec)
	]
	coclass DispCalculator
	{
		[default] interface IDispCalculator;
	};
};
```

At this point it would be easy to move on and think there is nothing noteworthy here, other than the 'default' attribute. That could not be further from the truth. The `IDispCalculator` interface is listed as the default interface. The default interface is the one that will be used by Automation clients that rely on IDispatch.

There is an important consequence here: only 1 interface can work as a dispatching interface. This is made explicit here by the 'default' attribute, but it also follows from the rules. We mentioned in the beginning that a QI request for IUnknown should always return the same pointer because it is used as the identity of the object. A similar requirement exists for IDispatch, which acts as the identity of a dispatching object (because late binding clients don't use IUnknown or query for interfaces). A QI request for IID_IDispatch must always return the same pointer because for a scripting client, that is the identity of the object.

A COM object can still expose multiple interfaces and support dispatching. But only 1 of those interfaces can be exposed for dispatching. In our example, that is also why it makes more sense to have an interface with the name '`IDispCalculator`' as the default interface for a '`DispCalculator`' COM object because from a late binding point of view, there is a 1 to 1 mapping of that specific interface and the methods that are implemented on the object.

If you look at the IDispatch interface methods, you see that the capabilities were there to support multiple dispatch interfaces, each with their own type library information.

It seems likely that having 1 interface per object sufficed for most automation scenarios and there was never enough market demand to force the standard to evolve and be adopted.

There are ways to work that limitation. An easy way is to modify the interface in such a way that an object has methods for handing out the other interfaces. For example, say that we have a trigonometry interface that we want to expose, but which is not part of the IDispCalculator interface. We support that in the following manner.

```
interface ITrigonometry : IDispatch
{};

interface IDispCalculator : IDispatch
{
      [id(1)] HRESULT Add(
                          [in] DOUBLE Arg1,
                          [in] DOUBLE Arg2,
                          [out] DOUBLE* Result);
      [id(2)] HRESULT Subtract(
                          [in] DOUBLE Arg1,
                          [in] DOUBLE Arg2,
                          [out] DOUBLE* Result);
      [id(3)] HRESULT GetITrigonometry(
                          [out] IDispatch* trig);
};

coclass DispCalculator
{
      [default] interface IDispCalculator;
      interface ITrigonometry;
};
```

Whether that is a smart strategy or not is a different question of course. Automation was conceived as a way to expose / implement an object hierarchy, with each object having an interface that exposes the functionality of that object, with the ability to hand out sub objects. For example, a COM object representing a selection of text might expose a Font property, allowing interaction with a separate font object's interface to manage the style of that selection. The text object itself wouldn't implement the font interface directly, as doing so would require it to support every possible interface related to text formatting. That would be an impractical and bloated design. From this perspective, it makes far more sense to design a clean object hierarchy with focused interfaces, rather than a monolithic object implementing countless interfaces. It's important to remember what IDispatch was designed for: enabling late-bound access to simple, scriptable interfaces, not simulating early-bound IUnknown behavior with multiple interfaces.

Implementing IDispatch

With the IDL part taken care of, we can compile it and implement a COM object in the same way as before, except now we also have to implement the IDispatch methods, just like we had to implement the IUnknown methods.

`GetTypeInfoCount` is the simplest of the bunch and returns either 1 or 0 to indicate whether the type information for the object is available or not.

```
HRESULT CDispCalculator::GetTypeInfoCount( UINT* pctinfo)
{
        if (pctinfo == NULL)
              return E_POINTER;
        *pctinfo = 1;
        return S_OK;
}
```

As mentioned before: when looking at the IDispatch interface, it is important to consider that when it was designed, COM and dynamic dispatching were still evolving. The interface was created with futureproofing and compatibility in mind. If the behavior needed to change at some point down the line, there was room to do so without breaking binary compatibility. This is why there is a method called '`GetTypeInfoCount`' even though in practice the count is always reported as either 0 or 1 as a sign of whether the type info is available or not.

`GetTypeInfo` can then be used to retrieve file info, with the ability to specify a locale ID in case the type library supports localized member names.

```
HRESULT STDMETHODCALLTYPE CDispCalculator::GetTypeInfo(
    /* [in] */ UINT iTInfo,
    /* [in] */ LCID lcid,
    /* [out] */ ITypeInfo** ppTInfo)
{
    if (!ppTInfo)
        return E_POINTER;
    return LoadRegTypeLib(
                LIBID_ComputerLib,1,0,lcid,&ppTInfo);
}
```

If we only support 1 set of type information, this implementation is trivial. It does require the type library to be registered correctly. This is something the COM server can do either when it registers itself, or it can be done manually using a tool like RegTlb.

`GetIDsOfNames` is used to retrieve the dispatch Ids (DISPID). These identifiers will be used when invoking methods and properties later. By using dispatch identifiers, the translation step to identify methods must be done only once. A simple implementation (assuming the type library info was loaded before, for efficiency) could be

```
HRESULT STDMETHODCALLTYPE CDispCalculator::GetIDsOfNames(
    /* [in] */ REFIID riid,
    /* [size_is][in] */ LPOLESTR* rgszNames,
    /* [range][in] */   UINT cNames,
    /* [in] */ LCID lcid,
    /* [size_is][out] */ DISPID* rgDispId)
{
    if (!rgDispId)
        return E_POINTER;

    m_pTInfo->GetIDsOfNames(rgszNames, cNames, rgDispId);
}
```

This snippet does not take the locale id into account. Instead, it assumes that the relevant type information was pre-loaded at some point. In a more complex implementation, the object would load the correct type library and return the locale specific information. And finally, there is the `Invoke` method which is used to translate a dispatch ID to an actual method call. Here, too, we can forward to the call (again, assuming the type library was loaded beforehand).

```
    HRESULT STDMETHODCALLTYPE CDispCalculator::Invoke(
        /* [in] */  DISPID dispIdMember,
        /* [in] */ REFIID riid,
        /* [in] */ LCID lcid,
        /* [in] */ WORD wFlags,
        /* [out][in] */ DISPPARAMS* pDispParams,
        /* [out] */ VARIANT* pVarResult,
        /* [out] */ EXCEPINFO* pExcepInfo,
        /* [out] */ UINT* puArgErr)
    {
        m_pTInfo->Invoke((IDispatch*)this,
            dispIdMember,
            wFlags,
            pDispParams,
            pVarResult,
            pExcepInfo,
            puArgErr);
    }
```

Looking at the code so far, you might wonder why IDispatch even has those members if the methods can be forwarded as is without really having to do anything special. Indeed, if we don't do anything special, there is no special benefit to doing this, but it makes it easier for the client because they can do everything through the interface pointer that they already have, without needing to manage type libraries and other complexities. And of course, the type library is optional and an object may instead want to implement its own dispatching routine.

To localize or not

You will have noticed that in the example code, the lcid parameter isn't used. Arguably, this is just code for the purpose of demonstration, but whether localization is good or bad, is a matter of perspective. To be precise: it's a matter of in what capacity you are making that judgement.

For an end user, it might seem like a non-starter. End user software is often provided in localized forms. Depending on the country, this can be a very sensitive topic, subject to legal requirements, and be considered a culturally non-negotiable situation. For example, a person in Belgium may have a French version of Windows, use a French version of Excel, and expect their VBA code to use French method names. Especially with late binding interfaces that are intended for scripting, that can be a strong expectation. At the same time, a different user in the same country but in a different language region could use a Dutch version of Windows, with a Dutch version of Excel, and expect Dutch method names. A Dutch language version of Excel can have a method name like 'Openen' for the same method that would be called 'Ouvrir'. This isn't typically a problem, and both users get exactly what they need and want on their respective sides of the language divide.

For a developer, the situation is going to be different. For a developer who must build something that can be deployed in different locales, this can cause all sorts of headaches. In the late 90's, I was working in a graphical development environment that supported the use of ActiveX objects. You would add an ActiveX object to your form and then select the appropriate method from a dropdown box. Upon selecting a method, the ActiveX node would generate an argument list where values could be supplied or retrieved. It worked very well, until the day we delivered the software to the customer.

The customer used a Dutch version of Windows and Office, We, being software developers in the late 90's, used the English versions of everything. The software we made worked as expected on the customer's systems because the development environment linked all code interface nodes to the DISPID. And the DISPID is platform independent. But if the environment detected any change, it would re-validate all interface nodes and refresh the DISPID. This process would fail because the localized names of the methods on those Excel objects were different and the English language type libraries were not installed, every interface node would break and had to be manually refreshed by selecting the Dutch language method from the relevant type libraries.

It can be argued that the world would overall be a better -or at least simpler- place for software developers if localization would not have to be considered. For COM objects that are intended for an audience of developers, a case can be made for only providing a language neutral interface. Otherwise, if your audience consists of a variety of user types, then you may want to consider providing localized versions.

Dispatch-only interfaces

Until now, we've covered all scenarios with the server supporting both types of binding, and clients being either one or the other. Supporting clients that do late binding doesn't affect the ability of the COM object to also support early binding. Or to put it differently: we've assumed that the infrastructure for early binding is a given, and we 'add' late binding support via the IDispatch interface which derives from IUnknown. IDispatch is a superset of IUnknown so instinctively we think that any object that supports IDispatch will be able to expose interfaces via QueryInterface. The client may not know what to do with that, but server would.

However, there are also scenarios where late binding is the only option. So far, we've considered all interfaces as being implemented on objects in a fully COM aware server. And this seems logical because if a server doesn't support the full COM plumbing, why would it be hosting COM objects?

The reason lies in the fact that when looking at automation clients, there are scenarios where a server needs to be able to notify a client that something happened. This is especially true with ActiveX controls that have a user interface component which needs to be able to send 'OnClick', 'OnMouseDown', 'FocusChanged' .... events to one or more clients that may or may not be subscribing to those events. Anyone who has ever used a user interface designer in any language is familiar with the concept of events. Underneath the syntactic sugar that makes an event appear differently from a method or a property, an event notification is only a method that is executed on an object inside the client which subscribed to the event.

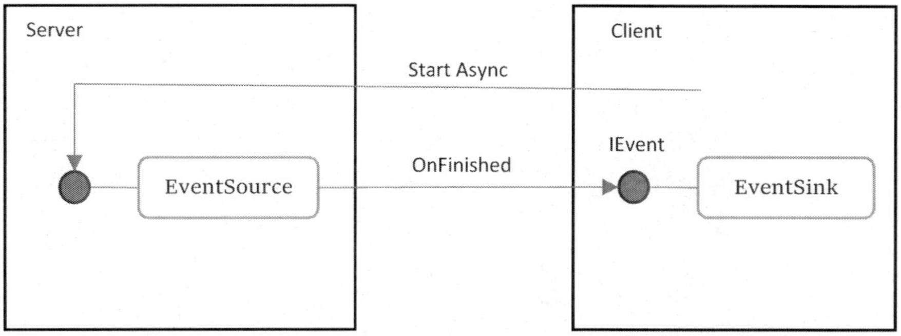

Consider a scenario where a client connects to a COM object in the server to start some sort of work that is executed asynchronously. When the work is done, the server reports back by executing the 'OnFinished' method on the client's implementation of the IEvent interface of which OnFinished is a member. We use source / sink terminology because that is a standard terminology which will come back later.

The key understanding here is that even if the server supports a standard dual interface, the client might be a late binding client which does not support calling IEvent::OnFinished by performing a QueryInterface first and then calling through the vtable. Even if such clients are not intended to host complex multi-interface objects, they need some way to allow calls to their internal objects. For this purpose, the dispinterface exists. The hypothetical interface in the example would be defined in IDL as follows:

```
[
	uuid(CA313502-3CEE-4FB0-B1A1-3FAB8BE50F05)
]
dispinterface IEvent
{
	properties:
	methods:
		[id(1)] HRESULT OnFinished();
};
```

If we compile this, MIDL still produces output.

```
#ifndef __IEvent_FWD_DEFINED__
#define __IEvent_FWD_DEFINED__
typedef interface IEvent IEvent;
#endif 	/* __IEvent_FWD_DEFINED__ */
```

And

```
MIDL_DEFINE_GUID(IID,
DIID_IEvent,0xCA313502,0x3CEE,0x4FB0,0xB1,0xA1,0x3F,0xAB,0x8B,0xE5,0x0F,0x05);
```

But that's everything really. There is no virtual class declaration to be found. The reason is that it would be wrong to create a declaration with virtual methods, similar to what would happen with a dual interface. A method call that would be called through the vtable could never work because in a late binding environment there is absolutely no way to map that call to the base pointer with the standard COM infrastructure. Any call must be dispatched via the 'Invoke' method. It's worth noting that even though no code is generated, for any call to happen in the COM world, a dispinterface must still follow the rules and 'fit' the shape of an IDispatch implementation. This includes an implementation of IUnknown. Any dispinterface has the following vtable layout:

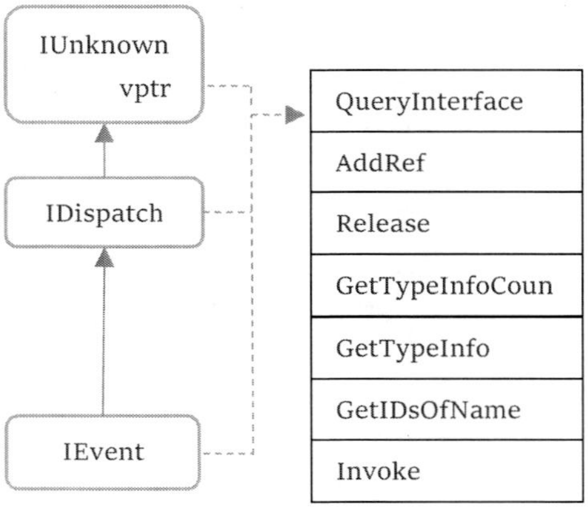

From a binary point of view, a dispinterface is identical to an IDispatch dual interface. The implementation will still need to support the reference counting primitives for example. Even an implementation that does not support flexible QI calls and vtable call routing will still need to implement the minimal functionality to uphold COM contracts, for example when the server wants to store a copy of the dispinterface pointer and call AddRef on it.

The only thing that is different is that purposely, no code is generated to help you implement IEvent. That is not the problem it might seem. We just need to provide a wrapper class that implements the OnFinished method by creating the appropriate Invoke call. There are ATL helper classes to take some of the work out of your hands, but it is actually much simpler. If the dispinterface is in a type library, then we can #import that type library and let Visual Studio do this for us. For example, if we import a type library with the IEvent dispinterface, Visual Studio creates the following code

```
// .tlh file
_COM_SMARTPTR_TYPEDEF(IEvent, __uuidof(IEvent));
struct __declspec(uuid("ca313502-3cee-4fb0-b1a1-3fab8be50f05"))
IEvent : IDispatch
{
    // Methods:
    HRESULT OnFinished ( );
};

// .tli file
inline HRESULT IEvent::OnFinished ( ) {
    HRESULT _result = 0;
    _com_dispatch_method(
                    this, 0x1, DISPATCH_METHOD, VT_ERROR, (void*)&_result, NULL);
    return _result;
}
```

So we get a convenient wrapper class with non-virtual methods that takes all the tedium of properly building the Invoke call out of our hands. This is the easiest way to do all this. Helper functions like _com_dispatch_method know that the vtable is fixed, and the Invoke method has a fixed offset position relative to the base pointer.

If you look at the declaration of the wrapper, you will also notice that the wrapper class derives from IDispatch, so aside from the fact that you can call the functional methods you are interested in, this means you can call AddRef and Release when you need to store these interface pointers.

Summary

In this chapter, we explained the differences between early binding and late binding, and showed how IDispatch can be used to support late binding clients such as PowerShell.

IDispatch is limited in the sense that only 1 interface can be dispatched, but that limitation can be remediated by designing a sensible object hierarchy where each object has a focused interface. There are also 'dispatch only' interfaces that make it possible to execute methods and properties on objects that are hosted by a late binding client which doesn't have the capability to work with the IUnknown paradigm of routing interface calls through the vtable.

9

Active Template Library

Having so far worked with raw C++ code, it has no doubt become painfully clear that working with naked C++ interface pointers is troublesome. Counting on software developers to always cover all scenarios and avoiding scenarios in which AddRef or Release are not called appropriately, is probably not a good idea. For smaller code snippets it is fine, but as soon as code becomes slightly more complex, nesting a lot of code based on the HRESULT and quickly leads to code that's hard to read and maintain correctly.

```
hRes = ift1->Foo();
if (SUCCEEDED(hRes)) {
    IItfA* iftA = NULL;
    hRes = ift1->QueryInterface(IID_IItfA, (void**)&iftA);
    ift1->Release();
    if (SUCCEEDED(hRes)) {
        hRes = iftA->Bar();
        iftA->Release();
    }
}
```

In the preceding code, there are 3 lines of 'useful' code, and they require 2 layers of nesting, with Release being called on 2 different levels. And in this case, it is still possible to oversee the correct Release behavior because all uses of these pointers are still close together. As soon as the program logic itself becomes non-trivial, it will quickly become non-trivial to look at the code and determine if Release is called in all the right places and at the right time.

To further complicate this, modern C++ programs make extensive use of exceptions for error handling. This makes explicitly calling Release impossible because the HRESULT based flow logic can at every point be broken if code can throw exceptions at some point. You'll remember that problems related to exceptions were covered in the first chapter. They were one of the reasons why HRESULT based control flow was conceived. Exceptions clearly couldn't be used with COM, but that doesn't mean they won't be used in the rest of a C++ application. So that is one serious class of problems that need dealing with.

At the same time, it has become clear that a significant amount of boilerplate code needs to exist for every class object or class instance. And to further complicate things, some of that boilerplate is going to depend on the type of server, whether it supports aggregation, etc. There is so much boilerplate code required that it quickly becomes impractical to implement everything manually. Soon after COM was brought to the main stage of software development, developers started to use various kinds of smart pointer and base classes to deal with the boilerplate stuff. Some of these were more reliable than others or tailored to specific types of use which might not be valid for all cases. It is easy to make subtle mistakes that lead to hard-to-diagnose errors.

To help developers deal with these issues in a more reliable and standardized way, as well as to improve coding efficiency, Microsoft released the Active Template Library (ATL). ATL has always been included with the Professional and Enterprise editions of Visual Studio. Since Visual Studio 2013 it was also added to the community editions of Visual Studio as an optional component to install.

The word 'Active' is meaningless here, and mainly used because when ATL was created, 'Active' was the buzzword of the day to indicate that something was internet ready and component based. and used in anything that was new at the time: Active Directory, Active Desktop, ActiveX, Active Server Pages, etc. The important information is the fact that ATL is a C++ template library.

For those who are not familiar with the concept: template programming is a way to implement classes and functions while providing placeholders for some of the data types that are used by the class. The template may be placeholder for a base class that the class derives from, or a data member that is stored internally. When a developer uses such a template class and provides the desired type, the compiler will substitute the template type for the supplied type and compile the new class as if it was written that way.

There are many benefits to this way of programming:

- The developer can work with 1 template class as if it is a generic class but at compile time, it will result in as many strongly typed classes as needed.
- Templates are strongly typed. Any mismatch in what the supplied template type supports vs. what is expected will result in a compile time error instead of a runtime error.
- Templates can be used with a variety of programming techniques so that upon compilation it can be specified which base class a higher-level class derives from or what sort of behavior is expected. The resulting class will not need to implement 'if' statements or have #ifdef clauses to modify its behavior. This is all sorted out during compilation in such a way that the resulting code is only the actual code that needs to run, within the constraints that were specified during compilation.

Going into the details of template programming is beyond the scope of this book. Template programming is an advanced topic about which entire books have been written. As interesting as it can be to go deeply into the implementation details, none of that really matters from the point of view of someone wanting to use the ATL. A benefit of template libraries in general is that they are human readable so if you want to know more about how it is implemented, you can read it all.

The goal of this chapter is not to document and explain every single class in ATL. Instead, the goal is to explain the structure and some of the more important techniques that underpin ATL and then use that understanding to use ATL to your benefit for both client and server development.

ATL Smart Pointers

For this section of the book, it's easiest to start with using ATL for client development because the concepts are easy to grasp and it immediately shows how to use the templates for developers who are not yet familiar with the concept of templates. No special project configuration needs to be done, other than including the main ATL header. The first ATL project is called AtlClient to make it easy to identify it in the solution but note that while the term 'ATL Server' is commonly used to identify a COM server developed in ATL, the term 'ATL Client' isn't a thing.

The 2 main classes that do most of the heavy lifting on the client side are CComPtr<T> and CComQIPtr<T>. They are very similar but serve slightly different purposes. CComPtr<T> is a smart pointer that encapsulates a raw COM pointer that was created someplace else. CComQIPtr<T> inherits directly from CComPtr<T> and can be used in the same way. The main difference is that it has a special constructor which initializes its internal interface pointer by performing a QueryInterface on the pointer that was passed as an argument.

The easiest way to understand the difference and their use is to take the CppClient application and convert it to use these ATL smart pointers. Let's start with the first example we had where we first get the class object, and then manually create the instance.

```
CComPtr<IClassFactory> classFactory;
hRes = CoGetClassObject(
    CLSID_Calculator,
    classContext,
    0,
    IID_IUnknown,
    (void**)&classFactory);

if (SUCCEEDED(hRes)) {

    CComPtr<IArithmetic> iArithmetic;
    classFactory->CreateInstance(
        NULL, IID_IArithmetic, (void**)&iArithmetic);

    if (iArithmetic) {
        double result;
        hRes = iArithmetic->Add(1.0, 1.0, &result);
        cout << "1 + 1 = " << result << endl;
    }
}
```

The first thing that stands out immediately is that a `CComPtr<IClassFactory>` can be used exactly like an `IClassFactory*`. The template class has all the right cast operations, conversions and operator overloads to make its behavior match to the point where you don't even know you're working with smart pointers.

The second thing that stands out is that there is no need any more to call Release manually. It will be called internally as soon as the smart pointer goes out of scope. To make sure there are no unintentional errors when raw interface pointers are replaced by smart pointers, CComPtr<T> overrides the Release method and makes it private so that any place where the Release would be called triggers a compiler error.

```
if (iArithmetic) {
    double result;
    hRes = iArithmetic->Add(1.0, 1.0, &result);
    cout << "1 + 1 = " << result << endl;
    iArithmetic->Release();     //C2248
}
```

The same is also true for AddRef, which makes sense because smart pointers can only work if you're not actively try to interfere with what those smart pointers are doing.

Looking at this code, you can already see it's less cluttered than the first implementation where we took the long road of going through the class object to get a class instance. However, you might still think that the CreateInstance method still looks ugly and has the potential for mismatching the IID and the interface pointer. This could have been resolved by having a custom specialization of `CComPtr<IClassFactory>` with a smarter implementation of CreateInstance. But there would be no real point to doing that because taking the long road isn't typically done. Instead, CComPtr<T> has a CoCreateInstance method that takes care of this.

```
CComPtr<IArithmetic> iArithmetic;
iArithmetic.CoCreateInstance(
    CLSID_Calculator, NULL, classContext);

if (iArithmetic) {
    double result;
    hRes = iArithmetic->Add(1.0, 1.0, &result);
    cout << "1 + 1 = " << result << endl;
}
```

In most situations, you're not going to have to anticipate the existence of in-process and out-of-process servers side by side, because most things only make sense either in-process OR out-of-process. In that scenario, the preceding code can be simplified even further.

```
CComPtr<IArithmetic> iArithmetic;
iArithmetic.CoCreateInstance(CLSID_Calculator);

if (iArithmetic) {
    double result;
    hRes = iArithmetic->Add(1.0, 1.0, &result);
    cout << "1 + 1 = " << result << endl;
}
```

In this case, `CoCreateInstance` uses NULL for the outer object, and CLSCTX_ALL for the proposed class context. This will make the COM runtime choose the type of server, in order of proximity. By using CComPtr<T>, all the boilerplate code concerning object creation and lifecycle management is shoved away to places where you don't have to look at it, and you only need to care about using the interfaces. `CoCreateInstance` does return a HRESULT which can be used in case you want to diagnose potential problems. If all you care about is whether it succeeded or failed, then evaluating the pointer value is a perfectly good solution.

CComQIPtr<T> only comes into play if we want to use the QueryInterface operation on another pointer. For educational purposes, the Calculator object has an interface that can be used to retrieve runtime information about the COM Server hosting the Calculator object

```
if (iArithmetic) {
    CComQIPtr<IComServer> iComServer( iArithmetic);
    if (iComServer)
    {
        //Do Something
    }
}
```

The QueryInterface operation takes place inside the constructor, so those details are hidden away as well. You might wonder about the fact that there is no HRESULT available this way, because the QueryInterface operation is handled in the constructor, and constructors don't have return values. This is less problematic than it might seem, because the object itself already exists.

```
if (iArithmetic) {
    CComPtr<IComServer> iComServer;
    if (SUCCEEDED(hr)) {
        hr = iArithmetic->QueryInterface(&iComServer);
        if (SUCCEEDED(hr)) {
            // QI succeeded
        }
        else {
            // QI failed, hr contains the error code
        }
    }
```

In older code and documentation, you might see the following use of CComQIPtr, which initializes its internal pointer through the assignment operator which takes an IUnknown* as right hand side.

```
CComQIPtr<IComServer> iComServer = iArithmetic;
```

This used to work because `CComPtr<IArithmetic>` can be converted to `IArithmetic*` which can be converted to `IUnknown*`. However, modern compilers do not allow this particular use of implicit conversion anymore. This changed with Visual Studio 2017 which started to enforce more strict behavior. The assignment method can be made to work, but you need the use of an explicit cast

```
CComQIPtr<IComServer> iComServer =
                  static_cast<IUnknown*>(iArithmetic);
```

or pass the raw pointer contained in `iArithmetic`.

```
CComQIPtr<IComServer> iComServer = iArithmetic.p;
```

Having casts when you don't really need them is not good practice, and neither is using the raw pointer unless you absolutely need to. Smart pointers can only be smart if you let them, so it's best to use them as they are intended.

CComPtr<T> and CComQIPtr<T> are without doubt 2 of the most important and useful tools in the ATL toolbox. But there are several others. As you might expect, they all serve the purpose of a) hiding away boilerplate code and b) managing the lifecycle of the underlying resources. The Microsoft online documentation is extensive, and it is not the intention of covering every single one of them in-depth. However, there are several that come in handy in almost every single project, and this is as good a place as any to introduce some of those.

CComPtrArray<T> This is a helper class for managing an array of CComPtr<T>
CComBSTR We first encountered the BSTR when talking about IDL data types. The special feature of BSTR is that there must always be a data field before the string pointer, and the memory allocation must be managed through APIs like SysAllocString. CComBSTR is a string class that behaves like a BSTR, provides string management functions, and hides away the memory management routines.
CComVariant Another data type commonly encountered in COM is the Variant. We briefly mentioned it in the IDL chapter as well. The nice thing about the variant is that it can be used for storing / passing almost every conceivable data type. The downside is that it can contain every conceivable data type and many of those data types need dedicated cleanup routines. CComVariant neatly encapsulates the Variant type and takes care of the resource management.
CComSafeArray SafeArray is another commonly used data type that provides the functionality of an array.
CComAutoCriticalSection This helper creates and deletes a critical section that can be used to protect code in a multithreaded environment. Because the critical section resource is managed internally, it is safe to use it to protect code which may throw exceptions.

There are many other helper classes that you can use in your client applications to make your code more robust. ATL is great for client applications because it takes away boilerplate pointer management. While it is not a typical requirement, you can extend these classes for more specific purposes by inheriting them.

For example, the CComPtr<T> has a CoCreateInstance method to help you create instances. This method suffices in most scenarios but if your application relies on creating remote instances based on runtime decisions, it would be convenient to extend CComPtr<T> in a way that supports this while also retaining all the convenience of CComPtr<T>. A possible way to implement this is as follows:

```
template <class T> class CComPtrAnywhere : public CComPtr<T>
{
public:
    HRESULT CoCreateInstanceEx(
        _In_ const std::wstring& remoteServer,
        _In_ REFCLSID rclsid,
        _Inout_opt_ LPUNKNOWN pUnkOuter = NULL,
        _In_ DWORD dwClsContext = CLSCTX_ALL)
    {
        COSERVERINFO info;
        memset(&info, 0, sizeof(info));
        info.pwszName = const_cast<LPWSTR>(remoteServer.c_str());

        MULTI_QI mqi[1];
        mqi[0].pIID = &__uuidof(T);
        mqi[0].pItf = NULL;
        mqi[0].hr = 0;

        HRESULT hRes = ::CoCreateInstanceEx(
            rclsid, pUnkOuter, dwClsContext, &info, 1, mqi);
        if (SUCCEEDED(hRes)) {
            hRes = mqi[0].hr;
            if (SUCCEEDED(hRes)) {
                this->Attach(static_cast<T*>(mqi[0].pItf));
            }
        }

        return hRes;
    }
```

The IP address or hostname is passed via the COSERVERINFO structure. CoCreateInstanceEx supports querying for multiple interface pointers at the same time, but we only need one. Should a necessity arise for working with multiple interface pointers, we can always add overloads of our own CoCreateInstanceEx method. And this is all there is to it. We now have a version of CComPtr<T> that supports remote activation and still has all the behavior that makes it work with the rest of the ATL which works with a CComPtr<T>.

Implementing a simple ATL Server

As convenient as ATL is for client applications, where it really shines is in the implementation of COM Servers. You will remember from previous chapters that the code for the value-added part of our Calculator was only a dozen lines or so, but we had to have hundreds of lines of code just to deal with

- Class object lifecycle
- Class instance lifecycle
- External connection management
- Server lifecycle management
- Locking
- Aggregation
- Registry manipulation for registration purposes

It's not that these things are massively complex, but they must be done repeatedly, require a lot of code, and are easy to get wrong. ATL makes it possible to implement servers without having to do any of that. Based on the choices you make when the project is created, your project will use certain base classes and implement certain interfaces. The benefit for ATL Server projects is that these base classes for the boilerplate code have received many man years of attention and all the edge cases and tricky problems are guaranteed to be handled correctly. That was the good news.

Now for the bad...

If you consult older books about ATL, (which really means ANY book on ATL at this point in time), you'll find that they talk about automated code generation, a wizard for doing things with your classes, and many other things that would make life a lot easier. Trying to follow these old tutorials and explanations is not always possible anymore. Sadly, some of those tools and wizards no longer exist. With the advent of .NET, DCOM and ATL have received progressively less love from the Visual Studio team. Over time, many things have fallen by the wayside because the cost and effort of maintaining them weren't justified anymore.

Some of the Wizards are still there, but may have reduced functionality, refuse to work in some cases, or contain visual artefacts that hint at things that no longer exist.

The 'Add new item' dialog in an ATL project used to look like this:

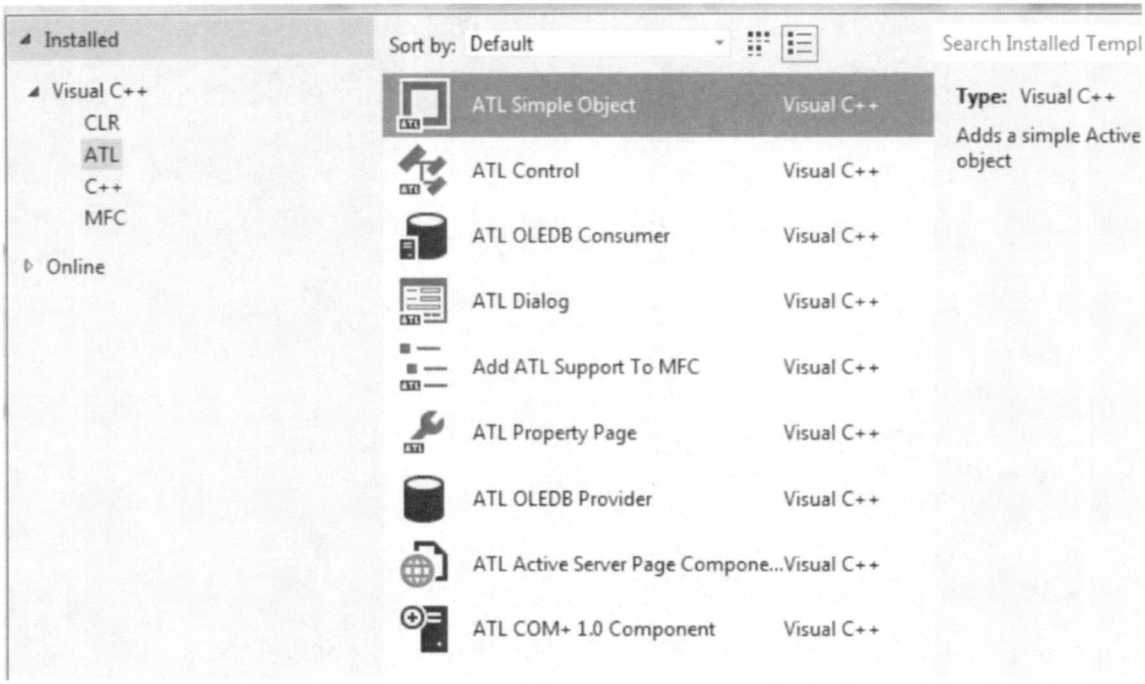

With Visual Studio 2022, it looks like this:

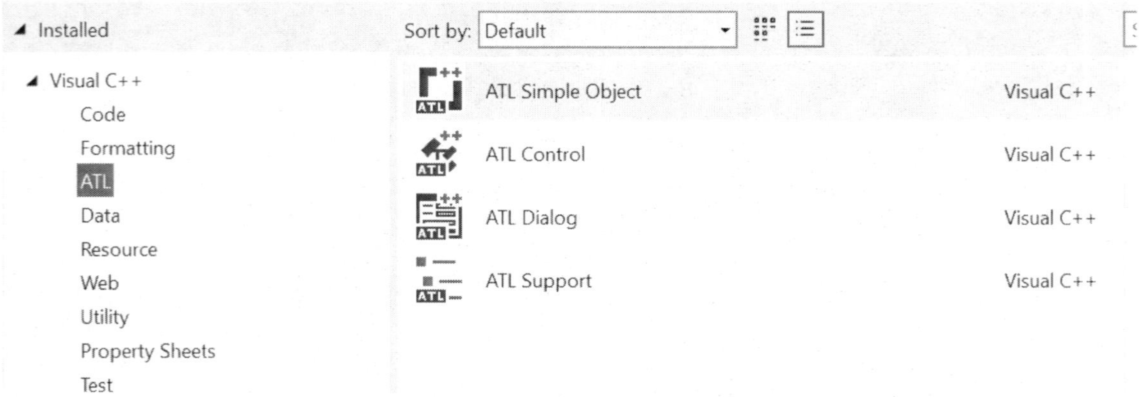

Less than half of the options remain. It's a rather sad realization that quite a bit of functionality seems to be lost. One of the notable victims is COM+. Granted, it has been legacy for a long time, and there's probably not a single aspect of COM+ compared to .NET which would even remotely justify starting a new project with COM+ as the infrastructure of choice. And that is without even thinking about the security implications. But it's like having a ratchet wrench set with the 14 mm socket missing. You probably never used it before, you will probably never ever need it in the future, but that empty placeholder in your toolbox looks wrong. You never needed it, but it was reassuring to know that it was there just in case, and it made the set look complete.

With Visual Studio 2019, the ATL COM+ wizard was defenestrated, and some of the other wizards and automated functions followed along. For now, basic ATL functionality remains supported though. With the items that were removed, whether something still works depends on the technology in question. For example, the ATL Active Server Pages project template for making lightweight Active websites is officially gone from Visual Studio. It has been released as open source by Microsoft, and is community maintained but you're essentially on your own for support. COM+ is still officially supported, in terms of interfaces, library support and runtime. But the wizards that used to make it convenient are gone. You may now have to use scripts for making registry changes and write configuration code yourself.

So, if you are working with ATL and find yourself asking "Hmm, this feels a bit clunky and could have been implemented in a much more convenient manner" then you are probably right, and it probably was implemented in a much more convenient manner at some time in the past. Still, in terms of baseline support, ATL still has a lot going for it for implementing and maintaining COM projects.

To show the convenience of using ATL, we are going to continue our calculator journey and build the Dispatching calculator we talked about earlier, before moving on with our work as a developer for CalculusInc, building a more comprehensive calculator. The dispatching calculator serves as a good jumping board because it will conveniently take us through the various elements of the ATL.

Creating an ATL project

To start with, we add a new ATL Server project to our solution.

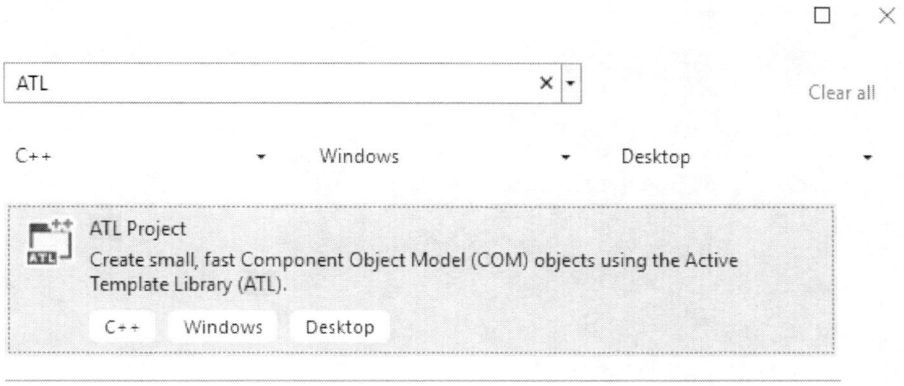

Give the project a proper name

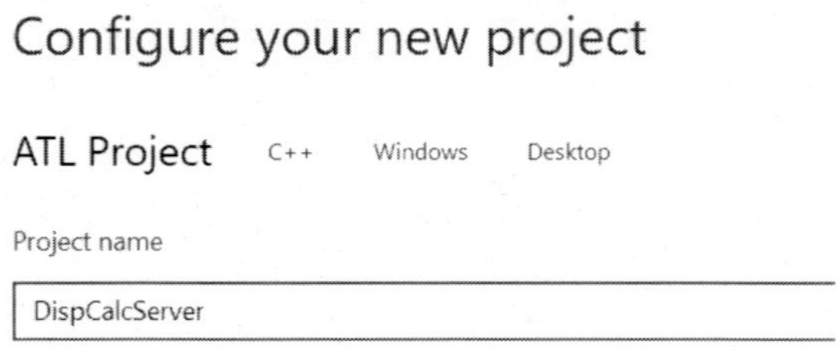

Then we can specify what kind of project we are building. This project dialog supports all 3 types of server we've covered so far: DLL (in-process), Executable (out-of-process application), and Service (out-of-process service).

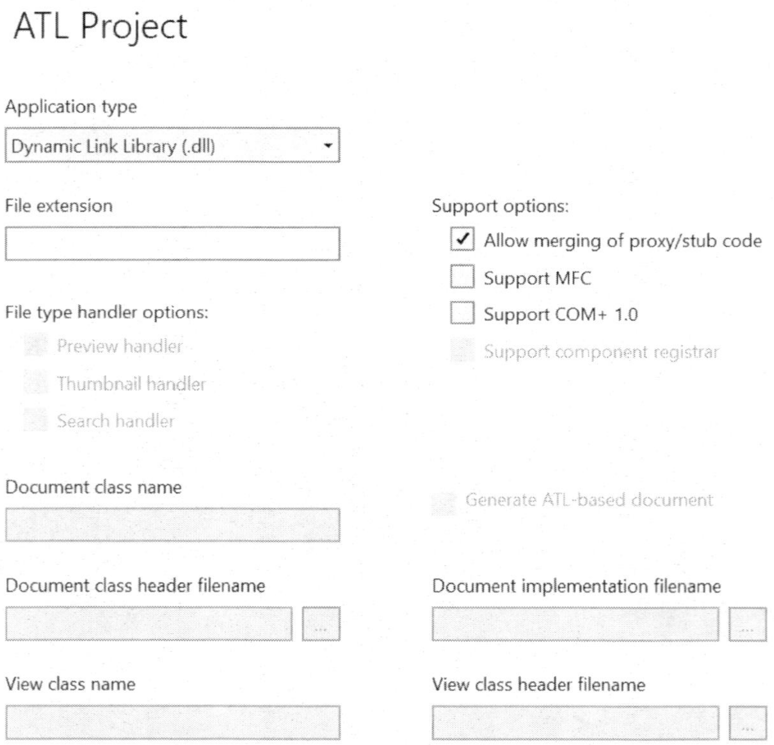

There are many settings available here, most of which are applicable only in certain cases. The following support options are available:

- Allow merging of proxy / stub code. The code for marshaling will not be built as a separate DLL but merged into the server. This only works for objects that implement the IDispatch interface. The 'Service' application type does not allow this setting. Not because it cannot work, but it is generally not an appropriate option for Service applications which typically require high performance and use complex data types. For the Dispatching calculator, we check this box because it makes things simpler (no separate proxy DLL). If we do not check this option, then the project wizard will create not 1 but 2 projects: 1 for the main project, and 1 for the proxy DLL.

- Support MFC. The MFC headers and libraries will be added to the project for use alongside ATL. This makes the entire MFC library available for things like GUI handling, working with MFC data types and so on. This is especially useful if the server needs to interact with the GUI.
- Support COM+ / Support Component Registrar. The project will support the COM+ interfaces and registration. These are beyond the scope of this book. COM+ is still supported, but you'll have to implement most things by hand.

The other settings will only be available if a file extension is filled in. If you fill in an extension such as ".abc", the project will be a Windows Shell extension that will be used to handle all files of the specified type. The following checkboxes are available:

- Preview handler. When you select a file with the specified extension, Windows Explorer can show a preview of that file.
- Thumbnail handler. The extension will be used to show a thumbnail when the files are listed.
- Search handler. The extension will expose searchable metadata.

If any of the preceding checkboxes are checked, the remainder of the fields become available. They concern the filenames for the Document / View implementation that will provide the specified functionality. Typically, this is done in MFC but will use ATL if the "Generate ATL based document" checkbox is checked to avoid loading the MFC libraries if there is a need for truly lightweight component.

Like COM+, MFC and Shell Extensions are out of scope for the purpose of this book. For our dispatching calculator, the only choice we really need to make is which type of server we're building. We choose the DLL because that is the most appropriate for a component that is loaded in the client for performing calculations. This project is created with a lot of boilerplate code.

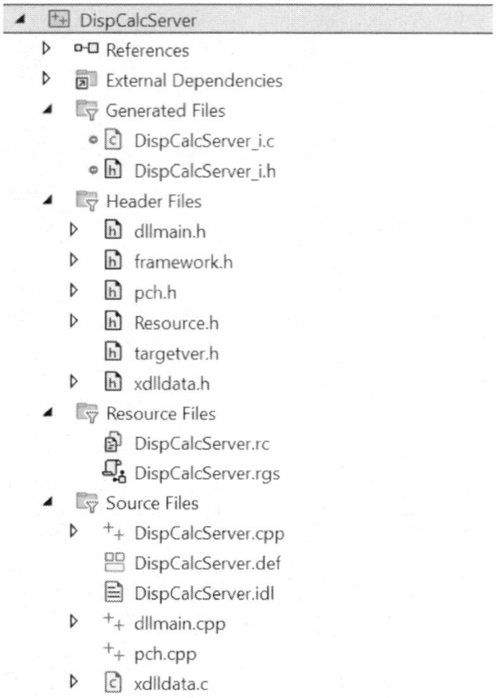

All of this is boilerplate for the sake of server registration, lifecycle management. It's a lot of code but the good thing is that we don't have to worry about it. Most of these files such as the generated files, the precompiled header files and the dllmain are recognizable from our earlier projects. The main file of interest is DispCalculator.idl which contains the IDL for the Library and the objects contained within. Any objects that are added to the server will be added there.

One thing that might seem different is that the IDL file with the Library declaration and the various COM objects is managed at the project level. In the earlier examples, that IDL file was shared between the different server implementations. With ATL projects, that is not the case. It's not that it was technically impossible to do things differently if Microsoft had wanted to, but in real-world scenarios there is almost never a reason to implement a server as both in-process and out-of-process server because the reasons why you might choose one over the other are usually mutually exclusive. There is also not really a good reason why it would be important for those 2 hypothetical servers to have the same CLSID or the same ProgID. From a COM point of view, only the interfaces matter. While working with the raw C++ code in the earlier projects, there was a lot of code that could be re-used between all server types. But with ATL, all boilerplate code is implemented via ATL. This means there is no real reason why you'd want to share COM related code between those projects. Code reuse is not really a consideration here.

Server Objects

Even without COM objects, there is already quite a bit going on. There is a server, which means there is a lifecycle that needs to be managed. There are 2 .cpp files that immediately come into play

```
// dllmain.cpp : Implementation of DllMain.
CDispCalcServerModule_AtlModule;

// DispCalcServer.cpp : Implementation of DLL Exports.
STDAPI DllCanUnloadNow(void)
{
#ifdef _MERGE_PROXYSTUB
    HRESULT hr = PrxDllCanUnloadNow();
    if (hr != S_OK)
        return hr;
#endif
    return _AtlModule.DllCanUnloadNow();
}

STDAPI DllGetClassObject(
    _In_ REFCLSID rclsid, _In_ REFIID riid, _Outptr_ LPVOID* ppv)
{
#ifdef _MERGE_PROXYSTUB
    HRESULT hr = PrxDllGetClassObject(rclsid, riid, ppv);
    if (hr != CLASS_E_CLASSNOTAVAILABLE)
        return hr;
#endif
    return _AtlModule.DllGetClassObject(rclsid, riid, ppv);
}

STDAPI DllRegisterServer(void)
{
    HRESULT hr = _AtlModule.DllRegisterServer();
#ifdef _MERGE_PROXYSTUB
    if (FAILED(hr))
        return hr;
    hr = PrxDllRegisterServer();
#endif
    return hr;
}

STDAPI DllUnregisterServer(void)
{
    HRESULT hr = _AtlModule.DllUnregisterServer();
#ifdef _MERGE_PROXYSTUB
    if (FAILED(hr))
        return hr;
```

```
    hr = PrxDllRegisterServer();
    if (FAILED(hr))
        return hr;
    hr = PrxDllUnregisterServer();
#endif
    return hr;
}

STDAPI DllInstall(BOOL bInstall, _In_opt_  LPCWSTR pszCmdLine)
{
    HRESULT hr = E_FAIL;
    static const wchar_t szUserSwitch[] = L"user";

    if (pszCmdLine != nullptr)
    {
        if (_wcsnicmp(pszCmdLine, szUserSwitch, _countof(szUserSwitch)) == 0)
        {
        ATL::AtlSetPerUserRegistration(true);
        }
    }

    if (bInstall)
    {
        hr = DllRegisterServer();
        if (FAILED(hr))
        {
            DllUnregisterServer();
        }
    }
    else
    {
        hr = DllUnregisterServer();
    }

    return hr;
}
```

All this is very similar to the boilerplate stuff we programmed before. The entry points are the same of course, and from a high-level view, ATL defers the calls to the `CDispCalcServerModule` class which represents the server. That is where we get a first glimpse into the ATL bag of tricks.

ATL makes extensive use of templates and macros to ensure that code is compiled according to the constraints and requirements we specified when we created the server and the COM object. C++ doesn't allow template declarations to be split from their implementations using the normal .h / .cpp paradigm like you'd do with regular classes. A language feature to support this briefly existed in the C++ standard. It was introduced in C++ (19)98 when ATL 3.0 already existed, and it was removed from the standard again in C++ (20)11 because it had almost no uptake among compiler vendors. Splitting template declaration from implementation turned out to be much more complex than expected, and didn't always work the way you'd think it'd do. Consequently, most of the interesting code in an ATL project is in C++ header files, because that is simply how templates work. So let's look at the code for the server module.

```
class CDispCalcServerModule :
        public ATL::CAtlDllModuleT< CDispCalcServerModule >
{
public :
       DECLARE_LIBID(LIBID_DispCalcServerLib)
       DECLARE_REGISTRY_APPID_RESOURCEID(IDR_DISPCALCSERVER, "{2b97fbfc-c11d-
46ed-89ca-1f2942b7854d}")
};
```

The careful observer immediately noticed something strange is going on here. `CDispCalcServerModule` derives from `CAtlDllModuleT`, yet `CAtlDllModuleT` itself relies on `CDispCalcServerModule` internally. On the face of it, it seems like it should be illegal for a type to derive from base classes that use the derived type in its base. However strange it may seem, this is legal C++ and is known as the Curiously Recurring Template Pattern (CRTP). According to Wikipedia, the CRTP was discovered when someone accidentally derived a base class from a derived class. Following the realization that it compiled, the ATL was programmed to make use of this language feature because it makes it much easier for base classes to delegate specific calls back to the derived class without having to use virtual base methods. Using this method means the vtable doesn't have to grow, and the method calls are direct calls instead of needing redirection via virtual functions.

This technique resembles the technique that we used for the non-delegating IUnknown implementation CNonDelegatingIUnknown in the chapter about aggregation. The main difference is that here, such a class is used as base class. Removing annotations and implementation details, this is the base class for our DLL module.

```
//atlbase.h
template <class T>
class ATL_NO_VTABLE CAtlDllModuleT :
       public CAtlModuleT<T>,
       private CAtlValidateModuleConfiguration<true, T>
{
public :
       // snip…
       HRESULT DllCanUnloadNow() throw()
       {
```

```
            T* pT = static_cast<T*>(this);
            return (pT->GetLockCount()==0) ? S_OK : S_FALSE;
        }

        HRESULT DllGetClassObject(
            _In_ REFCLSID rclsid,
            _In_ REFIID riid,
            _COM_Outptr_ LPVOID* ppv) throw() { // snip… }

#ifdef _ATL_USE_WINAPI_FAMILY_DESKTOP_APP

        HRESULT DllRegisterServer(
            _In_ BOOL bRegTypeLib = TRUE) throw() { // snip… }
        HRESULT DllUnregisterServer(
            _In_ BOOL bUnRegTypeLib = TRUE) throw(){ // snip… }
#endif // _ATL_USE_WINAPI_FAMILY_DESKTOP_APP

        HRESULT GetClassObject(
            _In_ REFCLSID rclsid,
            _In_ REFIID riid,
            _COM_Outptr_ LPVOID* ppv) throw() { // snip… }
};
```

The implementation of `DllCanUnloadNow` was left in place to demonstrate how the CRTP technique works. `CAtlDllModuleT` is designed to be a generic implementation of the functionality that makes up a server module. In the `DllCanUnloadNow` call, the 'this' pointer is cast to `T*` which is the derived class `CDispCalcServerModule`. To get the lock count here, the `CDispCalcServerModule:: GetLockCount` method is used. And this is where the CRTP comes in play. By default, `CDispCalcServerModule` does not have its own implementation of `GetLockCount` at the most derived level, which means that the `GetLockCount` method is executed on the `CAtlModuleT<T>` base. However, should `CDispCalcServerModule` override the `GetLockCount` method, then that would be called. And all of this would be achieved without having to declare all base methods as virtual and make the vtable size explode. In practice, this is not something that is usually done but the ATL makes aggressive use of CRTP to leave all options open without compromising in efficiency or memory footprint.

To give a concrete example, we could have a scenario where we implement our own lock counting or for example to log the calling pattern of lock related functions. If we want to trace this, we could simply implement the following:

```
 class CDispCalcServerModule : public
ATL::CAtlDllModuleT<CDispCalcServerModule>
{
public :
    //override at the most derived level
    LONG GetLockCount() throw() {
```

```
        ATLTRACE("GetLockCount\n");
        //explicitly send call to base class after logging
        return ATL::CAtlDllModuleT< CDispCalcServerModule >::GetLockCount();
    }
    //snip...
};
```

Using this pattern, we can effortlessly hook into the behavior of the ATL base classes without having to make any compromises.

The next base class in the hierarchy is `CAtlModuleT<T>` which is a template class that provides implementations of methods for functionality such as registering and unregistering the server; base functionality which a server might want to override. `CAtlModule` is a core implementation of basic COM functionality that does not need to know about derived types. Having a non-template base and a templated glue layer allows ATL to split the default baseline implementation of COM functionality from the CRTP mechanism that allows a developer to override many things. From a technical perspective these could have been merged into a single templated class. However, from a design perspective this is cleaner and more reusable. Lastly there is the CAtlValidateModuleConfiguration class which has no functional role. Instead, its inclusion in the hierarchy triggers a couple of checks that verify if the module is being built with valid settings.

That is in a nutshell the server object and how it is implemented. Had we chosen a different server type such as an executable module, the server module would have looked like this:

```
class CMyOOPServerModule : public ATL::CAtlExeModuleT< CMyOOPServerModule >
{
public :
       DECLARE_LIBID(LIBID_MyOOPServerLib)
       DECLARE_REGISTRY_APPID_RESOURCEID(IDR_MYOOPSERVER,
                 "{0fd815f3-24bb-4641-9046-878cbbbe4008}")
};

CMyOOPServerModule _AtlModule;
```

The only difference here is that instead of deriving from `CAtlDllModuleT`, the main server class derives from `CAtlExeModuleT`.

```
//atlbase.h
template <class T>
class ATL_NO_VTABLE CAtlExeModuleT :
       public CAtlModuleT<T>,
       private CAtlValidateModuleConfiguration<false, T>
{
};
```

If we follow the rabbit hole down the inheritance hierarchy, we find all the expected functionality such as the calls to `CoAddRefServerProcess` and `CoReleaseServerProcess`, the message loop, the shutdown event, and everything else we've explained in the first section of the book. Similarly, a COM service would look as follows (Note that the comment is proof that some of the code generation is a bit dated. As we'll cover in depth in the security chapter, the suggested impersonation level is no longer supported):

```
class CMySvcServerModule : public ATL::CAtlServiceModuleT< CMySvcServerModule,
IDS_SERVICENAME >
{
public :
	DECLARE_LIBID(LIBID_MySvcServerLib)
	DECLARE_REGISTRY_APPID_RESOURCEID(IDR_MYSVCSERVER,
		"{5811374d-118c-4f3b-a7bc-2d04af978edf}")
	HRESULT InitializeSecurity() throw()
	{
		// TODO : Call CoInitializeSecurity and provide the appropriate
		// security settings for your service
		// Suggested - PKT Level Authentication,
		// Impersonation Level of RPC_C_IMP_LEVEL_IDENTIFY
		// and an appropriate non-null Security Descriptor.

		return S_OK;
	}
};

CMySvcServerModule _AtlModule;
```

Because a service is also an out-of-process server hosted in an executable, the hierarchy simply piggybacks on to the default out-of-process hierarchy.

```
//atlbase.h
template <class T, UINT nServiceNameID>
class ATL_NO_VTABLE CAtlServiceModuleT :
	public CAtlExeModuleT<T>
{
};
```

Like the DLL module, there is a hierarchy that has all the recognizable pieces from the earlier explanation, and it uses CRTP to provide higher level access into the internals. It is not the purpose of this book to go into the entire hierarchy and branch out into all implementation details. This book is about helping you work with and navigate ATL projects and the generated code. With the knowledge of the previous chapters and using the 'Go to Definition' feature in Visual Studio, you have everything you need to investigate the details. If you want a detailed analysis of the ATL and a full architectural review, I recommend picking up a copy of 'ATL Internals, Second Edition'.

It's a bit dated on the topic of COM itself, but it's still by far the best and most detailed resource for learning the guts of ATL.

To get back to the topic at hand: at this point we understand how the server works and how the pieces of code fit together. But a COM server without objects is useless so let's do something about that.

COM Objects

The project still doesn't contain any code for the COM object we want. To add the DispCalculator object, right-click the project and select Add -> New Item. The Item we want is the ATL Simple Object

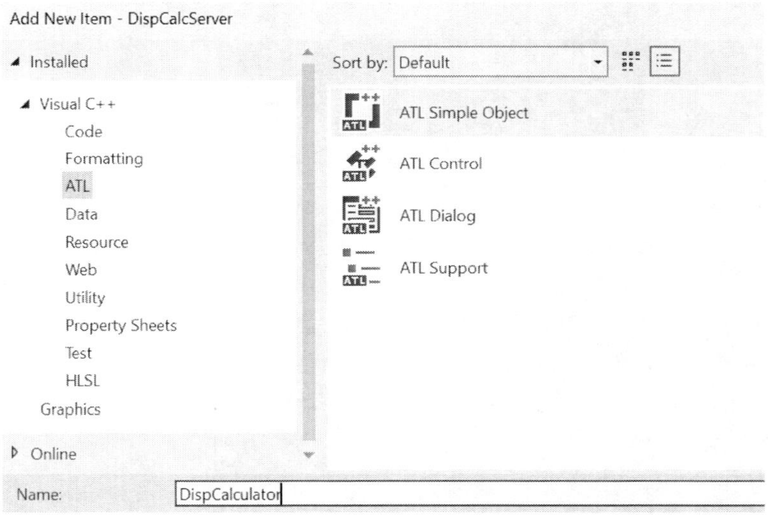

As with the creation of the ATL Server project, we now get a dialog for specifying the creation details of the COM object.

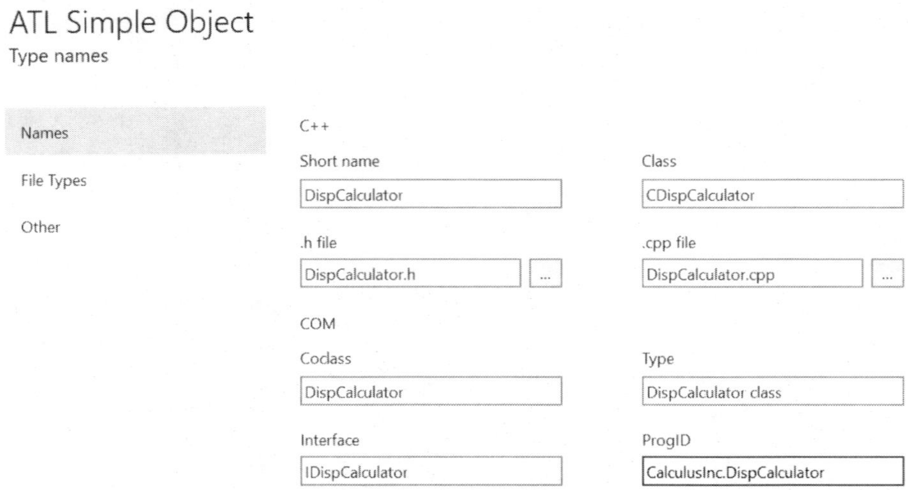

Contrary to the previous Calculator project, a dedicated interface is created for the version we're building in ATL. If you remember from the IDispatch chapter, All COM objects implement a single interface that derives from IDispatch. This is also why the interface is named specifically for the COM object we're implementing. There really is a 1 to 1 relationship between the dispatching interface and the object that implements that interface. For the ProgID we omit the version number. When the project is created, it will become obvious why. The file types section can remain default because it only has relevance to shell extension projects. The 'Other' section is where we can specify the requirements we have for our project.

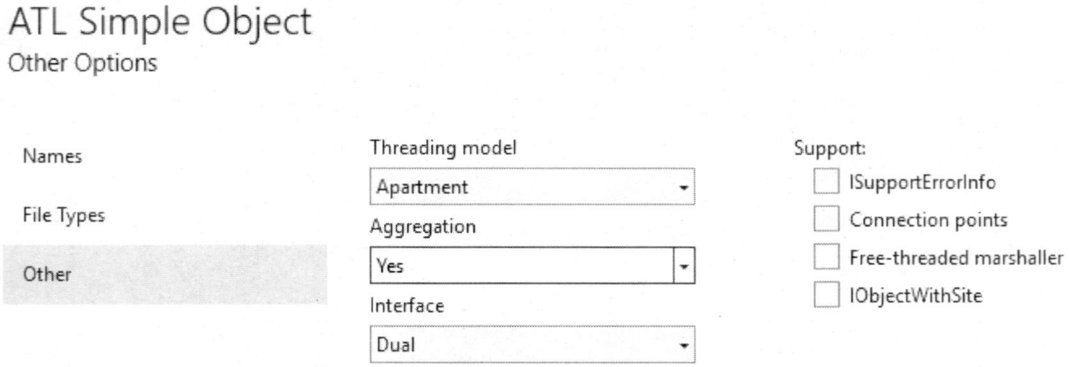

We'll ignore the support options for now. As you can see, even without those extra support options, the functionality we can pick and choose is phenomenal. Firstly, every possible apartment selection is available.

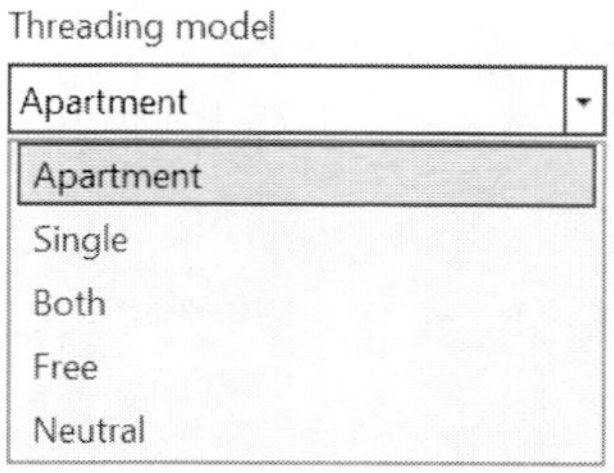

Based on the selection we make here, the C++ classes that define the COM object will inherit from base classes that implement the specified behavior, without having to even think about reference counting and thread safety. Out of the box, we also get aggregation for free if we want it. You could also choose not to allow aggregation or instead only allow aggregation. And finally, out of the box the COM server will support both the normal IUnknown based objects as well as the IDispatch based objects. For the calculator we choose ‘Both’ for the apartment model, aggregation support, and Dual interfacing. After creating the new object, the IDL for the server is updated.

```
[
	object,
	uuid(4ff14d8f-4d38-40d5-af67-e09b7a35bce5),
	dual,
	nonextensible,
	pointer_default(unique)
]
interface IDispCalculator : IDispatch
{
};

[
	uuid(2b97fbfc-c11d-46ed-89ca-1f2942b7854d),
	version(1.0),
]
library DispCalcServerLib
{
	importlib("stdole2.tlb");
	[
		uuid(6bd32af8-dd7d-4b68-8691-011a6704d9ec)
	]
	coclass DispCalculator
	{
		[default] interface IDispCalculator;
	};
};
import "shobjidl.idl";
```

Everything in the IDL so far has been covered before. The only new thing is the `"shobjidl.idl"` file which contains a lot of interfaces that are used with Shell Extensions. One thing that will become important later is how ATL projects deal with

IDL code. A lot can be learned from looking at the project settings that were configured by the project wizard.

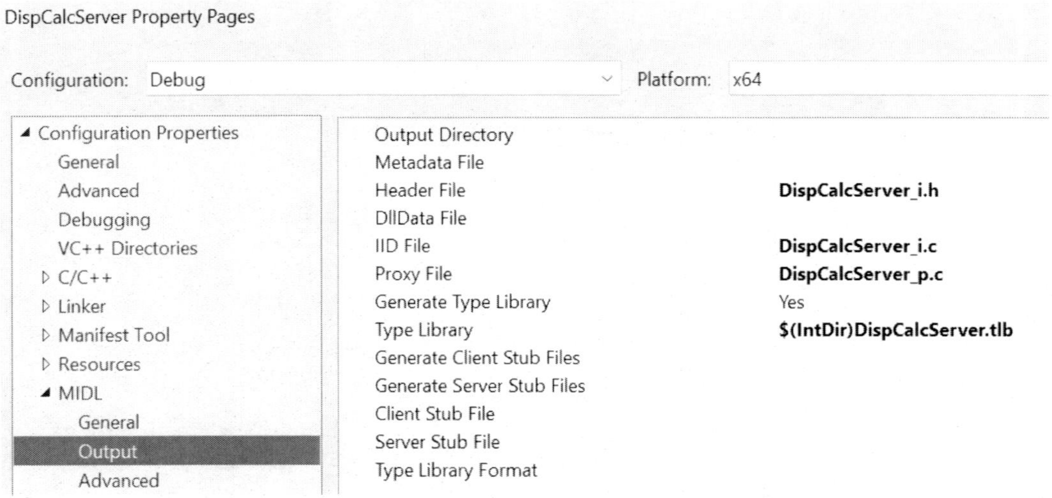

Unlike the project settings we had in the original Calculator project, here, the names of the output files are hardcoded. Not just the format of the names, but the names themselves are fixed. If we'd add multiple IDL files, the compilation project would just overwrite the output files with each extra IDL file that was compiled. As you can see, ATL projects are not meant to work with multiple IDL files. This is also why the ATL Simple Object wizard puts all new objects and interfaces in the same IDL file.

At this point, we have a server that is completely boilerplate, hosting a COM object that has no other interfaces than its default one, with no members. While ATL provides wizards to deal with many things, these wizards are not always reliable or working perfectly. In some cases, you will have to manually update the code. In order to make sense of any ATL project, let's take a look at some of the generated code.

Base classes

The declaration of the Calculator object has several base classes.

```
// DispCalculator.h : Declaration of the CDispCalculator
class ATL_NO_VTABLE CDispCalculator :
      public CComObjectRootEx<CComSingleThreadModel>,
      public CComCoClass<CDispCalculator, &CLSID_DispCalculator>,
      public IDispatchImpl<IDispCalculator,
                              &IID_IDispCalculator,
                              &LIBID_DispCalcServerLib,
                              /*wMajor =*/ 1, /*wMinor =*/ 0>
{
};
```

The behavior and traits of the COM object are determined by the base classes from which it inherits. CComObjectRootEx<CComMultiThreadModel> is the base class which implements reference counting and locking behavior that is appropriate for the COM object, based on the threading model that was specified. ATL has a philosophy of being 'just safe enough to fit the requiremenots'. In other words, if the COM object knows it will only be accessed in an STA, it will optimize its implementation at compile time to be as efficient as possible within those constraints. In the first Calculator implementation that we made, we used functions that were thread safe because we had to foresee all options. However, the template mechanism makes it trivial to tailor the behavior to the requirements, and to do it at compile time. A good way to illustrate how this works is by looking at how CComObjectRootEx is implemented (code trimmed to the essentials)

```
//atlcom.h
template <class ThreadModel>
class CComObjectRootEx :
	public CComObjectRootBase
{
public:
	typedef ThreadModel _ThreadModel;

	ULONG InternalAddRef()
	{
		ATLASSUME(m_dwRef != -1L);
		return _ThreadModel::Increment(&m_dwRef);
	}
};
```

Reference counting is 1 of the aspects that depend on the threading model. CComObjectRootEx implements the internal AddRef method by delegating the call to the threading model type which implements it as a static method. The STA model implements the counting using a simple ++ operation

```
//atlcom.h
class CComSingleThreadModel
{
public:
	static ULONG WINAPI Increment(_Inout_ LPLONG p) throw()
	{
		return ++(*p);
	}
};
```

Instead of using threadsafe interlocked functions like the MTA model.

```
//atlcom.h
class CComMultiThreadModel
```

```
{
public:
	static ULONG WINAPI Increment(_Inout_ LPLONG p) throw()
	{
		return ::InterlockedIncrement(p);
	}
};
```

In a similar vein, these models implement calls to critical sections for protecting code against race conditions. Only in the case of the STA model, these calls delegate to fake critical section classes whose methods are empty placeholders that don't do anything.

```
//atlbase.h
class CComMultiThreadModelNoCS
{
public:
	typedef CComFakeCriticalSection AutoCriticalSection;
};


class CComFakeCriticalSection
{
public:
	HRESULT Lock() throw()
	{
		return S_OK;
	}
	HRESULT Unlock() throw()
	{
		return S_OK;
	}
	HRESULT Init() throw()
	{
		return S_OK;
	}
	HRESULT Term() throw()
	{
		return S_OK;
	}
};
```

By employing mechanisms like that, a good amount of boilerplate can be implemented with a single base class, with behavior depending on the template arguments that can be specified as needed. `CComCoClass<CDispCalculator, &CLSID_DispCalculator>` is the next base class for consideration. It's also another place where the CRTP technique is used to let base classes delegate calls back to the derived class without the need to going through the vtable. CComCoClass is where the Class Factory is implemented, and creation is handled.

```
//atlcom.h
template <class T, const CLSID* pclsid = &CLSID_NULL>
class CComCoClass
{
public:
    DECLARE_CLASSFACTORY()
    DECLARE_AGGREGATABLE(T)
    typedef T _CoClass;
    //snip…
};
```

The DECLARE_AGGREGATABLE(T) macro expands to a type definition for a creator class that implements an object creation that supports aggregation.

```
//atlcom.h
#define DECLARE_AGGREGATABLE(x) public:\
Typedef ATL::CComCreator2<
  ATL::CComCreator<ATL::CComObject<x> >,
  ATL::CComCreator<ATL::CComAggObject<x>>> _CreatorClass;
```

The end result is that by default, all COM objects support aggregation in the ATL, but that doesn't mean that this is mandatory. If you selected the option for not supporting aggregation for example, the following line will be added to your class (or you can simply add it manually if you decide you don't want to support aggregation after all):

```
class ATL_NO_VTABLE CDispCalculator :
      public CComObjectRootEx<CComSingleThreadModel>,
      public CComCoClass<CDispCalculator, &CLSID_DispCalculator>,
      public IDispatchImpl<IDispCalculator,
                           &IID_IDispCalculator,
                           &LIBID_DispCalcServerLib,
                           /*wMajor =*/ 1, /*wMinor =*/ 0>
{
    // snip
    DECLARE_NOT_AGGREGATABLE(CAdvCalculator)
};
```

That macro expands to

```
//atlcom.h
#define DECLARE_NOT_AGGREGATABLE(x) public:\
typedef ATL::CComCreator2<
  ATL::CComCreator< ATL::CComObject< x > >,
  ATL::CComFailCreator<CLASS_E_NOAGGREGATION> > _CreatorClass;
```

At the level of the derived class, this typedef overrides the one in the base class. When CComCoClass creates the instance it uses the following method:

```
//atlcom.h
template <class Q>
static HRESULT CreateInstance(_COM_Outptr_ Q** pp)
{
  return T::_CreatorClass::CreateInstance(
                 NULL, __uuidof(Q), (void**) pp);
}
```

The Q template type is the type of the requested interface pointer. If our COM class used the `DECLARE_NOT_AGGREGATABLE(x)` macro to override the `_CreatorClass` type definition, `T::_CreatorClass` resolves to the non-aggregating typedef. If no macro is defined in the derived class, `T::_CreatorClass` resolves to the type definition in CComCoClass. By using techniques like this, CComCoClass can support all scenarios without needing different base classes. This concludes the list of boilerplate base classes. All next derivations concern the interfaces that are implemented.

Interfaces

On an object that implements a dual interface, interfaces are derived via `IDispatchImpl`. This base takes the interface type as a template parameter, together with the IID and the LIBID.

```
//atlcom.h
template <class T,
          const IID* piid = &__uuidof(T),
          const GUID* plibid = &CAtlModule::m_libid,
          WORD wMajor = 1,
          WORD wMinor = 0,
          class tihclass = CComTypeInfoHolder>
class ATL_NO_VTABLE IDispatchImpl :
    public T
{
public:
    typedef tihclass _tihclass;
    // Idispatch implementation
};
```

When `IDispatchImpl` is made concrete by the compiler, that specialization derives directly from the specified interface type so from that point of view, it's as if the class derives directly from that interface. Like the name suggests, `IDispatchImpl` implements the 4 methods of IDispatch in a very similar way like we covered earlier, except each method forwards the call to `CComTypeInfoHolder` instead of `ITypeInfo`. In the IDispatch explanation, we forwarded the calls to a cached `ITypeInfo` object. `CComTypeInfoHolder` is a class which performs that caching and performs correct loading of the type library based on locale ID and other pertinent information.

So far we've covered the locking, reference counting and object creation. That leaves just one part that has not been covered yet: querying for interfaces. Regardless of whether an object is a dual or single interface, it must support querying interfaces because at minimum, It needs to be able to satisfy a query of IUnknown. This is implemented via an interface map.

```
BEGIN_COM_MAP(CDispCalculator)
      COM_INTERFACE_ENTRY(IDispCalculator)
      COM_INTERFACE_ENTRY(IDispatch)
END_COM_MAP()
```

This set of macros implements the QueryInterface method for the `CDispCalculator` class. The entire source code of these macros is too extensive to post here but essentially, `BEGIN_COM_MAP` expands to a full QueryInterface implementation. This implementation is not a big if / else construction like our handcoded version but uses a map to translate IIDs to interface pointers. The `COM_INTERFACE_ENTRY` macros each expand into an entry in that map. There will be as many entries as there are interfaces for which the object can be queried. The `END_COM_MAP` macro closes the map.

There is also a `COM_INTERFACE_ENTRY2` macro which you might need. We've covered the fact that a COM object can only expose 1 IDispatch interface. In some cases, an object might need to implement multiple interfaces that derive from IDispatch. When we first tried to cast a COM object to an IUnknown*, we had the problem that this cast is ambiguous when multiple interfaces in the hierarchy derive from IUnknown*. The cast would be ambiguous. Trying to cast to IDispatch* when multiple interfaces derive from it, causes the same ambiguity. To work around that, `COM_INTERFACE_ENTRY2` can be used to indicate which interface is the one that gets exposed as IDispatch. To call this macro a kludge would be too strong an expression, but it is a sign that you're trying to do something that doesn't necessarily make a ton of sense. Any object that uses this macro will only expose some of its functionality. That would beg the question: why are those 2 interfaces on that object? It negates the reason why those interfaces support dispatching.

Still, there are cases where an object is required to support multiple interfaces that derive from IDispatch. In that scenario, you could use `COM_INTERFACE_ENTRY2` just to make everything compile even though semantically it doesn't make sense.

Adding methods and properties

With the boilerplate covered and a working server and COM object, we can finally flesh out the interface we want to support. We can do this manually, just like we did originally:

- Modify the IDL file to add methods and properties
- Compile the IDL
- Add the methods to the DispCalculator class in the header file
- Implement those methods in the DispCalculator cpp file

But Visual Studio can take that work out of our hands if we want. In an ATL project, a lot of help is provided through the class view where we see all major components. Using the class view and the object browser window, it's very easy to dive into the individual components.

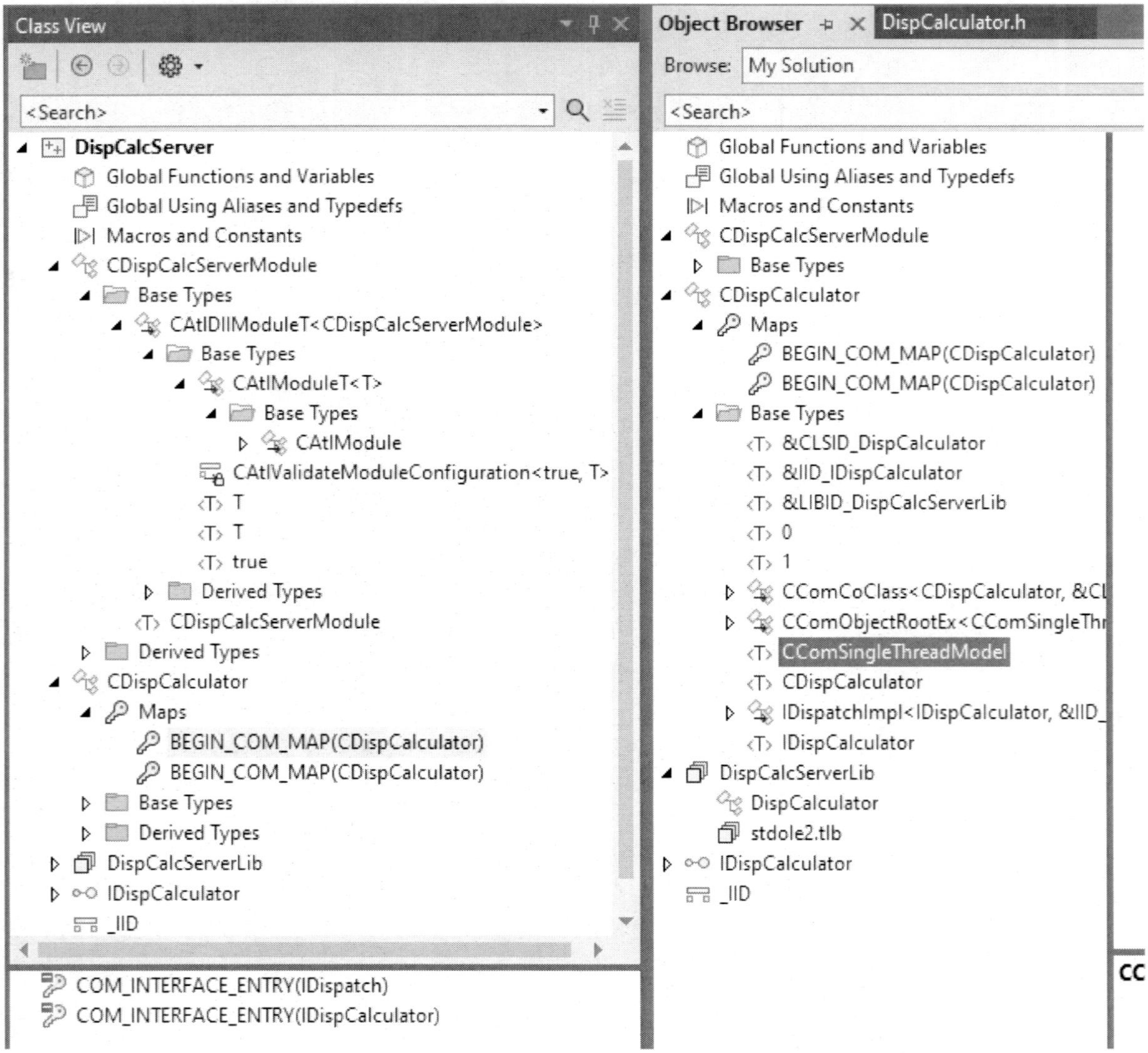

The 2 things that immediately become obvious are the COM object and the server module. Class View also shows the library definition that gives an overview of which

COM objects are going to be in the type library as well as which other type libraries it imports. Any interfaces are also going to be listed. Once you start expanding entries, you can fully explore the entire class hierarchy, relationships, and really the entire design. When used together with the Object Browser, you can take a complex ATL project and really get a good idea about how it all ties together without having to dive into thousands or lines of code.

The Class View window is also where we can ask Visual Studio to help us implement methods and properties. To do this, we right-click the interface and select 'Add Method'

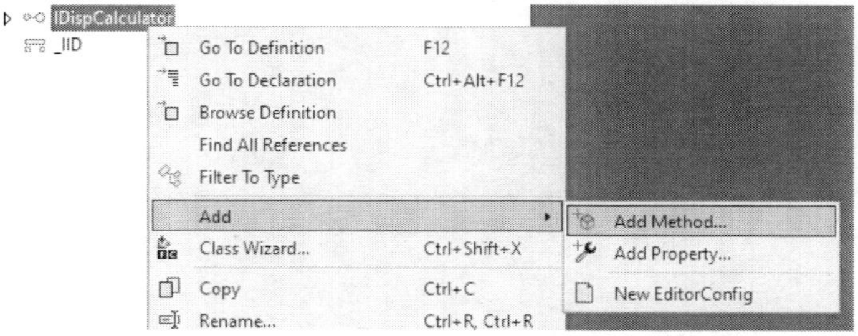

This brings up a dialog where we can define the new method.

Most of the functionality in this dialog is self-evident. The suggested ID is the DISPID of the new method call. call_as gives the option of redirecting a call to a different call if the runtime determines that it is a remote call to a different process. After we click 'OK', Visual Studio adds the method to the IDL file

```
interface IDispCalculator : IDispatch
{
	[id(1)] HRESULT Add(
				[in] DOUBLE Arg1,
				[in] DOUBLE Arg2,
				[out] DOUBLE* Result);
};
```

It also adds the following code to the C++ files

```
//DispCalculator.h
STDMETHOD(Add)(DOUBLE Arg1, DOUBLE Arg2, DOUBLE* Result);

// DispCalculator.cpp
STDMETHODIMP CDispCalculator::Add(DOUBLE Arg1, DOUBLE Arg2, DOUBLE* Result)
{
    // TODO: Add your implementation code here

    return S_OK;
}
```

We add the Subtract method in the same way. Adding the LastResult property is slightly different:

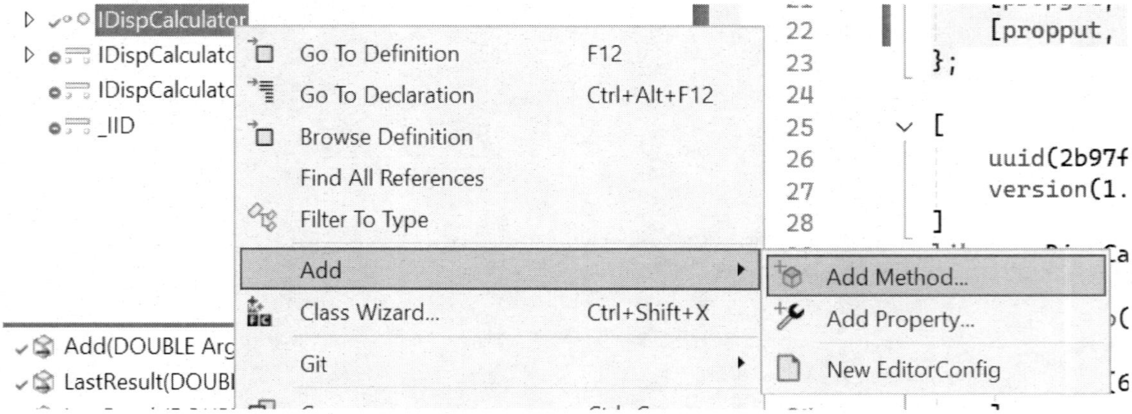

As before, the wizard will update the IDL file

```
interface IDispCalculator : IDispatch
{
      [id(1)] HRESULT Add(
                          [in] DOUBLE Arg1,
                          [in] DOUBLE Arg2,[out] DOUBLE* Result);
      [id(2)] HRESULT Subtract(
                          [in] DOUBLE Arg1,
                          [in] DOUBLE Arg2,
                          [out] DOUBLE* Result);
      [propget, id(3)] HRESULT LastResult([out, retval] DOUBLE* pVal);
      [propput, id(3)] HRESULT LastResult([in] DOUBLE newVal);
};
```

And generate the C++ code:

```
// DispCalculator.h : Declaration of the CDispCalculator
STDMETHOD(get_LastResult)(DOUBLE* pVal);
STDMETHOD(put_LastResult)(DOUBLE newVal);

// DispCalculator.cpp : Implementation of CDispCalculator
STDMETHODIMP CDispCalculator::get_LastResult(DOUBLE* pVal)
{
    // TODO: Add your implementation code here
```

```
    return S_OK;
}

STDMETHODIMP CDispCalculator::put_LastResult(DOUBLE newVal)
{
    // TODO: Add your implementation code here

    return S_OK;
}
```

At this point, you may also notice that the IDispCalculator is shown 4 times in class view.

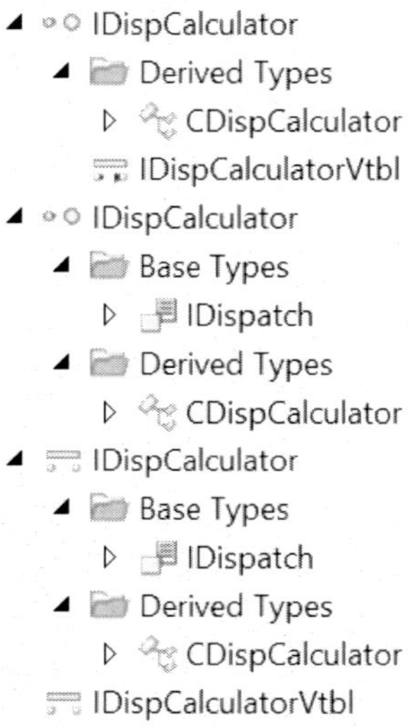

The reason is that the Class View picks up information from the IDL and from the generated interop or header files. The first item with the 2 connected circles icon represents the C style vtable definition in the header file that is the result of IDL compilation.

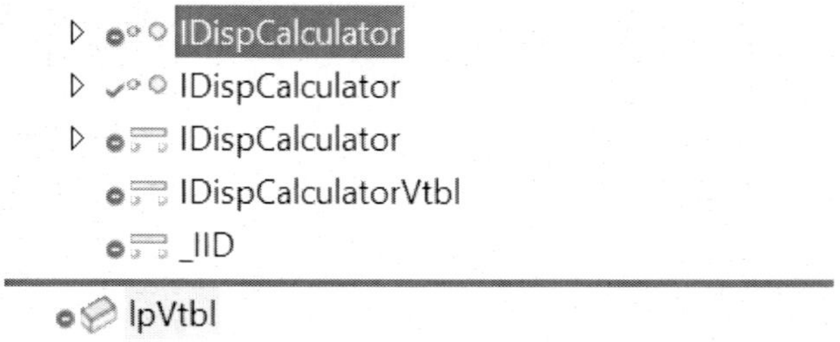

The second entry represents the definition in the IDL file itself. The 'Add Method' and 'Add Property' wizard is available from the context menu on each item.

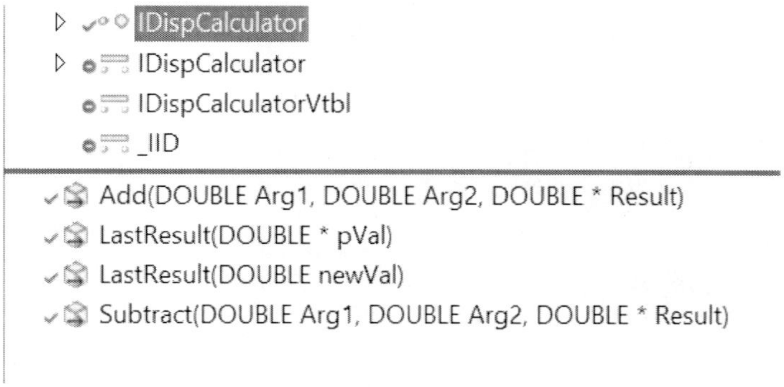

The 3d item represents the C++ declaration of the interface. From this item, the context menu allows you to add method and variables to that declaration instead of to the IDL file. However, this would be pointless because this code is re-generated each time you compile the IDL file so anything you add here would be wiped out. The reason the Class View still allows this is simply that to the Class View, this is a C++ class like any other. The fact that this is a generated file doesn't factor into it. The same applies to the 4th item which represents the full vtable of the interface. It shows the full list of methods that's available.

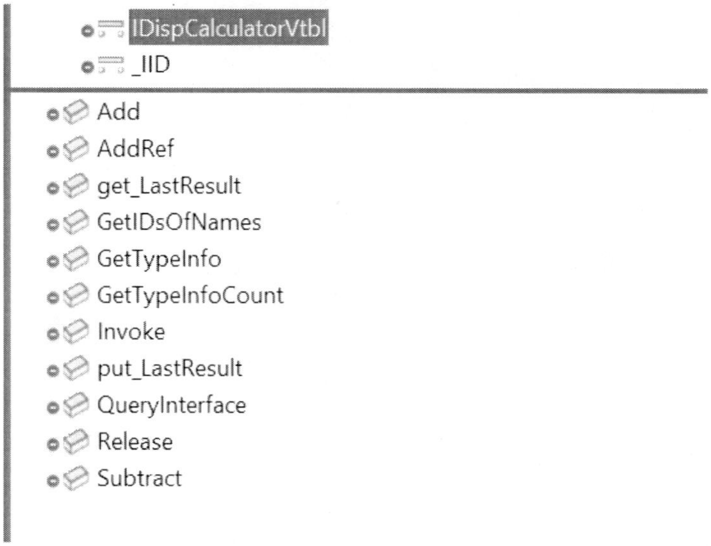

You can verify this by right clicking each of these items and selecting 'Go to definition' which will take you to the specific file and location where that data is pulled from. We need just 1 more step before we can implement everything. Since the COM object allows for getting and (re)setting the last result of an operation, our object needs a private instance variable. We can add that via the Class View as well.

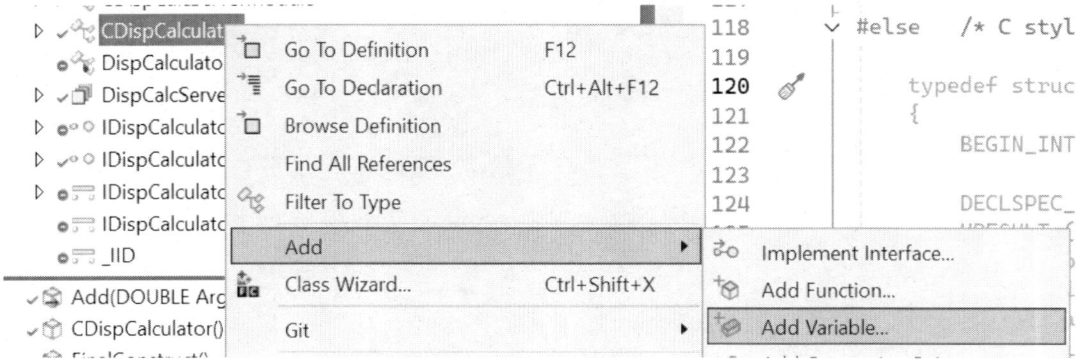

Note that it doesn't matter where we perform this action in the Class View. In the previous screenshot we did this from the main CDispCalculator entry, but it is just a valid to navigate via the interface and then the class which inherits from that interface.

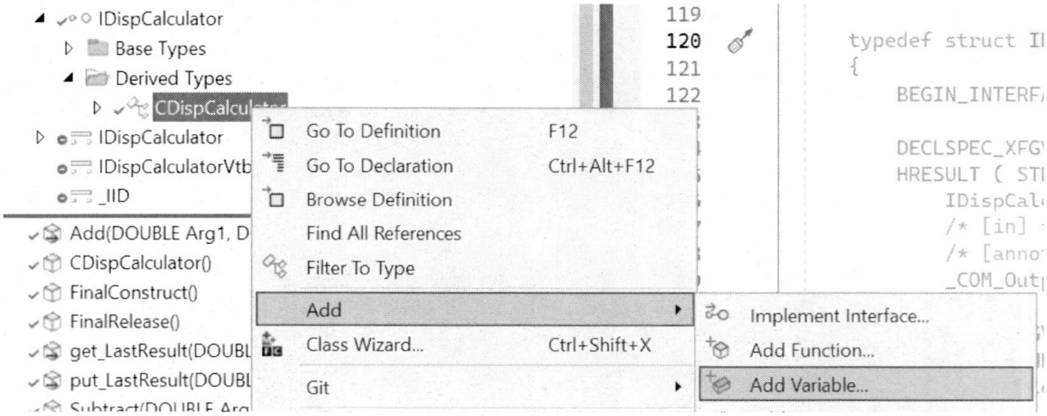

Either way a wizard pops up to implement that variable

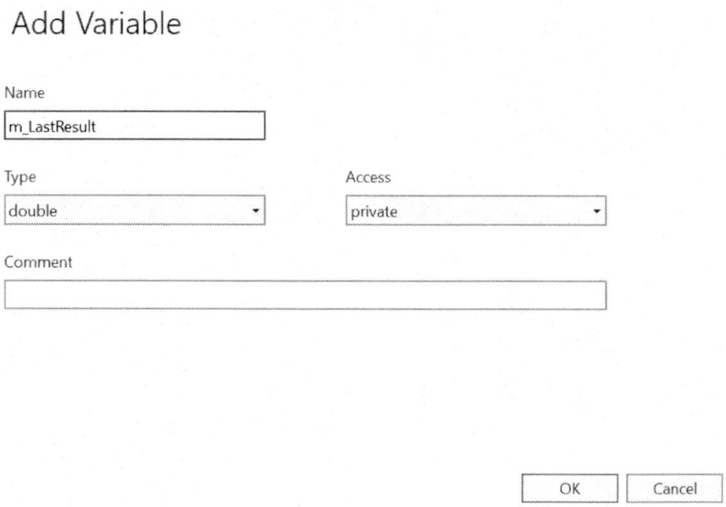

After which it is added to the class declaration

```
public:
    STDMETHOD(Add)(DOUBLE Arg1, DOUBLE Arg2, DOUBLE* Result);
    STDMETHOD(Subtract)(DOUBLE Arg1, DOUBLE Arg2, DOUBLE* Result);
    STDMETHOD(get_LastResult)(DOUBLE* pVal);
    STDMETHOD(put_LastResult)(DOUBLE newVal);
private:
    double m_LastResult;
```

With these things in place, we can flesh out the code that was generated for us.

```
STDMETHODIMP CDispCalculator::Add(DOUBLE Arg1, DOUBLE Arg2, DOUBLE* Result)
{
    if (!(std::isfinite(Arg1) && std::isfinite(Arg2)))
        return E_INVALIDARG;

    if (Result == NULL)
        return E_POINTER;

    *Result = Arg1 + Arg2;
    m_LastResult = *Result;
    return S_OK;
}

STDMETHODIMP CDispCalculator::Subtract(DOUBLE Arg1, DOUBLE Arg2, DOUBLE*
Result)
{
    if (!(std::isfinite(Arg1) && std::isfinite(Arg2)))
        return E_INVALIDARG;

    if (Result == NULL)
        return E_POINTER;

    *Result = Arg1 - Arg2;
    m_LastResult = *Result;
    return S_OK;
}

STDMETHODIMP CDispCalculator::get_LastResult(DOUBLE* pVal)
{
    if (pVal == NULL)
        return E_POINTER;

    *pVal = m_LastResult;
    return S_OK;
}

STDMETHODIMP CDispCalculator::put_LastResult(DOUBLE newVal)
{
    m_LastResult = newVal;
    return S_OK;
```

```
}
```

Server Registration

As we covered in the 'Server Objects' section, ATL projects have auto-generated registration code that defers to the CAtlModule for registration. These registration calls create the necessary information in the registry. For the objects we add to the project, this information is stored in the auto-generated *.rgs files. If we look at the DispCalculator.rgs file, this is the information that was generated.

```
HKCR
{
	DispCalc.Calculator.1 = s 'DispCalculator class'
	{
		CLSID = s '{6bd32af8-dd7d-4b68-8691-011a6704d9ec}'
	}
	DispCalc.Calculator = s 'DispCalculator class'
	{
		CurVer = s 'DispCalc.Calculator.1'
	}
	NoRemove CLSID
	{
		ForceRemove {6bd32af8-dd7d-4b68-8691-011a6704d9ec} = s
'DispCalculator class'
		{
			ProgID = s 'DispCalc.Calculator.1'
			VersionIndependentProgID = s 'DispCalc.Calculator'
			ForceRemove Programmable
			InprocServer32 = s '%MODULE%'
			{
				val ThreadingModel = s 'Apartment'
			}
			TypeLib = s '{2b97fbfc-c11d-46ed-89ca-1f2942b7854d}'
			Version = s '1.0'
		}
	}
}
```

Everything we see here is what we expect after we talked about Server registration. If we felt the need to add custom information that is pertinent to our project, we could add it here. If the project is an out-of-process server, the contents of the rgs file would be generated accordingly.

However, for Service applications, things don't quite work out that well. Let's look at the registration script that is generated when we generate a boilerplate ATL Service application.

```
HKCR
{
	Test.ServiceObject.1 = s 'ServiceObject class'
```

```
        {
                CLSID = s '{a0f23669-2ffc-427c-a566-d943fc6fc529}'
        }
        Test.ServiceObject = s 'ServiceObject class'
        {
                CurVer = s 'Test.ServiceObject.1'
        }
        NoRemove CLSID
        {
                ForceRemove {a0f23669-2ffc-427c-a566-d943fc6fc529} = s
'ServiceObject class'
                {
                        ProgID = s 'Test.ServiceObject.1'
                        VersionIndependentProgID = s 'Test.ServiceObject'
                        ForceRemove Programmable
                        LocalServer32 = s '%MODULE%'
                        {
                                val ServerExecutable = s '%MODULE_RAW%'
                        }
                        TypeLib = s '{a3e490a8-b6b8-44ea-9819-f4dd0c0d3fd0}'
                        Version = s '1.0'
                }
        }
}
```

You'll immediately notice 2 things:

- There is a LocalServer32 entry where you wouldn't expect one.
- There is no application ID with accompanying LocalService entry where you would expect one.

Things are clearly not all as they should be. When ATLService projects were added to Visual Studio, the wizards for regular out-of-process servers were re-used. This makes sense because they are similar. However, the above information is clearly not going to work. An APPID entry is vital to the service application but missing.

While I am not privy to the design decisions that led to this decision, there are a couple of reasons why the ATL team decided against having the wizard create an APPID section. APPID entries often contain machine specific security settings that need to be configured with knowledge of the local security. It would be difficult to make safe predictions for the initial configuration because it could be different for 2 similar machines, depending on how security was implemented.

Additionally, if security was manually configured as is expected for services, re-registration would stomp all over those settings. And then there is a situation that a developer would probably have different settings for their machine that are not necessarily valid on a client's machine.

That said, we may wonder why at the very least, the wizard doesn't create the key for an APPID section and puts the LocalService value inside. That way, at least there would be a registration that can be further fleshed out manually via DCOMCnfg. The answer is probably that this would have required updating the wizard and no one thought it was worth the effort. Services are typically installed via an MSI file or via a setup program, and it would easily create the necessary entries for COM registration as well as registering the executable with the Windows Service Manager. And in that case, the spurious LocalServer32 entry would be harmless dead weight because if a LocalService registration exists, the LocalServer32 entry is ignored anyway.

Certainly, it is easy enough to update the registration script for our purposes if we want to. We just add the relevant APPID information and remove the LocalServer32 info.

```
HKCR
{
	Test.ServiceObject.1 = s 'ServiceObject class'
	{
		CLSID = s '{a0f23669-2ffc-427c-a566-d943fc6fc529}'
	}
	Test.ServiceObject = s 'ServiceObject class'
	{
		CurVer = s 'Test.ServiceObject.1'
	}
	NoRemove CLSID
	{
		ForceRemove {a0f23669-2ffc-427c-a566-d943fc6fc529} = s
'ServiceObject class'
		{
			val AppID = s {6D815006-F399-4522-8ACA-57AD90D3143C}
			ProgID = s 'Test.ServiceObject.1'
			VersionIndependentProgID = s 'Test.ServiceObject'
			TypeLib = s '{a3e490a8-b6b8-44ea-9819-f4dd0c0d3fd0}'
			Version = s '1.0'
		}
	}
	NoRemove APPID
	{
		ForceRemove {6D815006-F399-4522-8ACA-57AD90D3143C} = s
'ServiceObject class'
		{
			val LocalService = s 'TestService'
		}
	}
}
```

Note that while this creates the appropriate COM entries, the service itself needs to be manually registered with the Windows Service Control Manager. The ATL certainly makes it possible to override the registration code and perform these actions manually and use the appropriate APIs to interact with the registration manager, such as OpenSCManager and CreateService. However, since this can be tedious and error prone and sidestep well-known and reliable tools such as sc.exe, this is probably never a worthwhile idea.

Registration and the Type Library

Because the new object supports dual interfacing which we intend to use with PowerShell, Type Libraries are very important. Having them registered properly is of critical importance to the overall usage of the server.

To ensure that these servers cannot accidentally be separated from their type libraries or registered only incompletely, an interesting design choice was made for ATL. When it comes to registration, we need to take a quick look at the snippet of boilerplate we glanced over when talking about the server. If we leave the comments in place this time, we see this:

```
// DllRegisterServer - Adds entries to the system registry.
_Use_decl_annotations_
STDAPI DllRegisterServer(void)
{
       // registers object, typelib and all interfaces in typelib
       HRESULT hr = _AtlModule.DllRegisterServer();
#ifdef _MERGE_PROXYSTUB
       if (FAILED(hr))
              return hr;
       hr = PrxDllRegisterServer();
#endif
       return hr;
}
```

The interesting thing here is the comment "registers object, typelib and all interfaces in typelib" in the DllRegisterServer function. Unlike our first, hand crafted COM server project, ATL projects register the server itself as a type library. In other words, the DLL file contains both the server and the type library.

There are several reasons why this is a good idea. First, it's convenient because there is only one file, and when you register your server with regsvr32, the type library is automatically registered. Remember that there is no separate readily available tool to register type libraries. This is probably an important reason why. After all, most classical COM servers are probably built with ATL, and ATL embeds the type library into the server module. While a separate registration tool like RegTlb can be useful, raw COM development is not really a thing in many real-world scenarios because ATL removes it from consideration.

The process of embedding the TLB works via a configuration in the project's resource.rc file. If you right-click the resource file in resource view, and select 'Resource includes', a dialog will pop up that has a compile time directive "TYPELIB ATLTest.tlb"

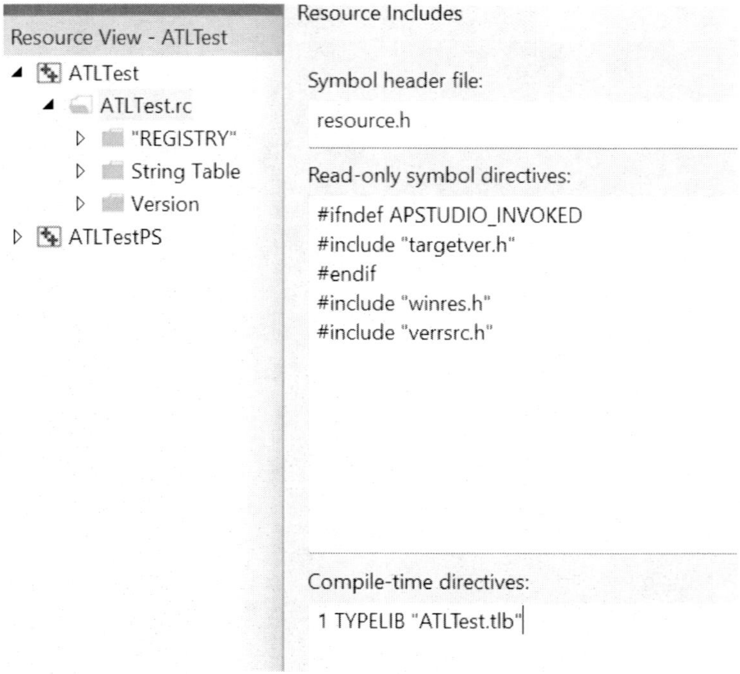

This directive will instruct the resource compiler to embed the specified type library into the module. If we look at the DllRegisterServer function we see it immediately delegates the call to the global server module.

```
STDAPI DllRegisterServer(void)
{
	HRESULT hr = _AtlModule.DllRegisterServer();
	return hr;
}
```

The ATL module has a method that has a boolean parameter that gives you the option of enabling or disabling the self-registration of the type library.

```
	//atlbase.h
	HRESULT DllRegisterServer(
		_In_ BOOL bRegTypeLib = TRUE) throw()
```

By default, your project will perform this registration but you can turn it off simply by putting in 'FALSE' as a parameter in the call to `_AtlModule.DllRegisterServer()`. If we right-click that method call and select 'go to definition' then we can follow that rabbit hole all the way down to the `AtlRegisterTypeLib` method.

```
//atlbase.h
ATLINLINE ATLAPIINL AtlRegisterTypeLib(
	_In_ HINSTANCE hInstTypeLib,
	_In_opt_z_ LPCOLESTR lpszIndex)
{
	CComBSTR bstrPath;
	CComPtr<ITypeLib> pTypeLib;
	HRESULT hr = AtlLoadTypeLib(
				hInstTypeLib, lpszIndex, &bstrPath, &pTypeLib);
	PFNREGISTERTYPELIB pfnRegisterTypeLib = NULL;
	// snip…

	hr = pfnRegisterTypeLib(pTypeLib, bstrPath, szDir);
	return hr;
}
```

First, the type library information is loaded from file into memory by calling AtlLoadTypeLib which uses the module HINSTANCE (a handle that identifies an executable module in memory such as a DLL or EXE) to identify the file.

```
//atlbase.h
ATLINLINE ATLAPI AtlLoadTypeLib(
	_In_ HINSTANCE hInstTypeLib,
	_In_opt_z_ LPCOLESTR lpszIndex,
	_Outptr_result_z_ BSTR* pbstrPath,
	_Outptr_ ITypeLib** ppTypeLib)
{
	// snip…
	GetModuleFileName(hInstTypeLib, szModule, MAX_PATH);

	// snip…
	HRESULT hr = LoadTypeLib(lpszModule, ppTypeLib);
	if (FAILED(hr)){
		// typelib not in module, try <module>.tlb
		const TCHAR szExt[] = _T(".tlb");
	// snip…
		hr = LoadTypeLib(lpszModule, ppTypeLib);
	}
	if (SUCCEEDED(hr)){
		*pbstrPath = ::SysAllocString(lpszModule);

	}
	return hr;
}
```

You can see that it retrieves the path of the module that is associated with the HINSTANCE and tries to load the TLB information from there. If that fails, it assumes that there is a TLB file next to the server module, with the same name and only a different extension. If either is true, the TLB information is returned to the caller, together with the actual path where it was found.

This information is then supplied to the `pfnRegisterTypeLib` registration function which is a function pointer to a function that either registers the type information per user or per machine, depending on how the installation was invoked.

Using the DispCalculator

Having built and registered the DispCalcServer, using it is as simple as opening a PowerShell window and simply telling PowerShell to create an instance of the object.

```
$comObject = New-Object -ComObject DispCalc.Calculator.1

[double] $arg1 = 1.0
[double] $arg2 = 1.0
[double] $result = 0
$comObject.Add($arg1, $arg2, [ref] $result)

"$arg1 + $arg2 = $result"
```

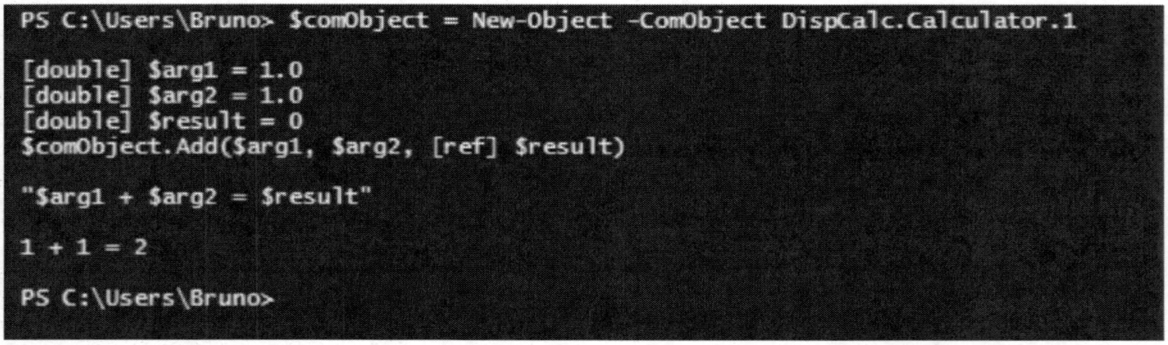

Interfaces and marshaling

At the beginning of this chapter, we used the 'Merge Proxy / Stub' option to avoid creating a separate project. And indeed, no separate project was created so we moved on with the explanation. We've successfully used the object, and you would almost believe that the picture is complete. However, there is another non-intuitive thing we still need to discuss. We selected the 'Merge proxy/stub' checkbox. It would seem sensible that the proxy code is merged into our project. And indeed, only 1 project is created, not 2. And the auto generated code seems to combine them. Let's take the DllRegisterServer exported function as an example here.

```
// DispCalcServer.cpp
```

```
STDAPI DllRegisterServer(void)
{
    HRESULT hr = _AtlModule.DllRegisterServer();
#ifdef _MERGE_PROXYSTUB
    if (FAILED(hr))
        return hr;
    hr = PrxDllRegisterServer();
#endif
    return hr;
}
```

It calls the DllRegisterServer functions of both the server and the proxy. This immediately brings up an interesting question because we've worked with the MIDL generated proxy code earlier, which didn't contain a `PrxDllRegisterServer` function. Instead it contains a simple `DllRegisterServer function`. So why isn't the `DllRegisterServer` function in the proxy code clashing with the `DllRegisterServer` in `DispCalcServer.cpp`? To answer that question we need to look at the xdlldata.c file that was generated by the project wizard.

```
// xdlldata.c
#ifdef _MERGE_PROXYSTUB // merge proxy stub DLL

#define REGISTER_PROXY_DLL //DllRegisterServer, etc.

#define USE_STUBLESS_PROXY      //defined only with MIDL switch /Oicf

#pragma comment(lib, "rpcns4.lib")
#pragma comment(lib, "rpcrt4.lib")

#define ENTRY_PREFIX      Prx

#include "dlldata.c"
#include "DispCalcServer_p.c"

#endif //_MERGE_PROXYSTUB
```

This file includes the dlldata.c and DispCalcServer_p.c files that contain the marshaling code that was generated by MIDL. If we did that without taking any special measures, there would indeed be name clashes. But this is where a bit of C style trickery comes to the rescue again, via the `ENTRY_PREFIX` macro which is defined before the dlldata.c file is included. If we dive into that file, we can follow the following trail of breadcrumbs:

```
//dlldata.c
DLLDATA_ROUTINES( aProxyFileList, GET_DLL_CLSID )
```

The `DLLDATA_ROUTINES` expands to

```
//rpcproxy.h
#define DLLDATA_ROUTINES(pProxyFileList,pClsID )    \
    \
    CLSID_PSFACTORYBUFFER \
    \
    CStdPSFactoryBuffer       gPFactory = {0,0,0,0};  \
    \
    DLLDATA_GETPROXYDLLINFO(pProxyFileList,pClsID) \
    \
    DLLGETCLASSOBJECTROUTINE(pProxyFileList,pClsID,&gPFactory)    \
    \
    DLLCANUNLOADNOW(&gPFactory)   \
    \
    CSTDSTUBBUFFERRELEASE(&gPFactory)    \
    \
    CSTDSTUBBUFFER2RELEASE(&gPFactory) \
    \
    DLLRPCDUMMYCALL    \
    \
    DLLREGISTRY_ROUTINES(pProxyFileList, pClsID) \
    \
```

If we then follow the DLLREGISTRY_ROUTINES macro for example, we find this.

```
//rpcproxy.h
#define DLLREGISTRY_ROUTINES(pProxyFileList,pClsID )
REGISTER_PROXY_DLL_ROUTINES(pProxyFileList,pClsID )
```

Which expands to a sizable section of code that contains the actual registration code. For our purpose we just look at the snippet that registers the proxy.

```
//rpcproxy.h
#define REGISTER_PROXY_DLL_ROUTINES(pProxyFileList, pClsID) \
    //snip
    /* DllRegisterServer registers the interfaces in the proxy DLL.*/ \
    HRESULT STDAPICALLTYPE DLLREGISTERSERVER_ENTRY() \
    { \
        return NdrDllRegisterProxy(hProxyDll, (const ProxyFileInfo
**)pProxyFileList, pClsID); \
    }  \
```

Finally, the DLLREGISTERSERVER_ENTRY macro expands to

```
//rpcproxy.h
#define __rpc_macro_expand2(a, b) a##b
#define __rpc_macro_expand(a, b) __rpc_macro_expand2(a,b)
#define DLLREGISTERSERVER_ENTRY __rpc_macro_expand(ENTRY_PREFIX,
DllRegisterServer)
```

The dlldata.c file that is generated by MIDL doesn't contain the various DLL entrypoints outright. It was designed to draw code from rpcproxy.h in such a way that other code files such as the generated code in the ATL project has the option of using macros to modify the MIDL code. By setting up this chain of macros with the `ENTRY_PREFIX` macro, the MIDL output can be merged without causing name clashes. In this case, they append the 'Prx' prefix to the DLL entry points, which allows ATL to use them as subroutines inside the general server entrypoints. This is also why you won't find MSDN documentation for e.g. `PrxDllRegisterServer`. It does not exist as such.

Now, this all seems sensible until you realize that at no point in the project is `_MERGE_PROXYSTUB` actually defined. In other words, there is code to ensure that the proxy / stub code is merged into the project, but it is purposely still excluded from the build. You would think that selecting the checkbox would take care of this, but all it does is ensure that the code to make this possible is generated. We still need to change a project setting to flip the switch. We can do this by adding a preprocessor macro that will enable the necessary code changes.

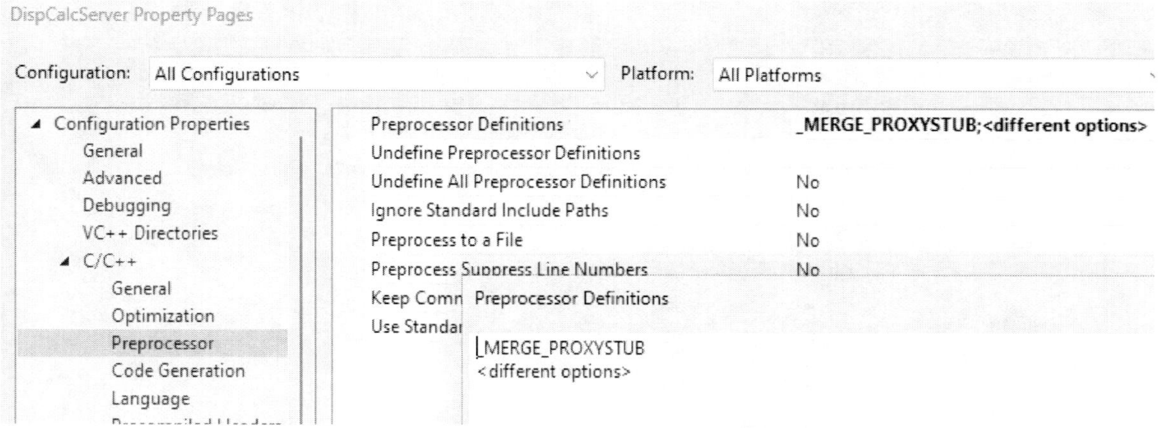

But there is a good reason why this is not the case by default. Between 70 and 80% of COM objects support IDispatch, which requires Type Library based marshaling. The marshaler for this is available on Windows by default because it only uses automation compatible types. If we enable the 'merge proxy / stub' checkbox, and our objects have a dual interface and are intended to be used via IDispatch, then there is no reason to build the marshaling code (dlldata.c, DispCalcServer_p.c) into the project. If we build the server without this switch, then it is immediately visible in the registration of the interfaces.

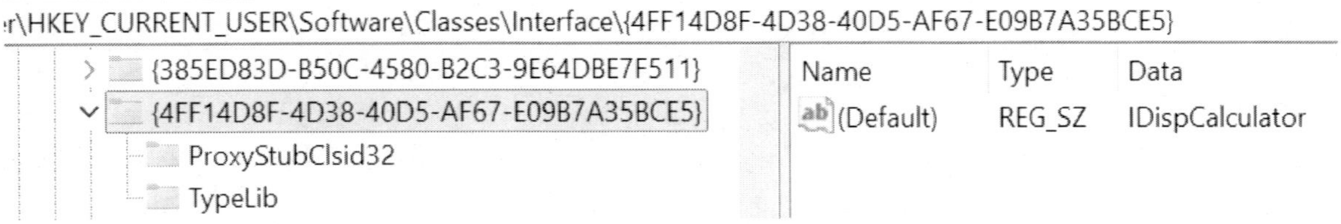

The ProxyStubClsid32 entry points to the CLSID of the universal marshaler in oleaut32.dll, not to the CLSID which we might have expected, based on the MIDL output. Not having the MIDL generated marshaling code baked in -can- be advantageous. The most immediate benefit is in registration. Trying to register a DLL with the per-user switch will fail if the MIDL generated code is linked into the DLL. To understand this, we need to look at the DllInstall entrypoint which will be used for per-user registration.

```
// DllInstall - Adds/Removes entries to the system registry per user per
machine.
STDAPI DllInstall(BOOL bInstall, _In_opt_  LPCWSTR pszCmdLine)
{
    HRESULT hr = E_FAIL;
    static const wchar_t szUserSwitch[] = L"user";

    if (pszCmdLine != nullptr)
    {
        if (_wcsnicmp(pszCmdLine, szUserSwitch, _countof(szUserSwitch)) == 0)
        {
            ATL::AtlSetPerUserRegistration(true);
        }
    }

    if (bInstall)
    {
        hr = DllRegisterServer();
        if (FAILED(hr))
        {
            DllUnregisterServer();
        }
    }
    else
    {
        hr = DllUnregisterServer();
    }
```

```
    return hr;
}
```

This function uses the optional commandline to scan for the 'user' command to determine whether the DllInstall function is called to perform a per-user registration. If that is true, the special function `AtlSetPerUserRegistration` is used to set a flag inside the ATL library that influences not only the DLL registration but also the type registration. Based on this flag, the ATL library does the same thing as our first Calculator server, which is to choose whether to register in HKLM or HKCU. After setting that flag, the registration is delegated to the `DllRegisterServer` function we covered previously.

Unfortunately, the `AtlSetPerUserRegistration` function only affects the server registration. As we showed earlier, the server DLL uses some macro magic to import the MIDL generated proxy registration code. And there is no support per-user registration in the proxy registration code. If we can accept dealing with the universal marshaler, avoiding custom proxy code means that per-user registration works as expected without having to open another bag of tricks. There is a downside of course. The universal marshaler only supports dispatch based marshaling. Which means our object won't work with early binding such as used by e.g. C++ clients. Even though our object theoretically is a dual interface object, the IUnknown based interface is effectively sheared off and it becomes an IDispatch-only object. If we flip the `_MERGE_PROXYSTUB` switch, our server can support both interfaces, but at the cost of not allowing per-user registration out of the box.

Note that this is also why the registration function calls the `_AtlModule.DllRegisterServer()` method first, and the `PrxDllRegisterServer` function second. By observing this order, the interface entries can be created first, pointing to the universal marshaler. If the proxy code was merged in, then that registration will overwrite those earlier values, and point the interface proxy values to the actual CLSID of the server module.
By default, ATL traps us in an either / or scenario where we can choose any 2 options from the following, without being able to choose them all.

- The convenience of having per-user registration of the server
- Merging the proxy / stub code into the main server
- Supporting full dual interfaces.

But just as we found a way to bypass this problem with our proxy DLL in the original Calculator project, we can apply a similar technique to an ATL project. We cannot just add the original dllinstall.c file to the project, for the simple reason that the ATL project already has an implementation of the DllInstall entry point. What we need to do is to avoid calling the ATL boilerplate code directly and instead use a custom implementation. There are several ways in which to implement this. One of the fundamental cornerstones of ATL is the concept of overriding things you don't want, to replace them with things you do want. The DLL entry points are not templates or type definitions, but in the spirit of ATL, the approach chosen here is to override the original DllInstall function and replace it with our own. The new function is defined in a new header file.

```
//DllInstallOverride.h
#pragma once

#include <atlbase.h>
#include <winreg.h>

STDAPI DllInstallBase(
    BOOL   bInstall,
    PCWSTR pszCmdLine);

HRESULT DllInstall(
    BOOL   bInstall,
    PCWSTR pszCmdLine)
{
    HKEY hkcuClasses = NULL;
    HRESULT hRes = S_OK;

    static const wchar_t szUserSwitch[] = L"user";
    if (pszCmdLine != nullptr)
    {
        if (_wcsnicmp(pszCmdLine, szUserSwitch, _countof(szUserSwitch)) == 0)
        {
            LSTATUS status = RegCreateKeyEx(
                HKEY_CURRENT_USER,
                L"SOFTWARE\\Classes",
                0,
                0,
                REG_OPTION_NON_VOLATILE,
                KEY_ALL_ACCESS,
                0,
                &hkcuClasses,
                NULL);

            if (status == ERROR_SUCCESS)
                status = RegOverridePredefKey(HKEY_CLASSES_ROOT, hkcuClasses);

            if (status != ERROR_SUCCESS)
                hRes = HRESULT_FROM_WIN32(GetLastError());
        }
    }

    if (SUCCEEDED(hRes)) {
```

```
        hRes = DllInstallBase(bInstall, pszCmdLine);
    }

    if (hkcuClasses)
        RegCloseKey(hkcuClasses);

    return hRes;
}

#define DllInstall DllInstallBase
```

The default registration code already has support for per-user registration, and we don't want to interfere with ATL if we don't have to. We use the same test that the default DllInstall function uses to determine whether the installation is per-user or not. If that is true, we set up the override for HKCR which causes the proxy registration to be redirected and delegate the actual registration to the `DllInstallBase` function. This function does not exist as such, but we end the header file with a macro that causes `DllInstall` to be replaced by `DllInstallBase`. All we have to do now is to include our header under the other header files.

```
#include "pch.h"
#include "framework.h"
#include "resource.h"
#include "RegTest_i.h"
#include "dllmain.h"
#include "xdlldata.h"

// inject new DllInstall, set up macro to rename the old one
#include "DllInstallOverride.h"

// snip

// DllInstall - will be renamed to DllInstallBase by the macro
STDAPI DllInstall(BOOL bInstall, _In_opt_  LPCWSTR pszCmdLine)
{
    // snip
}
```

This allows us to insert new registration code with no more modification than adding a single #include directive.

Creating an aggregate server

In this scenario, we use ATL to create a more complex server. In this new server, we continue with the Calculator journey by stepping in the role of a developer for the CalculusInc company. This developer is now tasked with creating a more advanced calculator that exposes the IArtihmetic interface as well as a new ITrigonometry interface. After reaching a deal with MathLibCo, the decision is made to aggregate their Calculator for the sake of exposing the IArithmetic interface.

Setting up the project

For that purpose, we start a new ATL project DLL server. Unlike last time, we do not merge the proxy / stub code this time. As a result, 2 projects are created by the wizard: the server project itself, and a proxy project.

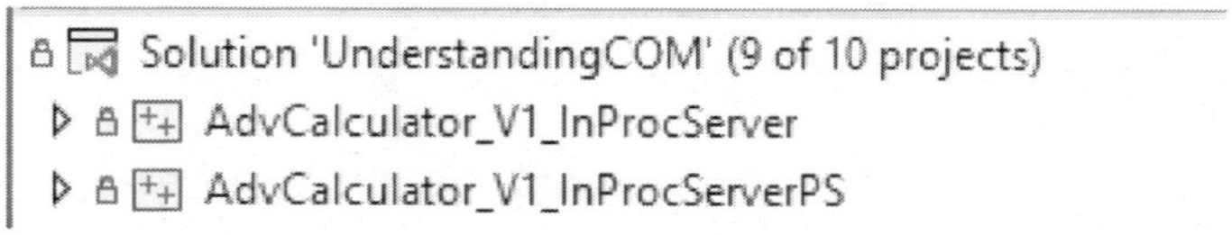

Creating the object is done in a similar fashion as before. When aggregating an object and exposing multiple interfaces, dispatching is not feasible in the same way as before. Switching between different interfaces is done via QueryInterface. So when you create the AdvCalculator object, you could also choose to use custom interfacing.

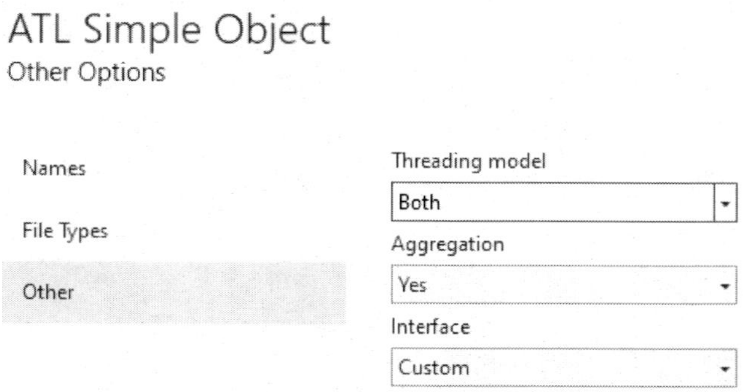

The resulting code would be similar to what we saw before, except the generated code will not derive from IDispatchImpl. Instead, it will derive directly from the main interface.

```
class ATL_NO_VTABLE CAdvCalculator :
	public CComObjectRootEx<CComMultiThreadModel>,
	public CComCoClass<CAdvCalculator, &CLSID_AdvCalculator>,
	public IAdvCalculator
{
};
```

However, choosing the dual option does not cost anything, and gives us more options later on because we can still choose to implement limited dispatching at a later point. After creating the object with the default options (except for the threading model), our project is created with the following IDL.

```
[
	object,
	uuid(066a4322-f272-45f7-8642-c89e31e3bcd9),
	dual,
	nonextensible,
	pointer_default(unique)
]
interface IAdvCalculator : IDispatch
{
};
[
	uuid(7307525a-1b23-4a4b-9bc8-c4860fa28004),
	version(1.0),
]
library AdvCalculatorV1InProcServerLib
{
	importlib("stdole2.tlb");
	[
		uuid(0ed7db13-b2e0-4db4-b20e-c23b7628c2e1)
	]
	coclass AdvCalculator
	{
		[default] interface IAdvCalculator;
	};
};
```

At this point we have a project with pure boilerplate and we could reasonably expect to be able to build the project. Indeed, the server itself builds just fine. However, when building the proxy project, we observe the following error in the messages window.

```
5): error MSB3073: The command "if exist dlldata.c goto :END
5): error MSB3073: echo Error: MIDL will not generate DLLDATA.C unless you have at least 1 interface in the main project.
5): error MSB3073: Exit 1
5): error MSB3073: :END
5): error MSB3073:
5): error MSB3073: :VCEnd" exited with code 1.
```

This is another ATL Visual studio quirk that exists because of legacy behavior. The pre-build step for the proxy project checks whether there is a dlldata.c file or not. However, it does not check this in the server project. Instead, it looks in the local project directory.

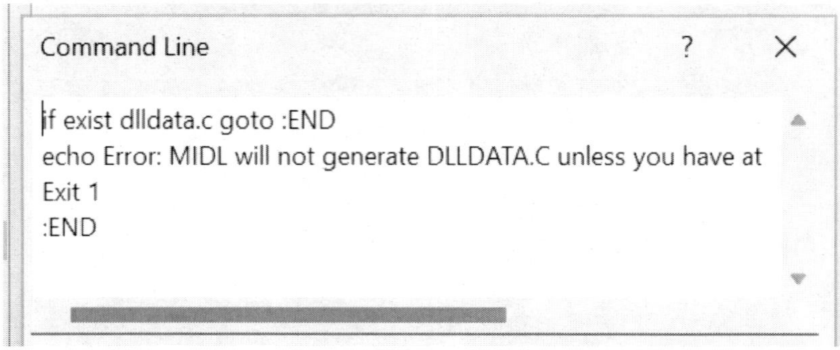

We could resolve this by editing the command to look in the server folder. However, there is not really much point to this step, other than to avoid a mildly confusing error if no interfaces were implemented on a COM object. So instead, we can just disable this step to get rid of it.

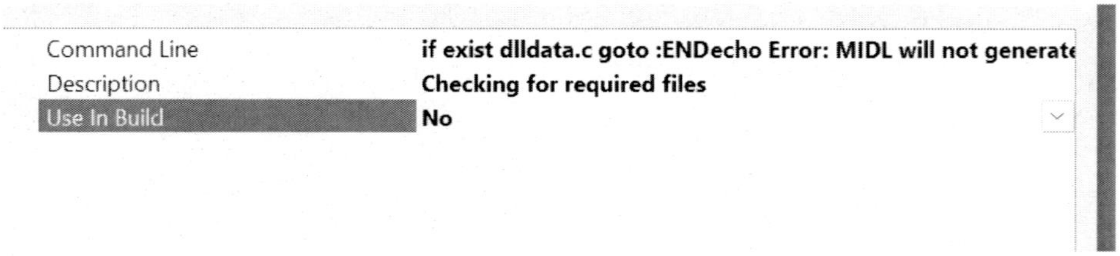

A similar problem props up in the linker settings. If we build the project after disabling the build event, we get the following error:

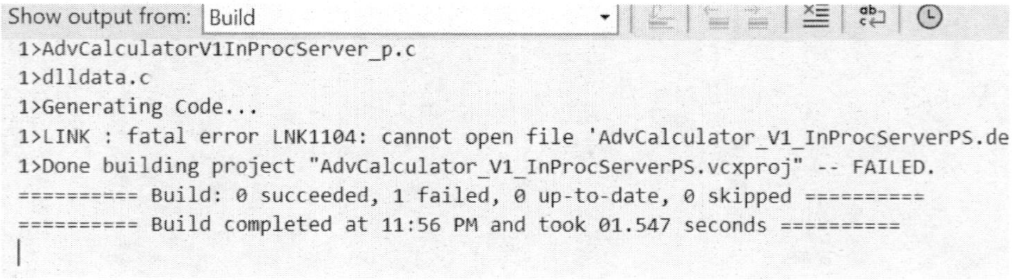

The reason is similar. The .def file is created in the server folder, but the proxy project is expecting that file in the local project folder.

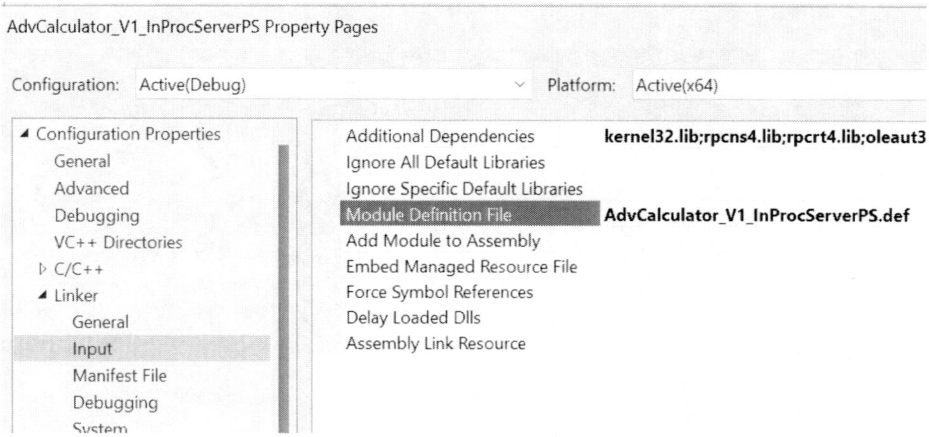

To fix this, we must change the file path so that it points to the server folder.

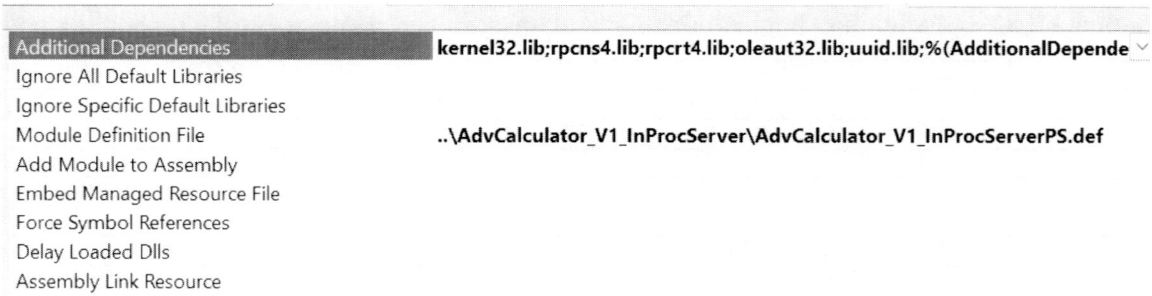

Registration still fails because the default DLL project does not support per-user registration. If Visual Studio is not running with administrative permission, that means an attempt is made to register the proxy in HKLM. To deal with this, we can add the DllInstall.c file to the project and add the DllInstall function to the def file. With that out of the way, we can successfully build both projects.

Implementing the ITrigonometry interface

As mentioned earlier, ATL projects are not wired up to work with multiple IDL files. Everything is built around the concept of working with single IDL file.

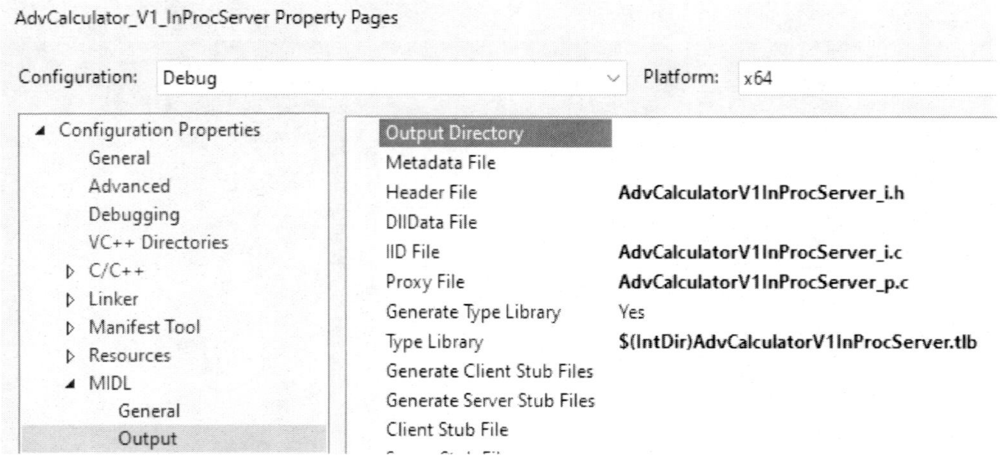

To work around this, you can add individual IDL files to the project and override the various MIDL settings so that the output of the compilation does not clash with the default project settings. However, if you do that, you need to manually add the generated files to the server project and the proxy project because that doesn't happen automatically. Alternatively, if the interface is under your own control, you can work with the ATL approach and add the additional interfaces to the main IDL file. That is the approach we will be using here.

```
[object, uuid (48CC2626-376A-4C9E-9777-75BDD101AF82)]
interface ITrigonometry : IUnknown
{
    HRESULT Sin(
        [in] double Arg1,
        [out] double* Result);

    HRESULT Cos(
        [in] double Arg1,
        [out] double* Result);

    HRESULT Tan(
        [in] double Arg1,
        [out] double* Result);
};
```

Instinctively, we might consider doing what we did before, which is to add the interface to our coclass and compile.

```
library AdvCalculatorV1InProcServerLib
{
      importlib("stdole2.tlb");
      [
            uuid(0ed7db13-b2e0-4db4-b20e-c23b7628c2e1)
      ]
```

```
        coclass AdvCalculator
        {
                [default] interface IAdvCalculator;
                interface ITrigonometry;
        };
};
```

But that is not the ATL way of working. Doing this will only update the IDL output files. We would still need to manually update the C++ declaration of the COM object, update the message map, and implement the method stubs. This is tedious and error prone for larger interfaces. Instead, the Class View provides a wizard for implementing interfaces.

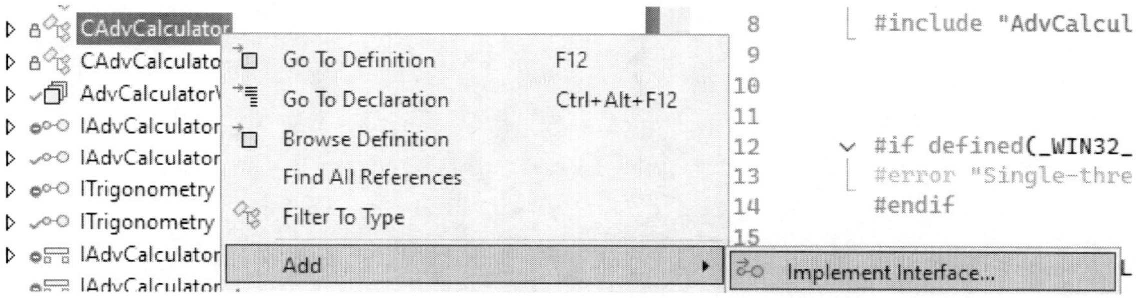

This wizard can collect type information from the registry, from specified TLB files, or from the project type library itself.

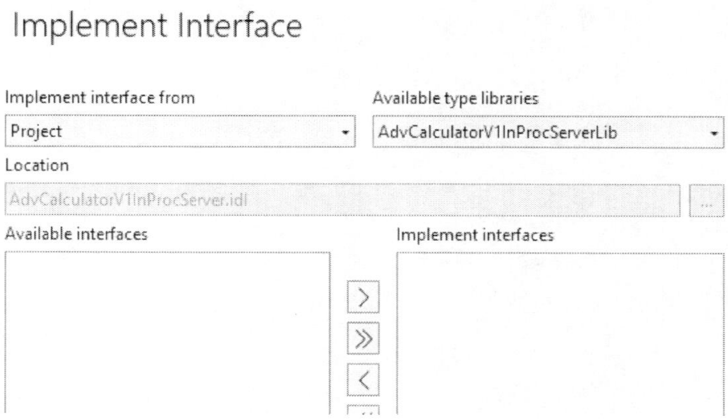

The only problem is that no interfaces are listed in the project type library. However, if we examine the project type library with OLEView, we can verify that the interface is really there.

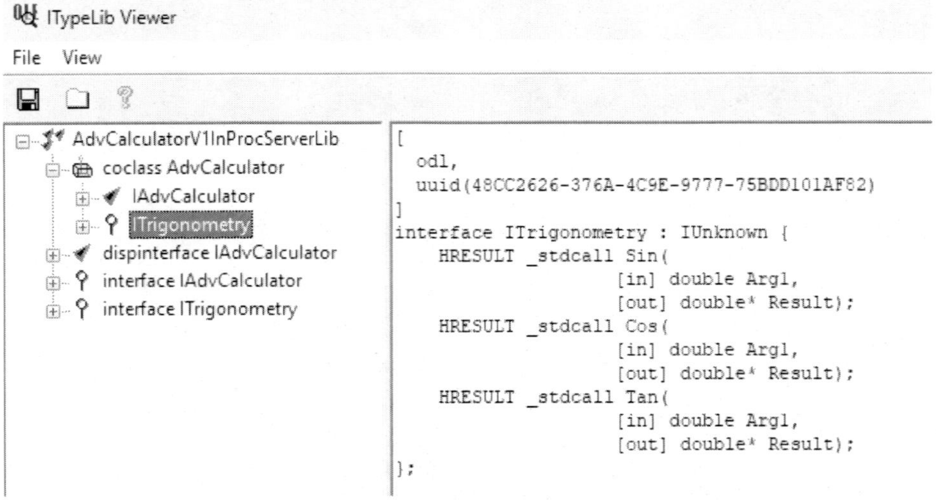

The reason it doesn't show up is that even though Visual Studio mentions the AdvCalculatorV1InProcServerLib type library, it doesn't actually look in the type library. Instead, it looks inside the library definition in the IDL file. And if the interface definition is not exported from the library, the 'implement interface' wizard considers it external to the type library, even though it is in the same IDL file. Exporting it isn't enough either.

```
library AdvCalculatorV1InProcServerLib
{
	interface ITrigonometry;

	importlib("stdole2.tlb");
	[
		uuid(0ed7db13-b2e0-4db4-b20e-c23b7628c2e1)
	]
	coclass AdvCalculator
	{
		[default] interface IAdvCalculator;
		interface ITrigonometry;
	};
};
```

The interface statement in the library block will cause it to be exported into the type library, even if the coclass wouldn't implement it. But this doesn't help with the problem. The ITrigonometry interface is still considered an external one because what the `interface Itrigonometry;` statement does is to export an interface that is defined outside the library. As such, it is still seen as external. If we work with the project IDL file, the way to do so is to put the interface definition itself inside the library block.

```
library AdvCalculatorV1InProcServerLib
{
    [object, uuid (48CC2626-376A-4C9E-9777-75BDD101AF82)]
    interface ITrigonometry : IUnknown
    {
        HRESULT Sin(
            [in] double Arg1,
            [out] double* Result);

        HRESULT Cos(
            [in] double Arg1,
            [out] double* Result);

        HRESULT Tan(
            [in] double Arg1,
            [out] double* Result);
    };

      importlib("stdole2.tlb");
      [
            uuid(0ed7db13-b2e0-4db4-b20e-c23b7628c2e1)
      ]
      coclass AdvCalculator
      {
            [default] interface IAdvCalculator;
            interface ITrigonometry;
      };
};
```

With this change, it finally shows up in the 'implement interface' wizard.

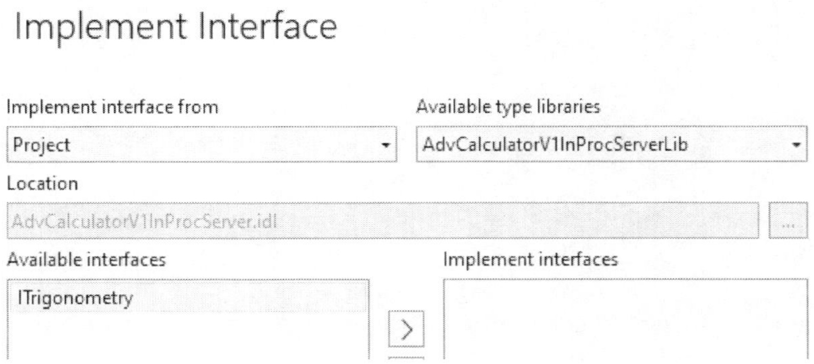

We can highlight the interface, use the arrow button to select it for implementation, and click 'OK' to make the magic happen… except the spell goes wrong, and now the project doesn't compile anymore. This is due to a combination of bugs in the wizard, one of which was already there in Visual Studio 2005, and it's still there in Visual

Studio 2022. The wizard blindly assumes that the selected interface derives from IDispatch, and alters the declaration of the COM object as follows:

```
class ATL_NO_VTABLE CAdvCalculator :
	public CComObjectRootEx<CComMultiThreadModel>,
	public CComCoClass<CAdvCalculator, &CLSID_AdvCalculator>,
	public IDispatchImpl<IAdvCalculator,
	                     &IID_IAdvCalculator,
	                     &LIBID_AdvCalculatorV1InProcServerLib,
	                     /*wMajor =*/ 1, /*wMinor =*/ 0>,
	public IDispatchImpl<ITrigonometry, &__uuidof(ITrigonometry)>
{
public:
	CAdvCalculator()
	{
	}

DECLARE_REGISTRY_RESOURCEID(106)

BEGIN_COM_MAP(CAdvCalculator)
	COM_INTERFACE_ENTRY(IAdvCalculator)
	COM_INTERFACE_ENTRY2(IDispatch, ITrigonometry)
    COM_INTERFACE_ENTRY(ITrigonometry)
END_COM_MAP()

	DECLARE_PROTECT_FINAL_CONSTRUCT()

	HRESULT FinalConstruct()
	{
		return S_OK;
	}

	void FinalRelease()
	{
	}

public:
};
```

Literally every single thing we asked the wizard to do, it did wrong:

1. The ITrigonometry interface is not a dual interface. It should not be derived by CAdvCalculator via `IDispatchImpl`.
2. The interface was added to the message map, which is what was needed. Only upon blindly assuming that ITrigonometry derived from IDispatch, the wizard also assumed it would be the interface we wanted to use as default dispatching interface and used the `COM_INTERFACE_ENTRY2` macro to make that happen.
3. No method stubs were created by the wizard despite the fact that it had all necessary information to do so.

Despite the high hopes we had of the 'Implement Interface', it didn't do anything. At this point the only way to implement the ITrigonometry interface is to manually derive from it, add it to the interface map, and add the method stubs to our class.

Implementing internal interfaces as external interfaces

It is definitely annoying that the 'Implement Interface' wizard didn't work for interfaces that are defined in the project IDL file. Until recently, it also didn't work for interfaces that are pulled in from a type library. This has now been fixed, and the 'Implement Interface' wizard allows us to select other type libraries and automatically generate the method stubs if we select the registry as a source of type definitions.

We saw previously that ATL embeds the type library in the server, so when we build and register the server, the type library will be automatically registered along with the server. Only if we check the list of type libraries, it isn't there.

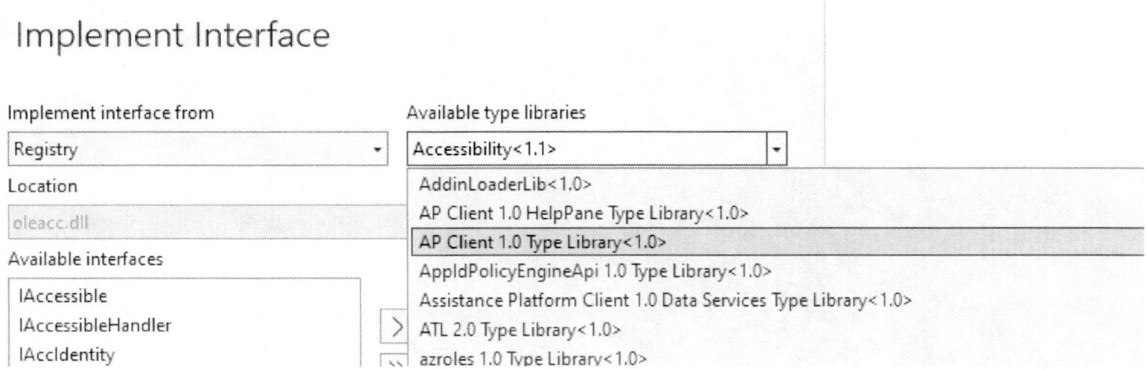

Yet if we use a tool like OLEView which can navigate all type libraries, it plainly shows up in the expected place, with the expected information.

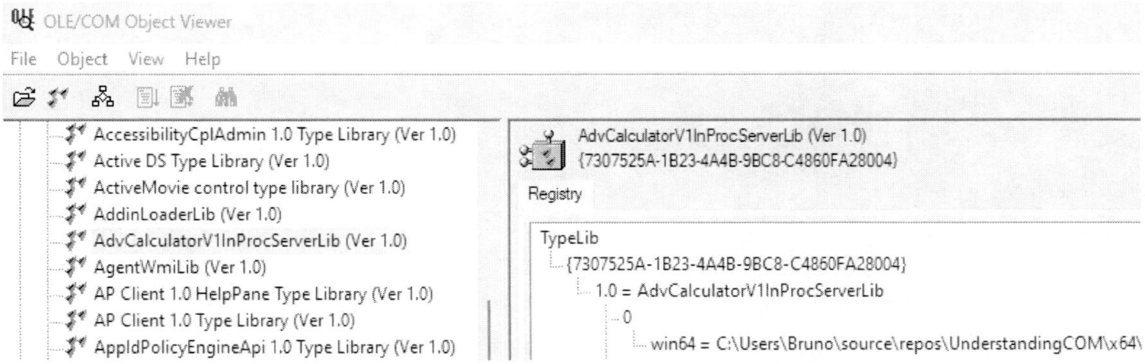

The problem here is not the type library but the Visual Studio tooling. In OLEView, the type library information refers to a win64 entry. The reason is of course that by default, our project settings are for an x64 server, which means the type library was generated for 64-bit architecture. And even though the embedded type information should be platform agnostic, Visual Studio refuses to look at type libraries that were compiled for another architecture than 32 -it. We can solve this problem easily by switching the build environment from x64 to x86 and rebuilding the project.

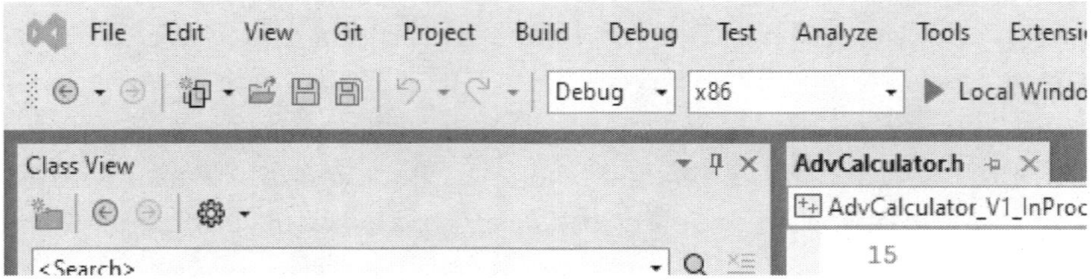

This will re-register the server and add the win32 entry to the TLB registration.

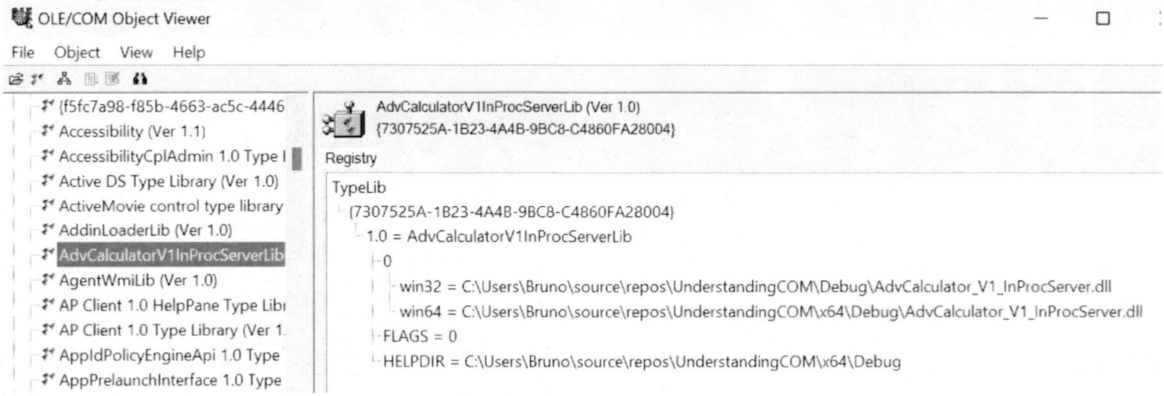

There are now 2 entries for the type library. An alternative approach would have been to simply rename the win64 key to win32 because the embedded information would be the same but this is a cleaner way to work and less hassle. Now, the project's type library shows up in the dropdown menu between the other librarie.

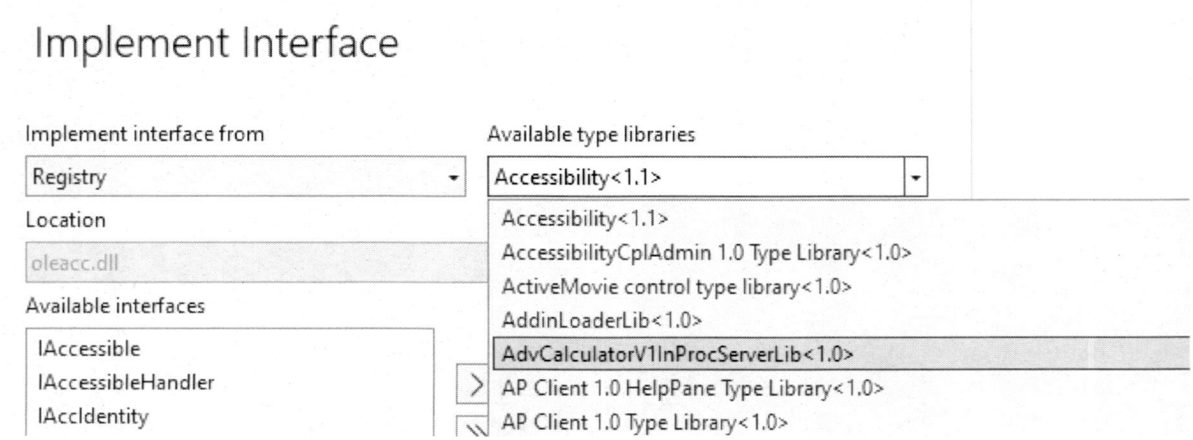

If we select that type library we can select the ITrigonometry interface and choose it for implementing.

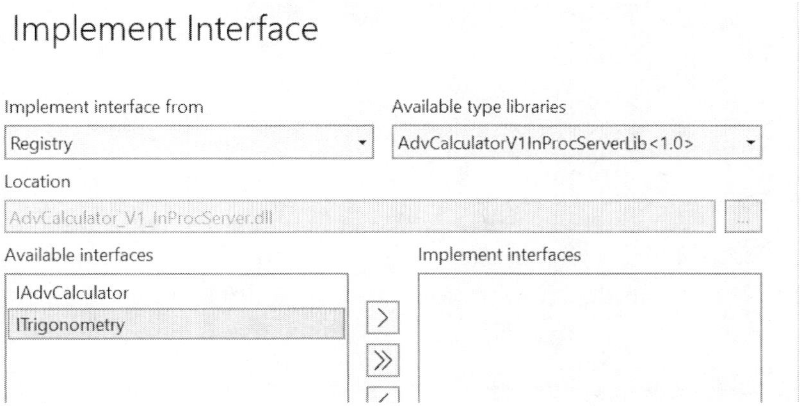

The result is still not quite perfect, but it's better than what we started with, in the sense that it's not completely broken.

```
class ATL_NO_VTABLE CAdvCalculator :
      public CComObjectRootEx<CComMultiThreadModel>,
      public CComCoClass<CAdvCalculator, &CLSID_AdvCalculator>,
      public IDispatchImpl<IAdvCalculator,
                           &IID_IAdvCalculator,
                           &LIBID_AdvCalculatorV1InProcServerLib,
                           /*wMajor =*/ 1, /*wMinor =*/ 0>,
      public IDispatchImpl<ITrigonometry,
                         &__uuidof(ITrigonometry),
                         &LIBID_AdvCalculatorV1InProcServerLib,
                         /* wMajor = */ 1, /* wMinor = */ 0>

{
//snip...
BEGIN_COM_MAP(CAdvCalculator)
      COM_INTERFACE_ENTRY(IAdvCalculator)
      COM_INTERFACE_ENTRY(IDispatch)
    COM_INTERFACE_ENTRY(ITrigonometry)
END_COM_MAP()

//snip...
// ITrigonometry Methods
public:
      STDMETHOD(Sin)(double Arg1, double * Result, HRESULT *Sin)
      {
             return E_NOTIMPL;
      }

      STDMETHOD(Cos)(double Arg1, double * Result, HRESULT *Cos)
      {
```

```
                return E_NOTIMPL;
        }

        STDMETHOD(Tan)(double Arg1, double * Result, HRESULT *Tan)
        {
                return E_NOTIMPL;
        }
};
```

On the upside, it did create method stubs and didn't mess up the interface map. On the downside, the base class is still wrong. And if you look carefully at the method stubs that were created, they erroneously have a HRESULT* parameter that shouldn't be there. To get it to compile cleanly, we need to manually replace the base class and remove those erroneous parameters.

```
class ATL_NO_VTABLE CAdvCalculator :
        public CComObjectRootEx<CComMultiThreadModel>,
        public CComCoClass<CAdvCalculator, &CLSID_AdvCalculator>,
        public IDispatchImpl<IAdvCalculator,
                        &IID_IAdvCalculator,
                        &LIBID_AdvCalculatorV1InProcServerLib,
                        /*wMajor =*/ 1, /*wMinor =*/ 0>,
        public ITrigonometry

{
//snip...
BEGIN_COM_MAP(CAdvCalculator)
        COM_INTERFACE_ENTRY(IAdvCalculator)
        COM_INTERFACE_ENTRY(IDispatch)
    COM_INTERFACE_ENTRY(ITrigonometry)
END_COM_MAP()

//snip...
// ITrigonometry Methods
public:
        STDMETHOD(Sin)(double Arg1, double * Result)
        {
                return E_NOTIMPL;
        }

        STDMETHOD(Cos)(double Arg1, double * Result)
        {
                return E_NOTIMPL;
        }

        STDMETHOD(Tan)(double Arg1, double * Result)
        {
                return E_NOTIMPL;
        }
};
```

You could ask yourself: is it really worth using that wizard anymore? That is certainly a valid question if you see the hoops we had to jump through to use it, in its broken state. For simple interfaces, there is certainly an argument to be made that implementing it manually is a lot faster. For complex interfaces, it could certainly be worth it because if an interface has many methods with complex signatures, manually creating the stubs is quite a bit more work than letting the wizard create them, and then cleaning up after the wizard. Speaking of cleanup, we still cannot build the project. If we try, then in the time-honored tradition of C++ we get a massive number of errors that all point to the same problem. One of those errors would be similar to thisnow seen using 'class'

```
1>C:\Users\Bruno\Source\Repos\UnderstandingCOM\AdvCalculator_V1_InProcServer\A
dvCalculatorV1InProcServer_i.h(240,5): error C2011: 'ITrigonometry': 'struct'
type redefinition
1>(compiling source file '/AdvCalculator_V1_InProcServer.cpp')
1>
C:\Users\Bruno\Source\Repos\UnderstandingCOM\AdvCalculator_V1_InProcServer\x64
\Debug\AdvCalculator_V1_InProcServer.tlh(37,1):
1>    see declaration of 'ITrigonometry'
```

This is caused by the fact that we used a loophole to implement the ITrigonometry interface as if it was an external interface. And that worked for the purpose of getting the wizard to do something reasonably useful, but that doesn't change the fact it's not an external interface. To understand what went wrong, we need to reexamine what really happened. And that means being a little more critical of what we assumed. We work in a C++ environment. We already know that our C++ code needs -among other things- a C++ declaration of the ITrigonometry interface. Something like this:

```
#ifndef __ITrigonometry_INTERFACE_DEFINED__
#define __ITrigonometry_INTERFACE_DEFINED__

/* interface ITrigonometry */
/* [uuid][object] */


EXTERN_C const IID IID_ITrigonometry;
#if defined(__cplusplus) && !defined(CINTERFACE)

    MIDL_INTERFACE("48CC2626-376A-4C9E-9777-75BDD101AF82")
    ITrigonometry : public IUnknown
    {
    public:
        virtual HRESULT STDMETHODCALLTYPE Sin(
            /* [in] */ double Arg1,
            /* [out] */ double *Result) = 0;

        virtual HRESULT STDMETHODCALLTYPE Cos(
```

```
            /* [in] */ double Arg1,
            /* [out] */ double *Result) = 0;

        virtual HRESULT STDMETHODCALLTYPE Tan(
            /* [in] */ double Arg1,
            /* [out] */ double *Result) = 0;
    };

#endif      /* C style interface */
#endif      /* __ITrigonometry_INTERFACE_DEFINED__ */
```

Suppose for a moment that we import a type library with an interface that is new to the project. If we ask the wizard to implement it, there needs to be a declaration for it somewhere. That is why the wizard silently inserts the following line in the precompiled header.

```
#import
"C:\Users\Bruno\source\repos\UnderstandingCOM\Debug\AdvCalculator_V1_InProcSer
ver.dll" raw_interfaces_only, raw_native_types, no_namespace, named_guids,
auto_search
```

Remember that the type library only showed up in the dropdown list of available libraries after we built the 32-bit version of our server. When we told the wizard to use that particular type library, it resolved the path and modified the precompiled header to import that library. As a result, there are now 2 competing definitions of that interface in our project: one comes from this import statement and the resulting TLH file. The other comes from compilation of the IDL file in our project. Since we only selected that type library as a loophole for the wizard to work, we can safely delete it from the precompiled header. This will remove the conflict, and the code will compile cleanly.

Declaring an interface of an aggregated object

With the ITrigonometry interface taken care of, it is time to modify the AdvCalculator class declaration in the project IDL file to declare that it implements IArithmetic. Even though our object doesn't implement the interface itself, it aggregates the object which does. The IDL file needs to reflect that the interface is part of its identity.

You could argue that technically, it doesn't 'have to'. Aggregation is almost by definition a process which is incompatible with dispatching. The IArithmetic interface is always going to be accessed via QueryInterface. If AdvCalculator would not declare that it implements this, clients could still query for it and use it regardless of what the IDL file says. But this is never a good idea. Someone who imports AdvCalculator's

TLB to start working with it, would be left blind to the parts that are not mentioned as part of the interface contract.

The simplest way to do this is to import the IArtithmetic IDL file like we did before.

```
import "IArithmetic.idl";

//snip...

coclass AdvCalculator
{
    [default] interface IAdvCalculator;
    interface ITrigonometry;
    interface IArithmetic;
};
```

But if we rebuild the project to force registration of the server and TLB file, we get a compiler error

```
\AdvCalculatorV1InProcServer_i.h(84,10): error C1083: Cannot open include file: 'IArithmetic.h': No such file or directory

\AdvCalculatorV1InProcServer_i.h(84,10): error C1083: Cannot open include file: 'IArithmetic.h': No such file or directory
```

Due to this piece of MIDL generated code in AdvCalculatorV1InProcServer_i.h.

```
/* header files for imported files */
#include "oaidl.h"
#include "ocidl.h"
#include "IArithmetic.h"
#include "shobjidl.h"
```

Upon encountering the `import "IArithmetic.idl"` statement, MIDL assumed we would compile it separately to generate those files. In the introduction chapter for IDL, we saw that IDL imports do not work like C++ includes. The imported IDL files had to be compiled individually because that doesn't happen as part of the compilation process. Note that if the compiler finds that file because it was created earlier as part of another project, the compiler will happily use that as if nothing is wrong, so watch out for that.

The IArithmetic interface is nowhere to be found. Not just the virtual base class, but the IID is missing as well. Adding the IDL files to our ATL project is not really an option because ATL projects are configured in the project properties to assume there is only 1 IDL file, which will create only 1 set of headers and C files. Stepping away from that principle would require a lot of additional manual configuration that has to be just right, for every interface we want to add this way. ATL projects are simply not meant to work this way. If an ATL project requires an external interface or external objects, the assumption is that someone else did all the work and delivered everything we need, in the form of a TLB file and a server. Instead of importing the IDL file, we use the calculator TLB.

```
//snip...
importlib("Calculator_V1.tlb");
importlib("stdole2.tlb");

[
    uuid(0ed7db13-b2e0-4db4-b20e-c23b7628c2e1)
]
coclass AdvCalculator
{
    [default] interface IAdvCalculator;
    interface ITrigonometry;
    interface IArithmetic;
};
```

Now the project builds cleanly. If we look at the TLB with OLEView we can see what is going on

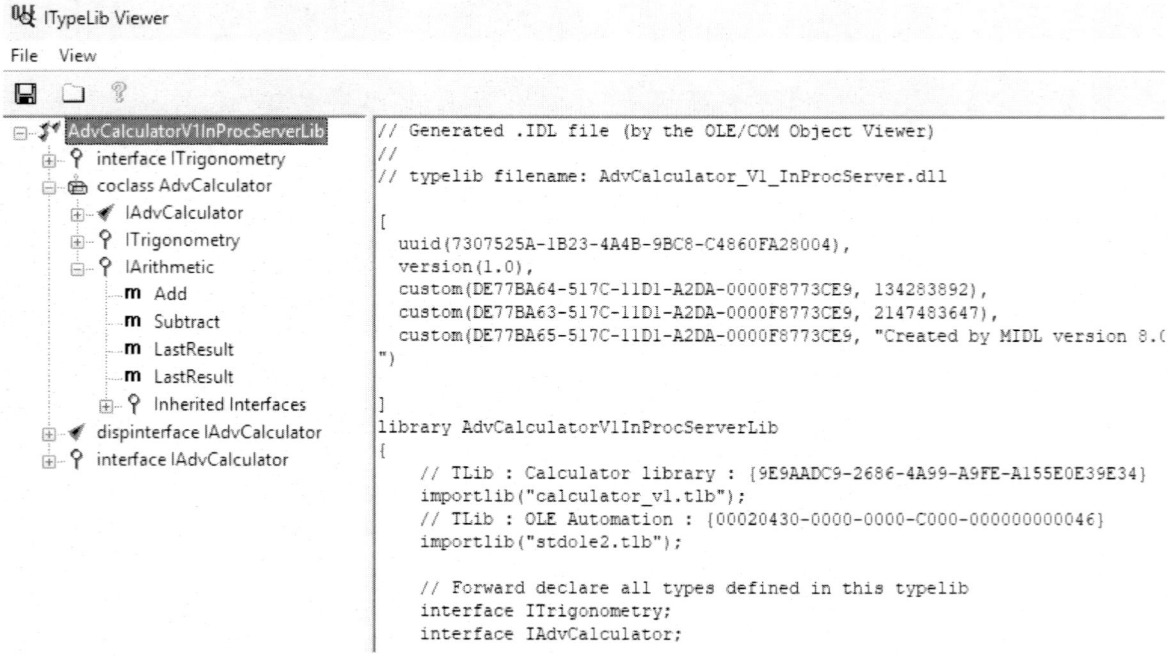

AdvCalculator implements IArtithmetic and the TLB can properly resolve that interface even though it is absent. As you can see on the left side, the importlib statement is carried over from the IDL file file into the type library. When AdvCalculatorV1InProcServerLib is opened to get the type information, the list of TLB dependencies is available inside the TLB to be used for resolving base types. This also implies that one any system where AdvCalculatorV1InProcServerLib is used, Calculator_v1.tlb needs to be present as well.

On the C++ side, IArithmetic is still completely absent. An IDL file is an interface contract and by importing if from a TLB file, MIDL will not generate code for it. However, as we have seen, you can just import a TLB file in the precompiled header.

```
#import "Calculator_V1.tlb" raw_interfaces_only, raw_native_types,
no_namespace, named_guids, auto_search
```

We don't have to change the AdvCalculator class declaration because it's not implementing the IArithmetic interface itself. It's aggregating the original Calculator. This involves 2 steps: creating the Calculator and aggregating it and updating the interface table so that QueryInterface calls are handled correctly. The first 2 things belong together. With ATL we get 2 placeholders that we can freely use to do any initialization and cleanup.

```
        HRESULT FinalConstruct()
        {
                return S_OK;
        }

        void FinalRelease()
        {
        }
```

These take the place of a regular constructor and destructor pair and similarly do not take any arguments. Using the FinalConstruct method instead of the constructor has the benefit that whatever initialization code is put inside can return a HRESULT and also access the 'this' pointer as a fully-fledged COM object.

First, we add a member for the IUnknown * of the inner object.

```
 private:
    CComPtr<IUnknown> m_inner;
```

We can then use it to hold the inner object pointer. Using the provided initialization and cleanup methods, we create and destroy the object.

```
HRESULT FinalConstruct()
{
    return m_inner.CoCreateInstance(
                            CLSID_Calculator, GetUnknown(),
CLSCTX_INPROC_SERVER);
}
void FinalRelease()
{
```

```
    m_inner.Release();
}
```

That takes care of the inner object. Updating the interface map is similarly trivial. ATL has a dedicated COM_INTERFACE_ENTRY_AGGREGATE macro for that which will tie an interface IID to an IUnknown* to which that particular QueryInterface request is delegated to.

```
BEGIN_COM_MAP(CAdvCalculator)
    COM_INTERFACE_ENTRY(IAdvCalculator)
    COM_INTERFACE_ENTRY(IDispatch)
    COM_INTERFACE_ENTRY(ITrigonometry)
    COM_INTERFACE_ENTRY_AGGREGATE(IID_IArithmetic, m_inner)
END_COM_MAP()
```

That is really all there is to it. We can now create a client application which consumes this server and use both the trigonometry interface.

Using the ATL smart pointers, this is trivial:

```
HRESULT hRes = iTrig.CoCreateInstance(CLSID_AdvCalculator, NULL, CLSCTX_ALL);
if (iTrig) {
    iTrig->Cos(std::numbers::pi/4.0, &result);
    std::cout << "Cos(pi/4.0) = " << result << std::endl;
    CComQIPtr<IArithmetic> iAr = iTrig.p;
    if (iAr) {
        iAr->Add(1.0, 1.0, &result);
        std::cout << "1 + 1 = " << result << std::endl;
    }
}
```

The client uses the object through the advertised interfaces, without knowing or caring about how those interfaces are implemented.

Attributed ATL

So far, the ATL we have used is also called classical ATL. Everything is implemented through macros and templates. This is reliable, predictable, and readable. But it is also enormously verbose. There is a ton of boilerplate code very noticeable in the project, and some information is present in the project multiple times. Granted, we didn't have to do anything to configure it, but it's still there. For example, the CLSID or the name of the class is present in the IDL file, in the generated .h and .c files, and in the registration (.rgs) files. If we wanted to change any of that information after the object was created, we'd have to manually go through all files and change things without making typos or forgetting something. Additionally, if we decide at some point that we want to support aggregation after all, or use a different threading model, we'd have to start editing the generated code, change base classes, and so on. It's messy.

When Visual Studio .NET was released in 2002, Microsoft came up with a new thing, called 'Attributed ATL'. When you started a new ATL project, you had to make a choice between Classic ATL and Attributed ATL.

The idea behind Attributed ATL was that you would define the interfaces and classes directly in C++ code and use attributes on those items to define the COM behavior you want. Visual Studio would then generate all the boilerplate code, the IDL, the registration code, and the type library on the fly. For example, our initial Calculator project could be implemented as follows.

```
[
	object,
	uuid("713E70B0-8E41-482C-80AB-0258CAA5350B"),
	helpstring("IArithmetic Interface")
]
__interface IArithmetic : IUnknown
{
	[id(1)]
	HRESULT Add([in] double Arg1, [in] double Arg2, [out] double* Result);

	[id(2)]
	HRESULT Subtract([in] double Arg1,[in] double Arg2, [out] double*
Result);

	[propget, id(3)]
	HRESULT LastResult([out, retval] double* pVal);

	[propput, id(3)]
	HRESULT LastResult([in] double newVal);
};


[
	coclass,
	threading(apartment),  // or "free", "both", "neutral"
	uuid("5AB4FB62-13B0-4370-AD0E-C9E6F989815F"),
	version("1.0"),
	helpstring("Calculator class")
]
class ATL_NO_VTABLE Calculator :
	public IArithmetic
{
public:
	Calculator() : m_lastResult(0.0) {}
```

```
    // Add method
    HRESULT Add(double Arg1, double Arg2, double* Result)
    {
        if (!Result) return E_POINTER;
        *Result = Arg1 + Arg2;
        m_lastResult = *Result;
        return S_OK;
    }

    // Subtract method
    HRESULT Subtract(double Arg1, double Arg2, double* Result)
    {
        if (!Result) return E_POINTER;
        *Result = Arg1 - Arg2;
        m_lastResult = *Result;
        return S_OK;
    }

    // Property getter
    HRESULT LastResult(double* pVal)
    {
        if (!pVal) return E_POINTER;
        *pVal = m_lastResult;
        return S_OK;
    }

    // Property setter
    HRESULT LastResult(double newVal)
    {
        m_lastResult = newVal;
        return S_OK;
    }

private:
    double m_lastResult;
};
```

Aside from the interface and a coclass, we also need library block, just like we had in the original IDL file. To solve this, we simply add a class to the project and give it the module attribute.

```
[
    module(name = "AttributedATL",
        uuid = "2826E620-A207-46C1-B2E1-5A0904A3E2B8",
        version = "1.0")
]
class CMyAttributedATLModule {};
```

If we do this, the project will generate the IDL code and MIDL code that represents the attributed ATL code.

vc140.h	10/15/2025 12:06 AM	C/C++ Header
vc140.idl	10/15/2025 12:06 AM	Interface Definition Language File
vc140.tlb	10/15/2025 12:06 AM	TLB File
vc140_i.c	10/15/2025 12:06 AM	C Source
vc140_p.c	10/15/2025 12:06 AM	C Source

If we look at the generated IDL code, we find the code that we expected. The IDL is also annotated with comments about where the definitions come from.

```
import "docobj.idl";

[
	object,
	uuid(713E70B0-8E41-482C-80AB-0258CAA5350B),
	helpstring("IArithmetic Interface")
]
#line 25 "c:\\users\\bruno\\source\\repos\\test\\server\\server.cpp"
interface IArithmetic : IUnknown {
#line 28 "c:\\users\\bruno\\source\\repos\\test\\server\\server.cpp"
	[id(1)] HRESULT  Add([in] double Arg1, [in] double Arg2, [out] double
*Result);
#line 31 "c:\\users\\bruno\\source\\repos\\test\\server\\server.cpp"
	[id(2)] HRESULT  Subtract([in] double Arg1, [in] double Arg2, [out]
double *Result);
#line 34 "c:\\users\\bruno\\source\\repos\\test\\server\\server.cpp"
	[propget,id(3)] HRESULT  LastResult([out,retval] double *pVal);
#line 37 "c:\\users\\bruno\\source\\repos\\test\\server\\server.cpp"
	[propput,id(3)] HRESULT  LastResult([in] double newVal);
};


[ version(1.0), uuid(2826E620-A207-46C1-B2E1-5A0904A3E2B8) ]
library AttributedATL
{
	importlib("stdole2.tlb");
	importlib("olepro32.dll");

	[
		uuid(5AB4FB62-13B0-4370-AD0E-C9E6F989815F),
		version(1.0),
		helpstring("Calculator class")
	]
#line 48 "c:\\users\\bruno\\source\\repos\\test\\server\\server.cpp"
	coclass Calculator {
		interface IArithmetic;
	};
```

```
}
```

With these rather small pieces of code, we could build the entire server. The attributes on the interface, together with the actual code, can be used to deduce what would go in the IDL file. Likewise, the attributes on the class and the inheritance declaration contain the progid, clsid, and threading model. Literally everything that was implemented through countless lines of boilerplate in the previous projects, is out of sight and out of mind. Everything would be generated on the fly, based on the attributes. Changing the threading model or progid or whatever, is as trivial as changing the attribute and rebuilding the code. The actual code is never there for you. Having the generated code be static would go against the reasons for having attributed code in the first place.

Attributed ATL was introduced with Visual Studio 2002 and promoted as 'Modern ATL' in Visual Studio 2003. With Visual Studio 2005, classical ATL began to regain favor and attributed ATL was no longer the default ATL type. With Visual Studio 2010 it became deprecated and now it's obsolete. Despite the clear benefits and initial push, it didn't deliver on the promises.

There are several reasons for this. We started this book with the idea of having an IDL file as the universal truth concerning an interface contract, and client and server would implement this contract. Additionally, generating the language specific binding for an interface would be done by MIDL, according to verifiable rules. By using attributed ATL, the cart would come before the horse. The idea of a predefined interface being immutable goes right out the window. Instead, you'd design a class and say 'the interface contract will be generated based on what the class happens to be during this build cycle'. Not only might the interface contract be slightly different than what you had in mind, but with the evolution of the program in its lifecycle and various rebuilds and compiler changes, it is too easy to accidentally end up with slightly different interfaces as time goes on. However, that isn't the biggest problem because after all you can easily verify the generated IDL.

The bigger problem was that the generated code was also hidden from the developer. You didn't get to see it, which in turn means it was hard to understand what was happening. Classic ATL can be intimidating and hairy but at least you get to read it. You can follow the entire trail of breadcrumbs down the class hierarchy, either in a code editor window or with a debugger and authoritatively say 'this is what happens'. With attributed ATL, you only knew in broad terms. And with everything you've seen in the past chapters vis-à-vis the reliability of code generation, how comfortable do you feel about the correct behavior of your code? Sure, this was at a time when

Microsoft was still throwing money at ATL and no doubt, it was ok most of the time. There is a compiler option that lets Visual Studio generate merge files with the code that was supposedly generated in the background but that was an imperfect process. Sometimes, the code was incomplete or wrong. On top of that, this approach also made debugging difficult.

What started as a grand vision and potentially phenomenal productivity enhancement eventually failed against the reality of C++ code complexity and compiler limitations. It's worth pointing out that eventually, the attributed approach would be very successful in the .NET world of COM wrappers around .NET classes and interfaces. There are several factors that undoubtedly contributed to this success. For starters, the .NET type system is much richer and internally consistent compared to the C++ world where anything is a pointer and type metadata doesn't really exist, let alone exist at runtime. And at the same time, lifecycle management in .NET is much more reliable than in COM, so anything that exists in the .NET world can be translated to the COM world much more easily.

There is no attributed ATL example program in this book because attributed ATL is fully obsolete and no longer supported. But it's worth knowing what it was about because here and there you will still find traces in Visual Studio. For example, in the 'Implement Interface' wizard, there is still an 'Embedded IDL' type source.

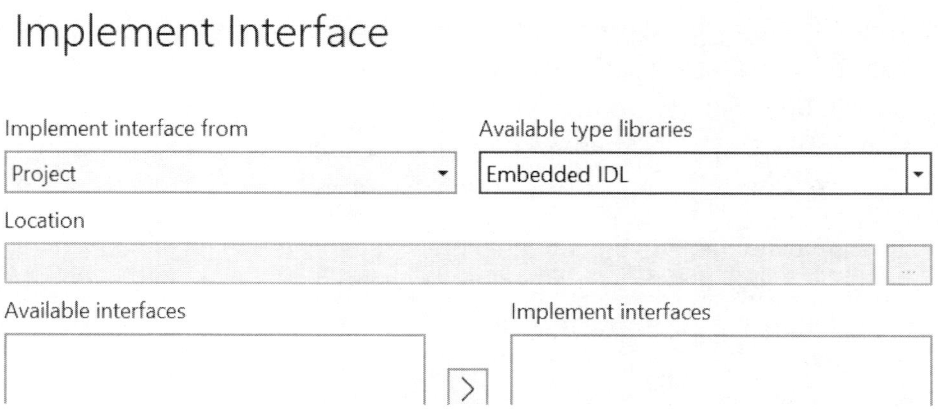

From what I could find in documentation, this is where you could select interfaces that were implemented via the attributed ATL C++ interfaces. This is not functional anymore. But the user interface item still exists and if you wondered what purpose it served: this is why. And if we look in the linker settings, we find an embedded IDL tab.

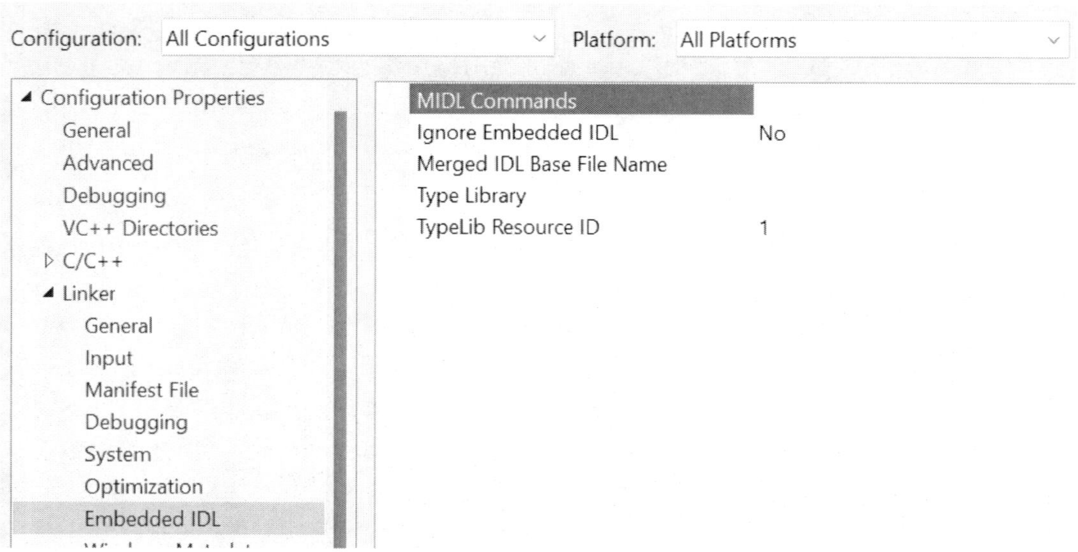

This is where you could define the names of the generated IDL and TLB, and custom commands and resource ID for the TLB. But like the interface wizard's Embedded IDL option, it still exists but is not intended to be used anymore. Like many other things, Attributed ATL has gone the way of the dinosaur and all we have to show for it are the fossils you find in the Visual Studio tools.

Summary

In this chapter we explored the tools that are used to develop COM objects and COM servers in real life. ATL is a set of macros and templates that takes much of the sting of programming boiler plate code away and lets you focus on actual functionality. Base classes, template arguments and overrides define the behavior and traits of the server and objects in a predictable and flexible manner.

ATL projects are built around the concept of a single IDL file that generates a TLB file which is embedded in the server module itself so that registration is simplified and more resilient. This is especially important because many ATL projects implement objects that derive from IDispatch. These rely on the availability of the correct type library to function correctly when used by late binding clients. Even so, ATL doesn't force you to use IDispatch. ATL is just as powerful when working with IUnknown derived objects and comes with several wizards that automate some of the work.

Many of the technologies that had ATL support no longer exist. ATL Server as an internet web server technology, COM+ and Attributed ATL are things of the past. Yet you will still find traces of them in documentation, build settings or user interfaces.

10

Marshaling revisited

At this point, we've implemented and installed a COM server, client applications, and have established a good start to finish understanding of what is going on. We've gotten used to things just working. Especially when working with ATL, you can almost get lulled into forgetting about apartments, marshaling, or the importance of design decisions.

All we've done so far is call into COM objects, using pointers we obtained from the COM runtime in the thread where we're using them. For a large portion of COM projects, that is all that is needed. If we expand the scope of requirements to include asynchronous programming and multithreading, things get more complex again. Not just because of the concurrency issues inherent in working with different execution threads, but also because marshaling requires consideration again.

During the editing phase of this book, I decided to cut the marshaling topic into 2 chapters. The first chapter in the beginning of the book covers things you must understand for reading the book up to this point, such as marshaling, apartments, types of server, etc. But that is not the entire story.

This chapter expands upon that and contains the things that are on topic for the remainder of this book, as well as some more niche things. The main reason for having 2 chapters about marshaling is that the topics in this chapter require working knowledge of interfaces and objects; things which were not yet covered when starting the first chapter about marshaling or apartments. I have strived to put the contents of this book in as much of a linear order as possible and that has generally worked out well except for marshaling which is why we revisit the topic before moving on.

How Proxy and Stub use RPC in default marshaling

If standard marshaling is used, the COM runtime will use the implementation of IMarshal that was generated by MIDL. This MIDL code uses RPC for efficiency because remote execution and data marshaling is expressly what RPC was designed for.

On the server side, COM will create a stub manager for the COM object from which an interface pointer is requested and create a stub for the requested interface. A packet of data is then sent to the client with the information that is needed to set up the proxy object and setting up a communication channel between the proxy and the stub.

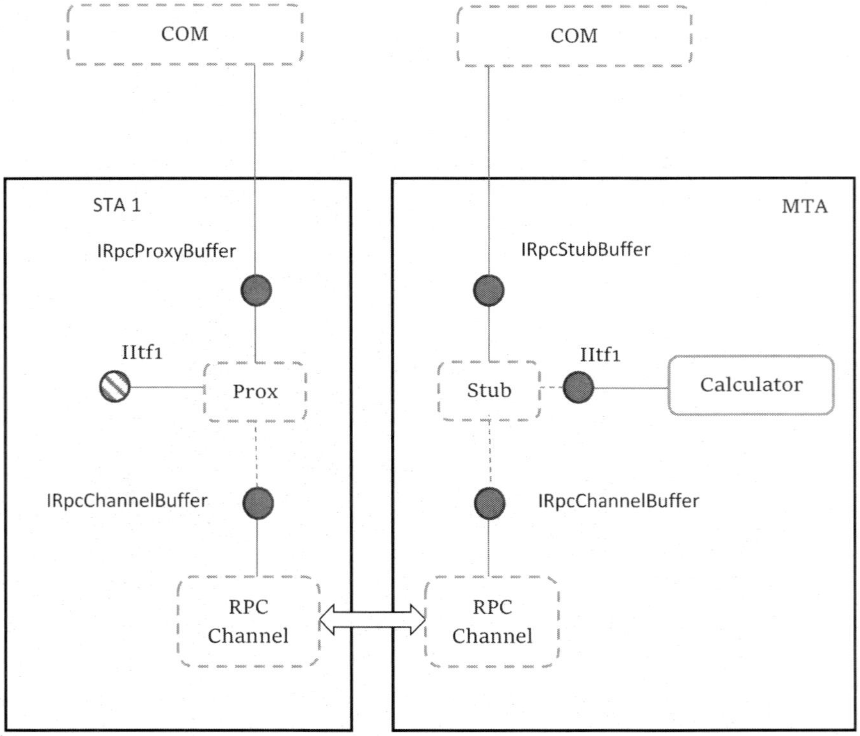

The proxy exports 2 interfaces: The interface that is being marshaled, in this case IItf1 (and implicitly the interfaces from which it inherits directly) and IRpcProxyBuffer. Client code cannot QueryInterface for IRpcProxyBuffer. It is only accessible to COM. IRpcProxyBuffer is a simple interface. It can only be used for connecting a proxy to, and disconnecting from an RPC channel. This is something that a client should not concern themselves with.

If an object supports multiple interfaces, then the different Interface proxies are aggregated into a larger proxy that represents the object as a whole. The reason an object proxy ties its interface proxies together is that different objects may export the same interface, and interface calls need to be marshaled to the interface stub connected to the correct object.

On the server side, the stub has an interface pointer for the object for which it was created. That is why stubs are not aggregated into a larger stub. There is no need because when a client call arrives, it is already targeting the correct object. It also implements the IRpcStubBuffer interface, which is more complex than the IRpcProxyBuffer interface. Not only does it need to connect and disconnect the stub to the object whose interface it is marshaling, but it needs to count references for external connections (we'll discuss that in depth later) as well as expose methods to allow COM to check if the stub supports a specific interface, and to invoke a call on that interface.

If a call is made, that call, its arguments and any necessary identification of the interface are translated into a wire protocol known as Network Data Representation (NDR). NDR is a platform independent definition of how any data value can be encoded in a byte stream in an unambiguous marshal data packet. This packet is sent through the RPC channel to the stub, which unwraps the NDR data, reconstitutes the argument data and then invokes it on the correct object through the interface pointer it is holding.

Both the proxy and the stub have an IRpcChannelBuffer pointer, supplied by COM after they were created, for the purpose of sending data to / receiving data from the channel that has been established by COM. The sequence of events looks like this at a high level:

1. A method call is executed on the proxy object.
2. The proxy builds a marshal data packet and sends it through the RPC channel.
3. One of the RPC threads received the data from the channel and reconstitutes the data for the method call.
4. The RPC thread locates the appropriate stub and uses it to invoke the method with the reconstituted data. With the invocation it passes a pointer to the IRpcChannelBuffer from which the call came, so that it can marshal any output parameters back though the channel.

How the invocation happens depends on the threading model of the object. Based on the requirements, the invocation can be done directly by an MTA thread or sent to an STA thread via the message queue.

IMarshal

When an object calls a method from a different apartment, the proxy and stub need to be set up to make this work. So far, every time we needed this to happen, we let the COM runtime take care of this. And indeed, barring specific requirements, there are few reasons to even want to take control. The complexity of doing so must be weighed against the increased design complexity, likelihood of making mistakes, etc. There is a cost – benefit analysis to be made.

To facilitate taking control of the marshaling process, an object can export the IMarshal interface. This interface exists to give a server the means to create, initialize and manage the proxy in a client process. The COM runtime queries for this interface to determine if a server wants that level of control.

If no custom marshaling is required, the COM runtime uses the standard marshaler which checks the Interfaces section in the registry to determine the CLSID of the object which performs the marshaling. That object will contain a default implementation of IMarshal that was generated by MIDL. The IMarshal interface is as follows:

```
//objidl.h
MIDL_INTERFACE("00000003-0000-0000-C000-000000000046")
IMarshal : public IUnknown
{
public:
    virtual HRESULT STDMETHODCALLTYPE GetUnmarshalClass(
        _In_  REFIID riid,
        _In_opt_  void *pv,
        _In_  DWORD dwDestContext,
        _Reserved_  void *pvDestContext,
        _In_  DWORD mshlflags,
        _Out_  CLSID *pCid) = 0;

    virtual HRESULT STDMETHODCALLTYPE GetMarshalSizeMax(
        _In_  REFIID riid,
        _In_opt_  void *pv,
        _In_  DWORD dwDestContext,
        _Reserved_  void *pvDestContext,
        _In_  DWORD mshlflags,
        _Out_  DWORD *pSize) = 0;

    virtual HRESULT STDMETHODCALLTYPE MarshalInterface(
        _In_  IStream *pStm,
        _In_  REFIID riid,
        _In_opt_  void *pv,
        _In_  DWORD dwDestContext,
        _Reserved_  void *pvDestContext,
        _In_  DWORD mshlflags) = 0;
```

```
    virtual HRESULT STDMETHODCALLTYPE UnmarshalInterface(
        _In_  IStream *pStm,
        _In_  REFIID riid,
        _Outptr_  void **ppv) = 0;

    virtual HRESULT STDMETHODCALLTYPE ReleaseMarshalData(
        _In_  IStream *pStm) = 0;

    virtual HRESULT STDMETHODCALLTYPE DisconnectObject(
        _In_  DWORD dwReserved) = 0;

};
```

In standard situations, unmarshaling on the client side is done with the help of the proxy object whose CLSID is retrieved from the registry. That works because both the client and server use the standard marshaler and follow the same process to figure out which object handles their side of things.

If a server takes control of the marshaling process, that also means that the unmarshaling process is non-standard. The server needs to communicate to the client what the correct (un)marshaler object is. GetUnmarshalClass is the method which is used for this. The server can tell the client which object implements the correct marshaling code for this particular situation, depending on the destination context.

From a client / server perspective, all that matters is whether the server object and the client threads are in the same apartment or not. That question determines whether there is need for marshaling or not. The actual process varies, depending on the distance between those apartments. It should be obvious that if those apartments are side by side in the same process, options for communicating are different than if they are on different machines. This is specified in the destination context. In ascending order of marshaling distance, the list goes:

1. MSHCTX_INPROC: marshaling happens between apartments in the same process. Both sides share the same memory space.
2. MSHCTX_LOCAL: marshaling happens between apartments on the same machine, and there is shared memory access allowed between the apartments.
3. MSHCTX_CROSSCTX: marshaling happens to a new context in the same apartment.
4. MSHCTX_NOSHAREDMEM: marshaling happens between apartments on the same machine, but there is no shared memory access allowed between the apartments. An example of this is when the server is a service running on the same machine. Services run in an isolated desktop session and cannot share memory by default.

5. MSHCTX_DIFFERENTMACHINE: marshaling happens between apartments on different machines. Memory access and security implications aside, this also means that the server cannot automatically assume that the same software is available on both machines. For example, an object might implement custom marshaling by value if it knows that certain values don't change in the object's lifetime. This would save on round trips and could be a huge potential timesaver in certain situations. It would also work only if the server is allowed to assume that the unmarshaling code on the server is also available on the client.

Depending on the context, the server can still decide to delegate the process to the default marshaling process and only customize the flow of data in specific cases where such optimizations make sense or certain things are possible. Delegating to the standard marshaler can be done via CoGetStandardMarshal which returns a pointer to the default IMarshal implementation for that interface.

The MSHFLAGS enumeration on the other hand deals with what we are trying to achieve with the marshaling operation.

1. NORMAL. An interface is being passed from 1 process to another. The interface can be unmarshaled only once.
2. TABLESTRONG. The marshaling data is stored in a table from which it can be unmarshaled multiple times. The fact that the marshaling data is in the table counts as a strong reference, meaning that even if no one else has a valid interface pointer anymore, the object will stay alive and another interface pointer can be unmarshaled.
3. TABLEWEAK. The marshaling data is stored in a table from which it can be unmarshaled multiple times, but it does not count as a strong reference. If no one has a valid interface pointer anymore, the entry in the table does not prevent the object from deleting itself.
4. NOPING Adding this flag when marshaling an original interface to an object (as opposed to a proxy) disables the PING protocol for the object.

Marshaling requires that data is transferred from the server to the client. This is done via a stream object that implements IStream. The amount of space that the COM runtime must provide in the stream is queried via a call to GetMarshalSizeMax. Note that this only concerns the amount of data that is needed to do the marshaling. Consider the hypothetical scenario where we want to marshal a large amount of data between apartments via shared memory. In that case, the max size is not the amount of data itself, but just the amount of data that is necessary to communicate the name of the file mapping that underpins the shared memory. If the data size that is communicated is too small, marshaling will fail and the stream may return errors such as STG_E_MEDIUMFULL. The communicated size is considered only valid between internal state changes of the object. The server must be prepared to handle errors gracefully.

DisconnectObject is used by the server as a normal part of the lifecycle during shutdown. It disconnects all external connections to its running objects.

That leaves MarshalInterface and UnmarshalInterface as the main points of interest. The sole purpose of MarshalInterface is to send the necessary information into the stream object to initialize the proxy on the client side. The sole purpose of UnmarshalInterface is to receive that information and initialize the proxy. Proxy objects may support more than 1 interface support one or more specific marshaling contexts. Barring special knowledge, the marshaling data would include a reference to the interface, marshaling flags, and whatever is needed to set up a connection between the proxy and the stub. Since you are implementing both sides of the tunnel, there are no hard restrictions, but it would be typical to set up a named pipe or RPC channel. Each side would manage their end of the connection and send data into the connection with a shared understanding of how a method call is serialized into the connection. On the server side, the stub would use this shared knowledge to deserialize the arguments and invoke the call in the correct apartment.

ReleaseMarshalData is used in scenarios where UnmarshalInterface is not called for whatever reason. During the call to MarshalInterface, data was put into the stream. This data must be purged from the stream, to allow cancellation to unwind the marshaling operation cleanly. Additionally, strongly marshal packets constitute a reference count that must be released properly so that the lifecycle management of the underlying objects is not disturbed.

Once the proxy and stub are created, MarshalInterface and UnmarshalInterface have done their job and are no longer playing an active role for every method call. IMarshal isn't involved in marshaling each and every method call. Its sole job is to set up the proxy which does. The actual method invocation is something you could implement any way you want.

Using IStream for marshaling

No matter which method a server may want to implement for marshaling, it will always require a means of passing instance specific and context dependent information to set up marshaling. The COM runtime sets up a secure and reliable communications channel between the client and server, in the form of an object which implements the IStream interface. The details of how this channel is implemented and managed are opaque to the marshaler. The only thing that matters is that it is a secure conduit for information between client and server. Bytes go in on the server side, and they come out on the client side. The exact meaning of those bytes is meaningless to the COM runtime.

There are a few restrictions:

- An object must state up front the maximum amount of data that it wants to put in the stream.
- An object cannot assume it has the stream to itself. An object being marshaled may be part of a hierarchy or collection of objects being marshaled. If multiple objects are marshaled into a stream, they must be unmarshaled in the same order because the stream is sequential.
- If an object puts X number of bytes into the stream, then the unmarshal operation must also remove X number of bytes from the stream. If the unmarshaling operation is cancelled and the marshaling data is released instead, the release operation must likewise remove X number of bytes from the stream. If a variable amount of data is put into the stream, then the proxy object is responsible for removing the exact number of bytes.
- The maximum amount of data into the stream is 4 GB.

A note on apartment requirements

An object which does the marshaling (in this case our own object) must support both STA and MTA apartments. When marshaling is performed, the COM runtime creates an instance of that object. What normally happens when any object is created, is that the runtime checks the current apartment type, and creates an object in that apartment only if the threading requirements match. If they don't, the object is created in a thread that is spun up as needed in a compatible apartment, and a proxy is created in the client apartment.

But if the object in question is the proxy object, and it does not support the client apartment type, this causes a recursive loop, where a proxy object is created in an apartment that is not the client's apartments. It will then create a proxy to that proxy object. Except that 2nd proxy is also not compatible with the client's apartment so it is created in a different apartment and a 3d proxy is created, etc. Eventually this causes an error and the entire operation is aborted with E_ABORT.

Any object that does implement its own marshaling should support both apartment types.

Marshaling interfaces between threads

So far, every time we used an interface pointer, be it a raw pointer or a proxy, has been handed to us either via one of the CoXxx type APIs, or via a marshaling operation by a proxy that we don't know about because it's transparent to us. In both situations, we received a pointer that is valid in the thread we're using it in. However, this may not always be the case. There are many situations where we get a pointer, and then use that pointer in a different thread such as a worker thread. As a rule of thumb, we only know that the pointer is valid in the current thread.

There is really only 1 scenario in which this does not pose a problem. If we receive that pointer in a thread in the MTA, and we know the worker thread is in the MTA, then that pointer is going to be valid for the worker thread, and we don't have to do anything. In all other cases, we must ask the COM runtime to give us a hand and transport that pointer to the target thread in a safe manner so that it is valid in the thread or apartment where it will be used.

To do this, the APIs CoMarshalInterface and CoUnmarshalInterface are used.

```
//combaseapi.h
WINOLEAPI
CoMarshalInterface(
     _In_ LPSTREAM pStm,
     _In_ REFIID riid,
     _In_ LPUNKNOWN pUnk,
     _In_ DWORD dwDestContext,
     _In_opt_ LPVOID pvDestContext,
     _In_ DWORD mshlflags
     );

WINOLEAPI
CoUnmarshalInterface(
     _In_ LPSTREAM pStm,
     _In_ REFIID riid,
     _COM_Outptr_ LPVOID  FAR * ppv
     );
```

The essence of what these APIs do is simple. CoMarshalInterface is supplied with a stream object, the IID of the specified interface, and the interface pointer that needs to be marshaled. dwDestContext and mshlFlags control the manner in which the marshaling is done, by specifying which assumptions can be used.

Through the supplied interface pointer, CoMarshalInterface queries whether the object implements the IMarshal interface. If it doesn't implement IMarshal like most objects, the COM runtime looks up CLSID of the proxy for the specified interface in the registry which does implement IMarshal. Either way, there will be an IMarshal whose methods would be called as follows:

1. GetMarshalSizeMax to determine how many bytes are needed to pass all necessary information for the operation.
2. GetUnmarshalClass to get the CLSID of the object which is going to perform the Unmarshal operation. Usually, marshaling and unmarshaling are done by the same class. However, this is not mandatory. A custom marshaling implementation may want to specify a different CLSID.
3. MarshalInterface to write all data into the stream that is necessary to initialize the proxy. If you implement your own proxy and stub, it is up to you to stream whatever data you need to set it all up as long as you don't write more data than was specified in GetMarshalSizeMax.

For unmarshaling, CoUnmarshalInterface will create the object that was identified during the call to GetUnmarshalClass. This object implements the specified Interface because it needs to mimic the marshaled interface as well as IMarshal. The UnmarshalInterface method receives the marshal stream, sets up the proxy internally and then queries itself for the requested interface to pass to the caller.

'Essential COM' by Don Box has a description of the data packet that is put in the stream when standard marshaling is used. I could not find the source information for this, so I am not going to cover that in detail here. Let it suffice to state that the information in the stream is whatever is needed to set up the RPC connection between the proxy and the stub. On the requesting side, CoUnmarshalInterface is called with the information that was put into the stream to set up the proxy object. It will create a proxy object whose methods are just forwarding each method invocation to the real object, using RPC.

In most circumstances, this process happens out of sight, and you would not use these lower-level APIs directly. A typical usage scenario where you would need to use them is to pass an existing interface pointer to a worker thread, which may be in another apartment in the same process. To use that pointer in an apartment for which may or may not be valid, we need to marshal it manually. There are a couple of approaches possible. A roundabout way is as follows:

```
HRESULT MarshalInterfaceIntoStream(
    REFIID riid, IUnknown* unkPtr, IStream ** stream)
{
    if (!stream)
        return E_POINTER;
```

```
    *stream = NULL;

    HRESULT hRes = CreateStreamOnHGlobal(
        NULL, TRUE, stream);
    if (FAILED(hRes))
        return hRes;

    hRes = CoMarshalInterface(
        *stream, riid, unkPtr, MSHCTX_INPROC, NULL, 0);

    if (FAILED(hRes)) {
        (*stream)->Release();
        *stream = NULL;
    }

    return hRes;
}
```

This code creates a new stream for receiving the marshal packet. We use CreateStreamOnHGlobal. This is a simple memory stream which the IStream acts as a funnel for the marshal data. The resulting stream can then be passed to another thread which can call

```
CoUnmarshalInterface(stream, riid, ppv);
stream->Release();
```

It doesn't matter what sort of apartment each side is in. COM will automatically do the right thing, based on the situation and create another proxy or raw pointer as appropriate. 'Essential COM' mentions that this type of marshaling will fail if the interface being marshaled is a proxy, but that is no longer the case.

In most cases where we need to marshal an interface, it is for the purpose of getting it from one thread to another. Rather than taking the manual approach outlined above, a real application would use the 2 APIs which are supplied specifically for this purpose:

```
//combaseapi.h
WINOLEAPI
CoMarshalInterThreadInterfaceInStream(
    _In_ REFIID riid,
    _In_ LPUNKNOWN pUnk,
    _Outptr_ LPSTREAM* ppStm
    );

WINOLEAPI
CoGetInterfaceAndReleaseStream(
    _In_ LPSTREAM pStm,
    _In_ REFIID iid,
```

```
    _COM_Outptr_ LPVOID  FAR * ppv
    );
```

The former API takes an interface pointer and creates a stream containing all required information to create a new interface pointer. The resulting stream is safe in the entire process, regardless of thread. The latter API takes that stream, rebuilds the interface pointer and releases the stream.

If you want to be able to unmarshal the pointer more than once, CoMarshalInterface needs to be called with the MSHLCTX_TABLESTRONG flag, and then send either a copy of the stream to each place where you want to unmarshal, or implement a synchronization method to make sure that each location can rewind the stream and unmarshal in peace without being interrupted.

Of course, this is just a simple example where we have the convenience of dealing with an in-process memory stream. When COM marshals an interface to a different process, or even a different computer, there will be a lot more going on, and the streams involved will require more internal bookkeeping and communication between the different subsystems, authentication, etc. But even then, CoMarshalInterface and CoUnmarshalInterface will be used.

For more complex scenarios where interfaces need to be marshaled to other apartments on a regular basis, there is an object known as the 'Global Interface Table'. As the name implies, this is a global table where an interface can be registered, resulting in a cookie of DWORD type. This cookie can then be sent to the destination apartment and simply be unmarshaled as needed, where needed. The GlobalInterfaceTable is a COM object, just like any other. You create it like any other COM object.

```
HRESULT hr = CoCreateInstance(
    CLSID_StdGlobalInterfaceTable,
    NULL,
    CLSCTX_INPROC_SERVER,
    IID_IGlobalInterfaceTable,
    (void**)&g_GIT);
```

Using that object is an alternative to using the CoMarshalInterThreadInterfaceInStream function and its counterpart. Instead of having to deal with single use streams, you can register a specified interface pointer in the GIT in return for a cookie.

```
//objidl.h
HRESULT RegisterInterfaceInGlobal(
    IUnknown* pUnk,
    REFIID   riid,
```

```
    DWORD* pdwCookie
);
```

You can then simply pass the cookie to any thread where the interface is needed. The thread can retrieve a copy of the interface upon showing the cookie.

```
//objidl.h
HRESULT GetInterfaceFromGlobal(
    DWORD  dwCookie,
    REFIID riid,
    void** ppv
);
```

This function returns an AddRef'ed pointer which the client can use until they are done with it. The registered interface itself can be used as many times in as many places as needed. Finally, when the interface is no longer needed, it must be revoked from the GIT.

```
//objidl.h
HRESULT RevokeInterfaceFromGlobal(
    DWORD dwCookie
);
```

It is up to the application itself to synchronize access to the GIT. You also don't need to reference it directly. It is process global, so the different xxxxGlobal functions can use it without having to pass it as input. The entire point of having 1 global interface table is that it is global.

Marshaling by value

The default proxy / stub architecture put in place by MIDL is highly optimized and debugged. It uses RPC functions that are supported directly by the operating system. Throwing all that overboard to implement your own marshaling is virtually never a good idea. You're not going to create anything that is more stable, secure, efficient or performant than what already exists. Especially not for general purpose method forwarding.

However, rolling your own can make sense and provide a measurable improvement in performance if you can marshal by value. Value marshaling means you can copy the internal state of an object into a clone of the object on the client side. The obvious benefit is that whenever you access the data, the proxy accesses the local copy of the data without requiring an RPC round trip to a remote apartment.

The restriction here is that it only works if the data of an object doesn't change after it is created or rather, after the first time it is marshaled. In cases where data objects are used with a high frequency for relatively simple operations, this can result in a huge performance gain. Especially if the object's apartment is in a different process or even a different machine. The typical example implementation uses the stream object as a conduit for data transport. Suppose we have an object that represents a spacetime coordinate, which is created by some coordinate provider. We can implement IMarshal on that object to provide a value marshaling solution.

The first order of business is to determine if we are in a situation where our proposed solution will work. Since this information is needed in several places we can implement it in a subroutine.

```
bool CSpaceTimeCoordinate::IsCustomMarshaled(DWORD dwDestContext)
{
    return (dwDestContext == MSHCTX_CROSSCTX ||
        dwDestContext == MSHCTX_INPROC ||
        dwDestContext == MSHCTX_LOCAL ||
        dwDestContext == MSHCTX_NOSHAREDMEM);
}
```

These are the 4 situations where we can safely use custom marshaling, because all 4 contexts indicate that both sides of the marshaling operation for the ISpaceTimeCoordinate interface are on the same machine. MSHCTX_DIFFERENTMACHINE would indicate that the operation crosses machine boundaries, and there is no guarantee that the custom operation can succeed on the other side. If the interface is an application specific interface, then obviously you could choose to also cover that scenario. If it is some industry standard interface, that assumption would not be safe because there can be many implementations and the other side might only support the standard MIDL generated marshaler.

To inform the COM runtime that we want to use custom marshaling, we must simply answer the QueryInterface call for IMarshal. To inform the client side which object implements the Unmarshal side of things, we must provide the CLSID of the proxy object.

```
STDMETHODIMP CSpaceTimeCoordinate::GetUnmarshalClass(
    REFIID riid,
    void* pv,
    DWORD dwDestContext,
    void* pvDestContext,
    DWORD mshlflags,
    CLSID* pCid)
{
    if (IsCustomMarshaled(dwDestContext)) {
        *pCid = CLSID_SpaceTimeCoordinate;
        return S_OK;
    }
```

```
    CComPtr<IMarshal> stdMarshal;
    HRESULT hr = CoGetStandardMarshal(
        riid, GetUnknown(),dwDestContext,pvDestContext, mshlflags,
&stdMarshal);
    if (SUCCEEDED(hr)) {
        hr = stdMarshal->GetUnmarshalClass(
            riid, pv, dwDestContext, pvDestContext, mshlflags, pCid);
    }

    return hr;
}
```

The documentation states that if you do custom marshaling, you handle only the specific cases you want to handle, and you must delegate to the standard marshaler in all other cases. In the case of our coordinate, we specify that the unmarshaler object has the same CLSID as the object we're marshaling. This is typical for objects in in-process servers, and it makes perfect sense. The object already implements IMarshal as well as the ISpaceTimeCoordinate interface we're marshaling. The COM runtime can just create another instance and ask it to unmarshal itself from a stream. For out-of-process servers, the unmarshaling object may be different because the proxy must be in a DLL that can be loaded by the client.

The object being marshaled must figure out how much data it requires in the marshal stream.

```
STDMETHODIMP CSpaceTimeCoordinate::GetMarshalSizeMax(
    _In_  REFIID riid,
    _In_opt_  void* pv,
    _In_  DWORD dwDestContext,
    _Reserved_  void* pvDestContext,
    _In_  DWORD mshlflags,
    _Out_  DWORD* pSize)
{

    if (IsCustomMarshaled(dwDestContext)) {
        //4 coordinate values
        *pSize = sizeof(ULONG) * 4;
        return S_OK;
    }

    // snip delegate to standard marshal
}
```

Our coordinate has 4 axis values

```
STDMETHODIMP CSpaceTimeCoordinate::MarshalInterface(
    _In_  IStream* pStm,
    _In_  REFIID riid,
    _In_opt_  void* pv,
```

```
    _In_  DWORD dwDestContext,
    _Reserved_  void* pvDestContext,
    _In_  DWORD mshlflags)
{
    if (IsCustomMarshaled(dwDestContext)) {
        HRESULT hr = S_OK;
        if (SUCCEEDED(hr)) hr = pStm->Write(&m_x, sizeof(m_x), NULL);
        if (SUCCEEDED(hr)) hr = pStm->Write(&m_y, sizeof(m_y), NULL);
        if (SUCCEEDED(hr)) hr = pStm->Write(&m_z, sizeof(m_z), NULL);
        if (SUCCEEDED(hr)) hr = pStm->Write(&m_t, sizeof(m_t), NULL);
        return hr;
    }

    // snip delegate to standard marshal
}
```

The stream now contains everything that is needed to create a clone of the object in the target apartment. COM creates an instance of the object with the specified CLSID, queries for IMarshal, and calls UnmarshalInterface with the stream as a parameter.

```
STDMETHODIMP CSpaceTimeCoordinate::UnmarshalInterface(
    _In_  IStream* pStm,
    _In_  REFIID riid,
    _Outptr_  void** ppv)
{
    HRESULT hr = S_OK;
    if (SUCCEEDED(hr)) hr = pStm->Read(&m_x, sizeof(m_x), NULL);
    if (SUCCEEDED(hr)) hr = pStm->Read(&m_y, sizeof(m_y), NULL);
    if (SUCCEEDED(hr)) hr = pStm->Read(&m_z, sizeof(m_z), NULL);
    if (SUCCEEDED(hr)) hr = pStm->Read(&m_t, sizeof(m_t), NULL);
    if(SUCCEEDED(hr)) hr = QueryInterface(riid, ppv);
    return hr;
}
```

The proxy is now a copy of the original object. You could think of this marshal / unmarshal operation as similar in nature to a C++ copy constructor. The final QueryInterface ensures that the client gets the correct interface pointer after the operation. If the operation is cancelled and the stream is not unmarshaled, the cleanup routine must remove from the stream what was put in.

```
STDMETHODIMP CSpaceTimeCoordinate::ReleaseMarshalData(
    _In_  IStream* pStm)
{
    return pStm->Seek(
        { sizeof(ULONG) * 4, 0 },
        STREAM_SEEK_CUR,
        NULL);
}
```

This can be achieved by moving the read pointer forward to the location in the stream where it would be after a successful Unmarshal operation.

Using shared memory

The preceding example uses the stream as a convenient way to pass the data. For small amounts of data, or data that does not change anymore after the initialization phase, this is the most efficient option because the stream will be created and used anyway. Even for non-trivial amounts of data, this is probably still the most efficient way to work. However, it is possible to use other approaches.

Suppose we work with large blocks of data that are initialized in some apartment, and we need to marshal them to a client. As efficient as the stream implementation is, it would still require significant amounts of data to be copied back and forth. Instead of storing the data on the normal heap, we could store it in a section of shared memory. Instead of copying the data into the stream and then copying it into another piece of heap memory in the proxy, we could simply map a pointer to the same piece of shared memory. No data would have to be copied, other than the bookkeeping data needed to identify the shared memory. For small objects this wouldn't be worth it but if it saves you from having to copy megabytes of data back and forth or marshal calls to access that data back and forth, it could be a significant time save.

For the sake of this example, we're going to work with 2 COM objects: A data object that supports memory access, and a generator object which creates data objects. Each object has just the one interface it needs.

```
[
      object,
      uuid(22256201-227f-40c8-87c5-760cc7e8d4d7)
]
interface IMyDataObject : IUnknown
{
    HRESULT GetAt([in] ULONG index, [out, retval] ULONG* value);
    HRESULT IsProxy([out, retval] ULONG* isProxy);
    HRESULT NumElements([out, retval] ULONG* elements);
};
[
      object,
      uuid(ee7e9a19-5209-425d-9c03-cd5d9ddd0efc),
]
interface IDataGenerator : IUnknown
{
    HRESULT GetDataObject([out] IMyDataObject** data);
};
```

Initializing the shared memory in the data object is simple (error handling removed for clarity).

```
HRESULT CMyDataObject::InitializeSharedMemory(const GUID& guid, ULONG size)
{
    wchar_t guidString[128];
    HRESULT hr = S_OK;

    int len = StringFromGUID2(guid, guidString, 128);
        m_handle = CreateFileMappingW(
            INVALID_HANDLE_VALUE,
            NULL,
            PAGE_READWRITE,
            0,
            size,
            guidString);

    m_ptr = (ULONG*)MapViewOfFile(m_handle, FILE_MAP_WRITE, 0, 0, size);
    m_size = size;

    return hr;
}
```

CreateFileMappingW creates a section of shared memory. The name seems odd but that is because originally, this function was used for mapping files into memory into a named region. When used with an invalid handle value, it created a section of shared memory instead. The name needs to be unique because it's meant to be used with a specific instance of CMyDataObject. Using a GUID as a name is an obvious choice. After creating the section, we can map it to a pointer. As long as there is an open handle to that named section, the contents will remain intact. The beauty of this arrangement is that to map the same section of memory somewhere else, all we need is that GUID. When we create a new CMyDataObject instance, we initialize the mapping and fill it with data.

```
HRESULT CMyDataObject::Initialize(ULONG elements)
{
    HRESULT hr = CoCreateGuid(&m_guid);
    if (SUCCEEDED(hr)) {
        hr = InitializeSharedMemory(m_guid, elements * sizeof(ULONG));
    }

    if (SUCCEEDED(hr)) {
        for (int i = 0; i < elements; i++)
            m_ptr[i] = i * 2;
    }
    return hr;
}
```

We create a new GUID, create a memory section with the GUID as its name, and put some data into it. The initialization routine is not part of the COM interface. It doesn't need to be. The data object is initialized directly by CDataGenerator after it is created.

```
STDMETHODIMP CDataGenerator::GetDataObject(IMyDataObject** data)
{
    if (!data)
        return E_POINTER;

    *data = NULL;
    CComObject<CMyDataObject>* object = NULL;

    HRESULT hr = CComObject<CMyDataObject>::CreateInstance(&object);
    if (SUCCEEDED(hr)) {
        object->AddRef();
        hr = object->Initialize(10);
        if (SUCCEEDED(hr)) {
            hr = object->QueryInterface<IMyDataObject>(data);
        }
        object->Release();
    }
    return hr;
}
```

We create an instance of CMyDataObject as a COM object, initialize it, and pass the pointer as an output parameter. From a functional point of view, there is nothing more to add so let's look at the first attempt at an IMarshal implementation. To evaluate the marshaling context, we remove the MSHCTX_NOSHAREDMEM option because logically, we can only marshal if shared memory is allowed.

```
bool CMyDataObject::IsCustomMarshaled(DWORD dwDestContext, REFIID riid)
{
    return ((dwDestContext == MSHCTX_CROSSCTX ||
        dwDestContext == MSHCTX_INPROC ||
        dwDestContext == MSHCTX_LOCAL));
}
```

GetMarshalSizeMax has no surprises.

```
STDMETHODIMP CMyDataObject::GetMarshalSizeMax(
    /* snip */
{
    if (IsCustomMarshaled(dwDestContext)) {
        *pSize = sizeof(m_guid) + sizeof(m_size);
        return S_OK;
    }
    return hr;
}
```

We need to marshal both the GUID that identifies the section as well as the size of the memory backing it. The marshaling implementation then becomes:

```
STDMETHODIMP CMyDataObject::MarshalInterface(
    /* snip */
{
    if (IsCustomMarshaled(dwDestContext)) {
        HRESULT hr = S_OK;
        if (SUCCEEDED(hr)) hr = pStm->Write(&m_guid, sizeof(m_guid), NULL);
        if (SUCCEEDED(hr)) hr = pStm->Write(&m_size, sizeof(m_size), NULL);
        return hr;
    }
    /* snip */
    return hr;
}
```

And to create a proxy, we get those values from the stream and initialize the shared memory section that is now being referenced in the proxy object.

```
STDMETHODIMP CMyDataObject::UnmarshalInterface(
    /*snip */
{
    HRESULT hr = S_OK;

    if (SUCCEEDED(hr)) hr = pStm->Read(&m_guid, sizeof(m_guid), NULL);
    if (SUCCEEDED(hr)) hr = pStm->Read(&m_size, sizeof(m_size), NULL);
    if (SUCCEEDED(hr)) hr = InitializeSharedMemory(m_guid, m_size);
    m_isProxy = true;

    if (SUCCEEDED(hr)) hr = QueryInterface(riid, ppv);

    return hr;
}
```

Everything looks good, all the pieces of the puzzle are in place, but when we run the client application:

```
    CComPtr<IDataGenerator> provider;
    provider.CoCreateInstance(L"SharedMemoryMarshaler.DataGenerator");

    CComPtr<IMyDataObject> dataObject;
    provider->GetDataObject(&dataObject);

    for (int i = 0; i < dataObject->NumElements(); i++) {
        wcout << L"Element " << dataObject->GetAt(i) << endl;
```

Things don't work out. Instead of a sequential list of numbers, all elements are 0.

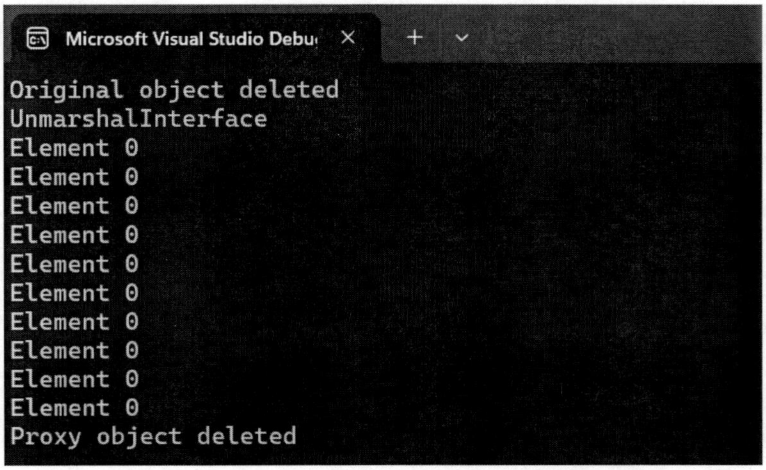

The clue as to what happens becomes visible if we print some debugging information concerning the lifecycle of the original object and the marshaling operation. We used the same approach as when we made a pure value marshaler. The underlying assumption in Value Marshaling is that whatever is in the marshal stream is everything needed to rebuild an object. But that is not entirely true in this case. The stream contains everything to build a proxy that references the same memory, assuming that the shared memory and its contents will still be around. In this case, with no other parties holding on to an AddRef'ed reference, the normal sequence of events is as follows:

1. CDataGenerator::GetDataObject passes an AddRef'ed IMyDataObject* as output.
2. The COM runtime queries the object for IMarshal and then use MarshalInterface to marshal the GUID and size into a stream.
3. Having no more use for the interface pointer, COM Release the interface. Because no one else is holding a reference, the object gets released and the shared memory handle is closed.
4. Client side, COM creates a new instance of the object, gets IMarshal and calls UnmarshalInterface which gets the GUID and size from the stream, and creates a shared memory section with that name.

Everything followed the rules to the letter. It's just unfortunate that the contents of the memory were linked to the lifecycle of the original object. What we need is to keep the original object alive long enough that when UnmarshalInterface does its thing, the shared memory still exists. Fortunately, no complex mechanism is needed because COM provides us with all the necessary tools. The solution is as simple as marshaling an IUnknown pointer along with the rest of the data. The only minor complication is that when we ask COM to marshal the IUnknown pointer, it will invoke our IMarshal implementation. For this to work, we need to ensure that only our data interface is marshaled using custom marshaling, and other interface via standard RPC marshaling.

```
bool CMyDataObject::IsCustomMarshaled(DWORD dwDestContext, REFIID riid)
{
    return ((dwDestContext == MSHCTX_CROSSCTX ||
        dwDestContext == MSHCTX_INPROC ||
        dwDestContext == MSHCTX_LOCAL) && IsEqualIID(riid,
IID_IMyDataObject));
}
```

GetUnmarshalClass stays the same, except it now also takes the requested riid into account.

```
STDMETHODIMP CMyDataObject::GetUnmarshalClass(
    /*snip */
{
    if (IsCustomMarshaled(dwDestContext, riid)) {
        *pCid = CLSID_MyDataObject;
        return S_OK;
    }
    /*snip */
}
```

GetMarshalSizeMax becomes a bit more complicated because the overall marshaling size is going to increase. We're no longer just streaming the GUID and the size, we're also streaming a marshal packet for the IUnknown pointer.

```
STDMETHODIMP CMyDataObject::GetMarshalSizeMax(
    /*snip */ )
{
    if (!pSize)
        return E_POINTER;

    CComPtr<IMarshal> stdMarshal;
    HRESULT hr = CoGetStandardMarshal(
        riid,GetUnknown(),dwDestContext,pvDestContext,mshlflags,&stdMarshal);
    if (SUCCEEDED(hr)) {

        if (IsCustomMarshaled(dwDestContext, riid)) {
            hr = stdMarshal->GetMarshalSizeMax(
                IID_IUnknown,
                pv, dwDestContext, pvDestContext, mshlflags, pSize);

            *pSize = sizeof(m_guid) + sizeof(m_size);
            return S_OK;
        }
        hr = stdMarshal->GetMarshalSizeMax(
            riid, pv, dwDestContext, pvDestContext, mshlflags, pSize);
```

```
    }

    return hr;
}
```

We need the standard marshaler no matter what we do here, because even in our custom marshaling solution, the IUnknown pointer needs to be marshaled, and the required size is going to depend on the context and the flags. Marshaling itself is going to be similar except for the additional step of marshaling the IUnknown pointer.

```
STDMETHODIMP CMyDataObject::MarshalInterface(
    /* snip */
{
    if (IsCustomMarshaled(dwDestContext)) {
        HRESULT hr = S_OK;
        if (SUCCEEDED(hr)) hr = pStm->Write(&m_guid, sizeof(m_guid), NULL);
        if (SUCCEEDED(hr)) hr = pStm->Write(&m_size, sizeof(m_size), NULL);
        if (SUCCEEDED(hr)) hr = CoMarshalInterface(
                                    pStm, IID_IUnknown, GetUnknown(),
                                    dwDestContext, pvDestContext, mshlflags);
        return hr;
    }
    /* snip */
    return hr;
}
```

Unmarshaling is going to have the have the same step added in reverse direction.

```
STDMETHODIMP CMyDataObject::UnmarshalInterface(
    /* snip */
{
    HRESULT hr = S_OK;

    if (SUCCEEDED(hr)) hr = pStm->Read(&m_guid, sizeof(m_guid), NULL);
    if (SUCCEEDED(hr)) hr = pStm->Read(&m_size, sizeof(m_size), NULL);
    CComPtr<IUnknown> sourceUnknown;
    if (SUCCEEDED(hr)) hr = CoUnmarshalInterface(
                                pStm, IID_IUnknown, (void**) &
sourceUnknown.p);
    if (SUCCEEDED(hr)) hr = InitializeSharedMemory(m_guid, m_size);
    m_isProxy = true;

    if(SUCCEEDED(hr)) hr = QueryInterface(riid, ppv);

    return hr;
}
```

And to complete the change, we must also modify the release of the marshal stream.

```
STDMETHODIMP CMyDataObject::ReleaseMarshalData(
    /* snip */
```

```
{
    HRESULT hr = pStm->Seek(
        { sizeof(m_guid) + sizeof(m_size), 0 },
        STREAM_SEEK_CUR,
        NULL);
    if (SUCCEEDED(hr))
        hr = CoReleaseMarshalData(pStm);

    return hr;
}
```

The DisconnectObject can stay the same because even though we now have situation where a remote reference exists, that connection is released either way during the marshaling process or when the marshal packet is released. If we build and run the code again, it now works as expected.

```
UnmarshalInterface for REFIID {22256201-227F-40C8-87C5-760CC7E8D4D7}
Original object deleted
Element 0
Element 2
Element 4
Element 6
Element 8
Element 10
Element 12
Element 14
Element 16
Element 18
Proxy object deleted
```

One thing that is very elegant about shared memory marshaling is its efficiency. In all scenarios where it is supported, we get instant data access with very little overhead. In all other scenarios, standard marshaling is used and we lose nothing because while the mechanism is slightly different to using the standard heap memory, shared memory is no different from heap memory. It's just managed in a different way.

A note on endian-ness

In 'Essential COM', Don Box performs an endian check as part of the unmarshal operation. The word 'endian' is a reference to Gulliver's Travels where different tribes fight wars about which end of an egg was the correct end to open an egg: the little end or the big end.

As quirky as it may sound, in the computing world this word was adopted and refers to the order in which the bits of a value are stored in memory. A 32-bit value consists of 4 bytes. If a 32-bit value starts at a given memory address, there needs to be agreement about the order in which those bytes are store: most significant first, or least significant first. Intel compatible architectures use little endian, meaning the least significant byte comes first. Motorola CPUs use big endian, meaning the most significant byte comes first.

Within a certain architecture, this doesn't really matter because if program A writes a 32-bit value into as stream and program B reads that 32-bit value, they're implicitly agreeing on the byte order because they run on the same platform. Any 32-bit value that goes into the stream will come out the other end with all its bits in the same order.

If marshaling is done to another machine, that is no longer guaranteed. If program A runs on an AMD compatible x64 CPU and program B runs on a similar CPU, things will work. They use the same endian-ness, meaning the individual bytes in a 32-bit value are stored in the same order. If program B runs a more exotic CPU such as an old Apple computer with a Motorola CPU, this is not the case.

In today's world, there are no COM environments which support anything but little endian. There are also no legacy environments which do. When 'Essential COM' was written, there was likewise no COM environment which supported anything but little endian. However, the COM landscape was still blossoming, and Apple was still using Motorola CPUs in big endian mode. Microsoft also had Windows NT running on MIPS, PowerPC and Alpha, which could theoretically operate in big endian mode. There was a realistic chance that at some point after COM was first created, there would be a big endian architecture running COM.

Any system which would support COM, would handle endian conversion at the infrastructure level and be generally transparent. However, any custom marshaling implementation which directly gets the marshaling byte stream would have to manually account for the possibility of endian differences. Don's example is a good example of defensive programming because at the time it seemed possible that COM would eventually run on big endian platforms. In such scenarios, any marshaling operation would need some sort of header with a known value that can be checked. For our coordinate, that might be implemented as follows:

```
//MarshalInterface side
ULONG header = 0xDEADBEEF;
pStm->Write(&header, sizeof(header), NULL);
pStm->Write(&m_x, sizeof(m_x), NULL);
//snip..

//UnmarshalInterface side
ULONG header = 0;
```

```
pStm->Read(&header, sizeof(header), NULL);
pStm->Read(&m_x, sizeof(m_x), NULL);
//snip...

if (header == 0xDEADBEEF) {
    //endianness OK
}
else if (header == 0xEFBEADDE) {
    //needs endian swap
    m_x = _byteswap_ulong(m_x);
}
```

History went in a different direction, and COM never spread to big endian systems. Or rather, industries slowly converged on little endian as a standard. Tracking down endian errors in a distributed system with different architectures can be a time consuming and complex task. Don Box made the right decision to anticipate it at that point in time. Today it is not necessary to consider this possibility because all systems supporting COM use little endian.

Free Threaded Marshaling

The custom marshaling situations so far have all centered around optimizing the access of memory content by value marshaling or shared memory marshaling to eliminate RPC round trips. The limitation is that the proxy is a completely new object which is independent of the original object.

Implementing a full custom marshaling approach to the original object that mimics standard marshaling is not something anyone would do because you wouldn't gain anything. Standard marshaling is as optimized as it's going to be while abiding by all security considerations, apartment restrictions, etc. However, there is one more option for an object to optimize that is worthwhile. And relatively cheap.

Standard COM marshaling abides by the normal apartment restrictions. If an object knows it is completely apartment-independent, it has the option to override marshaling and simply hand out a raw interface pointer, regardless of what the apartments are. This is called Free Threaded marshaling. Using it is trivial because COM provides us with the Free Threaded Marshaler (FTM).

We can manually add it to a COM object but in an ATL project, using the FTM is a simple checkbox option which produces the exact same configuration as if we had added it manually sometime after adding the object to the project.

The FTM is created upon construction and released upon destruction.

```
CComPtr<IUnknown> m_pUnkMarshaler;

HRESULT FinalConstruct()
{
        return CoCreateFreeThreadedMarshaler(
                GetControllingUnknown(), &m_pUnkMarshaler.p);
}

void FinalRelease()
{
        m_pUnkMarshaler.Release();
}
```

The FTM is aggregated into the object which uses it, because it provides an implementation of IMarshal that must follow the rules of COM. A QueryInterface through it must return the controlling IUnknown, which means it must be aggregated. The object's interface map is then modified to properly forward the request for IMarshal to the FTM.

```
BEGIN_COM_MAP(CSomeObject)
        COM_INTERFACE_ENTRY(ISomeObject)
        COM_INTERFACE_ENTRY_AGGREGATE(IID_IMarshal, m_pUnkMarshaler.p)
END_COM_MAP()
```

That is all there is to implementing it. Whether this makes sense or is even legal, depends on the object and the expected use case. Free threading has obvious performance benefits and it's simple. Adding the marshaler adds a number of bytes to the size of the object but that is no longer the concern it was in the late 90's. What matters more is the expected use case. If an object has method calls that happen only occasionally, or which cause a lot of processing, the relative performance gain of eliminating the marshaling may not be significant. If there are many repeated calls that are trivial, the relative performance gain could be big. For a small data object, that is only accessed once or twice, it may be preferable to value-marshal. Of course, optimization should be driven by need. In most cases, if objects are created in a sensible apartment, marshaling isn't needed at all.

The more important question is whether Free Threaded Marshaling is allowed in the first place. The object should be programmed in a fully thread safe manner. That is a requirement for any object that supports MTA so that should be a given. However, if the object uses any object to which it holds interface pointers, the situation becomes more complicated. If an object holds an interface pointer that is expected to be used in a specific apartment and it's now used in the wrong apartment because our object is free threading and hands out raw pointers to any apartment, various errors may occur.

Whether the Free Threaded Marshaler can be used or not must be evaluated carefully for the specific situation to ensure that there are no violations of apartment boundaries.

The case for MTA-only objects

When we first covered apartments, we covered that the main 2 types are STA and MTA, and the reason for having STA was to protect against multithreaded access as well as deal with cases where objects have thread affinity. Having STA-only objects makes sense for such cases. And if an object does not have those restrictions, it makes sense to support both apartment types and let the client choose which to use.

However, in some cases it makes sense to only support MTA and not STA. Sometimes an object uses worker threads to offload work. If that worker thread needs to use an interface pointer that comes from a client or from some internal object, making it safe for the worker thread is relatively easy if we have access to that pointer. CoMarshalInterThreadInterfaceInStream and CoGetInterfaceAndReleaseStream can be used for transporting that pointer.

The situation becomes more problematic if the object's worker thread needs a pointer to that object. To ensure that whatever the thread is doing is safe for all the interface pointers that may be used during worker thread's use of that object, the pointer must be marshaled to the apartment of the worker thread.

Consider the following scenario: A client creates an object which itself creates a worker thread for background processing. The worker thread exists solely for the purpose of supporting the object's background activities. A logical place to control the thread's lifecycle is to create it in FinalConstruct and terminate it in FinalRelease.

```
HRESULT FinalConstruct()
{
        //Create worker thread and pass IStream
        return S_OK;
}

void FinalRelease()
{
        //signal thread and wait until terminated
}
```

The exact implementation here is irrelevant. The important point is that the lifecycle of the worker thread is tied to the lifecycle of the object.

In the following example, a client creates an object in its own STA apartment. The worker thread exists in the MTA and uses a marshaled interface pointer for getting work items and reporting back.

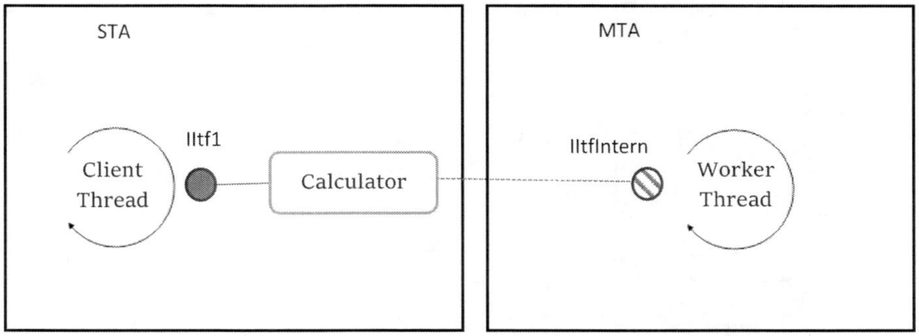

This setup follows the rules of COM and will work as expected. The problem starts when the client releases its interface pointer.

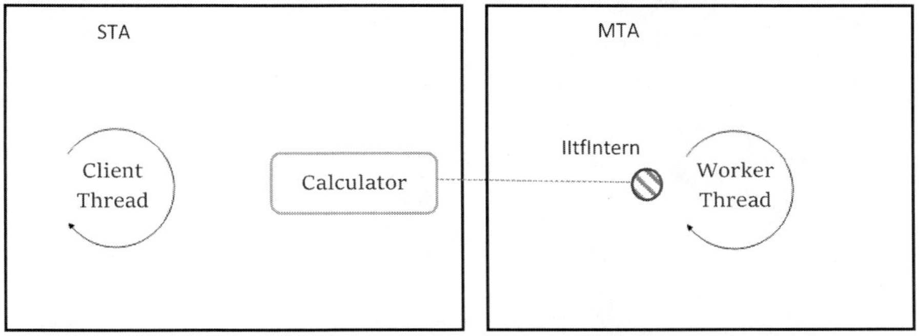

The client releases the last publicly owned pointer, and we'd expect the object to delete itself. However, the worker thread is holding a reference as well. The object will not delete itself and terminate the thread while there are outstanding references, and if the thread is running it won't release that last reference.

There are various ways we could attempt to solve this. One of those would be to marshal the reference as a weak reference, unmarshal it every time we need it and then release the unmarshaled pointer when we're done. Aside from the additional error handling and complexity it would work as advertised but we'd run into a second problem: interfaces are public. Anyone can query for them. It is conceivable that the IItfIntern interface exposes internals that are only intended for the worker thread and not any nosy client or application developer. Ideally, in such situations we'd simply use the object through its pointer. But that comes with the restriction that we can only safely do so if the worker thread and the object are in the same apartment. The simplest way to achieve this is to restrict the object to MTA only. The client can still use the STA and will automatically receive a marshaled interface pointer from the COM runtime. No one will be the wiser.

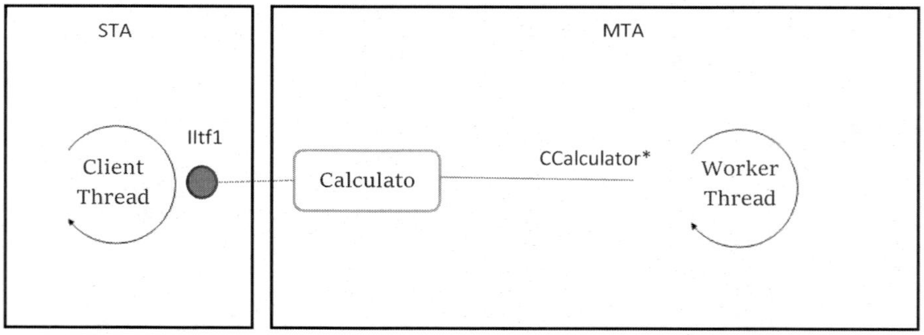

The downside is that each call will be marshaled, which may or may not be a performance issue. This could be solved relatively easily just by switching the client to MTA as well.

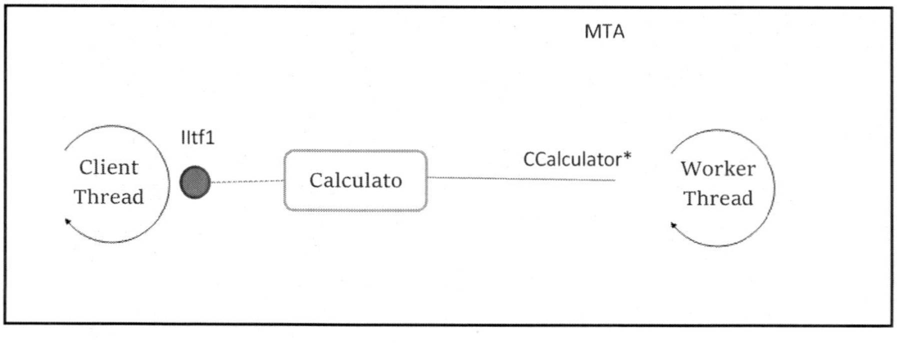

Whether this is possible depends on the situation. If the client is a Windows user interface object, this may be problematic because they are created in the STA. The flip side is that it may not even be necessary. If processing is sufficiently intensive that offloading to a worker thread becomes necessary, the marshaling overhead is probably going to be negligible in the bigger picture. Restricting your object to MTA only can solve a lot of design headaches because you're guaranteed that whatever worker threads are doing is safe with respect to any interface pointers held by the COM object.

Memory management

There is a final subtlety to be wary of if client and server are in the same apartment, and the marshaler is not involved. The marshaler always follows the IDL rules that follow from the interface declarations, meaning that if a parameter is only 'in', its value will not be copied back to the client, regardless of what the server does with the supplied arguments. The server may not follow those rules consider parameter directionality because there is no C++ enforcement mechanism.

Consider the following:

```
    HRESULT TestDirection(
        [in] double* Arg1,
        [in,out] double* Arg2,
        [out] double* Arg3);
```

And the server does this:

```
//Server side
HRESULT STDMETHODCALLTYPE IOTesterInstance::TestDirection(
    /* [in] */ double* Arg1,
    /* [out][in] */ double* Arg2,
    /* [out] */ double* Arg3)
{
    wcout << "Server side parameters : " << endl;
    wcout << "Arg1: " << *Arg1 << endl;
    wcout << "Arg2: " << *Arg2 << endl;
    wcout << "Arg3: " << *Arg3 << endl;
    *Arg1 = -1;
    *Arg2 = -2;
    *Arg3 = -3;
    return S_OK;
}
```

And the client does this:

```
        double arg1 = 1;
        double arg2 = 2;
        double arg3 = 3;
```

```
    hRes = ioDirTest->TestDirection(&arg1, &arg2, &arg3);
    wcout << "Client side parameters: " << endl;
    wcout << "Arg1: " << arg1 << endl;
    wcout << "Arg2: " << arg2 << endl;
    wcout << "Arg3: " << arg3 << endl;
```

Then what happens on the client may vary, based on the apartment situation. If client and server are in different apartments, then the results are exactly as expected, because the marshaler will enforce the interface contract.

```
Server side parameters:
Arg1: 1
Arg2: 2
Arg3: 0
Client side parameters:
Arg1: 1
Arg2: -2
Arg3: -3
```

The value of Arg3 is not copied to the server before the call, and the value of Arg1 that the server overwrites locally, is not copied back to the client. So far so good. But if we put client and server in the same apartment, things are different.

```
Server side parameters:
Arg1: 1
Arg2: 2
Arg3: 3
Client side parameters:
Arg1: -1
Arg2: -2
Arg3: -3
```

The client-side value of Arg3 is now visible on the server, and the server-side modification of Arg1 now makes it to the client. The reason is that without marshaler involved to enforce the contract, and the call just being a direct call, the pointers on client and server-side point to the same memory. C++ doesn't have the concept of directionality and any modification done to the memory will be immediate and permanent regardless of IDL definition.

When testing and validating your components, it's a good idea to use them in multiple apartment types to ensure that everything works as expected and the server is not doing anything it shouldn't.

Summary

In this chapter we revisited the topic of marshaling more in depth, exploring the mechanics happening under the hood. Using the IMarshal interface that is at the heart of everything, we implemented value marshaling and continued that effort with shared memory marshaling.

A good takeaway from this chapter is the understanding that in most cases, there is no added value to implementing custom marshaling. For general purpose marshaling, the auto-generated RPC code will be superior to anything you could do yourself. However, in specific cases where you are required to marshal large amounts of data or must deal with large amounts of cross-apartment use of value objects, it can be a significant performance enhancement.

11

Asynchronous programming

Everything we've seen so far centered around synchronous programming whereby a call was executed on a COM object in a server, and the results sent back. Depending on the client and server process as well as the apartments, this involved a certain marshaling strategy where everything happened in order and the client call finished only when the results were marshaled back.

For many things, this is the appropriate and expected scenario. This is also by far the simplest scenario. Not only because there is no concurrency to worry about, but also because it is guaranteed that any call related resources can be freed after the call. However, sometimes it is necessary to switch to an asynchronous model where the client starts an operation and is informed of the result at some time in the future.

It's all about the interfaces

To demonstrate a typical asynchronous worker process, we create a server with a worker object that starts a background task.

```
[
	object,
	uuid(5134abbe-18d3-4fa6-8daf-19a4e7500e03),
	dual,
	nonextensible,
	pointer_default(unique)
]
interface IWorkerNotificationHandler : IDispatch
{
```

```
    [id(1)]
    HRESULT ReportResult([in] LONG Result);
    [id(2)]
    HRESULT WasTriggered([out] LONG* triggered);
};

[
    object,
    uuid(b52780ff-c029-4b76-bb59-5ccb58b1c592),
    dual,
    nonextensible,
    pointer_default(unique)
]
interface IWorker : IDispatch
{
    [id(1)]
    HRESULT StartWorkAsync(
        [in] IWorkerNotificationHandler* callbackHandler);
};
library AsyncWorkerV1Lib
{
        importlib("stdole2.tlb");
        [
                uuid(18b7816f-54c0-4d2b-a3c4-555210ef6c57)
        ]
        coclass Worker
        {
                [default] interface IWorker;
        };
};
```

The concept is that we have an object that can perform work in an asynchronous manner while the client continues doing other things. In this case, the worker only has the `StartWorkAsync` method which starts this work. It takes an `IWorkerNotificationHandler` interface pointer which is used to report back to the client when the work is finished. Key here is that the server provides a Worker object and does the work, but it is the client which decides what happens when the result is reported. The library defines the interface contract between client and server, in terms of how the server can notify the client and which information it can report.

The client supplies an interface pointer. It is free to implement that interface on whatever object it wants. For example, an application with a GUI based interface may implement that interface on an object which performs graphical updates. With GUI based systems we know there is a restriction that GUI updates may only happen from within the thread which controls the message pump. If the client creates the callback object in the STA, then the COM marshaling infrastructure will automatically make this safe because the callback will always be executed on that particular thread, no matter where it originates.

Implementing the server-side object

For the purpose of this chapter, we're making a server with a worker object that starts some form of asynchronous processing and then uses the callback interface to inform the client that it's done. With most of the error handling and logging removed for clarity, this is the worker object:

```
STDMETHODIMP CWorker::StartWorkAsync(
                IWorkerNotificationHandler* callbackHandler)
{

    CComPtr<IStream> pStream;
    HRESULT hr = CoMarshalInterThreadInterfaceInStream(
        __uuidof(IWorkerNotificationHandler),
        callbackHandler,
        &pStream);

    if(- 1 != _beginthread(ASyncWorker, 0, pStream.p)) {
        pStream.Detach(); //async worker is now the owner
    }

    return hr;
}
```

The client supplies an `IWorkerNotificationHandler` interface pointer. The COM runtime marshals that interface pointer to whatever thread the `StartWorkAsync` method is running in so it is safe to use. However, we want to offload processing, and thus the use of the pointer, to a worker thread. Since we cannot know the threading constraints, we cannot assume anything and need to marshal that pointer manually into a stream which is then passed as a parameter to a worker thread. The stream pointer is passed as a raw pointer so if the thread was started properly, we detach the stream from the smart pointer because the worker thread is now the owner of that resource and it should not be cleaned up locally by the smart pointer.

The worker thread runs for 5 seconds to simulate some serious processing before finally reporting the result to the client.

```
void ASyncWorker(void* args)
{
    CoInitializeEx(NULL, COINIT_APARTMENTTHREADED);

    IStream* pStream = reinterpret_cast<IStream*>(args);
    IWorkerNotificationHandler* handler = NULL;

    HRESULT hr = CoGetInterfaceAndReleaseStream(
```

```
            pStream,
            __uuidof(IWorkerNotificationHandler),
            (LPVOID*)&handler);

    //simulate work
    Sleep(5000);

    if (SUCCEEDED(hr)) {
        handler->ReportResult(42);
        handler->Release();
    }

    CoUninitialize();
}
```

The newly created thread is not yet a COM thread. It needs to be initialized before the interface pointer can be unmarshaled because without a known apartment type, the COM runtime has no way to understand what it needs to do. The rules of marshaling depend on the client apartment and server apartment. Whatever the situation is, there will be a marshaling solution.

We can use `CoGetInterfaceAndReleaseStream` to unmarshal the interface pointer from the stream and release the stream in 1 operation. Regardless of the success of the operation, the stream is always released so there is no need to work with a smart pointer. Likewise, there is no real need to use a smart pointer for the handler because we release it immediately after the reporting call.

With this, the server side portion is complete. There is a public method which starts an asynchronous operation, a worker thread to do the work, and a way to signal completion of the task.

The client side

As mentioned, the client is completely free to implement the notification interface any way it wants. For the purpose of this example, we add an implementation of that interface in the form of a handler object in the same DLL as the worker object.

```
coclass WorkerNotificationHandler
{
        [default] interface IWorkerNotificationHandler;
};
```

It's important to realize that we add this object to the server module solely for convenience of the example and removing the need to implement a notification handler in a separate library. Any object which implements that interface would be valid and just because we supply a baseline implementation of that interface doesn't make it mandatory to use that reference implementation. The terminology here can also become a bit confusing. Because when the callback notification is done, the worker thread is the client, and the object in the client application is the server. The notification object has 2 methods.

```
STDMETHODIMP
CWorkerNotificationHandler::ReportResult(LONG Result)
{
    m_HasTriggered = true;
    wcout
        << L"Reporting result " << Result
        << L" in thread " << ::GetCurrentThreadId() << endl;
    return S_OK;
}

STDMETHODIMP
CWorkerNotificationHandler::WasTriggered(LONG* triggered)
{
    if (triggered == NULL)
        return E_POINTER;

    *triggered = m_HasTriggered;

    return S_OK;
}
```

The mechanism is simple. The worker reports a result and sets a flag that indicates the wait is over. On the client side, the client can check this flag. With error handling removed, a possible (but wrong) client side application could look like this:

```
CoInitializeEx(NULL, COINIT_APARTMENTTHREADED);
{
    CComPtr<IWorker> worker;
    hr = worker.CoCreateInstance(L"AsyncWorker.Worker");
    CComPtr<IWorkerNotificationHandler> callBackHandler;
    callBackHandler.CoCreateInstance(
                    L"AsyncWorker.WorkerNotificationHandler");

    worker->StartWorkAsync(callBackHandler);

    while (true) {
        long triggered = 0;
        callBackHandler->WasTriggered(&triggered);
        if (triggered) {
            wcout << L"callBackHandler was trigged" << endl;
            break;
        }
        else {
            Sleep(1000);
            wcout << L"Doing various things" << endl;
        }
```

```
    }
}
CoUninitialize();
```

What looks a bit odd here is the scope block between the CoInitializeEx / CoUninitialize calls. The reason is that without something like this, the smart pointers would release the interfaces after the call to CoUninitialize and this would cause errors. Logically, this seems to be in order: we create a worker object and a notification handler. The worker takes some time to process and eventually reports back while the client is doing other things. The only problem is that when we run this, the call to the notification interface never seems to arrive.

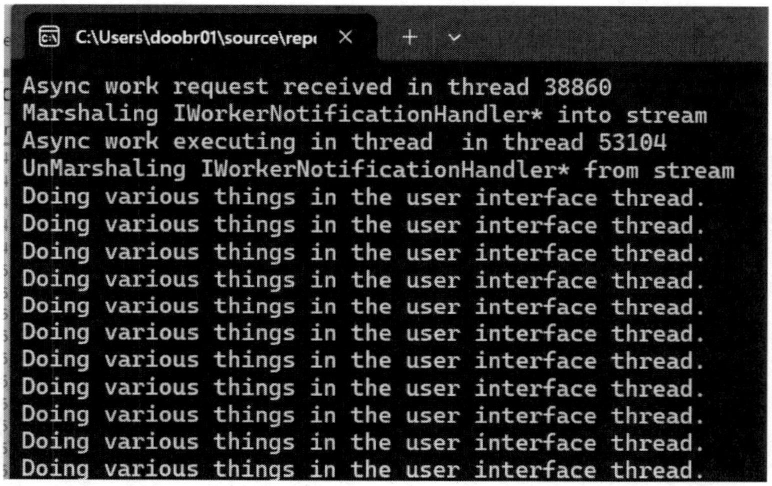

Everything seems to happen according to plan except the callback is lost in the aether. Historically, this has been a common problem in asynchronous COM scenarios. The problem here is that we're violating one of the core requirements of COM. The client application is not processing window messages. Window messages are essential to STA marshaling. Everything seems to work fine until the point where a call has to be marshaled. The messages are sent but no one is handling them, so the call is never executed. The call to Sleep is bad because it doesn't give the message pump a chance. To solve this problem, we have to replace the call to Sleep with one to the

```
while (true) {
    long triggered = 0;
    callBackHandler->WasTriggered(&triggered);
    if (triggered) {
        wcout << L"callBackHandler was trigged." << endl;
        break;
    }
    else {
        WaitProcessIOPumpMessages(1000);
```

```
        wcout << L"Doing various things." << endl;
    }

}
```

As soon as we do that, the program works as expected.

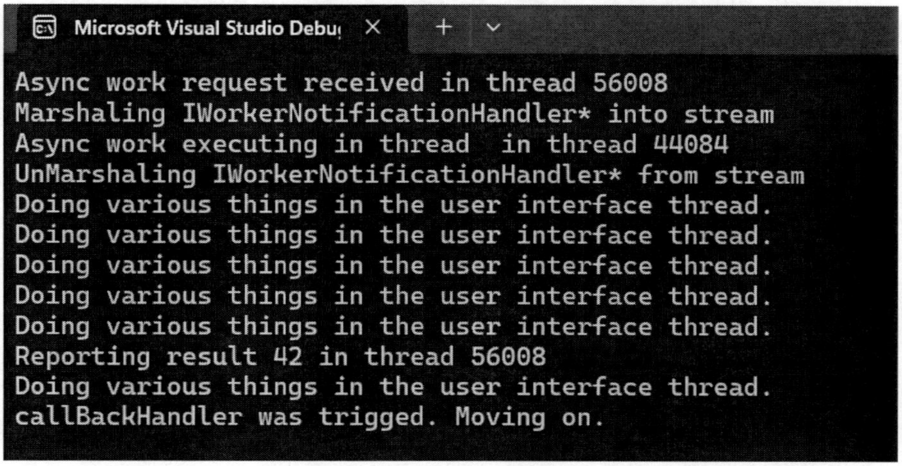

Note that in a production scenario, the Sleep call in the worker thread is just as bad because it too would interfere with marshaling to the worker thread of that should be needed at some point.

Summary

In this chapter we explored the concept of using a notification interface to enable a server to report back to a client in an asynchronous manner. The example here was very simplified. In a real implementation, there are several concerns that need to be addressed to avoid problems:

- If the number of concurrent asynchronous operations is subject to a limit, for example if only 1 call can be outstanding at the same time, a safe synchronization mechanism has to be implemented to ensure this limitation is enforced.
- There needs to be a cancellation mechanism so that if a call takes too long or the client initiates a shutdown, the worker needs to be able to stop.
- The cancellation could come just as the worker reports the result. This is a race condition that needs to be accounted for.
- If the worker fails or something goes wrong, there needs to be some mechanism that ensures the client isn't stuck in that wait loop for the rest of eternity.

And this is probably not the entire list. Asynchronous processing itself is a fairly straight forward concept. It's all the synchronization issues and problem scenarios that make asynchronous processing a complex thing to implement in a bullet proof fashion.

It's used in many real-world scenarios nonetheless because with any sort of operation that takes a long time to complete, tying synchronous operations to blocking user interface updates is just bad practice that feels clunky and freezes up the user interface for too long to be acceptable.

A defining characteristic of this programming paradigm is that the client is in control of the overall process. The client has knowledge about when and how many callbacks can be expected. It has knowledge about whether operations are running that may cause them and prepare its internal state and user interface accordingly.

12

Connection points

In the previous chapter we implemented asynchronous programming by passing interface pointers for callback handling. A defining principle was that the client is in the driving seat. But that is not always a representative use case. Sometimes, a server needs to inform a client of things happening inside. For example, a client application that has a GUI with and ActiveX control may need to know whenever the user clicks on that control, or whenever the control loses focus.

Whatever the case may be, this situation is fundamentally different because the client says 'I'd like to be informed whenever X happens'. X may happen once, never, or many times. And it may happen at any given time. The client might not be in a specific state that indicates it is waiting for something specific. For this use case, connection points were invented as a way to communicate events from a server to a client if the client subscribed to them. At the core of it, there is still an interface that is used for invoking callbacks. Let's say we have an IEvents interface that has methods for each type of notification that can be communicated via that interface.

The place where the event is triggered is called the source. The place where the event is consumed is called the sink.

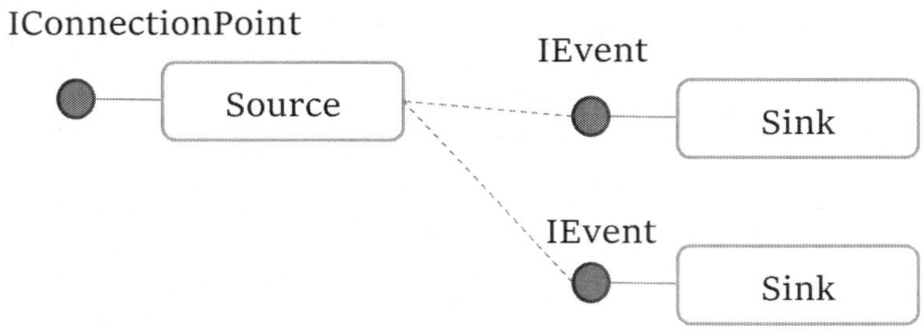

The concept of having an IEvents interface is similar to the callback mechanism we discussed earlier. But rather than using the interface in response to a specific client-initiated action, the concept is more like the client asking the server 'give me a heads up whenever X happens' without any indication of when or how often this is going to be. Another difference is that a connection point can support multiple sinks. Different clients or different objects inside a client may want to receive the same notification. The connection point interface has the following methods:

```
//atlcom.h
interface IConnectionPoint : IUnknown {
    HRESULT GetConnectionInterface(
        [out] IID* pIID
    );

    HRESULT GetConnectionPointContainer(
        [out] IConnectionPointContainer** ppCPC
    );

    HRESULT Advise(
        [in] IUnknown* pUnkSink,
        [out] DWORD* pdwCookie
    );

    HRESULT Unadvise(
        [in] DWORD dwCookie
    );

    HRESULT EnumConnections(
        [out] IEnumConnections** ppEnum
    );
}
```

The connection point allows a client to register and unregister an interface pointer for notifications, via the Advise and Unadvise methods. The client gets a cookie when the interface is registered so that it can easily unregister at a later point in time. EnumConnections is provided to give the source a convenient way to enumerate the registered interfaces and invoke one of the notification methods. GetConnectionInterface returns the IID of the callback interface which it supports. For the sake of dealing with sink interfaces, those 4 methods would be enough. But there is 1 more method.

The situation so far allows an object to support multiple sinks from a single source. That is still rather limiting. An object may implement many independent interfaces, and each of those interfaces may offer events through a different callback interface. To support that option, objects can implement the connection point container interface.

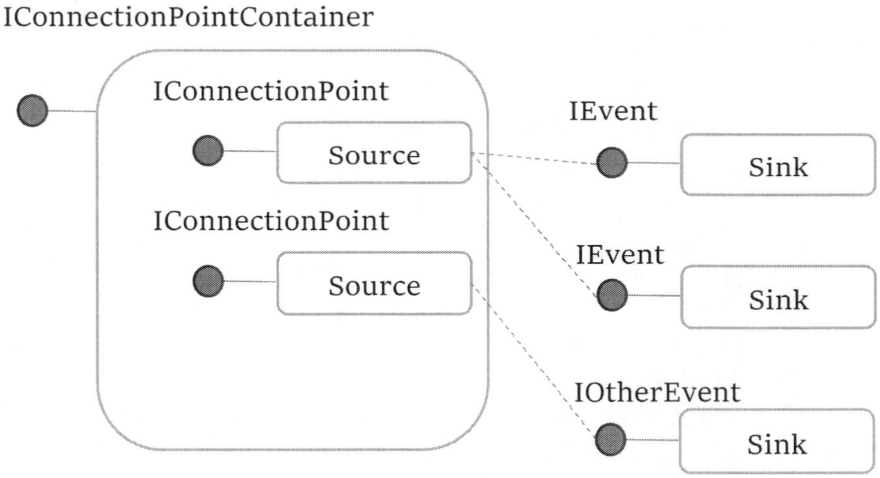

The GetConnectionPointContainer method of IConnectionPoint documents the link between the connection point, and the connection point container which contains all supported connection points of a specific object. Each supported sink interface will have a supporting IConnectionPoint implementation in the connection point container which has the following interface:

```
//atlcom.h
interface IConnectionPointContainer : IUnknown {
    HRESULT EnumConnectionPoints(
        [out] IEnumConnectionPoints** ppEnum
    );

    HRESULT FindConnectionPoint(
        [in] REFIID riid,
        [out] IConnectionPoint** ppCP
    );
}
```

EnumConnectionPoints enables someone to get a list of all supported connection points. This is primarily interesting for tooling and diagnostics. The main method for clients is the FindConnectionPoint method. If a client wants to register a sink interface with an object, it will first find the connection point and then use Advise to register that interface. The enumeration method is generally less interesting for clients because a client knows which sink objects it uses, and it will try to register those. Knowing which other interfaces are supported is not very useful.

Note that these 2 interfaces solely concern the management and registration of sink interfaces. They don't have any relation to the sink interfaces themselves. They are generic.

Supporting connection points

The connection point mechanism starts with the source object because that is where the sink interfaces are defined. Logically, these two are tied together at the hip because it is the server object that fires the methods of those sink interfaces when the conditions for doing so are met. To stay in the spirit of calculators, let say that we want to keep track of the number of times something happens, like a fishcounter, and every 5 events we want to report the number of to whoever wants to know.

While it is possible to add support for connection points after an object has been created, it involves a lot of tedious manual work. It's simpler by far to create the object in your project with connection point support baked in. We create a FishCounter_V1 project and then enable the connection points checkbox.

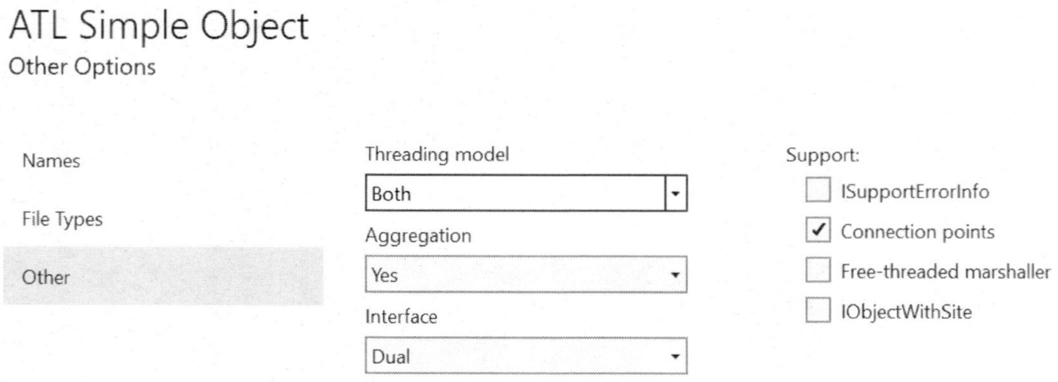

This simple checkbox has several consequences, starting with the contents of the IDL file. The object's main interface is still as expected.

```
[
    object,
```

```
        uuid(2f9bc024-57e3-4fc4-8c3f-8704716edd9f),
        dual,
        nonextensible,
        pointer_default(unique)
]
interface ICounter : IDispatch
{
};
```

We recognize this from the previous projects where the dual interface object has an interface with the same name. Supporting connection points has no effect on the object's dispatching surface. There interesting things are inside the library block and concern the coclass.

```
[
        uuid(04a27d17-9974-4c72-a3d9-8cf2e83a8748)
]
dispinterface _ICounterEvents
{
        properties:
        methods:
};
[
        uuid(174085bd-9c57-4ec3-ae87-3c188faec9f0)
]
coclass Counter
{
        [default] interface ICounter;
        [default, source] dispinterface _ICounterEvents;
};
```

The ATL wizard has auto generated the event interface. The leading underscore is a convention that helps tooling deal with the fact that it's an event interface and shouldn't be shown in various wizards or views. In the coclass it's listed in the interface list, but as a source. This makes MIDL treat it as an event source that is handled by the connection point container.

As mentioned earlier in the chapter covering Dispatch interfaces, the clients of an object may be automation environment that perform late binding and wouldn't know what to do with a vtable. Given that these environments needed to be able to subscribe to events, the only option was to require that those event interfaces be a dispinterface. This doesn't mean all late binding environments support this. Visual Basic did. Powershell does not. There are 2 important reasons for this.

Firstly, they serve very different purposes. A client like a Visual Basic application is meant to provide functionality to a user while running as a standalone program and presenting data. It needs to be able to respond to various things. A scripting language such as PowerShell, does not. Scripting languages are typically meant to automate tasks through the execution of a series of commands, accessing data and then finish.

Secondly, even though the event interface itself is a dispatching interface, it is not related to the main interfaces and there is no 'easy' way to register event sinks with the object. IConnectionPointContainer is not the default interface of a COM object, nor is it a dispatching interface. Both things complicate the process of registering event interfaces. Quite a bit of extra effort is required to enable sink interface registration that goes beyond the requirements for dispatching.

With Visual Basic, the effort was made to enable events because it's such a critical part of building user interfaces, especially considering that ActiveX controls were intended to be construction blocks of user interfaces and therefore any VB application would benefit from having them. Given that few late binding environments really implemented events, things would have been far simpler if event interfaces could have been dual interfaces but with VB being a late binding environment as well as dominating the user interface landscape, that was not to be.

In response to the connection points checkbox, the ATL wizard also modified the inheritance list of the C++ CCounter class.

```
class ATL_NO_VTABLE CCounter :
	public CComObjectRootEx<CComMultiThreadModel>,
	public CComCoClass<CCounter, &CLSID_Counter>,
	public IConnectionPointContainerImpl<CCounter>,
	public CProxy_ICounterEvents<CCounter>,
	public IDispatchImpl<ICounter,
	                     &IID_ICounter,
	                     &LIBID_FishCounterV1Lib,
	                     /*wMajor =*/ 1,
	                     /*wMinor =*/ 0>
{
    // snip
BEGIN_COM_MAP(CCounter)
	COM_INTERFACE_ENTRY(ICounter)
	COM_INTERFACE_ENTRY(IDispatch)
	COM_INTERFACE_ENTRY(IConnectionPointContainer)
END_COM_MAP()

BEGIN_CONNECTION_POINT_MAP(CCounter)
	CONNECTION_POINT_ENTRY(__uuidof(_ICounterEvents))
END_CONNECTION_POINT_MAP()

};
```

The first new base class is IConnectionPointContainerImpl<CCounter>, which is a boilerplate implementation of IConnectionPointContainer that performs all the generic management actions. Nothing it does, relies on the specifics of the event sources. It's just basic lookup and management of IID's and pointers in a similar fashion to how ATL deals with QueryInterface. That's why just like there is an interface map, the object now has a similar map for registering supported interfaces. This map doesn't work with an interface type but just with the IID because they're all dispinterfaces and as such they're really all IDispatch pointers.

The second new thing is the CProxy_ICounterEvents<CCounter> base class. This class is defined in the autogenerated _ICounterEvents_CP.h header file.

```
template <class T>
class CProxy_ICounterEvents :
        public IConnectionPointImpl<
                            T,
                            &__uuidof( _ICounterEvents ),
                            CComDynamicUnkArray>
{
        // WARNING: This class may be regenerated by the wizard
public:
};
```

Sooner or later, CCounter is going to have to be able to execute methods of the registered event interface, in this case _ICounterEvents, via calls to 'Fire_xxx' which will call the relevate method on each registered sink interface. To provide a sensible place for these 'Fire_xxx' calls, ATL provides us with an empty placeholder class which is the implementation that can access the list of registered sinks for a specific event interface. Regrettably, this is complicated by the fact that sink interfaces are not dual interfaces, and therefore there is no vtable and no base class whose methods can be executed. Instead, we're going to have to manually build a dispatch call with variant parameters and perform the Invoke call manually on every registered interface.

While the details are hidden away, it's important to understand a little bit of the details of how sink interfaces are managed inside a connection point. This will avoid confusion later on. We can get a ton of insight from the 'Advise' implementation which is a member of the IConnectionPointImpl base.

```
//atlcom.h
template <class T, const IID* piid, class CDV>
COM_DECLSPEC_NOTHROW STDMETHODIMP
IConnectionPointImpl <T, piid, CDV>::Advise(
    _Inout_ IUnknown* pUnkSink,
    _Out_ DWORD* pdwCookie)
{
    T* pT = static_cast<T*>(this);

        // snip
```

```
        IID iid;
    GetConnectionInterface(&iid);
    hRes = pUnkSink->QueryInterface(iid, (void**)&p);
    if (SUCCEEDED(hRes))
    {
        pT->Lock();
        *pdwCookie = m_vec.Add(p);
        hRes = (*pdwCookie != NULL) ?
                                    S_OK : CONNECT_E_ADVISELIMIT;
        pT->Unlock();
        if (hRes != S_OK)
            p->Release();
    }
    // snip
}
```

Apart from the input sanity checking and error handling, the crux of the Advise call is that we an IUnknown pointer of a dispinterface as input, which we try to register as sink interface for the IID for which that connection point is responsible. This relationship is verified with a QueryInterface call to the sink object. If it returns the specified interface, that interface is added to the internal array of sink pointers. At that point, ownership is in the IConnectionPointImpl class. When it is removed from the list in a call to Unadvise, it is released.

Adding the pointer to the array happens between calls to lock / unlock to ensure that the state of the internal array is not corrupted in case of multi-threaded access. This level of synchronization cannot be done inside the array itself because the array manages raw pointers. When we use a pointer from the list, we must use the same lock / unlock approach to ensure that it is not released while we're in the middle of using it.

A final important point is how the pointers are stored. The internal array used by IConnectionPointImpl is of the CComDynamicUnkArray type. Getting a cookie and finding a free spot in the list is done by walking the list, checking each position to determine if it is free or not.

Implementing the source side

Starting with the main interface, we use the class wizard to add and implement the methods and properties of ICounter in the same manner we used to develop the DispCalculator.

```
interface ICounter : IDispatch
{
    [id(1)] HRESULT Reset();
    [id(2)] HRESULT Increment();
    [propget, id(3)] HRESULT Value([out, retval] ULONG* pVal);
```

```
};

STDMETHODIMP CCounter::Reset()
{
    m_Count = 0;
    return S_OK;
}

STDMETHODIMP CCounter::Increment()
{
    InterlockedIncrement(&m_Count);
    return S_OK;
}

STDMETHODIMP CCounter::get_Value(ULONG* pVal)
{
    if (!pVal)
        return E_POINTER;
    *pVal = m_Count;
    return S_OK;
}
```

There is nothing noteworthy here except that we use InterlockedIncrement because our object supports both threading models and the regular ++ operation is not safe for multi-threaded use. The only thing left to implement is the code for firing the events. It starts with adding the IDL for the dispinterface.

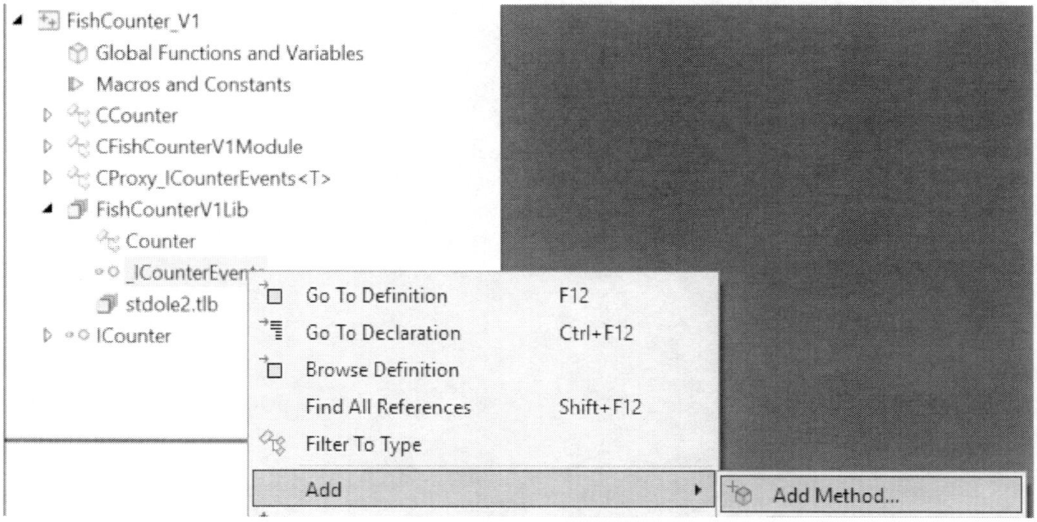

The _ICounterEvents interface is absent from the regular class view as intended, but it can be found in the list of library interfaces where we can add the OnCount method.

```
    [
        uuid(04a27d17-9974-4c72-a3d9-8cf2e83a8748)
    ]
```

```
dispinterface _ICounterEvents
{
        properties:
        methods:
                [id(1)] HRESULT OnCount([in] ULONG count);
};
```

The wizard doesn't add any C++ code because it's a dispinterface and there is nothing it can implement here because dispatching is an implementation detail. As a result, there's also no code yet for firing the events. Visual Studio has a wizard for generating this code and add firing support to the CCounter class.

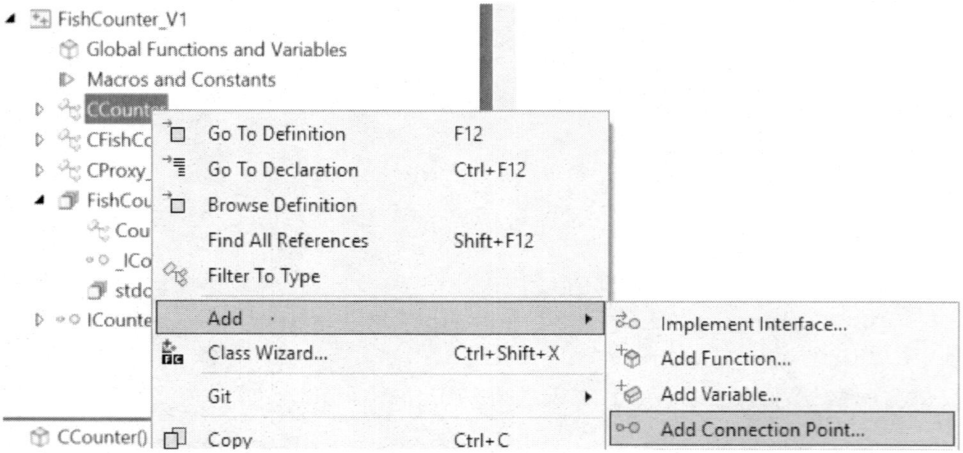

This starts the connection point wizard which looks a lot like the Implement Interface wizard.

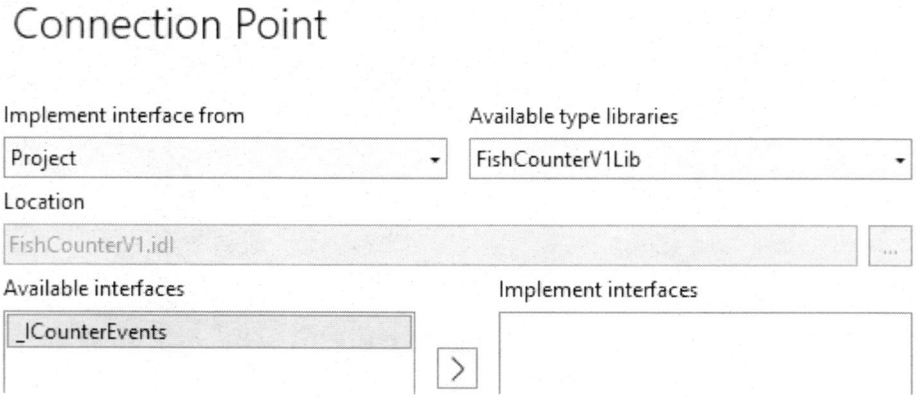

Unfortunately, this wizard is as broken as the Implement Interface wizard. Luckily, the same trick works to resolve this: build and register the x86 version, and load the library from the registry. This mostly works and is only slightly broken. Aside from removing the import statement from the precompiled header, the wizard also inserts a brand new connection point map at the bottom of the CCounter class declaration which needs to be removed.

```
class ATL_NO_VTABLE CCounter :
        // snip
{
public:



BEGIN_CONNECTION_POINT_MAP(CCounter)
        CONNECTION_POINT_ENTRY(__uuidof(_ICounterEvents))
END_CONNECTION_POINT_MAP()

public:
    STDMETHOD(Reset)();
    STDMETHOD(Increment)();
    STDMETHOD(get_Value)(ULONG* pVal);

    // remove this erroneously inserted map!!!
    BEGIN_CONNECTION_POINT_MAP(CCounter)
        CONNECTION_POINT_ENTRY(__uuidof(_ICounterEvents))
    END_CONNECTION_POINT_MAP()
};
```

Having to make the registry round trip and cleaning up after the wizard is still worth it because this is the generated code in the proxy class:

```
template<class T>
class CProxy_ICounterEvents :
    public ATL::IConnectionPointImpl<T,
                 &__uuidof(_ICounterEvents)>
{
public:
    HRESULT Fire_OnCount(unsigned long count)
    {
        HRESULT hr = S_OK;
        *pThis = static_cast<T*>(this);
        int cConnections = m_vec.GetSize();
        for (int iConnection = 0;
            iConnection < cConnections;
            iConnection++)
        {
            pThis->Lock();
            CComPtr<IUnknown> punkConnection =
                                    m_vec.GetAt(iConnection);
            pThis->Unlock();
            IDispatch *pConnection =
                    static_cast<IDispatch*>(punkConnection.p);
            if (pConnection)
            {
```

```
                CComVariant avarParams[1];
                avarParams[0] = count;
                avarParams[0].vt = VT_UI4;
                CComVariant varResult;

                DISPPARAMS params =
                                { avarParams, nullptr, 1, 0 };
                hr = pConnection->Invoke(0x1,
                                      IID_NULL,
                                      LOCALE_USER_DEFAULT,
                                      DISPATCH_METHOD,
                                      &params,
                                      &varResult,
                                      nullptr,
                                      nullptr);
            }
        }
        return hr;
    }
};
```

This code simply enumerates the available connections, formats the appropriate argument list, and then dispatches the call to each connected sink. Looking at the amount of code that was created, even with the minor code error and the need to clean up after the wizard, this is well worth the hassle. Given that you don't necessarily know the threading situation of the object, you might wonder how threadsafe this code is. Because while an object may be firing events, a client can register or unregister a connection point. That is why there is a lock / unlock pair around the call to m_vec.GetAt.

A similar mechanism is used in the calls to Advise / Unadvise where the lock is used before an interface pointer is added into and removed from the collection. This lock protects the life of the interface pointer until the smart pointer has made a copy of that pointer and stored it internally. If the lock would be used inside the GetAt call, there would be a window where the pointer is read from the collection but before it gets assigned to the smart pointer. During that admittedly brief window, the pointer could be removed from the collection and released so it needs to cover the read as well as the assignment. That part is now safe. Because the collection might have empty slots when sink interfaces are Unadvised, the loop checks for NULL in case that happens.

There is only 1 minor issue left: as-is, this code doesn't compile. There is a missing type.

```
    HRESULT Fire_OnCount(unsigned long count)
    {
```

```
        HRESULT hr = S_OK;
        *pThis = static_cast<T*>(this);
```

In this code, pThis is used as if it is a member of CProxy_ICounterEvents but that is not the case. It's a local variable with a missing type. Fixing this is trivial.

```
    HRESULT Fire_OnCount(unsigned long count)
    {
        HRESULT hr = S_OK;
        T *pThis = static_cast<T*>(this);     // Add T
```

There is also a minor change to the CProxy_ICounterEvents declaration itself. When this class was initially created, it had the following declaration

```
template <class T>
class CProxy_ICounterEvents :
        public IConnectionPointImpl<
                                 T,
                                 &__uuidof( _ICounterEvents ),
                                 CComDynamicUnkArray> {};
```

After importing the events interface from the type library, this changes to:

```
template<class T>
class CProxy_ICounterEvents :
    public ATL::IConnectionPointImpl<
                    T,
                    &__uuidof(_ICounterEvents)> {};
```

This is nothing to worry about because CComDynamicUnkArray is the default value of the 3d template argument and the only difference between both declarations is that the collection type is implicit instead of explicit. All we have to do now is to update our code to fire the event.

```
STDMETHODIMP CCounter::Increment()
{
    InterlockedIncrement(&m_Count);
    if (!(m_Count % 5))
        Fire_OnCount(m_Count);
    return S_OK;
}
```

Creating an event sink object

Now that we have an object ready to start firing events, we need to implement the other side of the coin and create a listener. This is where things get complicated again.

The event interface is a dispinterface. We can't just implement it like we did before because there is no vtable to work with.

Additionally, there are several scenarios in which events may be received. We may want to implement the event interface on a full-fledged COM object that does other things and which needs to be aware of things happening to other COM objects. Or we may be working on an ActiveX user interface element which needs to receive those events. Or we may have a client application which uses the source object and just wants to receive notifications without other hassle. The things you'd do in each scenario are a bit different.

The publicly available samples are a bit dated. There is an 'ATLEventHandling' sample for VS2008 which shows how to implement an event dispinterface on a full COM object which can then be consumed by an MFC application. It uses Microsoft Word as an event source. Unfortunately, it assumes you'll be importing DLLs from an Office version between Office 2000 and Office 2007, that a VBA6 DLL is available, and that these files can be found in hardcoded paths. It's only good as a reference to inspect the code. There is also a 'ComEvents' VS2010 example but that uses Attributed ATL for the source and sink. It serves no purpose expect to show how much easier life would have been if Attributed ATL had been a success.

For this chapter, I chose to implement the event interface on a local object that is not a full-fledged COM object with registration info and class factory. The reason for this is that it is an interesting use case to register for events in a plain C++ application in the same way we've been working with our client applications, and it opens the door to pointing out a few more peculiarities of ATL which would otherwise stay unnoticed.

There are 2 main things that we need to implement:

- The object handling the events needs to have the base functionality of a dual interface COM object, in the sense that it needs to support the base IUnknown and IDispatch behavior, which in turn means that it needs to support a threading model.
- It needs to be able to translate dispatch calls to actual method calls.

ATL can help us with both things. For the COM related behavior, we have the CComObjectRootEx<> class. To help with event dispatching, ATL has 2 helper classes: IDispEventImpl and its base class IDispEventSimpleImpl. The basics of our class look like this:

```
class ATL_NO_VTABLE CEventSink :
    public CComObjectRootEx<CComSingleThreadModel>,
```

```
    public IDispEventImpl<
                            1,
                            CEventSink,
                            &__uuidof(_ICounterEvents),
                            &__uuidof(__FishCounterV1Lib),
                            1,
                            0>
{
};
```

The only new thing here compared to the earlier ATL objects is the IDispEventImpl base. The first template argument is a simple numeric value that identifies that event sink interface. If the use case calls for it, a single object can receive events from different sources (either from the same dispinterface, or from different dispinterfaces). The second argument is the CEventSink type itself, in the same manner that a regular ATL class does. The other arguments uniquely identify the type library that holds the type definition of the dispinterface. _ICounterEvents and __FishCounterV1Lib are available after the import of the TLB. The major and minor versions are values that we must manually enter.

The way that IDispEventImpl and IDispEventSimpleImpl work together is that IDispEventSimpleImpl contains the code for the IDispatch::Invoke call that translates a dispatch call to an actual method call. At a high level, it's the opposite of what goes on in the source when the Fire_xxx call is translated to a dispatch call. To do this, it uses a table that matches a method with a dispatch ID as well as the parameter list. If we use IDispEventSimpleImpl by itself, it's up to us to populate that table and make sure the argument lists are correct. This is tedious and error prone, which is why IDispEventImpl implements the other IDispatch methods to load all that information from the type library to make it available to the IDispEventSimpleImpl base, thereby removing a lot of the manual work. I am not going to cover the inner workings here for the same reason other xxxxImpl classes aren't covered in detail: it's all boilerplate you don't have to worry about, and the source is there for you in the headers if you're interested.

From a practical point of view, all that's left here is to implement the method that handles the event and hook it into the dispatch routines.

```
const ULONG SOURCEID = 1;
const ULONG DISPID_ONCOUNT = 1;

class ATL_NO_VTABLE CEventSink :
    public CComObjectRootEx<CComMultiThreadModel>,
    public IDispEventImpl<
                            1,
```

```
                              CEventSink,
                              &__uuidof(_ICounterEvents),
                              &__uuidof(__FishCounterV1Lib),
                              1,
                              0>
{
public:
    BEGIN_COM_MAP(CEventSink)
    END_COM_MAP()

    BEGIN_SINK_MAP(CEventSink)
        SINK_ENTRY_EX(SOURCEID, __uuidof(_ICounterEvents), \
                      DISPID_ONCOUNT, OnCount)
    END_SINK_MAP()

    STDMETHODIMP OnCount(unsigned long count)
    {
        wcout << count << L" fish so far!" << endl;
        return S_OK;
    }
};
```

The COM interface map can remain empty. We're not implementing any interfaces, but the map must be there even if it's empty because otherwise our class doesn't compile.

The key element here is the sink map which provides a role that is similar to the interface map. The SINK entries build a table that matches methods to dispatch IDs. Each entry has 4 parameters: the identification number of the source interface, the IID of the dispinterface whose calls are dispatched, the DISPID that is tied to a method, and finally the method itself. It goes without saying that it's important that the method signature needs to match the one in the type library. By default, the import statement also creates a wrapper for the dispinterface which is not very useful by itself. You're not calling the interface so the wrapper doesn't do you much good, but you can copy the generated method signatures because they will match.

At this point, the internal logic for the event sink has been implemented but it's still an abstract class, missing the regular IUnknown members. The brains are still missing a body. In a regular scenario, an ATL creator class does this in response to a CreateInstance operation. This is usually invisible because at the client level we only ever see an interface pointer without being aware of where that pointer comes from. Since we're not using a class factory, we have to manually create an instance in a proper host body.

```
typedef CComObject<CEventSink> CEventSinkObject;
CEventSinkObject* sinkPtr;
```

```
if (SUCCEEDED(CEventSinkObject::CreateInstance(&sinkPtr))) {
        CComPtr<CEventSinkObject> sink = sinkPtr;

    //snip
}
```

ATL uses the CComObject class as a host for the event sink instance. The CreateInstance call creates a new object and returns a pointer to it. It must be noted that CreateInstance returns a pointer which is not AddRef'ed yet. In normal scenarios, we wouldn't have an object pointer, but an interface pointer obtained by a QueryInterface operation. To mitigate that, we need to AddRef it as well as ensure that the object isn't leaked. Luckily, we can use CComPtr for that. This line does both things.

```
CComPtr<CEventSinkObject> sink = sinkPtr;
```

Assigning the raw pointer to the smart pointer will store a copy of the pointer and call AddRef on the local copy. The lifecycle of the sink object depends on where the smart pointer exists and whether copies are made. We could skip the CreateInstance call completely and simply do this:

```
CComPtr<CEventSinkObject> sink = new CEventSinkObject();
```

The instance is going to be created just the same in both situations, but after the initial construction, things like FinalConstruct or FinalRelease will be skipped because those are called inside the standard CreateInstance call. Even if there is nothing there that has an impact, it's good practice to not rely on that.

Registering the sink interface

The sink object is now ready for action. All that's left it to Advise a source object to start receiving events, and then Unadvise sometime later to stop receiving events. IDispEventSimpleImpl has exposes 2 members to do this.

```
//atlcom.h
HRESULT DispEventAdvise(_Inout_ IUnknown* pUnk);
HRESULT DispEventUnadvise(_Inout_ IUnknown* pUnk);
```

These methods take a pointer to a source object and then call AtlAdvise and AtlUnadvise internally. You cannot do that yourself. At this point, you might also start to get a few doubts. We purposely left the COM interface map of the CEventSink empty. Yet when we advise a source object, IConnectionPointImpl performs a QueryInterface operation to get check that the correct dispinterace was supplied and to obtain the dispatch pointer. Additionally, if we support multiple sinks for the same type, a normal QueryInterface operation wouldn't know which IDispEventImpl was intended. The answer can be found in the inheritance hierarchy of IDispEventImpl.

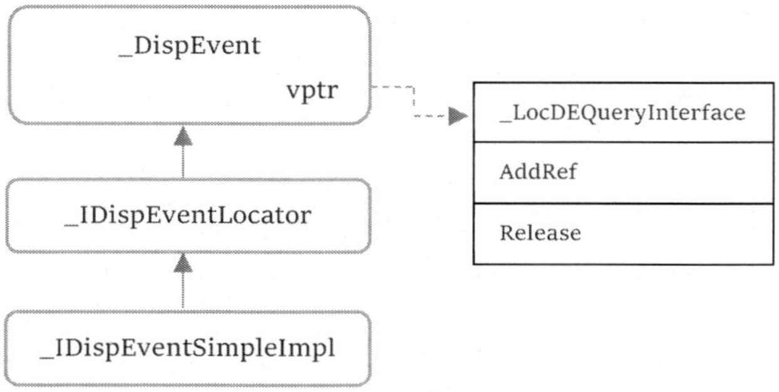

_DispEvent is the lowest base class of the IDispEventSimpleImpl inheritance tree. The first virtual method has the same index in the vtable as the QueryInterface method in the IUnknown vtable. It also has the same signature.

```
//atlcom.h
class ATL_NO_VTABLE _IDispEvent
{
public:
    // snip...
    //this method needs a different name than QueryInterface
    STDMETHOD(_LocDEQueryInterface)(
        REFIID riid,
        void** ppvObject )ATL_IUNKNOWN_NOEXCEPT = 0;
    virtual ULONG STDMETHODCALLTYPE
        AddRef(void) ATL_IUNKNOWN_NOEXCEPT = 0;
    virtual ULONG STDMETHODCALLTYPE
        Release(void) ATL_IUNKNOWN_NOEXCEPT = 0;
};
```

The AddRef and Release virtual methods are also at the index in the vtable where we would expect them in an IUnknown interface. Key here is that when CEventSink is compiled, AddRef and Release will point to the top implementations at the top of the hierarchy, because they have the same signature. The _LocDEQueryInterface vptr resolves to the implementation in _IDispEventSimpleImpl .

```
//atlcom.h
template <UINT nID, class T, const IID* pdiid>
class ATL_NO_VTABLE IDispEventSimpleImpl :
    public _IDispEventLocator<nID, pdiid>
{
public:
    STDMETHOD(_LocDEQueryInterface)(
        _In_ REFIID riid,
```

```
        _COM_Outptr_ void** ppvObject) ATL_IUNKNOWN_NOEXCEPT
    {
        // snip...
        if (InlineIsEqualGUID(riid, *pdiid) ||
            InlineIsEqualUnknown(riid) ||
            InlineIsEqualGUID(riid, __uuidof(IDispatch)) ||
            InlineIsEqualGUID(riid, this->m_iid))
        {
            *ppvObject = this;
            AddRef();
            return S_OK;
        }
        // snip...
    }
```

The end result is that a _IDispEventSimpleImpl* behaves very similar to an IUnknown* and can be used as one. It will use the same lifecycle routines. At the same time, any QueryInterface operation will be redirected. Instead of going to the higher level QueryInterface that has an empty COM interface map, it will go to this method which will succeed for either IUnknown, IDispatch or the IID of the dispinterface. This is why IConnectionPointImpl in the source object can query for the dispinterface and everything goes as planned. Whenever such a query is made, the returned interface pointer will point to the _IDispEventSimpleImpl base and events will always be dispatched to the correct sink.

When we call DispEventAdvise to register the sink to a source object, the call is delegated down the hierarchy.

```
//atlcom.h
HRESULT DispEventAdvise(_Inout_ IUnknown* pUnk)
{
    return _IDispEvent::DispEventAdvise(pUnk, pdiid);
}

HRESULT DispEventAdvise(
        _Inout_ IUnknown* pUnk,
        _In_ const IID* piid)
{
    ATLENSURE(m_dwEventCookie == 0xFEFEFEFE);
    return AtlAdvise(
            pUnk, (IUnknown*)this, *piid, &m_dwEventCookie);
}
```

This explains why we must advise through the DispEventAdvise calls. This way, the IUnknown* presented to AtlAdvise as event sink is the base _IDispEvent* which just happens to act like an IUnknown* for that specic dispinterface and everything works as expected.

An object's IUnknown* is its identity and one of the rules is that a query for IUnknown should always return the same pointer, so how is this trickery not a violation? The reason is that these classes carefully avoid that problem. The object is never queried through it's 'real' QueryInterface. When a 'faux' IUnknown pointer is used to advise a source, then any query through that pointer will always yield the same pointer. At no point is there any crossover. Conceptually, you can consider every sink interface to be just a small COM object that piggybacks onto a parent COM object for life support.

Counting fish

For the purpose of the example, we're having 2 threads. The main console thread is used to increment the number of fish, every time we press a key. The other registers the appropriate event interface to receive notifications until we press q to quit. Error handling removed for clarity.

```
CComPtr<ICounter> sourceObject;
sourceObject.CoCreateInstance(L"FishCounter_V1.Counter");

ICounter* rawPtr = sourceObject.p;
rawPtr->AddRef();
HANDLE thread = CreateThread(
                  NULL, 0, WorkerThreadFunc, rawPtr, 0, NULL);

HANDLE hStdin = GetStdHandle(STD_INPUT_HANDLE);
while (true) {
    WCHAR ch = WaitForInput(hStdin);
    if (ch == L'q' || ch == VK_ESCAPE) {
        g_IsShuttingDown = true;
        break;
    }
    else {
        sourceObject->Increment();
    }
}
WaitForSingleObject(thread, INFINITE);
```

The main thread creates the source object, and passes an interface pointer to a dedicated worker thread. Concerning reference counting, there are a couple of ways we could go about this, because we control what goes on in both threads. The main thread waits for the worker thread upon exit, with the help of a call to WaitForSingleObject. Under the 'special knowledge' rule, it would be perfectly safe to pass a pointer to the worker thread and use it there without putting any thought in pointer ownership. But that isn't a good idea in general.

Instead, we create an AddRef'ed copy of the pointer and pass that to the worker thread which will then own it for its entire lifetime and is responsible for releasing it when it no longer needs it. This is always the safer option because it no longer relies on dependencies between threads.

Inside the main thread, we keep responding to key presses and then either increment or quit as specified. Because we're working with COM, it is necessary to use an input method that doesn't block the message queue or stops APCs from firing. For that, we use the WaitForInput function we discussed earlier.

Meanwhile, the worker thread listens for counter events.

```
unsigned long WorkerThreadFunc(void* arg)
{
    CoInitializeEx(NULL, COINIT_MULTITHREADED);

    {
        CComPtr<ICounter> sourceObject;
        sourceObject.Attach(static_cast<ICounter*>(arg));

        CEventSinkObject* sinkPtr;
        CEventSinkObject::CreateInstance(&sinkPtr))) {
        CComPtr<CEventSinkObject> sink = sinkPtr;

        sink->DispEventAdvise(sourceObject);
        while (!g_IsShuttingDown) {
            WaitProcessIOPumpMessages(200);
        }
        sink->DispEventUnadvise(sourceObject);
    }
    CoUninitialize();
    return 0;
}
```

During the design phase we decided that the worker thread was going to own the supplied pointer so the first order of business is to attach it to a smart pointer so it doesn't leak. We create a new sink object, hook it up to the source, and then simply pump messages on the thread until it's time. As before, we use a scope block to ensure the pointer is released before the thread loses its apartment. Since this is an MTA thread and the pointer is a direct pointer, nothing bad would happen if we didn't observe this order of events. But it would be unsafe if the pointer was a marshaled pointer so it's good practice to follow.

Speaking about apartments, our sink object was declared to support the multi-threaded model. This is an important detail in light of the fact that we're not working with a full-fledged COM object. For a normal activation that involves the COM runtime functions like CoCreateInstance, the runtime ensures that we get an interface pointer which is appropriate for the apartment we're in. Through the object's declared threading model and current thread context, activation follows a certain route and at the end of the road, we get a pointer which may be a direct pointer or a proxy. The important consideration is that regardless of the thread context, whatever we end up with is safe for whatever we want to do.

But we're not using those routines. Ignoring the ATL niceties, the call to ComObject<>::CreateInstance boils down to a simple 'new' operation. The CComObjectRootEx<...> base class notwithstanding, the object is created in the apartment the thread is in at that particular time. If we are going to manually create objects like this, it is up to us to make sure they are compatible with that apartment.

The final little detail is that in order to use ATL, there needs to be an ATL module. It doesn't need to do anything except exist.

```
class CMyModule : public CAtlExeModuleT<CMyModule> {};
CMyModule _AtlModule;
```

With this out of the way we can build an example.

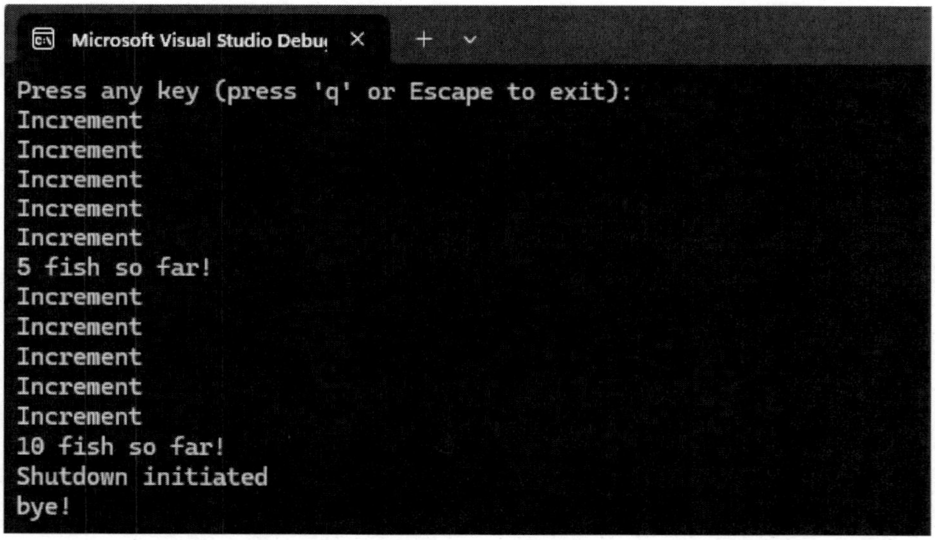

A final point of note is that if you want the Fire_xxx routine to fire events from a worker thread, it is imperative that the source object is in the MTA. Firing the event requires accessing interface pointers that were supplied by the client application. We don't know the apartment of the client, so we don't know if those interface pointers are safe to be used in whatever apartment the worker thread is in. The only way to guarantee safety is to ensure that the source object is an MTA only object, so that the worker can share it with the source object and safely use those sink interfaces.

Summary

In this chapter we continued with asynchronous programming, in the form of a well-defined connection point interface protocol with a concept of event sources and event sinks. This paradigm is available for custom events, but historically used predominately for the purpose of GUI applications and controls that need to be able to respond to events such as user input, as well as on things happening in the system or in other GUI controls.

13

.NET and COM

When .NET was released to the world in 2002, COM was still king. If .NET was to have any chance at surviving and taking over, it was extremely important that it could coexist with COM so that it could be introduced into the ecosystem without too much disruption or having to write off earlier development efforts. To that end, there was a lot of focus on interoperability. COM clients had to be able to consume a .NET object as if it was a COM object. Likewise, a .NET client had to be able to work with a COM object as if it was a .NET object. This was helped a lot by the fact that .NET and COM both have protocols for lifecycle management, and then both rely on having authoritative type information and interface contracts. The implementation differs a lot, but in both interoperability scenarios, it is conceptually easy to put a wrapper around objects in one technology stack so that it can be consumed by the other.

To help with this, Visual Studio and the .NET framework came with several tools to facilitate this. For example, there was a tool called tlbexp which could create a TLB file based on objects and interfaces that are marked for being visible to COM. There was also a tool called regasm which could register a .NET assembly for COM interoperability and create the various necessary registry entries. This greatly facilitated the coexistence of both technologies.

Unfortunately, due to the success of .NET, COM interoperability has become less and less important. Microsoft has also made a push to change from the .NET Framework to .NET Core as a way to refocus .NET as a true cross platform technology that is not tied as strongly to the Windows ecosystem. These 2 things combined have caused Visual Studio to drop support for several of these tools, in much the same way as portions of ATL were dropped along the way. It's still possible to use COM objects in a .NET project like it was before. Even when building new applications and services in .NET, the need to make use of certain old interfaces is still real. On the other hand, shoehorning a .NET project into a COM wrapper so that it can be consumed in a legacy environment has become less and less important, to the point where it's presumably not worth the time and investment anymore.

Visual Studio itself still supports the necessary code generation, but the rest of the tooling has fallen by the wayside. Thankfully, there is a strong opensource initiative to provide alternatives for those tools so that we can still continue on this journey without having to resort to hacks and undocumented behavior.

The 'core' naming was dropped eventually and now it's just '.NET' with a version number. In this chapter I will focus on working with .NET because that is the only supported way forward.

C++ / CLI

As a development tool, the .NET language of choice has always been C#. This is a C++ style language, purpose built for the .NET framework. It's what we will be using in this chapter. However, back when .NET was new, Microsoft made an effort to extend its C++ compiler so that it could combine native win32 code and managed .NET code in the same binary.

The first version of this was called 'Managed Extensions for C++', sometimes called 'Managed C++'. The language itself was an abomination unto mankind and combined a unique ugliness with syntactic ambiguity of the code. It was quickly replaced by C++/CLI which dropped the strict C++ language adherence and introduced a number of non-standard keywords and operators that made it a fun and intuitive language to play with.

With C# you already had the option to use .NET objects through COM wrappers or COM objects through an auto generated interop assembly. With C++/CLI you had an extra tool at your disposal because a single project could contain managed and unmanaged code. A single project could contain both. This was perfect for interoperability. It will not be covered here but deserves to be mentioned, because you will still find mentions about it. C++/CLI is still supported as a development choice for .NET Framework projects, but not for .NET Core or later. Using the techniques described below to create COM wrappers and extract TLB information from the assembly is not supported by Microsoft either.

Consuming a COM object in a .NET environment

The simplest scenario is if we want to consume a COM object in a .NET project. Suppose we want to implement the previous client application for the AdvCalculator object in C#. This is how we would go about it. First, create a new project:

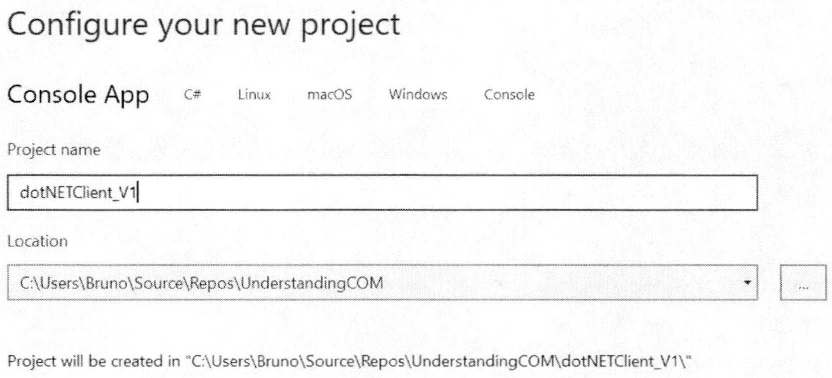

As the target framework, we choose one of the supported frameworks. The options here depend on what you have installed on your system. For this example, we choose the LTS version which is .NET 8.

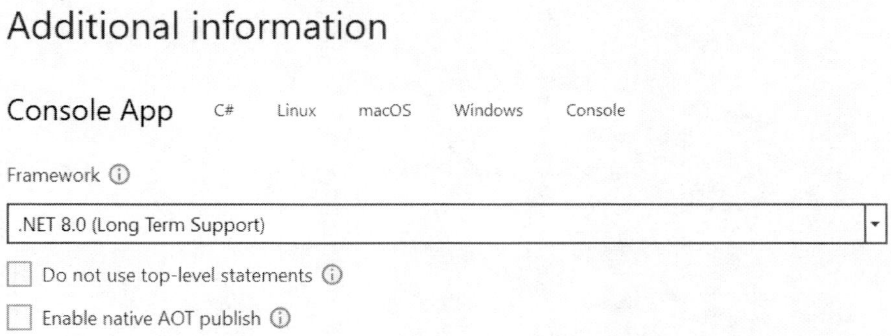

In the project settings, set the target OS to Windows because we will be working with COM after all.

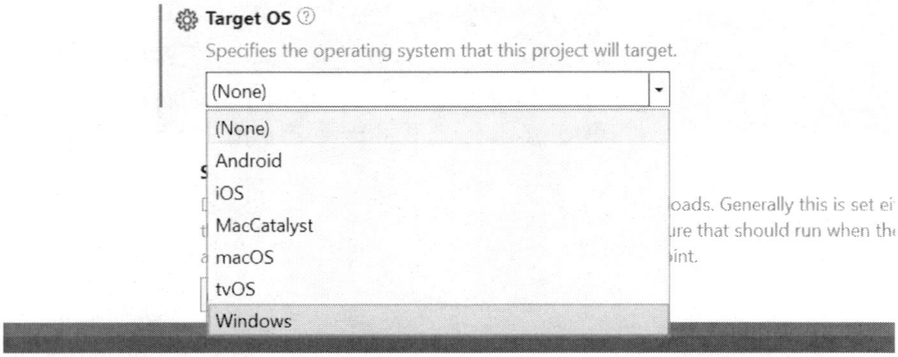

The first thing to do is to add a reference to the type library which holds the information we want to use. In a .NET project, this is called a COM reference even though it's really a Type Library reference. Unlike C++ projects, a .NET project cannot work with IDL files.

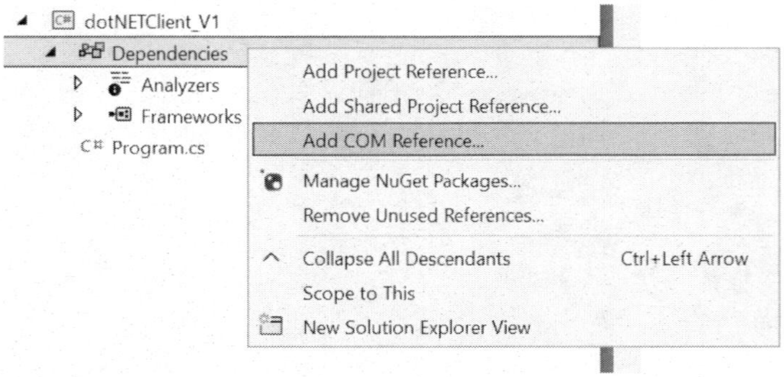

Incidentally, unlike the ATL 'Implement interface' wizard, the reference manager can work with type libraries that were created for a 64-bit architecture.

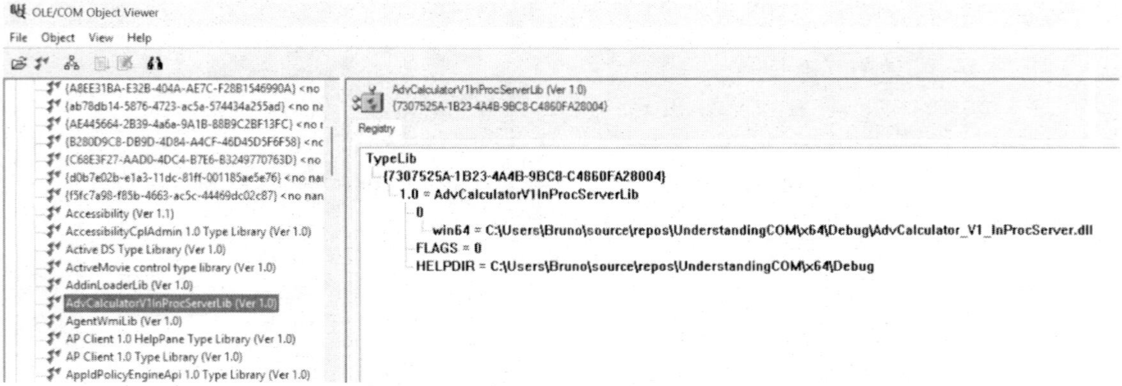

Even though the 32 bit version is not registered, the TLB shows up in the list of available type libraries.

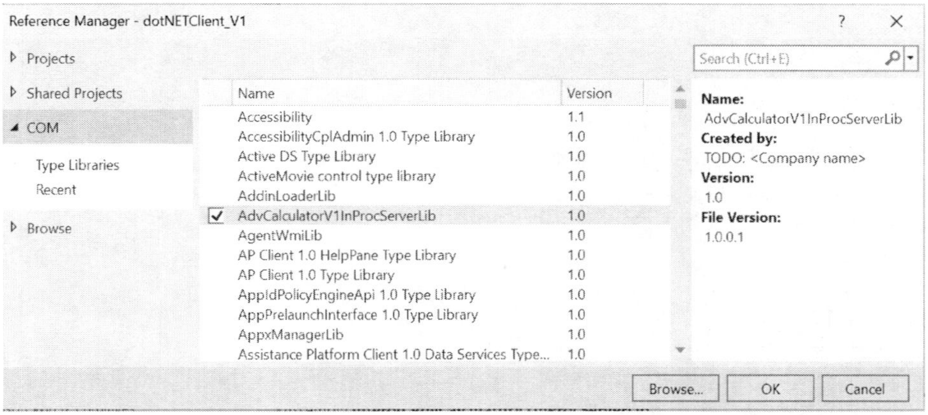

After we add it, it shows up in the COM dependency list. In object explorer, the contents of the type library show up, minus the IArithmetic interface which is recognized but missing. The reason it is missing is the interop assembly that was generated only contains types that are in the selected type library

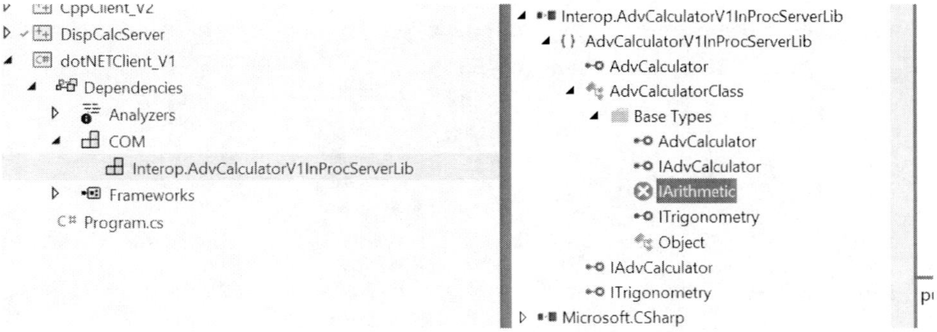

If we add a reference to the Calculator type library as well, the interface is resolved and our type is complete.

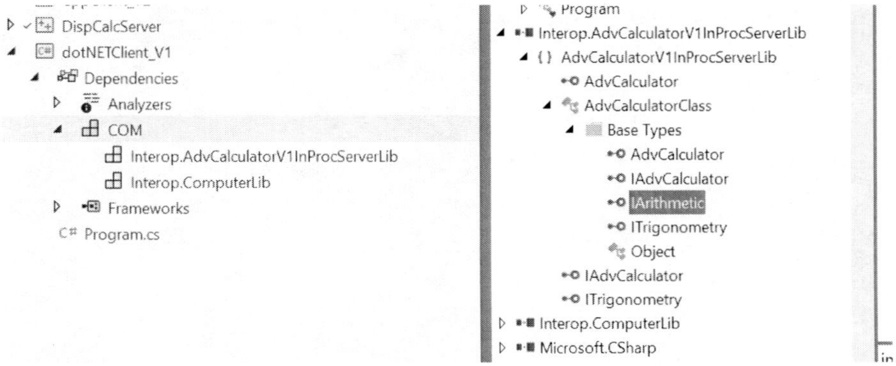

With that out of the way, using it is trivial. In many respects, the C# code strongly resembles the code of the C++ client (error checking removed for clarity).

```
using AdvCalculatorV1InProcServerLib;
using ComputerLib;

var calculatorType = Type.GetTypeFromProgID("CalculusInc.Calculator.1");
var comObject = Activator.CreateInstance(calculatorType);
IArithmetic? iAr =  comObject as IArithmetic; //internal QI
double result = 0;
iAr.Add(1, 1, out result);

Console.WriteLine("Result = {0}",result);
```

The most notable absence is the lack of reference counting which is taken care of by the internals of the COM wrapper. The QueryInterface calls are hidden away in the type cast which does that under the covers. Because it's a console program, the debug output of the original calculator DLL gets printed there as well before finally proving that 1 + 1 is still 2.

```
C:\ProgramData\DCOMDemoLogs\Calculator_V1_InProcServer.txt
2025-10-22 11:35:08    3608    Initialize Server
2025-10-22 11:35:08    3608    Classobject QueryInterface IID_IClassFactory
2025-10-22 11:35:08    3608    IClassFactory CreateInstance
2025-10-22 11:35:08    3608      Class instance created
2025-10-22 11:35:08    3608      Class instance QueryInterface for IID_IUnknown
2025-10-22 11:35:08    3608      Class instance QueryInterface for IID_IUnknown
2025-10-22 11:35:14    3608      Class instance QueryInterface for IID_IArithmetic
Result = 2

C:\Users\Bruno\Source\Repos\UnderstandingCOM\dotNETClient_V1\bin\Debug\net8.0-windows\dotNETClient_V1.exe
 exited with code 0 (0x0).
To automatically close the console when debugging stops, enable Tools->Options->Debugging->Automatically c
le when debugging stops.
Press any key to close this window . . .
```

And that's all there is to using a COM object in a .NET project. Note that because it's a DLL server, the bitness of the registered server needs to match the bitness of the application.

Consuming a .NET object in a COM environment

Using a COM object in a .NET environment was relatively easy. The other direction: to use a .NET object as a COM object, is possible too. It just requires some extra work on the side of the .NET object so that it can pretend to be a COM object. We're going to start with a .NET class library project.

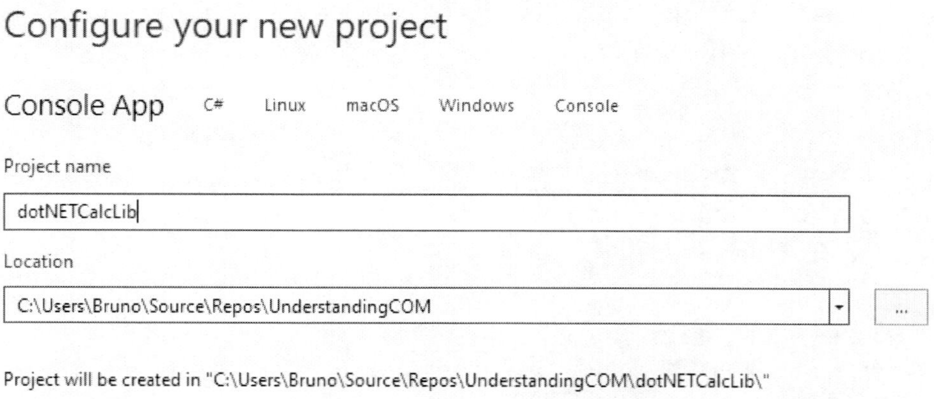

As mentioned, while the .NET framework release makes it a bit easier to do this, for the purpose of this book we're sticking to .NET 8.0 which is at present the long-term support branch.

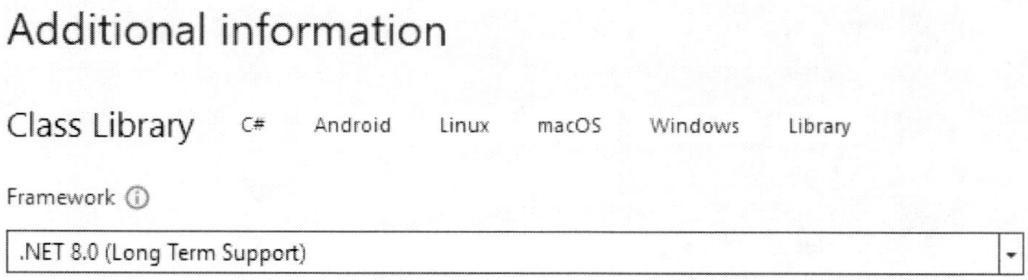

First order of business is to create a .NET interface. C# is nice in the sense that it has templates for everything. Granted, it's possible to add an empty .cs file and fill it in, but this way we have the proper keywords in place.

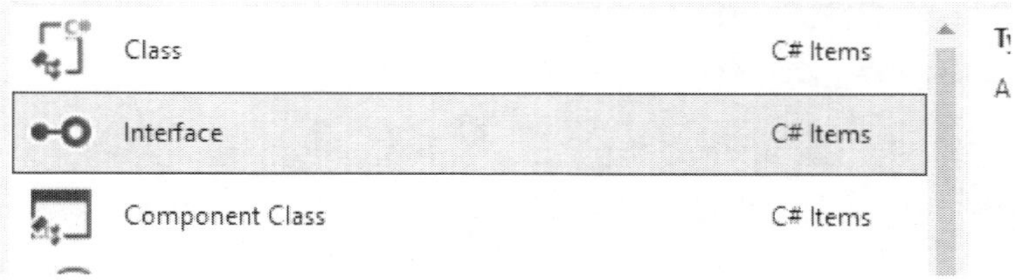


```
namespace dotNETCalcLib
{
    internal interface IDispCalculator
    {
    }
}
```

The default contents are an empty interface with only internal visibility. That needs to change to public. It also has to be marked ComVisible so that the proper interoperability code is generated, and decorated with the GUID that is used to identify the interface in COM. Lastly, we need to declare what sort of interface it has to be. The usual suspects are available: IUnknown based, dual, and dispinterface. For the purpose of this example, we're making a dual interface like we did in our earlier DispCalculator project.

```
[ComVisible(true)]
[Guid("A3B8A1FE-E198-42C3-9935-536032EC220F")]
[InterfaceType(ComInterfaceType.InterfaceIsDual)]
public interface IDispCalculator
{
    void Add(double Arg1, double Arg2, out double Result);
}
```

And like before, we need to put something interesting in there to implement, which is the 'Add' method again. Unlike before, we do not use a HRESULT return value. The .NET framework is firmly built around the notion or exceptions. The interop code that wraps this method call at runtime will catch any exception and return a HRESULT as appropriate. With the interface ready, we can turn our attention to the class object.

```
[ComVisible(true)]
[Guid("1E98E77B-4B1B-4C0F-9F3E-E8E3E148DB91")]
[ClassInterface(ClassInterfaceType.None)]
public class DispCalculator : IDispCalculator
{
    public void Add(double Arg1, double Arg2, out double Result)
    {
        Result = Arg1 + Arg2;
    }
}
```

The ComVisible attribute and Guid attribute are as expected. The interesting new thing is the ClassInterface attribute which can have 3 different values:

- None: No interface is generated for the class object itself.
- AutoDispatch: a dispatching interface is created that dispatches to all public members of the class object. If you remember our ATL project, dispatching was only implemented for the default interface. With .NET interop, there is the option to implement dispatching to every public member. On the face of it, this seems wonderful but there's a caveat. To avoid early binding or the caching of DispIDs, no type information is generated in the TLB file. This significantly reduces the usefulness because it's essentially a dispinterface.

- AutoDual: This is like AutoDispatch but it's a true dual interface and the type information will be available in the TLB. The caveat here is that this is strongly discouraged because there is no versioning system in place to deal with changes to anything in the public surface of the class. It causes the versioning problems described in the first chapter of this book. Any client that performs early binding to the type would break if the overall public interface of the class ever changes.

As a result of this, 'None' is the only choice that makes sense here. The entire point of what we're doing here is to ensure that a .NET object can work with the COM ecosystem. Following the same rules and abiding by the same restrictions is overall the best approach.

With the interface and the class object taken care of, there is still 1 piece of information missing from the puzzle: the LIBID of the type library that is going to contain the type information for this assembly. For that, we need to insert an assembly info file.

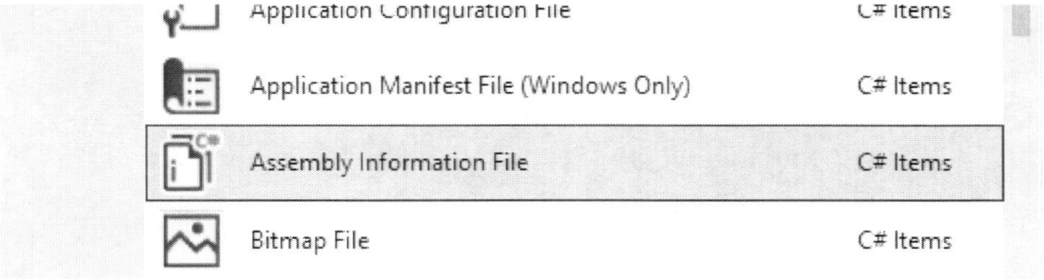

When the file is added, the following entries are automatically inserted. We just need to set the COM visibility to true.

```
[assembly: ComVisible(true)]
[assembly: Guid("a8c865ff-7f9c-4727-8bfd-b13888ff15b6")]
```

In terms of information, everything is there for the COM type generation. However, if we build this project, 1 thing is still missing: the actual COM wrapper. We need to tell the build process explicitly to generate it. This is not a setting in the standard project properties. We need to edit the project file itself as XML and add the required instructions ourselves.

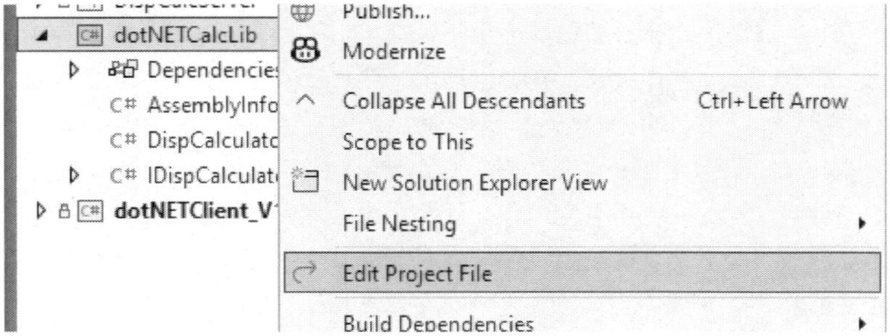

To create the COM wrapper and grant access to the embedded types, we have to add the EnableCOMHosting and ComVisible properties.

```
<Project Sdk="Microsoft.NET.Sdk">

  <PropertyGroup>
    <TargetFramework>net8.0</TargetFramework>
    <ImplicitUsings>enable</ImplicitUsings>
    <Nullable>enable</Nullable>

    <EnableComHosting>true</EnableComHosting>
    <ComVisible>true</ComVisible>

  </PropertyGroup>
</Project>
```

Upon building the project, the following files are generated.

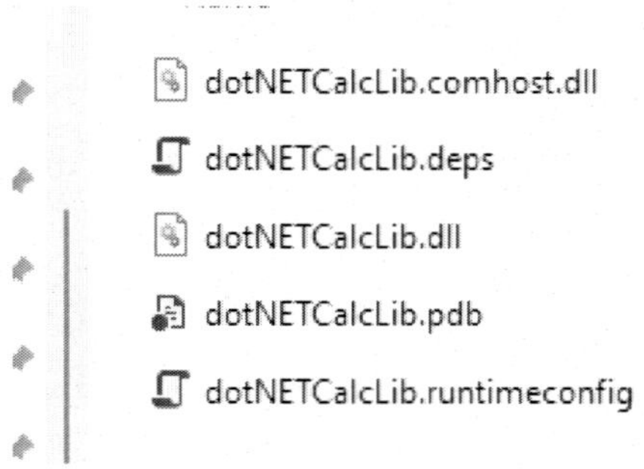

The files of main interest are the dotNETCalcLib.dll file which contains the class and the interfaces we've created. The dotNETCalcLib.comhost.dll is a wrapper with the COM entry points such as CoGetClassObject which then result in the interaction with the .NET class library. Unfortunately, this is where Microsoft abandons us, the developers. The next step in this process would be to generate the TLB file, using a tool called tlbexp.exe. Unfortunately, this is a .NET Framework tool, meant only for use with .NET Framework class libraries.

With the switch from .NET Framework to .NET, support for tlbexp was dropped. There is no longer an 'official' off the shelf tool to generate the TLB file from the assembly, and without it, we're stuck. Thankfully, there is an open-source project on GitHub by dSPACE group which provides an alternative.

https://github.com/dspace-group/dscom

dscom is a tool which can do a couple of interesting things. It can:

- Export the TLB from a .NET object
- Embed a TLB into a COM callable wrapper
- Register the com callable wrapper.
- In the case of the classic .NET Framework it could also register assemblies in the global assembly cache, but that is no longer relevant.

We can make a small PowerShell script that uses dscom to perform the actions that were done with framework tools in the past.

```
param
(
    $server
)

$dscom = "C:\program files\dscom\dscom.exe"

$server = (Resolve-Path $server).Path
$tlb = [System.IO.Path]::ChangeExtension($server, ".tlb")
$wrapper = [System.IO.Path]::ChangeExtension($server, ".comhost.dll")

& "$dscom" tlbexport $server
& "$dscom" tlbembed $tlb $server
& "$dscom" tlbregister $server
& regsvr32 $wrapper
```

After running this script, our calculator shows up as a registered Type Library with the correct information that allows a client application to use it like before.

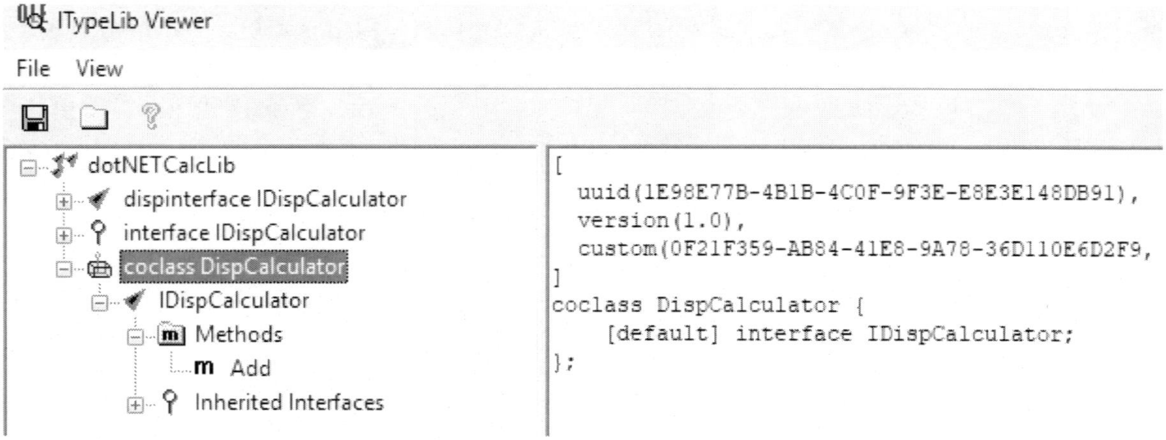

In fact, we can use the same Powershell script to use the new dotNET calculator. The only thing we need to change is the name of the calculator we want to use.

```
$comObject = New-Object -ComObject dotNETCalculator.DispCalculator

[double] $arg1 = 1.0
[double] $arg2 = 1.0
[double] $result = 0
$comObject.Add($arg1, $arg2, [ref] $result)

"$arg1 + $arg2 = $result"

$comObject | Get-Member
```

The results from this script are identical to what we got before.

```
PS C:\Users\Bruno> C:\Users\Bruno\Documents\Test-doNETDispCalc.ps1
1 + 1 = 2


   TypeName: System.__ComObject#{a3b8a1fe-e198-42c3-9935-536032ec220f}

Name MemberType Definition
---- ---------- ----------
Add  Method     void Add (double, double, double)
```

Summary

In this chapter we explored the interoperability options between COM and the .NET framework. It is possible to use COM objects in a .NET environment, and .NET objects in a COM environment. Realistically, the former is the most useful because new development is done in modern environments, and legacy objects are used until they can be replaced.

14

DCOM Security Model

The DCOM security model broadly consists of 2 different areas of security.

- Connection security. This is the security that is involved whenever data is marshaled between a client and a server and covers protection of that data to various degrees of security.
- Functional permissions. This is the configuration that is not covering the data, but the permissions that govern who is allowed to do what with specific servers.

Connection Security

When a client and a server communicate with each other, data is travelling back and forth between different processes, possibly traversing the network. This situation makes the data vulnerable. If data was sent unsecured, then it might be intercepted by network sniffers, or tampered with via man-in-the-middle attacks. The following settings are used to protect COM traffic:

- Authentication level
- Impersonation level
- Which authentication service to use
- Which identity or authentication information to use
- Which authentication capabilities of the system to use

We'll cover each of these in detail. The combined set of settings that are in use is called the security blanket. This blanket can be set either system wide, server specific, or at the level of specific interface proxies, to the following levels defined in the DCOM specification. The term sounds a bit like an inside joke because that term is also used to refer to the object toddlers use for feeling secure. In that sense the term is perfectly apt because the security blank covers our code and provides comfort and security.

Authentication level

At the heart, each marshaled call is flattened to a data packet; as series of bytes that is sent into a stream and unpacked at the other end to reconstitute the call.

To secure this data, authentication can be configured in increasing levels of data security to protect marshal calls

Level	Description
Default	Use the default authentication level
None	Use no authentication. In case of anonymous, unauthenticated users, this setting is required. Call data is unencrypted and origins are unverified.
Connect	Same as None, but the identity of the client is checked when the connection is made.
Call	Same as Connect, but the identity is verified with every call that is marshaled.
Packet	Same as Call, but identity is verified with every packet that is received.
Packet Integrity	Same as Packet, but a checksum is used with every packet, to ensure that the call is not tampered with, for example by a man-in-the-middle attack.
Packet Privacy	Same as Packet Integrity, but every packet is encrypted to make the contents unreadable to e.g. wire sniffers.

The server specifies the minimum level of authentication security it is willing to accept. The client specifies the level it wants to use. For example, if a client wants to communicate with a level of RPC_C_AUTHN_LEVEL_CONNECT and the server specifies that it requires RPC_C_AUTHN_LEVEL_PKT_INTEGRITY, authentication will fail.

If the client specifies RPC_C_AUTHN_LEVEL_PKT_INTEGRITY and the server level is RPC_C_AUTHN_LEVEL_CONNECT, they use RPC_C_AUTHN_LEVEL_PKT_INTEGRITY.

This has been a widely misunderstood situation. Both client and server have default settings that can be configured in DCOMCnfg. If the client initiates a connection, what happens depends on the security request from the client. If the client requests the default (in other words no actual permission is requested) then there is a round of negotiation between client and server when they establish a connection to determine the minimum level that can be used, even if the client default is less secure than what the server demands. However, if the client does specify a level, then there will be no negotiation and if the levels don't match, the request will fail as explained above.

For a long time, I couldn't think of any reason why someone had ever thought this was a good idea, but eventually a random comment from someone made me realize that I had been looking at this with the perspective of someone living in today's world instead of the late 90's. Today, we take it for granted that more security is considered better, and that there is no reason to not accept an upwards negotiation. But that could cause identity exposure. In the context of the internet accessible COM infrastructure that people thought the future would bring, it is understandable that clients might prefer to keep servers from getting information about their identity. Anonymity and encryption don't really go well together because encryption relies on keys, credentials, and security providers. Setting up a secure channel to exchange keys relies on authentication. And that would require the server and the client to learn identity details about each other. At the COM level the connection might be anonymous (assuming the server can be trusted) but at the infrastructure level there would be no anonymity.

For local security this matter has always been moot since Y2K because regardless of the value specified by this constant, same-system RPC traffic has always used RPC_C_AUTHN_LEVEL_PKT_PRIVACY. According to the github documentation for these RPC DCE constants, this behavior has been in place since Windows 2000. Remote-system calls otoh allowed the use of custom settings as described above.

Since the implementation of DCOM hardening, only Packet Integrity and Packet Privacy are supported because these are the only ones which have a guarantee that between the client and server, the packet contents have not been tampered with. The option of Default reverts the configuration to use the system default instead of server specific settings.

Impersonation level

The impersonation level determines whether a server is allowed to know the identity of a client, what it can know about a client, and whether it can operate using the client's identity. There are 4 levels.

Level	Description
Anonymous	The server cannot know anything about the client.
Identify	The server can identify the caller, find out which groups it is a member of for example, but not do anything with the identity token itself.

Impersonate	Same as Identify, but the server can also act as (impersonate) the client's identity for the purpose of accessing local resources.
Delegate	Same as Impersonate, but the identity can also be used for accessing network resources outside the system hosting the server.

Impersonation is a very useful and sometimes necessary feature. For example, a given server may be working as a middle-tier application, performing database updates on behalf of a client. This type of functional isolation is common in enterprise applications.

The database connection itself needs to be established with the client's credentials. This requires RPC_C_IMP_LEVEL_IMPERSONATE impersonation level if the database exists locally on the machine. If the database is instead on a different machine, RPC_C_IMP_LEVEL_DELEGATE is required because the identity needs to cross a security boundary and from a security perspective, that is markedly more sensitive. With Impersonate, a client at least knows on which system its identity can be used. With delegate, the server has the ability to fully act with the client's identity across the entire network.

For setting up the impersonation level of a connection, there is no negotiation process. The client determines what it wants to allow to happen with its credentials. The server accepts any level. At least, that was the situation until DCOM hardening.

Originally, having the lower-level options gave clients a guarantee that their identity could not be used in any meaningful way by a server it may not fully trust. The server might still attempt to impersonate and fail an operation if it was not able to impersonate at the required level. For example, if the server was asked to. perform a database update using client credentials, that could happen if the client doesn't allow it.

After DCOM hardening, only Impersonate or delegate are allowed for remote connections. This has shifted the level of trust from the client to the server. Now, it is the client which must trust the server. The server doesn't have to trust the client because it has the guarantee that the client's identity has been verified by the OS

Authentication service

COM allows you to specify programmatically which authentication service should be used. The list of possible values includes NTLM, Kerberos, SLL, and various others.

There is also an optional authorization level to go with each service, specifying how the authentication service should authenticate. The big services such as NTLM or Kerberos don't use it because the way identity management and authorization are implemented, are inherent in the protocol.

In a Windows landscape or mixed Windows - linux landscape, typically Kerberos would be used because it is one of the standard protocols in both OS landscapes. As a rule of thumb, the best approach is always to use the 'Default' and let the operating systems figure it out.

The only scenario in which there is ever a reason to use custom authentication authorization, is for example when interfacing with legacy systems that use Distributed Computing Environment (DCE) authorization.

Identity information

After specifying an authentication service to use, it follows logically that you can specify the identity that will be authenticated. This can be in the form of an explicit identity (username, domain, password), a certificate or the process identity.

Capabilities

The final piece of connection settings is a capabilities flag that allows a client to tweak the way security is handled. Some of these are obsolete. Some of these only apply with certain authentication providers. However, there are a couple that are worth mentioning.

Static / Dynamic cloaking. By default, the process identity (the user identity that started the process) is used for making the connection. In situations where a client application uses impersonation internally to perform actions as a different user, cloaking allows the thread identity to be used instead. Static cloaking means the identity is determined the first time a proxy call is made. With dynamic cloaking, the identity is determined with each call.

Disable AAA (Activate As Activator). This setting blocks the activation of any server that would be running under the identity of the client. Clients can use this setting to protect their identity they run as, to prevent potentially untrusted servers from running with client credentials and potentially abusing elevated privileges. This can be useful in scenarios where for example a client runs with an administrator account or the local system account, and wants to prevent

No custom marshal. This setting ensures marshaling is only done using CLSIDs that are implemented in Ole32.dll, ComAdmin.dll, ComSvcs.dll, or Es.dll, or which implement the CATID_MARSHALER category ID. Any service that is critical to system operation should set this flag. In earlier chapters we described that proxy DLLs are used to handle marshaling of interfaces that are used by a server. This requires the loading of the Proxy DLL which would mean that critical and sensitive processes would not be able to control which DLL would be inserted. After all, they can control which servers they load explicitly, but if someone were to replace an interface proxy, this would be invisible to the process for which marshaling is performed.

Permission Security

Permission security is the configuration of what is or is not allowed to be done with a COM object.

Launch and Activation permission

In the earlier chapter about COM Servers, we briefly explained the concept of Launch and Activation, and the fact that there are permissions assigned to those activities. Any COM server has an implicit (default) or explicit (specific to the server) security configuration. The default configuration is used if no specific configuration exists.

Security starts at this very first step in the COM Server lifecycle, with Launch and Activation permissions. To recap what we discussed earlier: Launch refers to starting an out-of-process server. Activation refers to the ability to use the class object inside that server. And while the term Activation may be used for in-process servers, the security configuration that may be done on the AppID does not apply to in-process servers.

At first glance it would seem sensible to put permissions on in-process servers, simply because we're used to thinking in terms of 'being allowed to...' when it comes to software. But the basic process management operating system principles don't translate neatly into COM specific restrictions. When all is said and done, an in-process server is just a DLL with known entry points such as DllGetClassObject.

Any process is allowed to load a DLL into its own memory space, if it has access to the physical location of the DLL. This means that any process could read the registry to find the location for a server, load the DLL using LoadLibrary, retrieve a pointer to the DllGetClassObject function, and start using the class object without the COM subsystem ever being formally involved. From an OS point of view, this is perfectly OK. The ability to load DLLs is fundamental to the correct functioning of the entire software ecosystem and couldn't be changed without breaking everything. And since the DLL itself has no notion of security, there is no practical way to enforce anything.

It would of course be possible to have COM itself honor the activation permission in calls to e.g. CoCreateInstance or CoGetClassObject, because when we use those APIs, COM is the gatekeeper. But it would only ever be a cosmetic security measure because any application would still be able to manually perform the required actions and there would be no way to put up a security measure against such things that wouldn't break a lot of software.

On the other hand, it makes perfect sense to restrict who can reach into a COM server process. And restricting access between 2 processes is completely natural and makes it trivial to enforce limitations through COM because COM is a non-negotiable gatekeeper when it comes to out-of-process servers.

Configuring Launch and Activation is done in the normal way of adding Windows principals, and then granting or denying access, with denial taking precedence. This is further split in local and remote launch and activation.

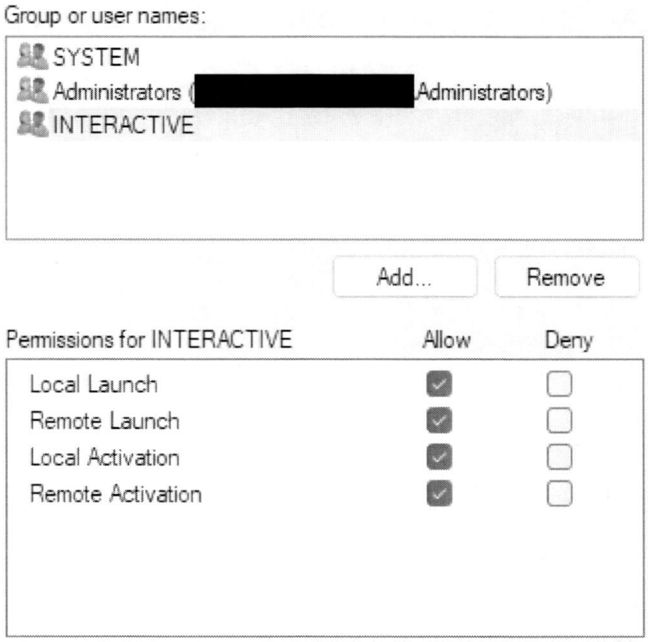

DCOMCnfg accepts specific named principal names such as Contoso\Users, as well as well-known principals such as SYSTEM and SERVICE. The well-known principal 'ANONYMOUS_LOGON' is still recognized but no longer honored. The well-known principal INTERACTIVE is commonly used to set permissions for any user that is logged on to an interactive desktop session.

Access Control

Aside from Launch and Activation permissions, Access permissions determine who is allowed to interact with objects. Like Launch and Activation permissions, these only apply to out-of-process servers.

In normal scenarios, any user with permission to launch or activate an object, will also be trusted to interact with it. The opposite is not always true. There may be out-of-process servers (such as application specific Windows services for example) which need to be started in a controlled manner by an administrator. As soon as they are running, users could be permitted to use the objects contained in that server. This is where access permissions come into play.

Here, too, well-known principals are often used. The use of 'SELF' is similar in nature to the 'CREATOR_OWNER' principal when dealing with file security. The default use of SELF is to define that anyone who started a COM server also has the right to access it.

It should be noted that in most scenarios, a client needs to have both Activation and Access permission to access objects in an out-of-process server. COM doesn't let you activate a class object without access permission. It also doesn't let you access a class object without access permission. At first glance, it appears that these 2 are completely overlapping. And in most cases that is correct. The exception is if the client is running with a different identity than the server. If that happens, then there is a scenario where we are allowed to Activate 1 object in the server, which in turn has the option to internally use instances of another object in the same server. In this scenario, the ability to access those objects through a marshaled interface pointer would be subject to the access permissions on that object. That would be a niche way to prevent external clients creating certain objects while still allowing those clients to use them, for example through a broker.

Configuration permissions

By default, only administrators can configure system wide settings and server specific settings. However, it is possible to delegate the right to configure specific servers to other users or principals. Specifically, this refers to the permission to configure the AppID settings for the server in the registry, which is also where launch and access permission lists are stored. If you use regedit to inspect the security settings of the specified AppID registry key, you can see that configuration permissions directly translate to permissions on that registry key.

For example, if we add 'INTERACTIVE' as a principal which has full control over the MathLib application

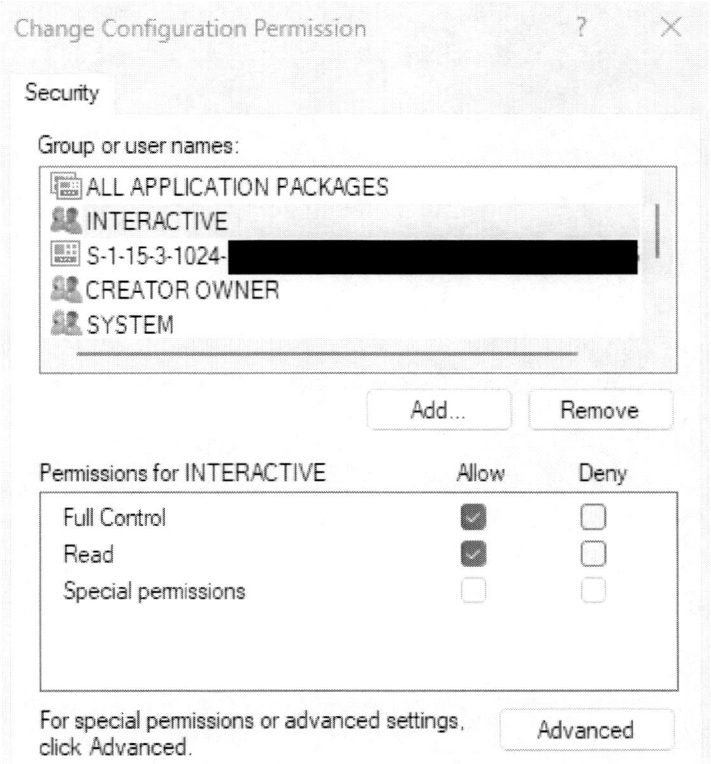

That principal is added to the registry settings for that key. You can see it is not an inherited permission; it is applied directly to the AppID key.

Note that this is only true in the HKLM hive. If you define the AppID in the HKCU hive, you can see it overrides the settings in HKCR but they will be ignored and modifying the ‘configuration security’ settings will only reflect in the HKLM registry, not HKCU. The HKCR settings will only reflect the HKLM situation if no HKCU AppID with the specified name exists

Granting configuration permissions is not something that is typically done because server configuration is system wide, but the option is there if it needs to be done.

Security limits

Launch, Activation and Access can all be configured either as system wide defaults, or server specific. And if configuration permission is granted to non-administrative users, those users can override existing launch and access permissions in a manner that is unsafe or might be undesirable. That is where security limits come into play.

In the system wide settings, administrators can specify a limit to the permissions that can be configured at the server specific level. Regardless of what is configured, the final set of launch and access permissions can never be more permissive than what is defined in the security limits. Limits can be applied on access level as well as launch and activation level.

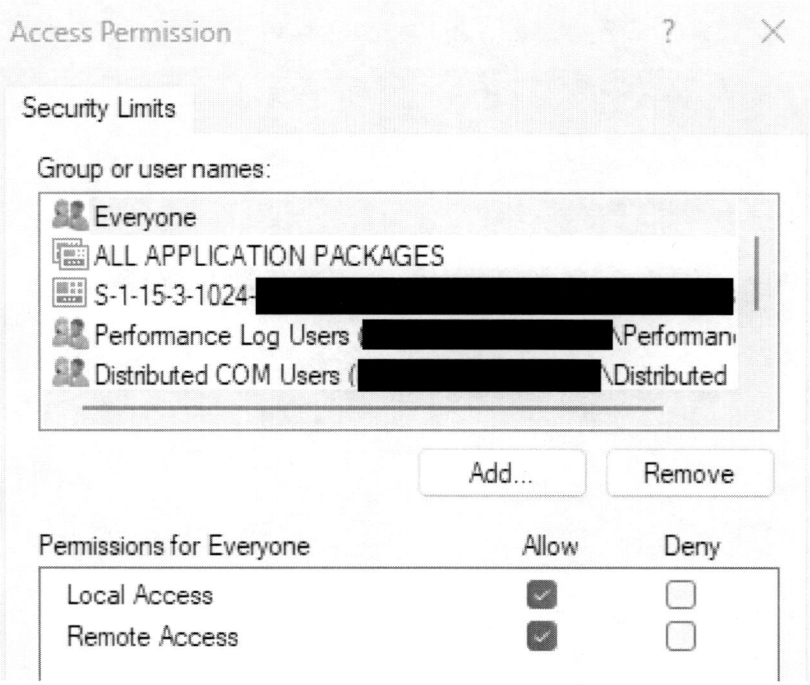

By default, the EVERYONE principal has both local and remote access limits, meaning that server specific levels can be configured to grant everyone all access. That doesn't mean that they automatically have those permissions if these are not explicitly defined.

The same default limits are defined for the Performance Log Users and the Distributed COM Users groups. If EVERYONE is allowed access, Performance Log Users and Distributed COM Users will also be included. However, administrators may wish to remove EVERYONE or limit that principal to local access only in some environments. In that case, there may still be a need to allow remote activation to users who need to monitor performance logs (which requires remote access) or who are explicitly configured as users who need Distributed COM access. By having those 2 groups predefined with appropriate limits, changes can be made without causing undue impact.

A similar mechanism exists for Launch and Activation permissions.

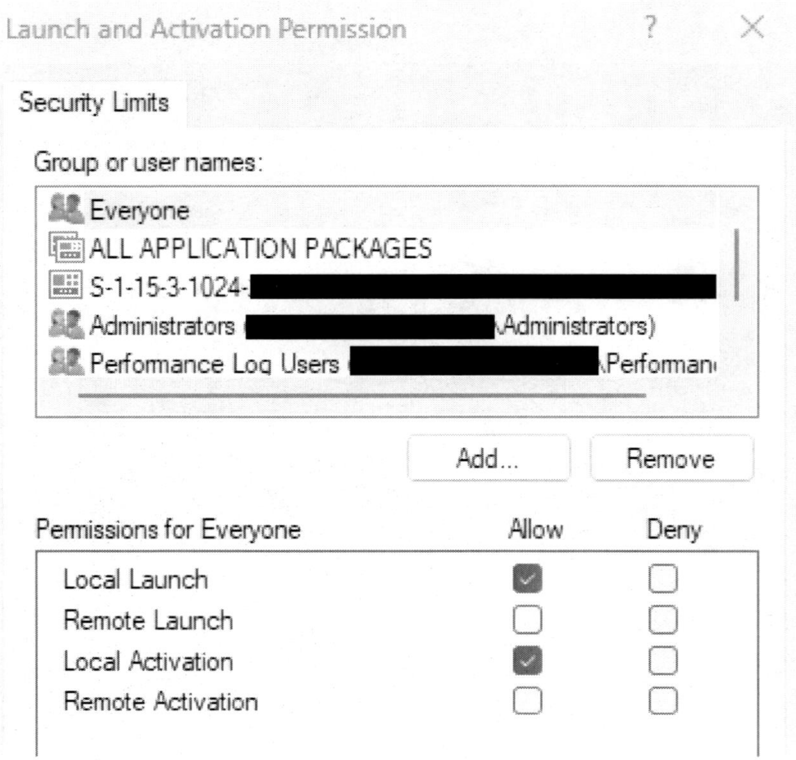

By default, EVERYONE is limited to only launch or activate locally. Otoh Performance Log Users and Distributed COM Users are not limited, meaning their default limit is to be able to launch and activate locally and remotely.

To re-iterate: Note that none of these limits grant any actual permission. They only define the limits for specified user principals in case they are used at the system wide or server specific level.

Configuring DCOM

Windows comes with a dedicated tool to configure COM connections. This tool is called DCOMCnfg. To be correct: there are also several non-security related parameters that can be configured in DCOMCnfg, such as network protocols and COM+ settings. But the main use for this tool is to configure security settings.

Technically, things like network port ranges and protocol settings could be argued not to belong in the security chapter. On the other hand, they have an impact on firewall configuration, which does belong in the security chapter. To keep all DCOM Configuration together, the author chose to keep all that information together instead of spreading it out among different chapters.

If you look online for information about this, there will be a lot of confusion, and you'll find statements that DCOMCnfg is used only to configure the 64-bit configuration of a server, and that a 32-bit version of the management must be used for managing the configuration of 32-bit servers via the command

```
mmc comexp.msc /32
```

However, that is not correct. Yes, you may load a 32-bit version of the DCOM snap in, but the documentation is very clear. The AppID key in HKLM or HKCU is shared between the 64-bit and 32-bit registry locations of those respective hives. There is only 1 configuration set for a DCOM application and no matter how you configure it, it is going to apply to both versions of the server. As a test, you can open the 64-bit and 32-bit configuration tools side by side and compare the entries. They will be identical. It is likely that this confusion stems from the origins of WOW64 in the XP timeframe when operations involving AppID settings were indeed redirected to architecture specific sections of the registry hive.

There are 2 types of setting to be configured here: global settings that apply to all COM servers (or are used as default if no server specific settings have been configured), and server specific settings that can override the global defaults.

Global settings

When you open DCOMCnfg, you are presented with a pretty basic user interface:

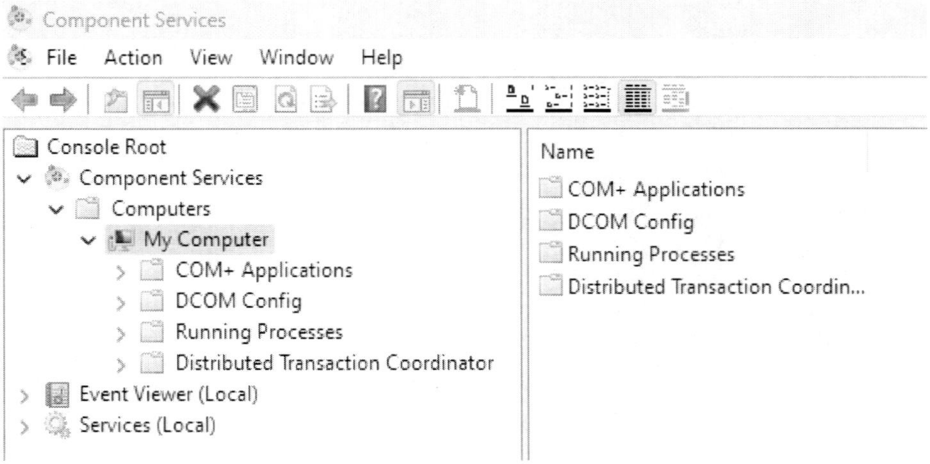

Underneath 'My Computer' there are 4 entries. COM+ Applications, Running Processes and Distributed Transaction Coordinator all pertain to COM+ servers. COM+ is out of scope for this book. It was introduced with Windows 2000, to provide support for distributed enterprise applications that work asynchronously and use transactions. As a technology it had mixed success in terms of adoption and was replaced fairly quickly by .NET which was released not too long after COM+ was introduced with Windows 2000.

DCOM Config is the folder where all server specific information can be managed.

For system wide configuration and defaults, right-click 'My Computer' and open the properties dialog where system wide settings reside. The 'General' tab doesn't contain anything useful.

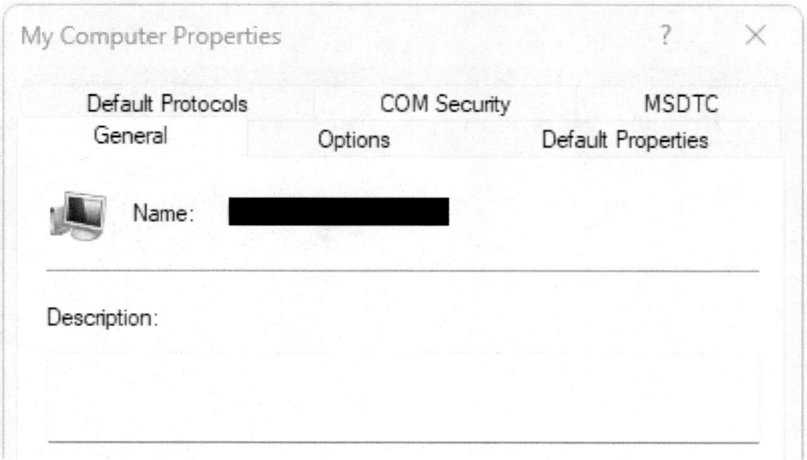

The 'options' tab lists options that are relevant only for COM+ applications which are out of scope for this book. For the sake of completeness these properties are explained briefly below.

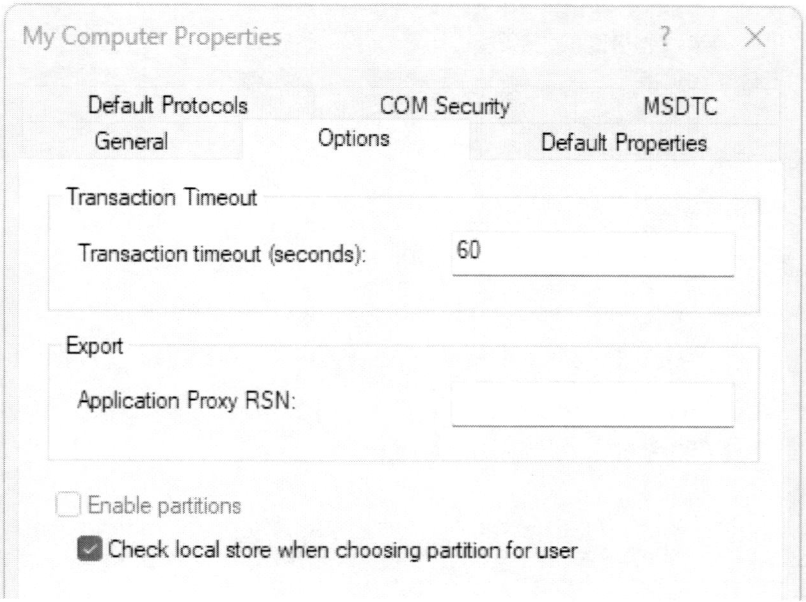

Transaction timeout concerns the maximum duration of a COM+ transaction. Partitioning is a feature that allows you to create isolated environments within a single COM+ application for the purpose of user isolation and resource management. 'Application Proxy Remote Server Name (RSN)' is the name of the default remote server for application proxies on that machine, if no specific remote server has been defined for a COM+ application.

Default Properties is where system wide connections are located for COM client-server connections across a network connection. This is an important page because these are the settings which will be used in the security blanket, if no server specific settings are found, and if the server itself doesn't override them.

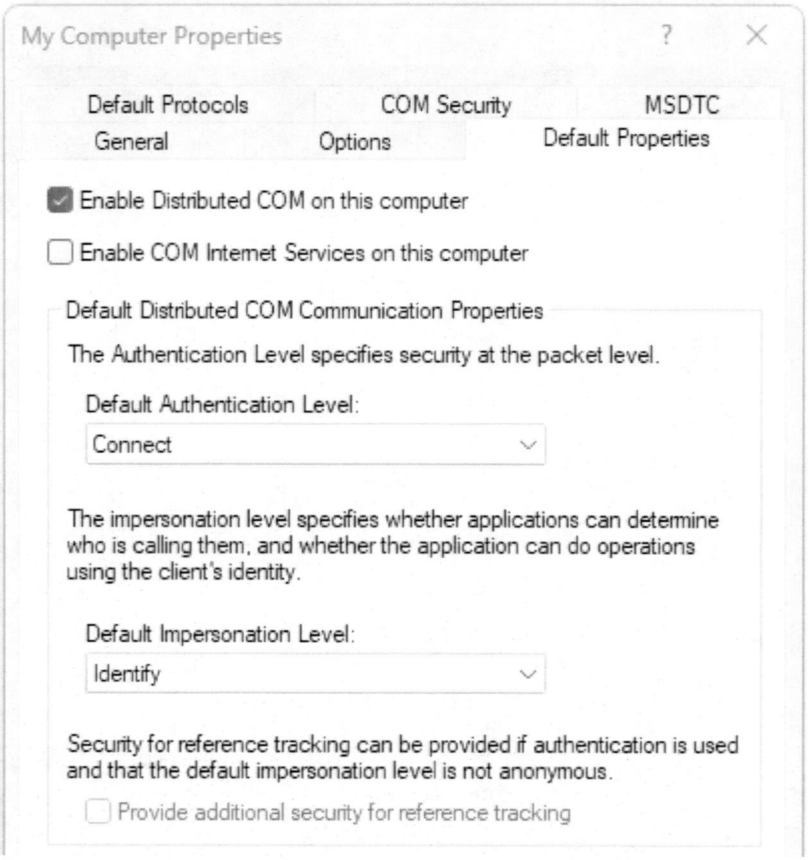

'Enable Distributed COM on this computer' can be used to enable or disable DCOM globally. This setting only has an impact on COM over network connections. Disabling DCOM will make it impossible to access class objects on this computer from a different location. This could be considered an upside from a security perspective, but the downside is that many Windows management tools use DCOM for remote administration purposes. If DCOM is disabled, not only client applications are impacted. Remote administration of the system is also no longer an option.

'Enable COM internet services (CIS) on this computer' can be used to enable DCOM over the internet using HTTP connections. CIS was an attempt in the late 90's early 2000's to make DCOM more internet friendly. We'll talk a bit more about this in the next section about DCOM hardening, but from a security perspective it is extremely unsecure, and should never ever be used unless you are connecting to a legacy system and can use additional mitigations such as network isolation or a VPN because by itself, such a setup offers less protection than a paper-mâché bulletproof vest. CIS is another topic which will not be covered in this book.

The 2 dropdown settings specify the system default settings for the authentication level and impersonation level. After DCOM hardening, whatever authentication level is selected, is silently updated to at least Packet Privacy. Whatever impersonation level is selected is silently updated to at least Impersonate.

The "Additional security for reference tracking" setting can be used to prevent denial of service attacks in scenarios where a server is used in a distributed scenario and multiple different users connect to the same object. By default, reference counting is a simple +1 / -1 operation without checks to ensure that every Release call matches an AddRef call by the same user. The COM Runtime will maintain this count and only allow Releases to be executed if the count of AddRef calls for that particular user is non-zero. In a multi-user scenario, this type of reference counting ensures that user B cannot deprive user A from using a class object by calling Release more times than it has called AddRef.

This setting is not enabled by default because it imposes a performance overhead, and not all servers warrant that level of paranoia. Additionally, this is not always necessary. For example if the class object is hosted in an out-of-process server that implements lifecycle management through IExternalConnection, the reference count of the class object does not contribute to the lifecycle management of the server. Additionally, if this setting is used, per-proxy configuration of the security blanket could fail.

The 'MSDTC' tab lets you specify whether COM+ uses the local transaction coordinator or a remote one. As mentioned, COM+ is out of scope for the purpose of this book.

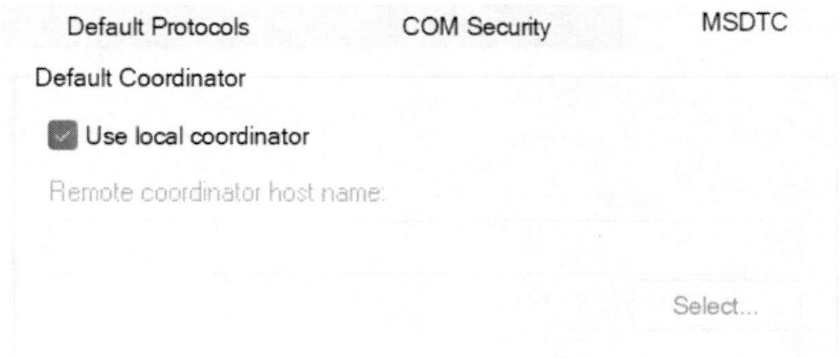

For the sake of completeness, if the checkbox for using the local coordinator is checked, the configuration can be found in the properties of the Local DTC node in DCOMCnfg.

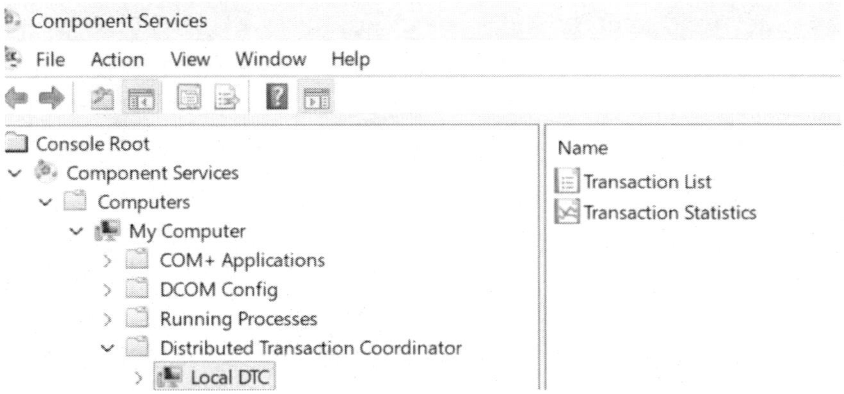

The final tab that can be configured concerns the communication protocols that will be used for DCOM.

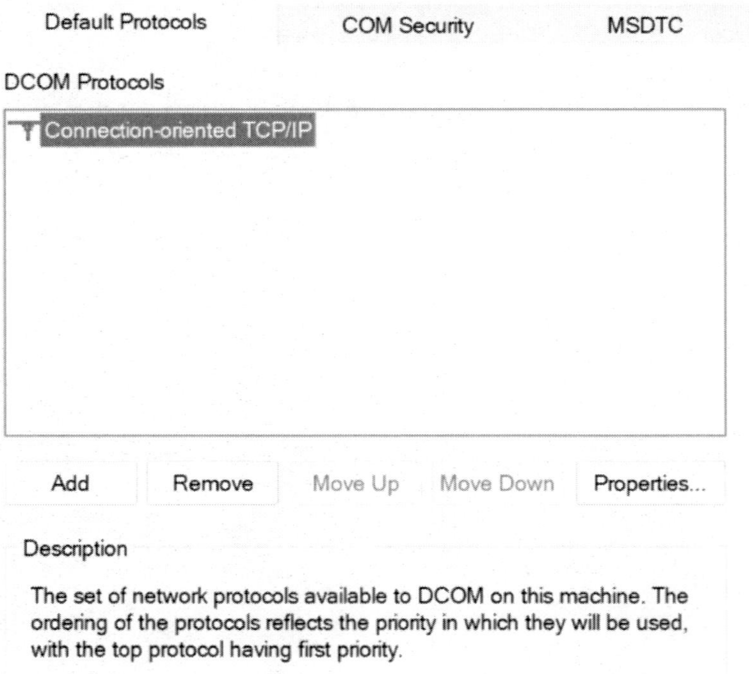

The default option is to use DCOM over TCP/IP. It is possible to configure specific port ranges to be used. By default, the following ports are used.

TCP Port	Purpose	Description
135	RPC Endpoint Mapper	COM makes use of the RPC protocol. Port 135 is the RPC port so it the initial contact point for DCOM. This port must be open on client and server.
49152–65535	Dynamic RPC ports	After initial contact, DCOM dynamically assigns a port in this range for actual communication.
1024–4999	(Older systems)	Used on systems prior to Windows Server 2008.

This is a rather large set of ports to use. This makes DCOM a very firewall-unfriendly protocol because it requires thousands of ports to be open. Network administrators are allergic to things like that because it drastically increases a potential network attack surface. It is possible to decrease this number, but that would require manual configuration to the protocol settings that must match the firewall configuration. To deal with that, it is possible to configure the use of a tunneling tcp/ip protocol which doesn't require all those ports top be open. However, tunneling tcp/ip is a part of CIS, and if CIS is disabled as it should be, then tunneling won't work either. A minor point of clarification is warranted if you want to specify custom port ranges for regular connection based tcp/ip. The title of the dialog says "Properties for COM Internet Services"

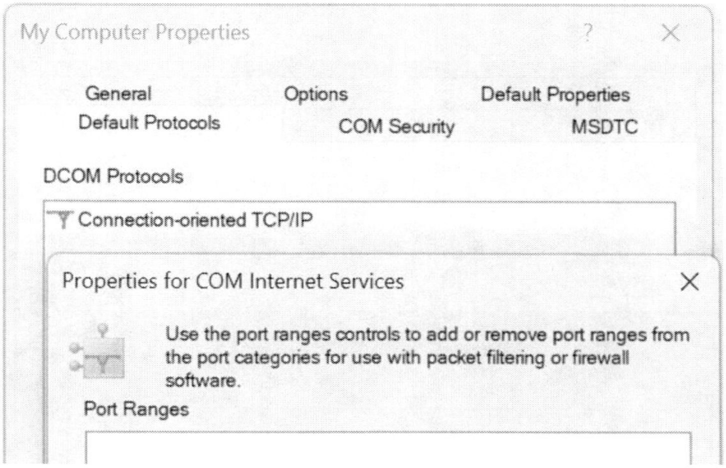

This is a legacy GUI artifact from a dialog box that once served a different purpose. The dialog box may say it is CIS, but you're not using CIS just because the dialog box says so.

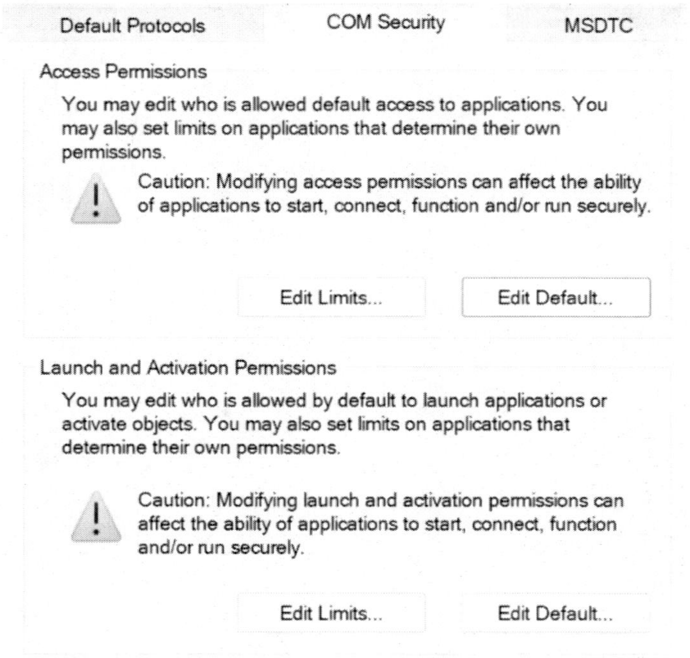

The final tab page covering global settings is the security tab. Using this tab, an administrator can configure the default permissions for launching / activating, and accessing COM Servers, as well as their limits, as explained in detail in the previous section about the permission security.

Server settings

Let's examine the entry that was created for the calculator server.

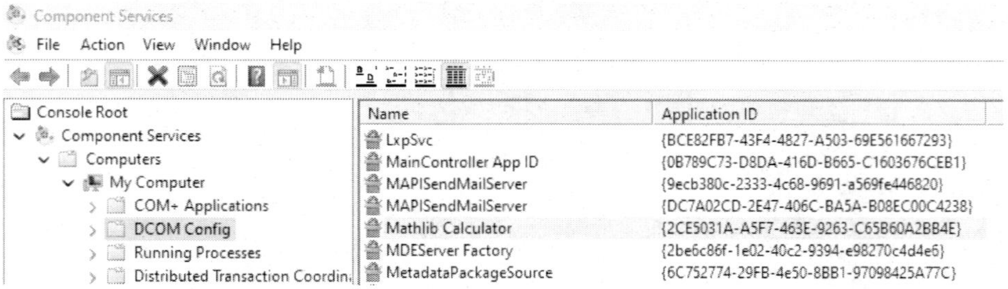

Even though the registry uses the GUID to link the ClsID entry to the AppID, the default value of the AppID is used as displayname in DCOMCnfg so it is still easy enough to find the Calculator application. The application dialog has several configuration tabs.

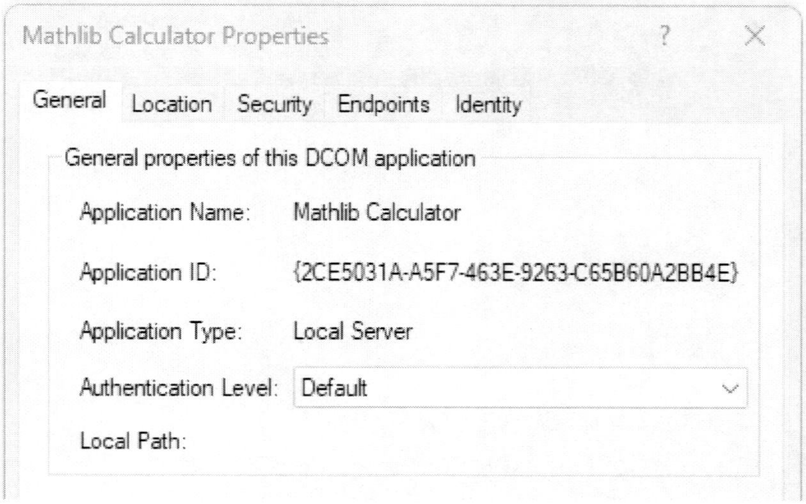

The first tab lists only the Authentication level. This can be left default, in which case the global authentication level will apply. Since the minimum level of authentication after DCOM hardening is Packet Integrity, the only reason to change this setting is if the server needs to ensure that Packet Privacy is used.

The Location tab is used to configure the computer on which the COM server will actually run, even if the activation request is a local activation request. Configuring which computer to use for which server is one of the ways in which an administrator can configure the topology of a distributed application.

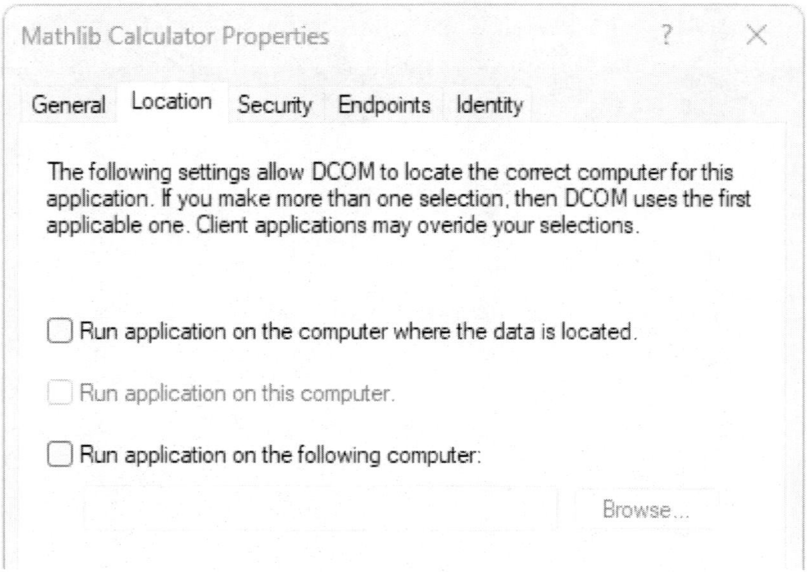

Bottom to top, there are 3 options available:

- Run application on the following computer. If an application requests the server to run, the server is launched on the specified computer, and any calls are marshaled back and forth. Normally the client will be unaware of this. This gives administrators a great amount of leeway in configuring and balancing distributed applications.
- Run application on this computer. Just like a server can be configured to run on another computer, it can be prohibited from running locally. This setting is only available for AppID settings that are linked to an executable server. It doesn't apply to a DLL server because DLLs are not launched but loaded into the client's address space.
- Run application on the computer where the data is located. This setting is not documented very well. DCOM itself has no special knowledge about where application data is located or which connections are made. When this setting is enabled, the ActivateAtStorage registry value will be set. This in turn will cause various APIs to try and locate a COM object in the running object table that is on the same system as the system from which data is loaded via e.g. the IStorage parameter in a call to CoGetInstanceFromIStorage API. There are no hard guarantee but the attempt will be made to activate the COM server in a way that local file IO is used instead of network IO to load its state from the file in which it was serialized. The reason to use this option would be primarily a performance improvement in scenarios where performance depends less on

where the server runs, and more on the IO distance between the data and the server.

For security, there are 3 options as well":

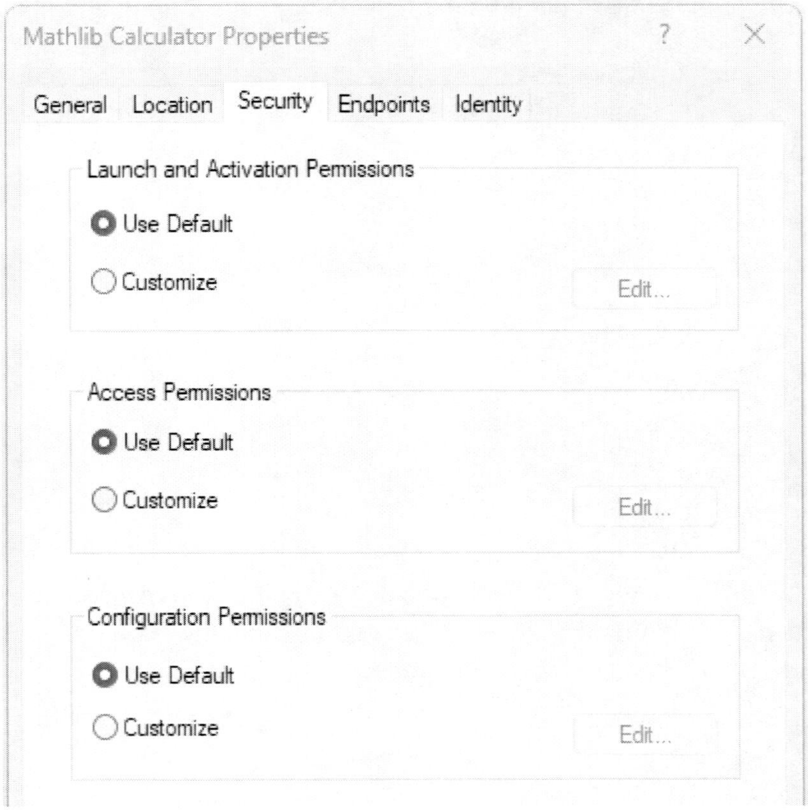

- Launch and Activation permissions. This refers to the permission for launching the COM server and activating the class object. These permissions distinguish between launching the server as a response to a client on the same machine and coming from a remote machine.
- Access permissions. This refers to the permission for using the class object after a server is launched or activated. A user or group may not have permission to launch the server process (for example if the COM server is a Windows service for a special purpose) but are allowed to interact with it while it is running.
- Configuration permissions. This refers to the right to configure AppID settings.

The effect of customizing these settings is as described in the previous section. ‘Endpoints’ allows you to configure the network protocol that is used for communication between client and server.

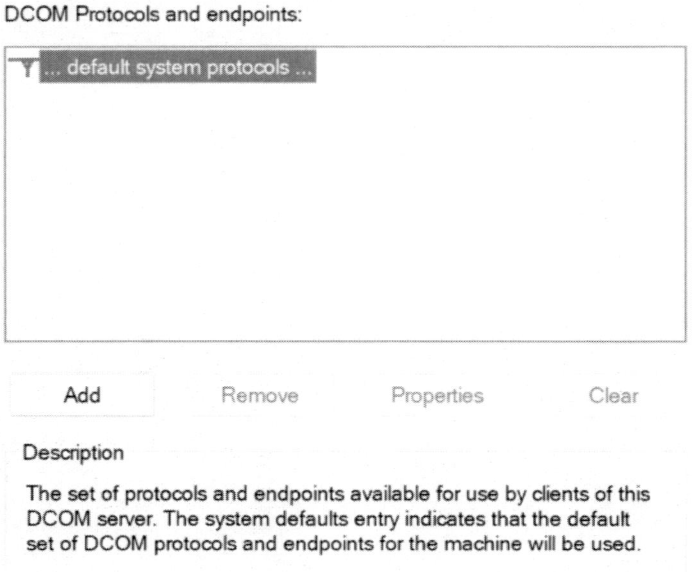

The same remarks apply to the server configuration as to the global system settings. You can configure port ranges or the use of tunneling, but you’ll run into the same problems, and should avoid tunneling for the same reason.

The final tab here is the identity tab.

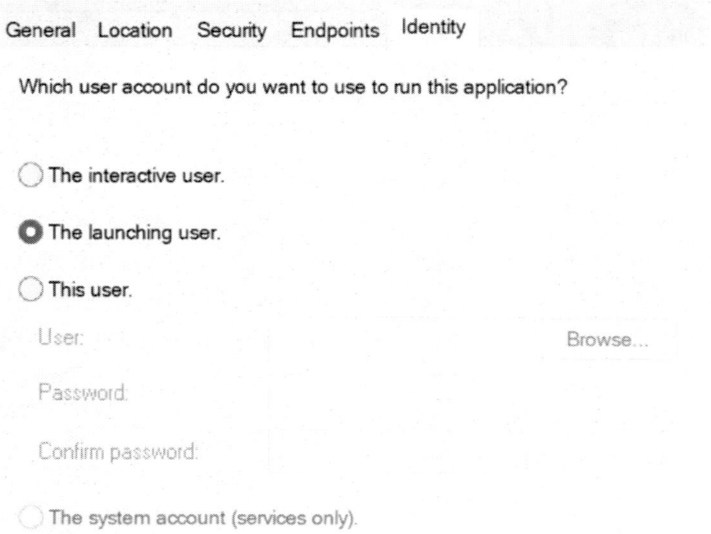

The default option is to run the server with the identity of the client, aka 'the launching user'. This is the logical default, because if a client wants to user the Calculator server for example, then logically the Calculator server is working on behalf of the client, using resources for the client, and it should be subject to the same rights and permissions as the client.

'Interactive user' is a legacy setting to enable working with servers that require some sort of user interface interaction from the session in which they are running. For example if a client starts under a different identity but still in a user's desktop session via the 'run as' command, a COM server configured to run as interactive user could use a GUI to interact with the user. This approach is bad from a security perspective because the server runs with the user's identity, even if the user didn't explicitly want that. Additionally, this doesn't work if the server is launched from inside a service application because services are isolated from the desktop session. And of course, if no user is logged in, then there is no interactive user whose identity can be used.

'This user' creates the option of forcing a server to use under the identity of a specific user. When this user is set, the password is verified so it is impossible to abuse a user identity without knowledge of the password. This option can be used at all times and can be especially useful when the actions that are performed by the server need to happen under a specific user account for security reasons. You would then combine this setting with a list of access permissions for the server, to configure which users are allowed to use the server and thus piggyback onto the identity of the server.

In the past it was possible for an administrator to specify that the local system account could be used as an identity, but as a security improvement, that can now only be done for servers that run as a Windows service, but no longer for regular servers because the local system account is too powerful to be used this way. If a server needs to run with a very privileged account, then an explicit user account must be created, and granted those permissions. Of course it's still possible to configure a server with administrative privileges, but at least it will be visible and subject to the procedures for handling administrator accounts.

Programming DCOM Security

If you compare the section about the DCOMCnfg with the plethora of settings that were described earlier, you will undoubtedly notice that there are many things that can go into the security blanket which cannot be configured through DCOMCnfg. For example, there is no way to configure which authentication service is used, or which authorization info is used.

There is not a single design decision which led to this situation. Back when DCOMCnfg was created, DCOM was a different beast, and the Windows system administration tools were much more limited. Central administration of network security with group policy and local policy was also not as prevalent as today. We must be careful to not look at this situation with today's eyes. Not only do we expect protocol and configurations to be decided by an administrator instead of a developer, and not only do we expect to have the management tools to do so, but in a networked environment we fully expect any security level configuration to be handled by group policy.

But the 90's were a different era. Networking technology evolved very quickly, and in many different directions. As inconceivable as it sounds today, technology like COM predates the inclusion of a tcp/ip stack in Windows. Likewise, protocols like NetBEUI or IPX/SPX were commonly used alongside tcp/ip because many network environments were heterogenous and required custom configuration. The security landscape was similarly heterogenous, which is why Windows supported the use of pluggable security packages via the Security Support Provider Interface (SSPI). Custom packages could be installed to provide authentication that was tailored to a specific environment.

In such an environment, with custom authentication providers which all require specific configuration information, and which may or may not support certain capabilities, it is understandable that DCOMCnfg can't be used as a configuration tool because it was a general-purpose tool which would have no knowledge or understanding of the various security packages which could be installed. That is why COM supports programmatic configuration of the security blanket.

A security blanket can be configured at the process level and at interface level. It is unavoidable that if a process uses COM, there has to be a process level security blanket because if no proxy specific one was provided, there must be a blanket to fall back on, even if the programmer didn't yet provide one.

Configuring the process level security blanket

The process level blanket can be set exactly once per process. To give the programmer the opportunity to explicitly provide one, the COM runtime waits until the first call needs to be marshaled before it insists there must be one. If no process level blanket exists at that time, then the COM runtimes of the client and server use each other's system default settings and supported authentication protocols to figure out which authentication service should be used, how identity is managed, what the impersonation level and authentication level are, etc. Until that time, a programmer has the opportunity to explicitly provide a security blanket using the following API

```
//combaseapi.h
WINOLEAPI
CoInitializeSecurity(
    PSECURITY_DESCRIPTOR pSecDesc,
    LONG cAuthSvc,
    SOLE_AUTHENTICATION_SERVICE* asAuthSvc,
    void* pReserved1,
    DWORD dwAuthnLevel,
    _In_ DWORD dwImpLevel,
    _In_opt_ void* pAuthList,
    _In_ DWORD dwCapabilities,
    _In_opt_ void* pReserved3
    );
```

The first parameter is used only in server processes, and can be either:

- A pointer to an AppID GUID
- A pointer to an IAccessControl structure which contains access control settings.
- A pointer to a Windows security descriptor with access control settings.

If a server calls `CoInitializeSecurity`, it is strongly discouraged to leave this setting blank because in that case, COM will ignore the AppID settings of the server, and instead use default permissions for the various permissions settings, which may not be advisable. At the very least, it is advised to specify the AppID GUID so that the correct settings are loaded from the registry.

All other settings in the parameter list cover the configuration of the security blanket settings we covered earlier. If client and server specify different settings, then the situation will either resolve itself or fail, according to the rules that were explained in the section about connection security.

In general, in the modern programming era, it is strongly preferable to NOT call `CoInitializeSecurity` explicitly. Not calling it explicitly has benefits which cannot be overstated:

- Security configuration is placed in the hands of the system administrators (and in larger companies the cyber security experts) who are really the only appropriate people to make decisions about what is or is not acceptable.
- Security configuration can change as times or situations change. Registry settings and group policy can change. Hard coded security can't. And while there is no rule that says software developers can't map all these settings to some registry key with the necessary values to avoid this problem, a) typically that won't happen and b) if they do, then there is really no reason to explicitly go through all that effort to put control back in the hands of the administrators

when you'd achieve exactly the same thing by just not calling `CoInitializeSecurity`. As will be explained in detail in the section that covers DCOM hardening, Hardcoded `CoInitializeSecurity` parameters caused mayhem of apocalyptic proportions in certain industries; mayhem which could all have been resolved effortlessly if only developers had left security configuration to the administrators.

- Aside from whether settings are appropriate or not, protocols come and go. Back when Essential COM was written, NTLM was the only supported authentication service out of the box. Kerberos was talked about but not yet released. Any application that explicitly requests NTLM authentication may fail if NTLM is disabled in an overall push to switch to Kerberos. At this point in time, Windows 11 24H2 and Server 2025 will disable NTLM out of the box. There is no announced hard cut-off date yet, but it will happen. When it does, it's going to be Y2K / DCOM Hardening type mayhem all over again for applications that have a hard coded request for NTLM.
- Not calling `CoInitializeSecurity` explicitly will leave client and server to figure things out among themselves through negotiation. Not only is this by far the easiest option for developers, but it's also the most flexible because if the client default settings would not be secure enough, they will be raised automatically instead of failing. Given that after DCOM hardening only secure settings are left and the server is in charge of defining the minimum accepted settings, most of the settings have become largely irrelevant.

All these things combined make it best to simply not use it. The only reason why you would still call `CoInitializeSecurity` is in very specific scenarios. For example:

- in a self-hosted COM server (an executable that registers class objects but which was not started by the COM runtime in response to an activation request), `CoInitializeSecurity` must be called explicitly because the COM runtime will do so with default settings which -may- not be what you want, for example in terms of access permissions. However, in that scenario it would still be best to specify an AppID for the first parameter. That would bring the DCOMCnfg configuration of the server back into driving seat.
- At first, it might appear that another good reason would be to connect to legacy systems. After all if a client needs to connect to a legacy sever that requires DCE authorization via a custom authentication service, it is hard to avoid. But doing so would make this a global setting. And as a global setting it would also be used if the client tried to also communicate with a server on a modern system that doesn't support DCE. In a mixed environment, it would be better

to leave the process blanket alone, to be negotiated by the OS, and cover interfaces to non-standard servers with a proxy specific blanket instead. Note that either way, if you need to configure explicitly security settings for either the process blanket or a proxy specify blanket, you implement registry bindings and document them well so that their values can be updated and managed by an administrator as the situation requires.

Client Side Proxy level security configuration

Security configuration of a proxy can be done at 2 different times: by the COM runtime when the object is created, or by the client at a later time. It may seem weird to make this distinction but it's important.

If we want to connect to a COM object on a remote legacy system, we cannot do so using `CoCreateInstance`. Instead, we must use `CoCreateInstanceEx`. It does essentially what `CoCreateInstance` is doing, but with optional parameters

```
//combaseapi.h
HRESULT CoCreateInstanceEx(
  [in]       REFCLSID     Clsid,
  [in]       IUnknown     *punkOuter,
  [in]       DWORD        dwClsCtx,
  [in]       COSERVERINFO *pServerInfo,
  [in]       DWORD        dwCount,
  [in, out] MULTI_QI     *pResults
);
```

The first 3 arguments are the same as before. CoCreateInstanceEx has the ability to return multiple interfaces in 1 go, instead of having to query for each of them individually. That is why instead of specifying 1 riid and have 1 output pointer, there is a C style array of MULTI_QI structures or a specified number of elements.

```
//objidl.h
typedef struct tagMULTI_QI {
  const IID *pIID;
  IUnknown  *pItf;
  HRESULT   hr;
} MULTI_QI;
```

Since each interface request can fail individually (because it may not be implemented), there is an individual HRESULT for each request. That part is irrelevant for now because in this case that's not why we want to use it. That leaves the pServerInfo variable which is of the type `COSERVERINFO`.

```
//objidl.h
```

```
typedef struct _COSERVERINFO {
  DWORD      dwReserved1;
  LPWSTR     pwszName;
  COAUTHINFO *pAuthInfo;
  DWORD      dwReserved2;
} COSERVERINFO;
```

This structure has 2 reserved parameters that should be NULL and 0 respectively. The pwszName argument is used for the name or IP address of the server where we want to run the COM server. pAuthInfo is of type `COAUTHINFO`, which can be used for configuring how the client and server authenticate each other. Here we recognize the entire set of parameters that we know go into the security blanket.

```
//wtypesbase.h
typedef struct _COAUTHINFO {
  DWORD          dwAuthnSvc;
  DWORD          dwAuthzSvc;
  LPWSTR         pwszServerPrincName;
  DWORD          dwAuthnLevel;
  DWORD          dwImpersonationLevel;
  COAUTHIDENTITY *pAuthIdentityData;
  DWORD          dwCapabilities;
} COAUTHINFO;
```

If we want to connect to a remote object on a legacy system which needs custom parameters, this is the correct time to specify those parameters because this will inherently be the first time the requested interface(s) will be marshaled and that can only work if the settings such as authentication service and authorization service are configured correctly.

In most circumstances, this will be the last time you would need to touch those settings for that particular proxy. After all, if they work for the first marshal call, there is typically no need to alter those settings. And if they don't work, then there is no interface pointer whose blanket can be adjusted. However, there could be scenarios where the security blanket of a particular object instance needs to be changed after the interface pointer was created.

Note that obviously, it doesn't make sense to try to change the authentication service that is used. If the authentication service and authorization for a legacy object required special configuration just to work, then there is no point in trying to change those things after the interface pointer was created because the interface proxy wouldn't work anymore.

However, it is conceivable for example that a client may want to configure a specific interface to use Packet Privacy authentication level to protect sensitive data when it traverses the network, without wanting to impose the resulting performance overhead on all network traffic if multiple different DCOM objects are used on different servers. Such a scenario is perfectly plausible in modern distributed systems that use otherwise system default security settings.

Configuring per-proxy information is done via the interface pointer itself. In the chapter about aggregation, we briefly mentioned that the proxy manager for a specific remote object doesn't just aggregate the individual interface proxy objects, but it also exports an IClientSecurity interface.

```
//objidlbase.h
IClientSecurity : public IUnknown
{
public:
    virtual HRESULT STDMETHODCALLTYPE QueryBlanket(
        _In_  IUnknown *pProxy,
        _Out_  DWORD *pAuthnSvc,
        _Out_opt_  DWORD *pAuthzSvc,
        __RPC__deref_out_opt  OLECHAR **pServerPrincName,
        _Out_opt_  DWORD *pAuthnLevel,
        _Out_opt_  DWORD *pImpLevel,
        _Outptr_result_maybenull_  void **pAuthInfo,
        _Out_opt_  DWORD *pCapabilites) = 0;

    virtual HRESULT STDMETHODCALLTYPE SetBlanket(
        _In_  IUnknown *pProxy,
        _In_  DWORD dwAuthnSvc,
        _In_  DWORD dwAuthzSvc,
        __RPC__in_opt  OLECHAR *pServerPrincName,
        _In_  DWORD dwAuthnLevel,
        _In_  DWORD dwImpLevel,
        _In_opt_  void *pAuthInfo,
        _In_  DWORD dwCapabilities) = 0;

    virtual HRESULT STDMETHODCALLTYPE CopyProxy(
        _In_  IUnknown *pProxy,
        _Outptr_  IUnknown **ppCopy) = 0;

};
```

The settings themselves don't need much explanation at this point. They are the same ones we've covered already. This interface provides a way to query the current safety blanket, and to modify those settings.

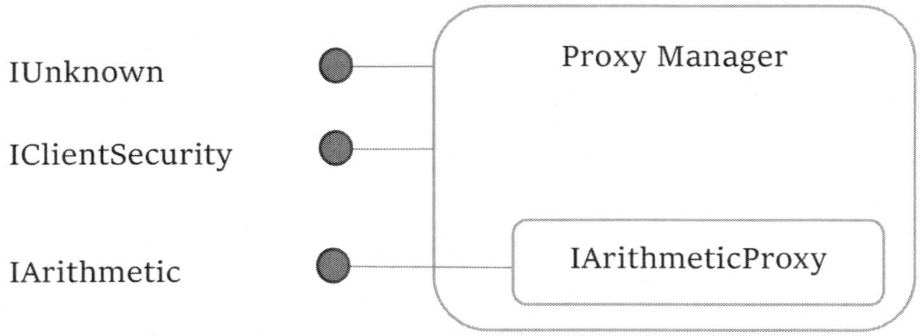

Consider a situation where we have an interface pointer, and we want to manually modify certain security settings, such as the authentication level. Because the interface pointer really belongs to an aggregated object which also implements the IClientSecurity interface, this makes it trivial for anyone with access to that pointer to modify or query its security configuration because as an aggregated object, we can simply use QueryInterface to retrieve the IClientSecurity interface and do something with the security settings.

```
CComQIPtr<IClientSecurity> clientSecurity(itf1);
if (clientSecurity) {
    hRes = clientSecurity->SetBlanket(itf1,
        RPC_C_AUTHN_DEFAULT,
        RPC_C_AUTHZ_DEFAULT,
        COLE_DEFAULT_PRINCIPAL,
        RPC_C_AUTHN_LEVEL_PKT_PRIVACY,
        RPC_C_IMP_LEVEL_DEFAULT,
        NULL,
        EOAC_NONE);
}
```

Even though we obtained the security interface through the original interface pointer, we must still present the interface pointer as an argument because the proxy manager manages all interface proxies for a specific COM object, and we can configure the blanket per interface, instead of for all interfaces simultaneously. The other parameters can be configured as needed. And if we only want to specify 1 specify parameter, the others must be set to default to let the COM runtime control them. Alternatively, you could use the QuerySecurity method first to get all actual values, modify the one you want, and then pass them all back.

The CopyProxy method is provided to give the programmer a convenient way to make a copy of whatever interface we're working with, so that we can modify the settings for that interface. The copy is a private copy, meaning it has 1 reference, and it is the responsibility of the caller to make sure it gets freed. This copy is also not aggregated into the proxy manager because only 1 implementation of an interface can be aggregated. This also means that if you call QueryInterface on the copy, the query gets resolved to the original interfaces that are aggregated into the proxy manager. Conversely, a QueryInterface on the proxy manager for GUID of copied interface pointer will always result in a pointer to the original interface proxy, not to the copied interface. The copy is always private and only accessible to the one holding it.

If the original interface pointer we're working with is not a proxy but a direct, non-marshaled interface pointer, the QueryInterface operation will fail with an error of E_NOINTERFACE because our COM object, like most, does not implement that interface. It pays to be aware of this because in a COM application, objects may reside anywhere and for many scenarios, the object may or may not reside in a different apartment. Therefore, it may legitimately fail the QueryInterface without it being indicative of an error.

For the sake of convenience and to cut down on the boilerplate code required to deal with IClientSecurity, the COM runtime has 3 helper APIs which encapsulate the QueryInterface operation and the method call.

```
//combaseapi.h
WINOLEAPI
CoQueryProxyBlanket(
    IUnknown* pProxy,
    DWORD* pwAuthnSvc,
    DWORD* pAuthzSvc,
    LPOLESTR* pServerPrincName,
    DWORD* pAuthnLevel,
    DWORD* pImpLevel,
    RPC_AUTH_IDENTITY_HANDLE* pAuthInfo,
    DWORD* pCapabilites
    );

WINOLEAPI
CoSetProxyBlanket(
    IUnknown* pProxy,
    DWORD dwAuthnSvc,
    DWORD dwAuthzSvc,
    OLECHAR* pServerPrincName,
    DWORD dwAuthnLevel,
    DWORD dwImpLevel,
    RPC_AUTH_IDENTITY_HANDLE pAuthInfo,
    DWORD dwCapabilities
    );

WINOLEAPI
CoCopyProxy(
    IUnknown* pProxy,
    IUnknown** ppCopy
```

```
    );
```

By using these functions, you can improve your code readability and reduce the risk of mistakes.

Server-Side Proxy level security configuration

Any marshaling setup has a client side and a server side. So far, we've considered everything from the client perspective because logically, it's the client that initiates a connection. From the server side, things are a little different. If the server is running, then the RPC connection was set up correctly and whatever security configuration was in play, worked. A server has no need to worry about whether the COM connection was authenticated successfully. If the server is running, that question answers itself. Also, inside a COM object, the object has no interface pointer to deal with. The object doesn't even know where the client is or how many pointers are extant in how many client apartments. Still, it may be important for a server to get connection details of the call that is currently in progress. For that purpose, there is the CoGetCallContext API.

```
//combaseapi.h
WINOLEAPI
CoGetCallContext(
    _In_ REFIID riid,
    _Outptr_ void** ppInterface
    );
```

This is used to retrieve the IServerSecurity

```
//objidlbase.h
IServerSecurity : public IUnknown
{
public:
    virtual HRESULT STDMETHODCALLTYPE QueryBlanket(
        _Out_opt_  DWORD *pAuthnSvc,
        _Out_opt_  DWORD *pAuthzSvc,
        __RPC__deref_out_opt  OLECHAR **pServerPrincName,
        _Out_opt_  DWORD *pAuthnLevel,
        _Out_opt_  DWORD *pImpLevel,
        _Outptr_result_maybenull_  void **pPrivs,
        _Inout_opt_  DWORD *pCapabilities) = 0;

    virtual HRESULT STDMETHODCALLTYPE ImpersonateClient( void) = 0;

    virtual HRESULT STDMETHODCALLTYPE RevertToSelf( void) = 0;

    virtual BOOL STDMETHODCALLTYPE IsImpersonating( void) = 0;

};
```

The blanket information is the same we covered at the client level. However, the server introduces an interesting new feature: impersonation.

When a process starts, Windows associates a security token with that process. This token represents the identity of the user that has started the process. By default, all threads in a process run with that token. Every interaction with the operating system, such as opening a file or opening a database connection, is allowed or disallowed based on the rights and permissions associated with that user. This becomes problematic for COM Servers that need to perform such actions on behalf of a client application, such as in business applications that act as a middle tier between clients and protected resources. If a client requests access to a resource secured by an ACL (Access Control List), the server must temporarily assume the client's identity to perform the action with the correct permissions.

COM supports this by temporarily replacing the thread's security token with the client's token using the `ImpersonateClient` method. This allows the server to perform actions as if it were the client, ensuring proper access control and auditing. When the server is done with those actions, `RevertToSelf` is used to revert the thread back to its original security configuration.

```
CComPtr<IServerSecurity> serverSecurity;
HRESULT hRes = CoGetCallContext(IID_IServerSecurity,(void**)&serverSecurity);
if (serverSecurity) {
        hRes = serverSecurity->ImpersonateClient();
        if (SUCCEEDED(hRes)) {
                //do stuff as client
                serverSecurity->RevertToSelf();
        }
}
```

IServerSecurity has a couple of helper functions to help with impersonation.

```
//combaseapi.h
WINOLEAPI CoImpersonateClient(void);
WINOLEAPI CoRevertToSelf(void);
```

These are meant for simple scenarios where you want to impersonate a client, perform some actions and revert. If you are dealing with complex code where it is uncertain whether impersonation is already happening or not, you'll have to deal with IServerSecurity directly. Speaking about complex code, there is an issue with the impersonation code above. We're using CComPtr to make sure that the pointer is released properly in all scenarios. But that doesn't take care of cleaning up the impersonation that may or may not be in progress. Just like we use smart pointers to take the risk and uncertainty out of their lifecycle, we can use a similar approach to making sure that if an impersonation session starts, it is not left dangling if an exception is thrown. The following is a possible way to implement this.

```
class ScopedImpersonation {
public:
	ScopedImpersonation() {
		m_hr = CoImpersonateClient();
	}

	~ScopedImpersonation() {
		if (SUCCEEDED(m_hr)) {
			CoRevertToSelf();
		}
	}

	bool IsImpersonating() const {
		return (SUCCEEDED(m_hr));
	}

	HRESULT GetImpersonationStatus() {
		return m_hr;
	}

private:
	HRESULT m_hr;
};
```

Based on that, we could implement impersonation like this:

```
ScopedImpersonation impersonation;
if (impersonation.IsImpersonating()) {
	//do stuff as client
}
```

This would be safe and convenient. It may seem counterintuitive that a piece of code can just decide to pretend to be the client. This is not something that any piece of software can do when it has a connection. It is a built-in functionality for RPC, COM, and a couple of other technologies that are available in the Windows world, and subject to the relevant administrative control and security policies.

In the case of COM, the client can set limits, though since DCOM hardening was implemented, the client can only choose between allowing impersonation and delegation. This might seem like a security problem because a client must trust an opaque piece of code with its identity and just hope that nothing bad is going to happen. This is true. But on the other hand, it would be equally true if the client loaded a DLL that exports some functionality it uses. A regular DLL is equally opaque. And if a server needs to access resources that are protected, there is no way to avoid the requirement for impersonation.

The call-back trap

At this point we've talked about clients and servers being able to configure the security blanket. In an environment where client and server run on Windows, there shouldn't be much of a problem to set up secure infrastructure because both sides support Kerberos or NTLM. In a mixed environment with legacy authentication services, security providers may need to be installed, and client and server can use interface specific blanket configuration to set up security so that even in a mixed environment, all components can talk to each other. This makes it seem as if with enough poking and prodding, every scenario can be made to work. Unfortunately for those tasked with writing code in such an environment, there may be scenarios where callback functionality is required.

In some designs, clients communicate with a remote server and at some later point, the server tries to call back into the client asynchronously. Effectively, the client would also act as a server for the purpose of receiving callback calls. And the remote server would also act as a client.

DCOM only supports one authentication service per process for inbound calls. The authentication service used for inbound calls is determined by the client's CoInitializeSecurity configuration (whether it was called explicitly or determined by defaults). Suppose there are 2 different servers with different authentication configuration, trying to do a callback into the client. The client has the luxury of being able to set up authentication for each outgoing interface. But if those 2 servers use different authentication services, then not all of them are going to be compatible with the client. You might see one server's callbacks working perfectly while the other's fail with errors like 0x80070721 – A security package specific error occurred. Or there may not be an error, just missing data updates. In industrial process control networks, legacy DCOM protocols such as OPC (OLE for Process Control) are commonly used even today. OPC makes extensive use of callback mechanisms because it is usually configured for asynchronous updates where data is sent when it changes, to reduce traffic. It is also common for OPC data collectors (clients) to acquire data from different OPC servers in different networks. Callback scenarios are not uncommon in the process world, and cannot always be resolved without workarounds.

A common workaround is to run separate client processes, each configured for a specific authentication service or with specific credentials, for use with a specific server. This allows you to tailor the setup of each connection. This is one of those architectural edge cases that's easy to overlook until you're deploying or testing.

There is no singular solution because there is no singular problem. If you are designing a distributed application with COM connections to different remote components, take your time to evaluate the security setup of the entire application, and perform proof of concept testing early in the development process. Not every scenario can be made to work in every manner, but if you have the freedom to tweak local components, there is usually a way to make things work.

DCOM Hardening

Of all the things that have changed over the years in the COM landscape, security is by far the most pertinent one. COM became DCOM to enable remoting for interface-based functionality, which gave rise to a fantastic landscape of scalable distributed applications. This expressed itself not only in an ecosystem of applications that could integrate with each other, but also a plethora of management tools that could be used to manage systems remotely with the same ease as managing them locally.

However, the late 90's and early 2000's was a time when that computing landscape was evolving rapidly. There was at times a serious disconnect between system administrators and software developers. Systems were often configured according to certain security models, but without consideration for requirements of individual software packages. System security configuration was often either set in stone or didn't exist in any meaningful way.

As a developer for enterprise software, a given security context was often something you would comply with if you could, or work around or bypass if you couldn't. As a developer for consumer software there was not a whole lot to consider because security was pretty much nonexistent and users often logged in as administrator.

In terms of the overall Windows ecosystem, reality was as follows:

- Users logging in as administrator was common.
- DCOM was even supported on Windows 98; An operating system with the barest notion of security or authentication to begin with.
- Windows systems at the time didn't have built-in firewalls. On the consumer side, systems were often plugged in directly to the internet with a public routable IP address, making them publicly accessible for direct contact. If you visited a malicious website, that server would have enough information to directly contact your system and probe for known vulnerabilities or even just attempt to connect the management interface via DCOM to see if it would

accept anonymous logon. In fact, because the addresses would be publicly routable, the bare fact of connecting to the internet meant that you were guaranteed connection attempts from anyone scanning IP ranges.

- Automatic security updates didn't exist. At enterprise level, service packs (a big set of cumulative patches and feature updates) might be installed eventually after they were released. But that was not a given, and especially developers tended to be skeptical about doing so because service packs might have their own issues and the last thing a developer wanted was to brick the development system they spent days setting up just right. This sentiment wasn't entirely unwarranted. For example, Service Pack 2 for NT4 was infamous for the issues it caused after installation. At the consumer level, things were even worse because internet connections were slow. As impossible as it sounds to people under 30, 56 kilobits per second was considered top of the line high speed. Downloading a service pack could take hours, if no one picked up the receiver of the phone or otherwise interrupted the connection because you'd need to start over. Consumer systems were often simply not patched at all.
- Network traffic was often unencrypted, making it extremely susceptible to data leaks or man-in-the-middle attacks.
- Network authentication was weak.

Those are just some of the severe security issues that were recognized as a problem even then. Some of the intentional features were not much better.

- For a while, there was the notion that websites could publish COM servers and they would download, install and run as requested by a client application, web page, browser or Visual Basic application. There was even -very briefly- something called Active Desktop which was a one-way upgrade that enabled such objects to embed themselves into your desktop.
- Aside from DCOM, there was even a concept of computers exposing themselves to the internet in a way similar to web servers today, using technology known as COM Internet Services (CIS). Just like DCOM enabled remote administration, CIS could be used to leverage http as transport protocol, bypassing firewalls and internet proxy servers by essentially hijacking the http protocol.
- DCOM could be (and was often) configured to accept anonymous and unauthenticated connections. This was often the only way to get it to work between non domain-joined computers or computers in different domains. Especially in industrial process control networks that were not connected to

the office network, it was not uncommon to see DCOM servers configured to run as administrator at the request of an anonymous logon.

The result of all this was inevitable. There was the Blaster worm in 2003 which used a vulnerability in RPC handling, allowing it to spread across the internet and infect millions of machines. There was the Sasser worm in 2004 which exploited a vulnerability in LSASS and also used DCOM to propagate to millions of machines. And there was the Conficker botnet in 2008 which also exploited DCOM vulnerabilities to some extent and infected an estimated 10 million machines.

Those are only some of the more notorious examples but in the 2000's, there was a literal ecosystem of botnets contending with each other to take over computers for nefarious purposes. It got to the point where botnets like Conficker and Zeus actually patched security vulnerabilities on computers after infecting them to keep other botnets from taking control of the same computer.

If you are under 30 and have never known a world without internet, it may seem unfathomable that anyone ever thought it was a good idea to have DCOM features like bypassing firewalls, unencrypted internet traffic, install and run on demand, supporting anonymous logon or for that matter allowing DCOM to face the internet.

The key to understanding this is that you must remember that at the time, the primary focus of any technical development was the benefit or usefulness, and not the risk. Security was often an afterthought in the design process, added to a finished concept like black pepper to a steak that is already on your plate.

This is not because engineers then were not smart. On the contrary. But when COM became DCOM, most networking was either an internal matter completely (such as office networks) or used dedicated leased lines between sites. There was no real paranoia about attacks or malware because all clients, servers, and network peripherals were under centralized control. Not only was there no 'outside' world as far as general-purpose networking went, but when internet adoption started to accelerate, nothing important was on it yet, like it is today. There were no online government services, no online banking, no online administration of your utilities, etc. The stakes were much lower because there was no massive financial incentive to hack consumer computers. Security wasn't that big a deal and the risks were on a different level. At the same time, computing hardware was extremely limited. When you must support an OS on systems like an Intel 386 with 4 Megabytes of RAM, on a closed office network with no significant risk from the outside world, giving customers the option to not encrypt DCOM network is entirely justifiable.

With the benefit of hindsight and 25 years of cynicism, we look at computing and DCOM in a different light. Due to several DCOM security related vulnerabilities, and the fact that many vendors still installed software in a terribly unsafe configuration as recent as 2022, Microsoft implemented several security measures that had a severe impact on many enterprise and industrial systems. Impact on home systems was limited, because the changes only affected Distributed COM (which required networking) and the vulnerable configurations occurred predominately in enterprise class software.

The issue that triggered the update that became known as 'DCOM Hardening' was a security feature bypass that is documented in security bulletin CVE-2021-26414. Information about these changes was described in knowledge base article KB5004442, which also links to various Microsoft pages containing practical information for system administrators. The contents in this chapter describe the state of COM security in compliance with the hardening changes. The process that happened to implement this change from concept to release will be covered later in this chapter. At the time of writing, hardening changes have been active for 3 years, but at the enterprise level there may still be private networks where hardening continues to be an issue, and there are still enterprises where Windows 2008 servers are still running in a forgotten corner, waiting to be decommissioned.

The DCOM hardening process was done in several phases and took over 2 years until completion. The intention was to mitigate network vulnerabilities by removing all but the 2 strongest authentication options from being used. Additionally, the minimum impersonation level was raised to 'Impersonate'

As mentioned earlier, some of the lower authentication levels make no sense anymore in today's networking landscape and existed solely to accommodate hardware limitations in scenarios where the risk was otherwise mitigated, for example because outside connections to untrusted networks did not exist or because people simply didn't care about security at all and performance was the only consideration. Unfortunately, even though computers have gotten orders of magnitude more powerful since the inception of COM, standard practice even in 2020 was to leave everything unsecured especially in industrial distributed environments where security was often not even an afterthought.

Over time, several DCOM related vulnerabilities were found, such as RemoteMonologue which exploits DCOM objects to coerce NTLM authentications without touching LSASS. Such exploits could have specific remediations such as NTLM hardening. However, In June 2021, Microsoft published CVE-2021-26414 to document mitigation for a DCOM man-in-the-middle security bypass. Unlike previous targeted fixes, this led to a broad hardening initiative that addressed systemic weaknesses in DCOM's trust and authentication model. The resulting changes, rolled out in phases, enforced stricter authentication levels and effectively brought remote DCOM activation under the Windows security perimeter.

This process had 3 distinct phases:

1. June 8, 2021 Hardening changes disabled by default, but with ability to enable them using a registry key.
2. June 14, 2022 Hardening changes enabled by default but with ability to disable them using a registry key.
3. March 14, 2023 Hardening changes enabled by default with no ability to disable them

As previously indicated, the 2 specific infrastructure changes were:

1. To invalidate all authentication levels except Packet Integrity and Packet Privacy.
2. To invalidate all connection levels except Impersonate and delegate.

The initial result of activating hardening changes in a complex industrial network was pure mayhem. Virtually all process control software and lab application software used the default unsecured options. And as is common with industrial software, much software that was still in use was over a decade old at least. A common problem was that there was either no support contract with the vendor, the vendor didn't exist anymore, or there was simply no viable alternative that could be upgraded to. And that was a situation that could not be changed easily.

The initial hardening change was that after enabling the hardening change, all servers were configured to have RPC_C_AUTHN_LEVEL_PKT_INTEGRITY as the minimum accepted security level. We know from the previous section that if an application accepts the default (by not requesting a specific level), a round of negotiation would happen to figure out the appropriate minimum level. But if a specified a value and that value was not the same as or higher than RPC_C_AUTHN_LEVEL_PKT_INTEGRITY, the connection would fail.

Unfortunately, back when much COM software was created, example code and documentation would often explicitly advise developers to initialize security with RPC_C_AUTHN_LEVEL_CONNECT for the level, and 'Identify' as the impersonation level. The result of this is all software that did this, stopped working.

To help with mitigation of the impact of hardening changes, over the roll-out period of DCOM hardening, the hardening approach consisted of the following changes:

- The COM infrastructure layer was modified on all supported operating systems so that a server will never accept anything less than RPC_C_AUTHN_LEVEL_PKT_INTEGRITY regardless of what is specified
- Any client request will automatically be elevated to RPC_C_AUTHN_LEVEL_PKT_INTEGRITY regardless of how it is configured or what level it requests. The client may still specify an authentication level of RPC_C_AUTHN_LEVEL_CONNECT but between doing so and the connection going out, that level will be raised transparently

The combination of these 2 changes ensures that DCOM hardening is applied, even with legacy client software.

Or at least, that is true if both the client and the server run on systems that both have received the hardening updates. At the time of the roll-out, the lowest supported Windows client was Windows 8.1 and the lowest supported Windows Server was 2012. These systems did receive both halves of the hardening change and were fully functional. However, in industrial environments, there is a tendency to keep legacy systems alive for business reasons. At the time DCOM hardening came on the radar, some companies still had Windows 2008 R2 or even earlier systems running. In that case, there was no good solution.

It was not impossible to mitigate a client running on a Windows 2008R2 or even Windows 2003 system. It just required a high enough degree of desperation. For example, one approach which was tested and verified by me for the sake of it, on a Windows 2008 system, concerned a .NET application which used CoInitializeSecurity with settings that were not supported. Since it was a .NET application, it was possible to run it through a disassembler, alter the assembly file, recompile it, and then disable code signing verification for that specific assembly in the registry because the assembly was no longer signed by the original vendor. It should be obvious that this is not best practice.

There are a couple of other approaches one might take, but that would lead us further into the realm of what my daughter calls 'going through the firewall' aka computer hacking, and is not the goal of this book.

Connection security is something which in my opinion you should never ever mess with as a programmer. In the late 90's, early 2000's, security was developer-driven. Developers could set authentication and impersonation levels in code, register COM servers with minimal or no security descriptors, control access permissions via CoInitializeSecurity or registry settings, etc.

This made sense at the time because security was seen as a feature, not a baseline requirement, if it was even considered at all. Enterprise IT was less centralized, and developers often deployed directly to production, with not a lot of interaction with the IT Admins. The threat landscape was less mature, and local trust was assumed.

But there arose 2 huge problems with this. The first is that it led to a situation where security was usually scaled to the lowest possible option because that was both the most performant solution as well as the easiest way to get things to run. Sometimes security was actively bypassed on purpose. In online discussions you will even find quotes like "*By using tunneling, you can implement DCOM calls across most any TCP port (if allowed by your firewall). That means if you want to use DCOM but your firewall administrator won't allow 135 and a custom range, you can sneak the DCOM across port 80*". The second problem is that allowing developers to hard-code these security settings in the application made it impossible for IT admins to alter security settings, and this caused the fallout when Microsoft rolled out DCOM hardening.

In today's landscape, this situation has flipped completely. In today's enterprise IT, security is often the first consideration, not the last, and security baselines are enforced by administrators, through Group Policy. Developers are expected to comply with, instead of making security decisions.

The transition from a developer driven model to a security administrator driven model was a painful but necessary one that took control of application security away from application code and placed it in the hands of policy and infrastructure management. This is especially critical in today's world because the threat landscape can change not just from day to day but from hour to hour and fitting security changes to a software development lifecycle is simply not acceptable anymore.

Summary

In this chapter, we covered the various security related settings that are involved when using COM. We covered how to configure security both from an administrative point of view, as well as from a programmatical point of view.

All in all, it is best to not play with security programmatically and instead let security be set through administrative tools and group policy.

We also took a look at DCOM hardening and the historical reasons for things happening the way they did.

15

Miscellaneous

One of the challenges in writing a book like this is knowing when to stop. Even though a lot of material has been covered, there are a couple of topics that are still worth mentioning, even if they're not going to be covered as fully worked out examples.

Pointers, arrays, and more pointers

When IDL was introduced, we covered basic data types that included arrays, and we saw several types of array. However, the rabbit hole goes quite a bit deeper, and we have the C language to thank for that, because it has ambiguity baked in. If you are already familiar with this topic, feel free to skip slightly ahead because you'll still want to read about the sizing and.

```
double val = 42;            //this is a double
double* pVal = &val;        //pointer to a double
```

A pointer is a memory address. A pointer to a value is just the memory address where that value is located.

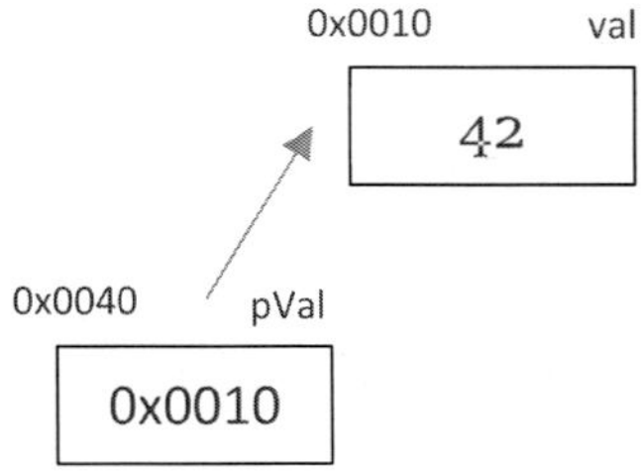

In this case, the value 42 is located at memory address 0x0010. The pointer is located someplace else, and has a value of 0x0010. The problem is that due to the way the C language was conceived, an array is also just a pointer to the first element in the array.

```
double val[] = { 42, 43, 44 }; //this is an array
double* pVal = anArray;     //this is also an array
```

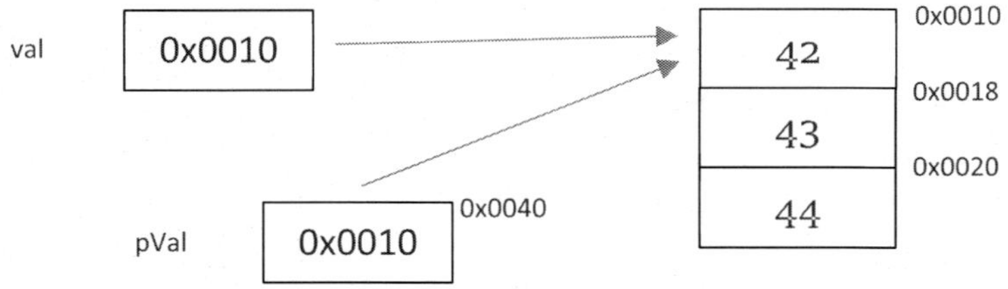

In both examples, pVal points to the same location, which also has the same value in it. As you can see, conceptually there is literally no difference between an array, and a pointer to a double. Just from looking at the code, there is no knowing what `double* pVal` really means without special knowledge that cannot be gleaned from the declaration itself.

`double* pVal` and `double pVal[]` are the same. The different notation is just syntactic sugar. `double* pVal` is the notation you will most commonly see.

We already mentioned that we can use the `size_is` attribute to designate a parameter as array size. Naively, we could say that if a size is specified, pVal is an array, and if there isn't, then it's a pointer to a single value. And indeed, that is how it works. But that would be extremely limiting. Because there are plenty of scenarios where we need to have an interface that doesn't just use an array, but a pointer to an array. The most common reason would be to support a method where the caller supplies an array to the COM component, and gets a different array back. That seems like a simple enough concept. But looks can be deceiving. Even declaring the array itself is counter intuitive, because the following:

```
double* Values[]
```

Is not a pointer to an array. Instead, it's an array of pointers. `double* Values[]` Is equivalent to `double** Values`. And that leads to ambiguity. Because this can lead to multiple interpretation of what it is we're looking at.

`double** Values` could mean this

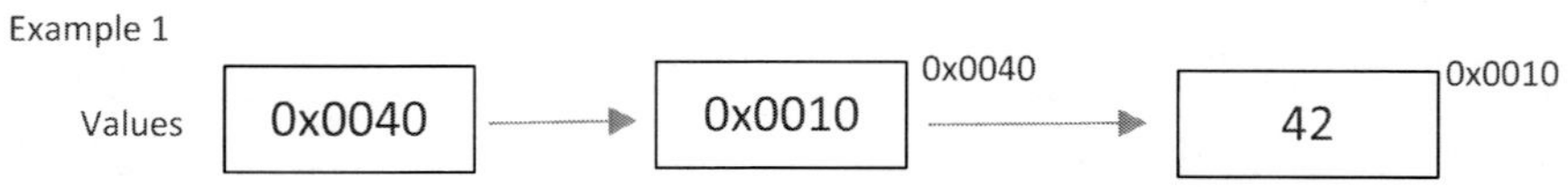

But it could also mean this

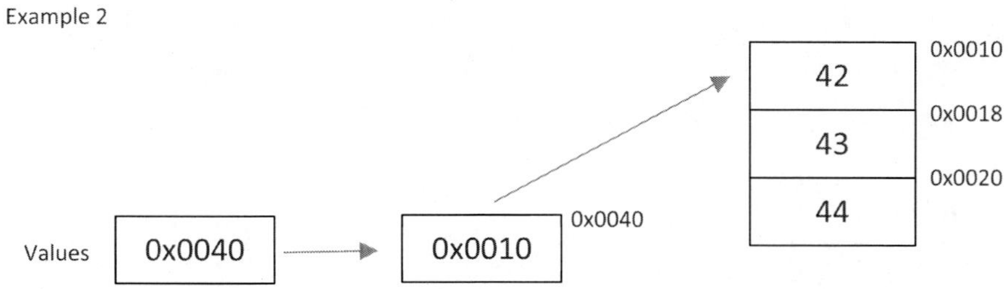

Or this...

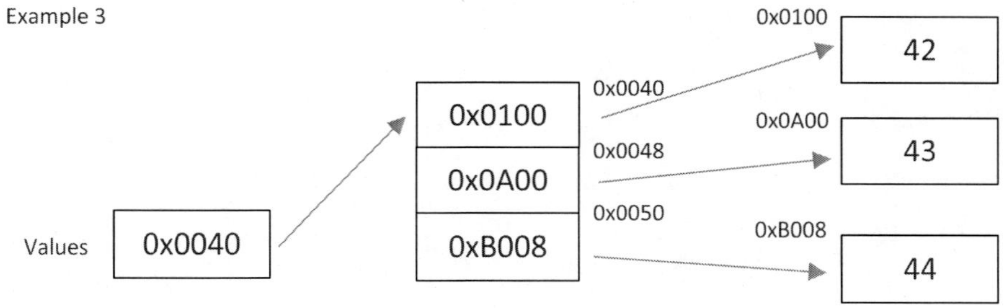

Or this...

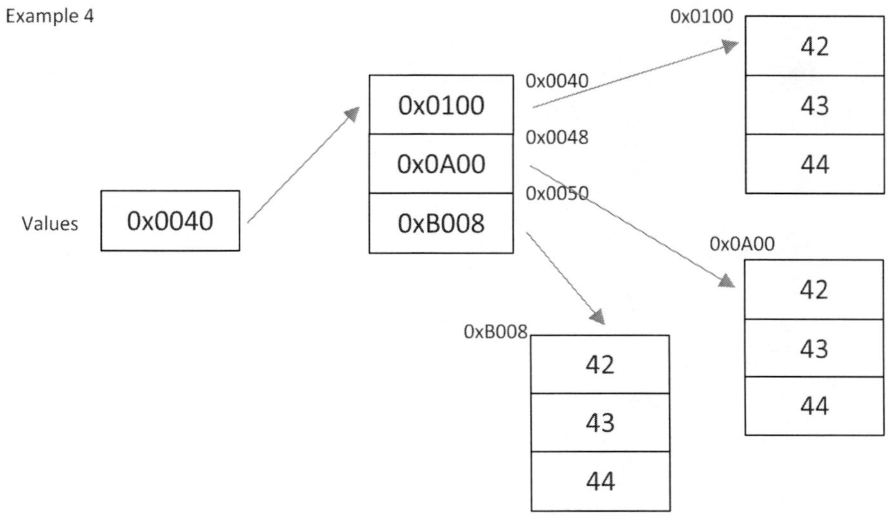

The only hard information that `double** Values` conveys is that Values points to a memory location where 1 or more consecutive pointers are stored, and that each of those pointers points to 1 or more `double` values. So it makes sense that without a lot more information, a parameter declaration like `double** Values` cannot make sense.

That is why the `size_is` attribute can take multiple, comma separated values. For each level of indirection (which is a fancy way of saying 'for every target of a pointer') there needs to be a size provided by the `size_is` attribute. For example, `size_is(1,1)` indicates that Values is simply a pointer to a single pointer, which points to a single value. That would cover Example 1.

```
//Example 1
HRESULT GetArray(
    [out, size_is(1,1)] double **Values);
```

By varying the values in the attribute list, we can indicate which situation is happening.

```
//Example 2
HRESULT GetArray(
    [out, size_is(1,3)] double **Values);

//Example 3
HRESULT GetArray(
    [out, size_is(3,1)] double **Values);

//Example 4
HRESULT GetArray(
    [out, size_is(3,3)] double **Values);
```

The only limitation is that at each level of indirection, the pointers point to the same number of items. So the following is illegal.

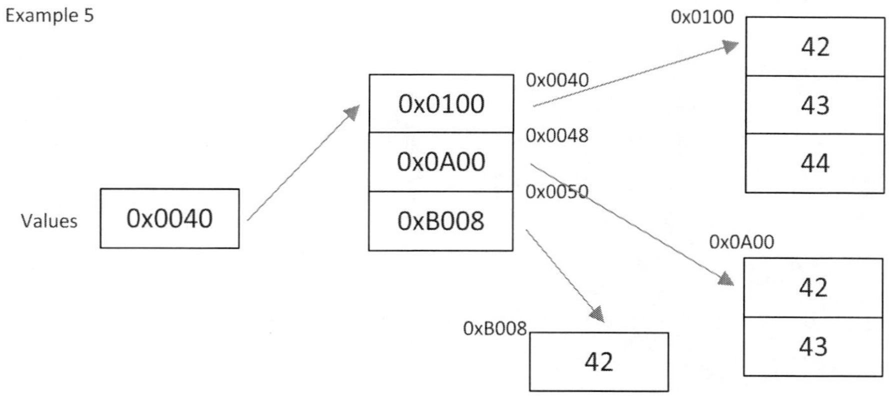

That makes sense because the `size_is` attribute can specify only 1 number per level.

As a special exception to the numbering rule, if the number is 1 and the pointer is effectively just a pointer to a single thing and not a pointer to the first element of multiple elements, it can be left out as long the comma remains to make it clear which of the levels can be regarded as just a pointer to 1 thing.

```
//Example 1
HRESULT GetArray(
    [out, size_is(,)] double **Values);

//Example 2
HRESULT GetArray(
    [out, size_is(,3)] double **Values);

//Example 3
HRESULT GetArray(
    [out, size_is(3,)] double **Values);
```

If you leave away all specifications like in Example 1, then you're also allowed to leave away the attribute altogether.

```
//Example 1
HRESULT GetArray(
    [out] double **Values);
```

For completeness's sake, we need to revisit my earlier statement that `double* Values[]` Is equivalent to `double** Values`. It is, but MIDL looks at the following statement

```
//Example 1
HRESULT GetArray(
```

```
        [out] double *Values[]);
```

And throws a compiler error to chastise you for leaving away the `size_is` attribute in a declaration that is 'obviously' meant to be an array of pointers. You can fix that by specifying the attribute, but my personal preference it to not use this notation to begin with, and stick to the `double**` notation because it is more generic and doesn't lull you into making assumptions.

The only place where using the `[]` is really useful is if you're working with fixed size arrays or multidimensional arrays.

```
    HRESULT SetArray(
        [in] double Values[10]);

    HRESULT SetMatrix(
        [in] double Values[4][4]);
```

Admittedly, here I used an example where the array or matrix are use as input parameters so I can avoid having to specify a pointer to said array or matrix, because that would lead to Values being regarded as an array of `double *` values instead of an array of `double`. Thankfully, there is a relatively simple way around that, which is to use a type definition.

```
    typedef double MATRIX[4][4];

    HRESULT GetMatrix(
        [out] MATRIX* Matrix);
```

By taking this approach, it is clear to both the programmer and the IDL compiler what is meant.

IClassFactory2

So far, we covered the class factory as the means to create new instances, using the IClassFactory interface. For most situations, there is no need to think about a different way of creating instances. However, there is an IClassFactory2 interface which brings extra capabilities to the table. It has the following definition:

```
    //ocidl.h
    MIDL_INTERFACE("B196B28F-BAB4-101A-B69C-00AA00341D07")
    IClassFactory2 : public IClassFactory
    {
    public:
```

```
    virtual HRESULT STDMETHODCALLTYPE GetLicInfo(
        LICINFO *pLicInfo) = 0;

    virtual HRESULT STDMETHODCALLTYPE RequestLicKey(
        DWORD dwReserved,
        BSTR *pBstrKey) = 0;

    virtual HRESULT STDMETHODCALLTYPE CreateInstanceLic(
        IUnknown *pUnkOuter,
        IUnknown *pUnkReserved,
        REFIID riid,
        BSTR bstrKey,
        PVOID *ppvObj) = 0;
};
```

The method names make it clear that its purpose has to do with licensing. Back when COM was the hot new thing, a main driver of its adoption was the ability to distribute libraries and components as building blocks. Making components for others to use was a profit model. Development environments were much more basic, and making user interfaces or database bindings represented a significant development effort if you had to use only the standard tools at your disposal.

Entire industries emerged that revolved around development outfits creating software components for other development outfits. In other words, the customer for such components was not the eventual end user of the product, but the developer integrating it into their application. This required a licensing model that was suited to the situation. Any component vendor could obviously implement an internal check in their activation code to see if a license has been installed on the current machine or for the current user, but that would require the end user to purchase and install the license. Consider a complex application which uses 10 components that are licensed in that manner. The end user would need to install 10 different licenses, possibly in different ways. Some universal and more robust licensing method was required.

The licensing concept behind IClassFactory2 is that there are 2 types of licenses: full licenses and runtime licenses. A component developer can take 2 approaches. The first approach is to simply always require a full license. This would mean the component itself needs to perform some sort of licensing check and fail or succeed instance creation. In that scenario, using IClassFactory2 doesn't really add value except for having the GetLicInfo method to show licensing information for diagnostic purposes.

The second approach is to allow the object to be activated without full license and instead use runtime licenses. In this scenario, an application developer needs to license their development machine with a full license. During the development phase, the developer (or their development environment) can use the class object to create a runtime license via the RequestLicKey method. This key is then stored with the application, for example in a key file or embedded into the application as a resource or constant value. The standard CreateInstance method would fail unless the full license is installed. Instead, the application would create instances via the CreateInstanceLic method with the previously created license key. To take Visual Basic as an example: if a developer dropped a licensed control on a form, the IDE would query the class object to generate a license key. It would then embed that key in the form code and generate the code to create the control via CreateInstanceLic with that key.

The profit model behind IClassFactory2 was to have an ecosystem of commercial modules that make software development easier. In today's world, that notion seems outdated. There is a vast landscape of professional grade opensource libraries and software that provides a full suite of user interface features, database components, audit and video processing, etc. In today's world, that no longer makes much sense, especially in the COM landscape where no one is trying to get into the market anymore. ATL supports the use of IClassFactory2 if you create an ATL Control. The wizard gives you the option to support licensing.

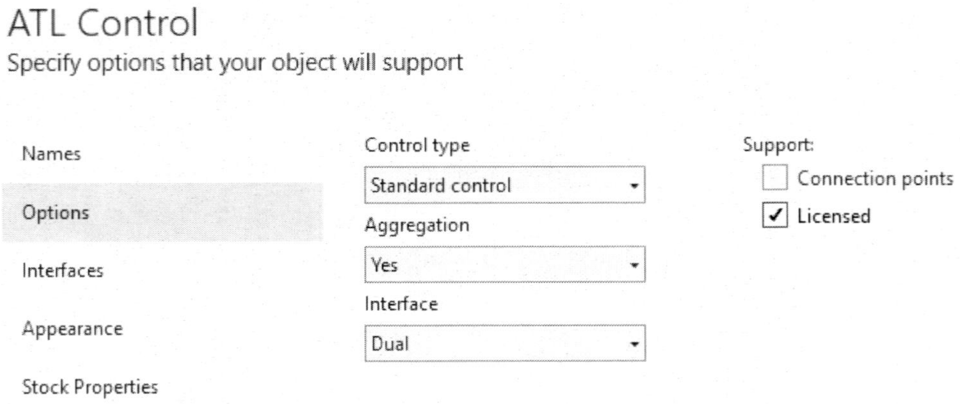

If you create the control like that, the declared class factory is an implementation of IClassFactory2.

```
class ATL_NO_VTABLE CMyControl :
      // snip...
{
public:
```

```
DECLARE_CLASSFACTORY2(CMyControlLic)
        // snip...
};
```

Licensing can then easily be implemented via the CMyControlLic class which is automatically generated for you to add actual license mechanics.

```
class CMyControlLic
{
protected:
    static BOOL VerifyLicenseKey(BSTR bstr)
    {
        return !lstrcmpW(bstr, L"MyControl license");
    }

    static BOOL GetLicenseKey(DWORD dwReserved, BSTR* pBstr)
    {
        if( pBstr == nullptr )
         return FALSE;
        *pBstr = SysAllocString(L"MyControl license");
        return TRUE;
    }

    static BOOL IsLicenseValid()
    {
        return TRUE;
    }
};
```

IClassFactory2 does have a different use case though. I know of at least one vendor of a large distributed application which is built on an internal ecosystem of COM objects, with a roadmap spanning decades. They use IClassFactory2 to prevent developers or admins from using the components in scripts or custom applications, instead allowing only the use of validated tools who provide a secret runtime license key to enable the object for approved use.

Directory Based Activation

When 'Essential COM' was first published, it mentioned that starting with Windows NT5 aka Windows 2000, it would be possible to register COM objects not just in the local registry under HKCR, but also in Active Directory. The book is understandably light on details because Active Directory was still in development.

The idea sounded cool. Based in part on the flags that are used during activation, a client application would try to find a given object or control in the local store, and if it wasn't found, it would look in AD and install the component on demand. This methodology paints a picture of software as a dynamic ecosystem that evolves and grows as needed.

The class store in AD would be managed through a plugin for mmc. The object installers needed to be published in a public location such as an IIS server or a file server and referenced in the class store. In Windows 2000 and 2003, this mechanism was supported. With Windows Vista and 2008, the plugin for managing the class store was marked deprecated, and eventually it was removed from standard installs. The AD schema still supports the class store but there is no support and no tooling. There are several factors which caused the demise of this idea:

- It could be complicated to set up.
- The installation packages had to be tailored to work as intended.
- Security policy had to be configured to allow it.
- Due to network latency or local configuration issues, installation could be slow or fail.

As a concept it faded away through disuse. There seem to be 2 main contributors why this idea never caught on. The first is simply a practical one: if we install an application on a computer that relies on specific components, there is not a good reason why you wouldn't install the dependencies as well. In 2000, disk space was still costly but not so costly that a handful of COM objects would matter.

The second issue is that the world learned the hard way that downloading and installing COM objects on demand was an extremely dangerous idea. Granted, downloading from the intranet via the class store is less troublesome than downloading from the internet. But at the same time any breach that affects the class store could potentially give an attacker a main line into the entire network, especially in the mid 2000's when the Windows ecosystem was much less security oriented than it is today.

Aside from that, there is also the shift in mindset that happened between a developer CoGetClassObject oriented process vs an administrator-oriented process. We also touched on that in the discussion about COM security. It's no longer up to developers to decide ad-hoc what is or is not loaded on a client machine. If code is needed on a client machine, the machine will be configured to get it automatically via MSI packages that are deployed through group policy, SCCM, any of the other enterprise level deployment management systems, or even manually in response to an internal support ticket.

Tear-off interfaces

There is no real limit on how many interfaces are implemented on an object, but one of the real-world consequences is that every interface that gets added to the object's inheritance hierarchy increases the total size of the vtable. In today's world, that may be of little concern but in the late 90's, vtable bloat could have a measurable impact on overall resource usage. If an application uses many instances of the same object, and rarely used interfaces take up a significant percentage of the total vtable, then removing those interfaces can make a measurable difference.

You still need to implement them somewhere to use them in those rare cases, which is where tear-offs come into play. A tear-off is an interface that is implemented on a helper object which can be created as needed. This takes the interface out of the main vtable. You can think of it as a 'light' version of aggregation. Consider the following interface and its implementation:

```
class IRarelyUsedIF : public IUnknown
{
public:
    virtual HRESULT Method1(void) = 0;
    virtual HRESULT Method2(void) = 0;
    //...
};

template<class T>
class CRarelyUsedIFImpl : public IRarelyUsedIF
{
    T* m_owner;
    ULONG m_refCount;
public:
    CRarelyUsedIFImpl(T* owner) {
        m_owner = owner;
        m_refCount = 0;
        m_owner->AddRef();
    }

    ~CRarelyUsedIFImpl() {
        m_owner->Release();
    }

    HRESULT  QueryInterface(REFIID riid, void** ppvObject) {
        if (riid != IID_RarelyUsedIF) {
            return m_owner->QueryInterface(riid, ppvObject);
        }
        *ppvObject = static_cast<IRarelyUsedIF*>(this);
        AddRef();
    }

    ULONG AddRef(void) {
```

```
        return InterlockedIncrement(&m_refCount);
    }

    ULONG Release(void) {
        ULONG count = InterlockedDecrement(&m_refCount);
        if (!count) {
            delete this;
        }
    }

    HRESULT Method1(void) {
        //implementation
        return S_OK;
    }
    HRESULT Method2(void) {
        //implementation
        return S_OK;
    }
    //...
};
```

In 'Essential COM', the implementation for the rarely used interface is a subclass of the main COM object for which it is a helper. The reason is that this was a reliable way for CRarelyUsedIFImpl to reference the main object without using template programming which was still not properly standardized at the time. That approach would still work here but I prefer the template approach because it allows you to separate the main object and the helper object.

CRarelyUsedIFImpl takes a pointer to the main object and AddRefs it. This ensures that the main object is alive at least as long as the tear-off. As soon as the tear-off deletes itself, it releases the main object.

The tear-off can recognize the QueryInterface call for its own tear-off interface, and simply delegate any other query to the main object. This is important because of the COM identity requirements. A tear-off is considered part of its owning object and as such has the same identity. This means that a query for IID_IUnknown must return the IUnknown* of the main object.

Leaving out error handling and input validation, the main object could then be implemented like this:

```
class CSomeObject :
    public IItf1,
    public IItf2
{
    //snip...
    HRESULT  QueryInterface(REFIID riid, void** ppvObject) {
        //snip...
```

```
        if (riid == IID_RarelyUsedIF) {
            CRarelyUsedIFImpl<CSomeObject> * helper =
                new CRarelyUsedIFImpl<CSomeObject>(this);
            return helper->QueryInterface(riid, ppvObject);
        }
        //snip...
    }
};
```

The benefit of this approach is that the rarely used interface has no effect on the memory footprint of the object, either via the vtable or as a member variable which holds a pointer to the tear-off. The downside is that each repeated query for the rarely used interface will create a new instance. This can quickly negate any memory benefits there might have been if that interface is not truly rarely used.

An alternative implementation might be to cache the pointer to the tear-off in the main object. Of course, this requires a modification to the lifecycle management because if the tear-off is allowed to delete itself, a cached pointer might become invalid. Instead, the cached tear-off is integrated with the lifecycle management of the main object.

```
template<class T>
class CRarelyUsedIFImpl : public IRarelyUsedIF
{
    T* m_owner;
public:
    CRarelyUsedIFImpl(T* owner) {
        m_owner = owner;
    }

    HRESULT  QueryInterface(REFIID riid, void** ppvObject) {
        if (riid != IID_RarelyUsedIF) {
            return m_owner->QueryInterface(riid, ppvObject);
        }
        *ppvObject = static_cast<IRarelyUsedIF*>(this);
        AddRef();
    }
    //snip...
    ULONG AddRef(void) {
        m_owner->AddRef();
    }

    ULONG Release(void) {
        m_owner->Release();
    }
    //snip...
};
```

The main difference here is that the pointer to the main object is not an AddRef'ed pointer, and the tear-off doesn't maintain and independent reference count.

```
class CSomeObject :
    public IItf1,
    public IItf2
{
    CRarelyUsedIFImpl<CSomeObject>* m_RarelyUsedIFImpl;
public:
    CSomeObject() {
        m_RarelyUsedIFImpl = NULL;
    }

    CSomeObject() {
        if (m_RarelyUsedIFImpl) {
            delete m_RarelyUsedIFImpl;
        }
    }

    HRESULT  QueryInterface(REFIID riid, void** ppvObject) {
        //...
        if (riid == IID_RarelyUsedIF) {
            if (!m_RarelyUsedIFImpl) {
                m_RarelyUsedIFImpl =
                    new CRarelyUsedIFImpl<CSomeObject>(this);
            }
            return m_RarelyUsedIFImpl->QueryInterface(
                                              riid, ppvObject);
        }

        //...
    }
};
```

The main object creates a tear-off when it's needed, and keeps it around until the object itself deletes itself. It then cleans up the tear-off if there is one. This is also why the tear-off doesn't AddRef the pointer to the main object. If the tear-off stored an AddRef'ed pointer, the main object's reference count would never reach zero. And because the main object stores a pointer to the tear-off, the tear-off cannot be allowed to delete itself.

Tear-off interfaces never saw a lot of uptake. On one hand, they are only ever useful in very niche circumstances. And on the other hand, they are fundamentally incompatible with dual interfaces. When we explored IDispatch, one of the key limitations was that an object could support only 1 main interface. Since dual interfaces became mainstream in many situations, the idea of supporting multiple interfaces in general became less relevant than it was in the 90's.

This topic was included in the book not because it has practical relevance, but because it presents a different way to think about interfaces and objects.

16

Afterword

Ending this book is in some ways more difficult than beginning this book. When I began writing this book, I didn't know what I was getting into. I thought this would take me a year and a half, 2 at the most. And I thought I would have to really stretch go get to 200 pages if I included everything and the kitchen sink, and added a lot of verbose example code. And here we are. 4 years, roughly 450 pages, and approximately 120000 words later.

My goal in writing this book was to comprehensively cover the basics of COM, both in how things work, and how to work with it. I also wanted anyone to be able to pick up this book to learn about COM without having to be an experienced developer. If you read this book, I suspect you are likely to fall into 1 of 3 categories:

- A seasoned veteran developer who worked with COM in the past and is interested in learning what has changed since the late 2000's.
- A junior developer who hasn't really had a lot of experience with COM and who finds themselves staring at decades old code, wondering what on earth an apartment is. If this is you, I truly hope my book was of benefit to you.
- An IT professional who is interested in learning enough COM basics to make sense of a design document of a legacy application.

Keeping this audience in mind helped me in selecting which topics made it into this book, and how to organize the content. Obviously, anyone reading this book should take away a solid understanding of topics like reference counting, lifecycle management, apartments, marshaling, and interface management. From there, I switched to ATL to talk about specific programming techniques and topics you are likely to encounter if you are still working with COM, such as dispatching, aggregation, asynchronous execution, connection points and .NET interoperability.

There are also some topics which have no practical value anymore. I could have completely avoided talking about attributed ATL or Directory Based Activation for example. I included them because they are interesting concepts and you might find references to them in older books or leftover GUI artefacts in Visual Studio.

The topic of security was the odd one out. It required a massive amount of historical context to explain why someone ever thought that anonymous execution of code with administrative privileges was a good idea. And at the same time, it contained a lot of detailed information about programmatically configuring security with a side note explaining that it's probably best to never do this. Still, security is an important topic and even if you don't programmatically mess with it, it's good to understand what is going on. Especially if you are looking at an old codebase and wondering what the easiest way it to make it work, post DCOM hardening.

There are also topics that didn't make it into this book. ActiveX is one of them. It existed for GUI purposes. There is still a massive amount of COM running in back ends, but not in front ends. Most things that are customer facing have been replaced by other technology.

I also purposely avoided any topics such as monikers, containers, activators, persistence, and several others. Technically, those topics are general purpose COM concepts that could be used for many purposes. In reality, they are almost exclusively used in the realm of Object Linking and Embedding (OLE). OLE is a subset of COM focused on compound documents and data linking. Today, its use is limited to a handful of very large applications such as Office, AutoCAD, CorelDraw. Not only is the use of OLE marginal in the remaining COM landscape, but presumably, if you work for one of the companies which publish those applications, you have access to proper design documents and information to help you make sense of those projects.

A chapter about marshaling is useful for anyone working with COM. A chapter about monikers and activators may be equally interesting, but only useful for a very small segment of people still doing anything with COM. Additionally, adding all those topics to this book would easily make it a few hundred pages longer, and add several years to this project which already took almost 4 years to write.

If you reached the end of this book, I hope you found it interesting, useful, or both.

17

Index

D

E

F

G

H

I

K

L

M

N

O

P

Q

R

S

T

U

V

W